Sport Tourism and Sustainable Destinations

Destinations include the places, landscapes and communities where sport tourism development takes place. Whether sport tourism development takes the form of sport events, active participation in sport, and/or sports nostalgia/heritage, it draws on local resources, and forms part of the complex dynamic of daily life. As such, sports tourism has implications for residents, with destination communities in a position to benefit from, or absorb the costs of, the extent to which development is sustainable. Subsequently, this book features contributions that focus on sport tourism and destination sustainability. Issues covered include, though are not limited to, destination management, surf localism, the production of space, event sustainability in national parks, utilisation of sport heritage for destination promotion, enhancing the attractiveness of destinations through sport tourism, destination development and sport tourism, utilising sport to motivate travel to destinations and environmentally responsible behaviour in sports tourism destinations. The unique contribution of this edited volume is the multi-disciplinary approach applied to enhance conceptual understanding of issues surrounding sport tourism and destination sustainability.

The chapters in this book were originally published as a special issue of the *Journal of Sport & Tourism*.

The authors would like to acknowledge the contribution of Professor Mike Weed from the Canterbury Christ Church University in the UK, specifically for his vision to compile the four special issues that made this edited book possible.

B. D. Moyle is Associate Professor of Tourism at the University of the Sunshine Coast, Queensland, Australia. Dr Moyle's research focuses on three interrelated streams, sustainable tourism, visitor experience design and evaluation, and sport tourism. He is an Adjunct Professor at Southern Cross University, Australia.

T. D. Hinch applies a multidisciplinary approach to the understanding of sport tourism, leisure and conceptually related fields. He is a Professor Emeritus at the University of Alberta, Canada, and a Distinguished University Professor in the Faculty of Tourism at Wakayama University, Japan.

J. E. S. Higham is a Professor at the University of Otago, New Zealand, specialising in tourism and environmental change, with long standing interests in the field of sport tourism. He is Co-Editor of the *Journal of Sustainable Tourism* and holds the positions of Visiting Professor of Sustainable Tourism at the University of Stavanger, Norway and Jim Whyte Fellow, University of Queensland, Australia.

Sport Tourism and Sustainable Destinations

Edited by
B. D. Moyle, T. D. Hinch and J. E. S. Higham

LONDON AND NEW YORK

First published 2018 by Routledge

2 Park Square, Milton Park, Abingdon, Oxfordshire OX14 4RN
52 Vanderbilt Avenue, New York, NY 10017

Routledge is an imprint of the Taylor & Francis Group, an informa business

First issued in paperback 2020

Copyright © 2018 Taylor & Francis

All rights reserved. No part of this book may be reprinted or reproduced or utilised in any form or by any electronic, mechanical, or other means, now known or hereafter invented, including photocopying and recording, or in any information storage or retrieval system, without permission in writing from the publishers.

Notice:
Product or corporate names may be trademarks or registered trademarks, and are used only for identification and explanation without intent to infringe.

British Library Cataloguing in Publication Data
A catalogue record for this book is available from the British Library

ISBN 13: 978-0-8153-8022-1 (hbk)
ISBN 13: 978-0-367-51383-2 (pbk)

Typeset in Myriad Pro
by RefineCatch Limited, Bungay, Suffolk

Publisher's Note
The publisher accepts responsibility for any inconsistencies that may have arisen during the conversion of this book from journal articles to book chapters, namely the possible inclusion of journal terminology.

Disclaimer
Every effort has been made to contact copyright holders for their permission to reprint material in this book. The publishers would be grateful to hear from any copyright holder who is not here acknowledged and will undertake to rectify any errors or omissions in future editions of this book.

Contents

Citation Information	vii
Notes on Contributors	ix

1. Sport tourism and sustainable destinations: foundations and pathways 1
   Tom D. Hinch, James E. S. Higham and Brent D. Moyle

2. The role of travel conditions in cycling tourism: implications for destination and event management 13
   Richard J. Buning and Heather J. Gibson

3. Surf localism in Costa Rica: exploring territoriality among Costa Rican and foreign resident surfers 33
   Lindsay E. Usher and Edwin Gómez

4. Local identities in a global game: the social production of football space in Liverpool 55
   Daniel Evans and Glen Norcliffe

5. Factors effecting destination and event loyalty: examining the sustainability of a recurrent small-scale running event at Banff National Park 71
   Elizabeth A. Halpenny, Cory Kulczycki and Farhad Moghimehfar

6. Leveraging sport heritage to promote tourism destinations: the case of the Tour of Flanders Cyclo event 101
   Inge Derom and Gregory Ramshaw

7. Serious about leisure, serious about destinations: mountain bikers and destination attractiveness 123
   Julie Moularde and Adam Weaver

8. Sports tourism development and destination sustainability: the case of the coastal area of the Aveiro region, Portugal 143
   Maria João Carneiro, Zélia Breda and Catarina Cordeiro

9. Motivation of active sport tourists in a German highland destination – a cross-seasonal comparison 173
   Alexander Hodeck and Gregor Hovemann

10. Determining the influence of the social versus physical context on environmentally responsible behaviour among cycling spectators 187
Elizabeth A. du Preez and Ernie T. Heath

Index 209

Citation Information

The chapters in this book were originally published in the *Journal of Sport & Tourism*. When citing this material, please use the original page numbering for each article, as follows:

Chapter 1
Sport tourism and sustainable destinations: foundations and pathways
Tom D. Hinch, James E. S. Higham and Brent D. Moyle
Journal of Sport & Tourism, volume 20, issue 3–4 (2016), pp. 163–174

Chapter 2
The role of travel conditions in cycling tourism: implications for destination and event management
Richard J. Buning and Heather J. Gibson
Journal of Sport & Tourism, volume 20, issue 3–4 (2016), pp. 175–194

Chapter 3
Surf localism in Costa Rica: exploring territoriality among Costa Rican and foreign resident surfers
Lindsay E. Usher and Edwin Gómez
Journal of Sport & Tourism, volume 20, issue 3–4 (2016), pp. 195–216

Chapter 4
Local identities in a global game: the social production of football space in Liverpool
Daniel Evans and Glen Norcliffe
Journal of Sport & Tourism, volume 20, issue 3–4 (2016), pp. 217–232

Chapter 5
Factors effecting destination and event loyalty: examining the sustainability of a recurrent small-scale running event at Banff National Park
Elizabeth A. Halpenny, Cory Kulczycki and Farhad Moghimehfar
Journal of Sport & Tourism, volume 20, issue 3–4 (2016), pp. 233–262

Chapter 6
Leveraging sport heritage to promote tourism destinations: the case of the Tour of Flanders Cyclo event
Inge Derom and Gregory Ramshaw
Journal of Sport & Tourism, volume 20, issue 3–4 (2016), pp. 263–284

Chapter 7
Serious about leisure, serious about destinations: mountain bikers and destination attractiveness
Julie Moularde and Adam Weaver
Journal of Sport & Tourism, volume 20, issue 3–4 (2016), pp. 285–304

Chapter 8
Sports tourism development and destination sustainability: the case of the coastal area of the Aveiro region, Portugal
Maria João Carneiro, Zélia Breda and Catarina Cordeiro
Journal of Sport & Tourism, volume 20, issue 3–4 (2016), pp. 305–334

Chapter 9
Motivation of active sport tourists in a German highland destination – a cross-seasonal comparison
Alexander Hodeck and Gregor Hovemann
Journal of Sport & Tourism, volume 20, issue 3–4 (2016), pp. 335–348

Chapter 10
Determining the influence of the social versus physical context on environmentally responsible behaviour among cycling spectators
Elizabeth A. du Preez and Ernie T. Heath
Journal of Sport & Tourism, volume 20, issue 2 (2016), pp. 123–143

For any permission-related enquiries please visit:
http://www.tandfonline.com/page/help/permissions

Notes on Contributors

Zélia Breda is a member of the GOVCOPP – Research Unit on Governance, Competiveness and Public Policies, and is based at the University of Aveiro, Portugal.

Richard Buning is based at the School of Business at the University of Queensland, Australia.

Maria João Carneiro is based at the Department of Economics, Management, Industrial Engineering and Tourism, University of Aveiro, Portugal.

Catarina Cordeiro is a based at the Department of Economics, Management, Industrial Engineering and Tourism, University of Aveiro, Portugal.

Inge Derom is based at the Department of Movement and Sport Sciences, Vrije Universiteit Brussel, Belgium.

Elizabeth du Preez is based at the Division Tourism Management, Department of Marketing Management, University of Pretoria, South Africa.

Daniel Evans is based at the Department of Geography, York University, Toronto, Canada.

Heather Gibson is based at the Department of Tourism, Recreation and Sport Management, University of Florida, USA.

Edwin Gómez is based at the Department of Human Movement Sciences, Old Dominion University, USA.

Elizabeth Halpenny is based at the Faculty of Physical Education and Recreation, University of Alberta, Canada.

Ernie Heath is based at the Division Tourism Management, Department of Marketing Management, University of Pretoria, South Africa.

James Higham is a professor in the Department of Tourism, University of Otago, New Zealand and Visiting Professor at the University of Stavanger, Norway.

Tom Hinch is a Professor Emeritus at the University of Alberta, Canada and a Distinguished University Professor (visiting) at Wakayama University, Japan.

Alexander Hodeck is based at the Sports Science Faculty, Department of Sports Management and Sports Economy, Leipzig University, Germany.

Gregor Hovemann is based at the Sports Science Faculty, Department of Sports Management and Sports Economy, Leipzig University, Germany.

NOTES ON CONTRIBUTORS

Cory Kulczycki is based at the Faculty of Kinesiology and Health Studies, University of Regina, Canada.

Farhad Moghimehfar is based at the Outdoor Recreation and Tourism Management, Ecosystem Science and Management Program, University of Northern British Columbia, Canada.

Julie Moularde is based at the School of Management, Victoria University of Wellington, New Zealand.

Brent Moyle is based at the University of the Sunshine Coast, Queensland, Australia.

Glen Norcliffe is based at the Department of Geography, York University, Toronto, Canada.

Gregory Ramshaw is based the Department of Parks, Recreation and Tourism Management, Clemson University, USA.

Lindsay Usher is based at the Department of Human Movement Sciences, Old Dominion University, USA.

Adam Weaver is based at the School of Management, Victoria University of Wellington, New Zealand.

Sport tourism and sustainable destinations: foundations and pathways

Tom D. Hinch, James E. S. Higham and Brent D. Moyle

Introduction

Destinations serve as the spatial context and reference point for this book. They are, in essence, the place where sport tourism is produced and consumed (Higham, 2005). Whether sport tourism development takes the form of sport events, active participation or sport heritage activities, it draws on local resources and forms part of the complex dynamic of community life (Weed, 2008; Preuss, 2015). Sport tourism therefore has implications for destination residents who may benefit from, or incur the costs of this development, with potential impacts ranging across the local–global spatial spectrum (Giampiccoli, Lee & Nauright, 2015). As such, it is essential that the academic community critically question the sustainability of sport tourism destinations.

Sustainable development has been an ongoing concern for both tourism (McCool, 2015) and sport (Tak, 2013) scholars. However, despite mounting focus in these parent fields there has been limited effort to neither clearly articulate nor theoretically and empirically address critical questions associated with the ways in which sport and tourism interplay in relation to sustainability at the destination level. Acknowledgement must be made of the *Journal of Sport & Tourism* which is in the process of publishing a series of special issues dedicated to highlighting and beginning to address these gaps. This book is drawn from the special issue on sports tourism and sustainable destinations (issue 3 and 4 volume 20), one of a series of four special issues designed to mark the twentieth anniversary of the *Journal of Sport & Tourism*. The other three issues address events, active sport tourism and theoretical perspectives of sport tourism, which has recently been published in issue 2 volume 20 of the *Journal of Sport & Tourism*. Clearly, there is a strong interrelationship between the four special issues.

This book, then, reflects upon the three fundamental questions addressed in the special issues series: (1) What do we know? (2) What do we not know? and (3) What do we need to know? We introduce this book by providing a summary of what we know about destination sustainability from the parent fields of tourism (e.g. Gössling, Hall & Weaver, 2009; Ruhanen, et al., 2015) and sport (Lindsey, 2008; Mallen, Adams, Stevens & Thompson, 2010) followed by insights from the emerging sport tourism literature. We then consider gaps in the existing literature before introducing and contemplating the ways in which the chapters that follow address these gaps. It concludes with our views on what we still need to know or the research directions that should be pursued to provide further insight into the sustainability of sport tourism destinations.

What we know

Although the sport literature does not focus on destinations it has increasingly explored issues of sustainability at a local level that can be categorized in terms of a triple bottom line approach (Andersson & Lundberg, 2013). Much of this work has been concentrated in the socio-cultural realm with Lindsey (2008: 2) suggesting that sustainability has 'become ubiquitous in sports development policy and practice.' For example, the role of participatory sport programmes in fostering community is a popular area of research (e.g. Schulenkorf, 2012; Spaaij, 2009) as are the social impacts of sport events (e.g. Taks, 2013). Similarly, the economic impacts of major sport events such as the Olympics and the development of large-scale sport facilities have been another area of research related to local dimensions of sustainability (Gratton, Shibli & Coleman, 2005).

Here the outcomes of hosting mega sports events remain a bone of contention. The recent Rio 2016 Olympic Games were subject to negative media associated with the displacement of lower socio-economic residents to make way for the development of Olympic facilities including the athlete's village; actions that triggered violent protests (Watts, 2016). Debate also swirled around the wisdom of hosting the Olympic Games at substantial cost, in a country in political and economic turmoil with a significant proportion of the population living in extreme poverty (Zimbalist, 2016). Economists generally question the logic of hosting the Olympic Games (Dale, 2016), particularly if Olympic profits are redirected away from the hosts by the granting of tax exemptions to Olympic sponsors such as Visa, McDonalds and Coca-Cola. Cultural and environmental programmes have emerged as a strong focus of events management, pointing to the world-making role of sports events; a term that describes the 'creative/inventive role and function of tourism in the making of culture and place' (Hollinshead, 2009: 139). A focus on legacies aimed to facilitate post-event sports participation has also become a more common feature of mega sports events.

While the findings have been mixed, highlighting both positive and negative impacts, these studies suggest that the predicted economic benefits of such developments are often overstated (Mills & Rosentraub, 2013). Sport event-related tourism interests are subject to an array of displacement effects that are described by Weed (2008) using terms such as 'homestayers', 'runaways', 'changers', 'extensioners', 'time-switchers' and 'cancellers'. While it is recognized that the tourism possibilities associated with sports events need to be carefully planned and managed (Preuss, 2015), the manner in which these effects play out are almost impossible to predict in advance (Weed, 2008).

Finally, much less attention has been directed toward the ecological sustainability of sport although there are increasing calls for more research and debate in this area (Mallen & Chard, 2011). More generally, there has been a trend for this scholarship to incorporate the dynamic of tourism, including destination impacts, into studies on the sustainability of sport tourism (e.g. Gibson, Kaplanidou & Kang, 2012; Taks, Chalip & Green, 2015). The local environmental impacts of sports vary between nature-based sports, and those that take place in centrally located built facilities. The former can be long-term and irreversible while the latter tend to be more fleeting, causing temporary inconvenience to residents (e.g. Bale, 2003). Both categories of impact must be closely managed, however far less attention has been paid to the national or global impacts of sports events. The 2006 FIFA World Cup in Germany was an exception with its attempt to stage a carbon neutral event (Higham & Hinch, 2009).

The sustainable tourism development literature is also well established and dynamic. Much of this literature considers the tourism system within its wider socio-cultural, political and economic contexts (Ruhanen, 2013). These efforts have not been without criticism, given the reality that interests in and understandings of sustainability differ with perspective (Hallsedt, Thompson & Lindahl, 2013). Much focus has centred on environmental dimensions of sustainability, but there is a growing recognition of the fact that tourism systems are set within the wider socio-cultural, political and economic dimensions of sustainable development (Bramwell, Higham, Lane & Miller, 2017). Research in this field was also initially characterized by a focus on small-scale local tourism development, which has been more aligned with interests in sustainability (Cater, 1993). There is now greater recognition that all forms of tourism development, from specific niches to mass tourism phenomena, challenge and are challenged by notions of sustainability.

The framing of the field of sustainable tourism has also evolved over time (Bramwell et al., 2017). It has been noted that initially sustainable tourism was addressed in terms of the management of environmental impacts at the local scale of analysis. This framing has been challenged in various important ways. The focus on environment has, by necessity, expanded to accommodate society (politics, economy, community) (Moyle, McLennan, Ruhanen & Weiler, 2014). Tourism destinations have come to be conceived by some to function within wider socio-ecological systems (SES), which has given rise to interests in system resilience and the conceptual development of sustainability in relation to resilience theory (Bec, McLennan & Moyle, 2016; Farrell & Twining-Ward, 2004; McCool, 2015).

The framing of sustainable tourism has also moved beyond the local scale of analysis which Becken and Schellhorn (2007) described as the 'reading glass' (local) approach, to an 'open system' (global) perspective of sustainability. Accommodating the global scale of analysis has raised a raft of new questions and challenges. The relevance for sustainable tourism development is significant, not only in terms of the movement of tourists from generating to destination regions to engage in sports, but also in terms of the greenhouse gas emissions associated with movement of spectators (Heath & Kruger, 2015). Indeed it is not only the movements of tourists that cause impacts that are dispersed and global. The emissions associated with the movement of elite athletes, which are considerable, need to be accounted for under the provisions of the Paris (2015) global climate agreement. These emissions may ultimately become part of the energy inventory and emissions profile of the destinations that host sports events and benefit from the flows of tourists, both spectators and elite athletes, associated with those sports.

Super Rugby provides an eye-opening illustration. Originally involving teams from New Zealand, Australia and South Africa (Super 12), the competition – which now runs over the course of a season from February–July (Super 18) – has been extended in the interests of sponsors and television broadcasters to include teams from Japan and Argentina. The CO_2 consequences of this commercial decision are profound. As an example, in the last six rounds of the 2016 Super 18 competition, the Highlanders (Dunedin, New Zealand) contested matches in Wellington (New Zealand), Port Elizabeth (South Africa), Buenos Aires (Argentina), Dunedin (New Zealand), Canberra (Australia) and Johannesburg (South Africa). The aggregate distance between these host destinations is 53,495km[1]. The Super 18 involves 18 teams travelling and playing each week in squads of around 25 personnel. The aggregate carbon emissions associated with the movement of teams in this competition are too significant to ignore under the urgent emission reduction targets set out in the Paris Climate Agreement.

At the intersection of this topic lies the sport tourism literature. Fyall and Jago's (2010) special issue on sport tourism sustainability in the *Journal of Sport & Tourism* highlighted the active role of sport tourism researchers in exploring this topic. Key contributions in this issue included the recognition of the need to move from rhetoric to substance, the merit of a triple bottom line approach within a sport tourism context and the fact that sport tourism was not only responsible for impacting sustainability but also was impacted by events in the social, environmental and economic realms that lie outside of its direct influence. The present issue seeks to build on this base by examining the sustainability of sport tourism from a destination perspective.

More generally, there is a well-established body of knowledge that sport tourism destinations are part of complex, adaptive and multifaceted systems (Hinch & Higham, 2011; Schientz & Kavanagh, 2008). Seminal work on the tourism system identified that an attraction, or a destination, consists of an empirical connection between a tourist, a nucleus and a marker (Leiper, 1990). Academic discourse has advanced this understanding, with scholars exploring various components of the tourism system (Espiner & Becken, 2014). For example, studies have sought to understand what motivates people to travel, with sport identified as a critical factor for destination selection (Kozak, 2002; Kurtzman & Zauhar, 2005). Similarly, sport tourism has been identified as a critical factor in many destination development strategies (Klenosky, 2002). In particular, sport tourism has been identified as an important strategy in rejuvenating tourism destinations (Agarwal, 2002).

Despite the importance of sport in contemporary society, sport tourism has only relatively recently emerged as an area of scholarly enquiry (Hinch & Higham, 2003). This is especially true for the area of sport tourism destinations (Getz, 2008). Previous literature on sport tourism destinations has covered a range of core areas (Higham, 2005). One such area was dedicated to understanding sport tourism experiences in destinations with studies predominantly focused on visitor satisfaction (Shonk & Chelladdurai, 2008). Within this particular stream of research, studies on market segmentation suggested that the active sport tourism market is growing in prominence (Gibson, Attle & Yiannakis, 1998; Tassiopoulos & Haydam, 2008). This body of work includes, though is not limited to, the understanding of the sport tourism experience at the destination level, with contemporary studies covering issues such as sport tourism authentication (Lamont, 2014).

Sport tourism destination planning and policy has also received substantial attention in scholarly discourse (Flagestad & Hope, 2001). For instance, sport tourism planning was discussed by Hall (2004), who argued that it is critical for destinations to engage in appropriate policy and governance, if sport tourism is to serve as a mechanism for urban regeneration. Strategic destination partnerships are seen as critical for operationalizing sport tourism at different scales (Weed & Bull, 2012). Public and private sector partnerships are also considered essential to ensure the delivery of a high quality visitor experience (Andersson & Getz, 2009; Dolnicar, 2004). The bundling (Chalip & McGuirty, 2004) and leveraging (Chalip, 2006; Chalip & Leyns, 2002) of sports events (and sports more broadly) to maximize tourism industry benefits has become an important aspect of destination planning.

Image making and marketing have also been identified as essential for sport tourism destinations (Funk & Brunn, 2007). Specifically, research has considered the role of marketing, media and place promotion in the formation of destination image (Kaplanidou & Vogt, 2007). There is a need, however, to link destination image more strongly to the concept of place in terms of sport's role in infusing destinations with meaning (Higham & Hinch, 2009; Gammon, 2015). Of course, different sport tourism contexts have been the subject of scholarly discourse, with examples of sports in winter and summer destinations prevalent in extant literature (Hallman, Zehrer & Muller, 2013). Urban areas have also been the focus of much research in sport tourism destinations with host community perceptions towards events receiving substantial attention (Hritz & Ross, 2010). Given the different spatial scales of sport tourism destinations, the resources required at this level to support sport tourism in different spatial locations and at geographic scales have also come under considerable debate (Weed & Bull, 2012). Scholars have recognized that a different set of material, social and physical resources and infrastructure is required in different scales of sport tourism destinations.

Although an appropriate context to validate existing theories from multiple disciplinary contexts, questions have been raised about the propensity of the sport tourism field to generate new theory (Gibson, 1998). In addition, sport tourism has been criticized for being quite descriptive, at times atheoretical and lacking a core disciplinary grounding (Chalip & Costa, 2005). However, Weed (2005) argues that sport tourism research, especially at the destination level is underpinned by various epistemological standpoints, consisting of a range of theories and methodologies that are constantly evolving. As such, this volume positions sport tourism as a field of research, within which multiple disciplines can address issues critical for the sustainability of the planet (Weed, 2006).

Consequently, it is somewhat surprising that one area of research on sport tourism destinations that has received scant attention in academic literature is the area of sustainability, especially across different geographic scales. Sustainability is critical for the success of sport tourism destinations (Higham, 2005) although there is considerable debate as to whether sustainability is achievable or rhetoric (Moyle, McLennan, Ruhanen & Weiler, 2014). As such, sustainability has been recently redefined from the traditional triple bottom line approach to consider a broader range of issues, such as politics and technology (Cohen, Higham, Gossling & Peters, 2014). Notwithstanding this increasing interest toward broad based sustainability, economic studies continue to dominate the literature (Gratton, Shibli & Coleman, 2005; Ponting & O'Brien, 2014; Weed et al., 2014).

What we don't know

Many questions relating to the sustainability of sport tourism destinations remain to be addressed by the academic community. For sport tourism destinations, research has tended to focus on the impact of major events, particularly those relating to economic impacts, social impacts and destination image. Research into the wider role of sports tourism in destination development strategies has been more limited (Gibson, Willming & Holdnak, 2002). It remains unclear, for example, whether a portfolio of smaller sport tourism events in a range of seasonal contexts events may serve the interests of destinations more so than a mega sports event hosting strategy (Gratton, Shibli & Coleman, 2005). Similarly, the harnessing of active sport tourism products may provide a greater return for destinations than investment in one-off major events. The extent to which destinations of different sizes might benefit from developing single or multi-product sports has not been thoroughly addressed by researchers nor has its implications for sustainability. How such strategies may interface with the development of public sports resources, and tourism destination products has not been critically addressed. The development of Mediterranean golf resorts, which can irreversibly transform the environmental and cultural character of distinctive and historic coastal landscapes, is a case in point. In fact, it is not entirely clear how destinations should decide how or why they should develop a sport tourism strategy at all.

Those destinations that do implement sport tourism development strategies have further pause for thought relating to the various framings and dimensions of sustainability touched upon above. In terms of infrastructure and investment, critical consideration of civic investments in facilities to host sports will continue to be important (Scherer & Sam, 2008). Such considerations should extend to sport and destination lifecycles. All sports are subject to evolving lifecycles (Hinch & Higham, 2011), which need to be understood and accommodated in the development of tourism strategies for destinations. Indeed these lifecycles, which have in the past been driven largely by social forces, are now subject to the factors of global environmental change (Higham & Hinch, 2009). The links between climate change, sport and tourism destinations merits further attention from the research community. Local and regional manifestations of global environmental change include changing abundance and availability of natural resources for sports, shifting seasonal weather patterns and the frequency and intensity of extreme weather events (Gössling, 2002; Gössling & Hall, 2005). The implications of the availability of snow for the sustainability of winter destinations are already being felt (Hopkins, Higham & Becken, 2012). Challenging questions arise relating to climate, sport and sustainability strategies at tourism destinations. These will include manifestations of, and responses to, changing climatic regimes. More fundamentally, while some progress has been made in response to Gibson's (2006) lament about the lack of theoretical underpinnings in sport tourism research, there remains considerable room for advances in this area.

What we need to know

Clearly, there is much work that needs to be done in order to meet the gaps in the literature on sustainable sport tourism destinations. A partial list of research needs includes studies that address: (1) differing scales both in terms of activity and destination; (2) single versus multisport destinations; (3) sport destination resources and civic investment; (4) the interplay of sport and destination lifecycles; (5) sport tourism's contribution to and impacts of climate change; and (6) more explicit theorizing.

The chapters presented in this book reflect significant progress in these areas of need. Table 1 summarizes key characteristics of each chapter with an emphasis on the contributions they make to our understandings of sustainability in sport tourism destinations. At an aggregate level these contributions are found in the chapters of this book that focus on local destinations versus those that have a wider macro-regional focus. National and global scales of destination require further attention.

As reported, much of the existing literature in this area examines the sustainability of major sporting events so this issue intentionally focuses on smaller scale events (e.g. Buning

Table 1. Contributions and implications for sustainable sport tourism destinations.

Title	Authors	Context	Theory/concepts	Contribution	Implications for destination sustainability
Local scale					
The role of travel conditions in cycling tourism: Implications for destination and event management	Buning, Gibson	Cycle tourism	Active Sport Event Travel Career	Travel conditions surrounding a trip were found to be more important than the comparative advantage and characteristics of an event	Sport tourism destinations need to target participants most likely to engage in sustainable behaviour while in the destination. This includes developing event portfolios geared towards sustainable event practices
Surf localism in Costa Rica: Exploring territoriality among Costa Rican and foreign resident surfers	Usher, Gómez	Surf tourism	Territoriality and localism	The social sustainability of sport tourism destinations is impacted by the participant groups' sense of territoriality. While crowding is a major source of conflict it is also clear that different versions of localism exist amongst indigenous local surfers, long-term migrant surfers and short-term visitor surfers	Sport tourism destinations need to manage potential sources of conflict to ensure surf tourism is socially sustainable
Local identities in a global game: The social production of football space in Liverpool	Evans, Norcliffe	Football/soccer	Production of space, local identity, and globalization Lefebvrian theory	The contestation of football space by locals is an attempt to control the production of space and assert that the global game can have a Liverpool-specific inflection	Sport tourism destinations should consider leveraging the contests embedded within the local context to harness global potential
Factors effecting destination and event loyalty: Examining the sustainability of a recurrent small-scale running event at Banff National Park	Halpenny, Kulczycki, Moghimehfar	Running in National Parks	Destination and event loyalty Place attachment	Event attachment was shown to be an antecedent to place attachment at the local level	Sports tourism destinations should harness small-scale sport events to build attachment to places and to encourage future visits

(Continued)

Table 1. Continued.

Title	Authors	Context	Theory/concepts	Contribution	Implications for destination sustainability
Regional scale					
Leveraging sport heritage to promote tourism destinations: The case of the Tour of Flanders Cyclo event	Derom, Ramshaw	Cycling tourism	Event leverage, heritage sport tourism	The study contributes to the conceptual framing of event leverage by identifying active sport heritage as an important resource	Sports tourism destinations should leverage heritage as a mechanism to reduce the seasonality and enhance sustainability, particularly across the triple bottom line
Serious about leisure, serious about destinations: Mountain bikers and destination attractiveness	Moularde, Weaver	Mountain biking	Serious leisure	Destination characteristics facilitate the pursuit of serious leisure and, in turn, destination image is shaped by the capacity of destinations to strengthen the commitment of serious leisure participants	Sports tourism destinations need to consider the role of image in shaping sustainability, specifically by demonstrating a commitment towards serious leisure participants
Sports tourism development and destination sustainability: The case of the coastal area of the Aveiro region, Portugal	Carneiro, Breda, Cordeiro	Managers of small to medium sized operations in Aveuri region of Portugal	Triple bottom line approach with the addition of technological and political dimensions	Confirmation of the complex and multifaceted character of sustainability through the identification of additional dimensions in a sport tourism context	Sport tourism destinations should harness collaborative partnerships to build strong potential to foster social cohesion and build capacity to increase sustainable practices
Motivation of active sport tourists in a German highland destination – a cross-seasonal comparison	Hodeck, Hovemann	Active sport tourists	Destination choice, segmentation, seasonality, climate change	Identified seasonal differences in active sport tourists to different regions in the German highlands using a market segmentation approach	Sport tourism destinations should market with sustainability in mind in order to promote to desired market segments
Determining the influence of the social versus physical context on environmentally responsible behaviour among cycling spectators	Du Preez, Heath	Spectators at road race and mountain bike events in South Africa	Environmental behavioural intention, place attachment, subculture identification and subjective norms	The social setting of the event (sub-culture) outweighs place attachment and subjective norms as a predictor of environmental behavioural intention	Sport tourism destinations have an opportunity to leverage the social setting of the event to influence pro-environmental behaviour

& Gibson) and activities (Derom & Ramshaw). Three of the nine chapters (Carneiro, Breda & Cordeiro; Du Preez & Heath; Hodeck & Hovemann) address multi-sport destinations while the balance examine destinations from a single sport perspective. Several chapters focus on sport tourism destinations that draw on public resources such as national parks (Halpenny, Kulczycki & Moghimehfar), marine environments (Usher & Gómez), heritage landscapes (Derom & Ramshaw) and an assortment of other natural and cultural resources found in the public domain.

While none of the chapters explicitly examines the nature of destination and sport life-cycles, several emerging sports such as surfing (Usher & Gómez) and mountain biking (Moularde & Weaver) are highlighted, as are traditional sports such as football/soccer (Evans & Norcliffe) and cycling (Du Preez & Heath). Seasonality is addressed directly in Hodeck and Hovemann's chapter although climate change only receives passing reference. Finally, the majority of the chapters draw on strong theoretical foundations with examples including theories related to active sport event careers (Buning & Gibson), territoriality and localism (Usher & Gómez) and Lefebvre's ideas on the production of space and identity (Evans & Norcliff). Finally, while this issue provides important new insights into sport tourism destinations, the authors consistently ended their chapters with detailed calls for further research.

Note

1. By comparison, the circumference of the earth is 40,075km.

Acknowledgements

The editors gratefully acknowledge the contributions of the anonymous reviewers who contributed their expertise to the peer review processes underpinning the special issue that this book is founded upon. We also acknowledge Professor Mike Weed (Editor, *Journal of Sport & Tourism*) for his vision for the anniversary special issues series, which lead to our special double issue on 'Sport, Tourism and Sustainable Destinations,' and to this book.

References

Agarwal, S. (2002). Restructuring seaside tourism: The resort lifecyle. *Annals of Tourism Research*, *29*(1), 25–55.
Andersson, T. D., & Getz, D. (2009). Tourism as a mixed industry: Differences between private, public and not-for-profit festivals. *Tourism Management*, *30*(6), 847–856.
Andersson, T. D., & Lundberg, E. (2013). Commensurability and sustainability: Triple impact assessments of a tourism event. *Tourism Management*, *37*, 99–109.
Bale, J. (2003). *Sports Geographies*. London: Routledge.
Bec, A., McLennan, C. L., & Moyle, B. D. (2016). Community resilience to long-term tourism decline and rejuvenation: A literature review and conceptual model. *Current Issues in Tourism*, *19*(5), 431–457.
Becken, S., & Schellhorn, M. (2007). Ecotourism, energy use and the global climate: Widening the local perspective. In J.E.S. Higham (Ed.), *Critical issues in ecotourism: Understanding a complex tourism phenomenon* (pp. 85–101). Oxford: Elsevier.
Bramwell, B., Higham, J. E. S., Lane, B. and Miller, G. (2017). Twenty-five years of sustainable tourism and the Journal of Sustainable Tourism: Looking back and moving forward. *Journal of Sustainable Tourism*, *25*(1): doi; 10.1080/09669582.2017.1251689.

Cater, E. (1993). Ecotourism in the third world: Problems for sustainable tourism development. *Tourism Management, 14*(2), 85–90.

Chalip, L. (2006). Towards social leverage of sports events. *Journal of Sport & Tourism, 11*(2), 109–127.

Chalip, L., & Costa, C. A. (2005). Sport event tourism and the destination brand: Towards a general theory. *Sport in Society, 8*(2), 218–237.

Chalip, L., & Leyns, A. (2002). Local business leveraging of a sport event: Managing an event for economic benefit. *Journal of Sport Management, 16*(2), 132–158.

Chalip, L., & Mcguirty, J. (2004). Bundling sport events with the host destination. *Journal of Sport & Tourism, 9*(3), 267–282.

Cohen, S. A., Higham, J. E., Stefan, G., & Peeters, P. (2014). *Understanding and governing sustainable tourism mobility: Psychological and behavioural approaches* (Vol. 43). New York: Routledge.

Dale, C. (2016). Economists question wisdom of hosting Olympics. Retrieved 10/9/16 from: http://www.cnbc.com/2016/08/04/rio-olympics-2016-economists-question-wisdom-of-hosting-olympics.html.

Dolničar, S. (2004). Beyond "commonsense segmentation": A systematics of segmentation approaches in tourism. *Journal of Travel Research, 42*(3), 244–250.

Espiner, S., & Becken, S. (2014). Tourist towns on the edge: Conceptualising vulnerability and resilience in a protected area tourism system. *Journal of Sustainable Tourism, 22*(4), 646–665.

Farrell, B. H., & Twining-Ward, L. (2004). Reconceptualizing Tourism. *Annals of Tourism Research 31*(2), 274–295.

Flagestad, A., & Hope, C. A. (2001). Strategic success in winter sports destinations: A sustainable value creation perspective. *Tourism Management, 22*(5), 445–461.

Funk, D. C., & Bruun, T. J. (2007). The role of socio-psychological and culture-education motives in marketing international sport tourism: A cross-cultural perspective. *Tourism Management, 28*(3), 806–819.

Fyall, A., & Jago, L. (Eds.) (2009). Sustainability in sport & tourism. *Journal of Sport & Touirsm, 14* (2–3), 77–81.

Gammon, S. (2015). Sport tourism finding its place? In S. Gammon & S. Elkington (Eds.), *Landscapes of Leisure* (pp. 110–122). London: Palgrave Macmillan.

Getz, D. (2008). Event tourism: Definition, evolution, and research. *Tourism Management, 29*(3), 403–428.

Giampiccoli, A., Lee, S. S., & Nauright, J. (2015). Destination South Africa: Comparing global sports mega-events and recurring localised sports events in South Africa for tourism and economic development. *Current Issues in Tourism, 18*(3), 229–248.

Gibson, H. J. (Ed.) (2006). *Sport tourism: Concepts and theories* . New York: Routledge Taylor & Francis Group.

Gibson, H. J. (1998). Sport tourism: A critical analysis of research. *Sport Management Review, 1*(1), 45–76.

Gibson, H. J., Attle, S. P., & Yiannakis, A. (1998). Segmenting the active sport tourist market: A life-span perspective. *Journal of Vacation Marketing, 4*(1), 52–64.

Gibson, H., Willming, C., & Holdnak, A. (2002). Small-scale event sport tourism: College sport as a tourist attraction. In S. Gammon & J. Kurtzman (Eds.), *Sport tourism: Principles and practice* pp. 3–19, Eastbourne: Leisure Studies Association.

Gibson, H. J., Kaplanidou, K., & Kang, S. J. (2012). Small-scale event sport tourism: A case study in sustainable tourism. *Sport Management Review, 15*(2), 160–170.

Gössling, S. (2002). Global environmental consequenses of tourism. *Global Environmental Change, 12*(4), 283–302.

Gössling, S., & Hall, C. M. (Eds.). (2005). *Tourism and environmental change: Ecological, economic, social and political interrelationships*. Oxford: Routledge.

Gössling, S., Hall, C. M., & Weaver, D. (Eds.). (2009). *Sustainable tourism futures: Perspectives on systems, restructuring and innovations*. Oxford: Routledge.

Gratton, C., Shibli, S., & Coleman, R. (2005). Sport and economic regeneration in cities. *Urban studies, 42*(5–6), 985–999.

Hall, C. M. (2004). Sport tourism and urban regeneration. S*port Tourism: Interrelationships, Impacts and Issues, Channel View, Clevedon*, 192–205.

Hallmann, K., Zehrer, A., & Müller, S. (2013). Perceived destination image: An image model for a winter sports destination and its effect on intention to revisit. *Journal of Travel Research*, 0047287513513161.

Hallstedt, S. I., Thompson, A. W., & Lindahl, P. (2013). Key elements for implementing a strategic sustainability perspective in the product innovation process. *Journal of Cleaner Production, 51*, 277–288.

Heath, E. T., & Kruger, E. A. (2015). *Spectators' contribution to the environmental dimension of sustainable event sports tourism* (Doctoral dissertation).

Higham, J. (Ed.). (2005). *Sport tourism destinations: Issues, opportunities and analysis*. Oxford: Elsevier Butterworth Heinemann.

Higham, J., & Hinch, T. (2009). *Sport and tourism: Globalization, mobility and identity*. London: Elsevier.

Hinch, T. D., & Higham, J. E. S. (2003). Sport, space and time: Effects of the Otago Highlanders franchise on tourism. *Journal of Sports Management, 17*(3), 235–257.

Hinch, T. D. & Higham, J. E. S. (2011). *Sport tourism development* (2nd ed.). Bristol: Channel View Publications.

Hollinshead, K. (2009). The "worldmaking" prodigy of tourism: The reach and power of tourism in the dynamics of change and transformation. *Tourism Analysis, 14*(1), 139–152.

Hopkins, D., Higham, J. E. S., & Becken, S. (2013). Climate change in a regional context: Relative vulnerability in the Australasian skier market. *Regional Environmental Change, 13*(2): 449–458.

Hritz, N., & Ross, C. (2010). The perceived impacts of sport tourism: An urban host community perspective. *Journal of Sport Management, 24*(2), 119–138.

Kaplanidou, K., & Vogt, C. (2007). The interrelationship between sport event and destination image and sport tourists' behaviours. *Journal of Sport & Tourism, 12*(3–4), 183–206.

Klenosky, D. B. (2002). The "pull" of tourism destinations: A means-end investigation. *Journal of Travel Research, 40*(4), 396–403.

Kozak, M. (2002). Comparative analysis of tourist motivations by nationality and destinations. *Tourism Management, 23*(3), 221–232.

Kurtzman, J., & Zauhar, J. (2005). Sports tourism consumer motivation. *Journal of Sport Tourism, 10*(1), 21–31.

Lamont, M. (2014). Authentication in sports tourism. *Annals of Tourism Research, 45*, 1–17.

Leiper, N. (1990). Tourist attraction systems. *Annals of Tourism Research, 17*(3), 367–384.

Lindsey, I. (2008). Conceptualising sustainability in sports development. *Leisure Studies, 27*(3), 279–294.

Mallen, C., Adams, L., Stevens, J., & Thompson, L. (2010). Environmental sustainability in sport facility management: A Delphi study. *European Sport Management Quarterly, 10*(3), 367–389.

Mallen, C., & Chard, C. (2011). A framework for debating the future of environmental sustainability in the sport academy. *Sport Management Review, 14*(4), 424–433.

McCool, S. (2015). Sustainable tourism: Guiding fiction, social trap or path to resilience? In T.V. Singh (Ed.), *Challenges in tourism research* (pp. 224–234). Bristol: Channel View.

Mills, B. M., & Rosentraub, M. S. (2013). Hosting mega-events: A guide to the evaluation of development effects in integrated metropolitan regions. *Tourism Management, 34*, 238–246.

Moyle, B. D., McLennan, C. L. J., Ruhanen, L., & Weiler, B. (2014). Tracking the concept of sustainability in Australian tourism policy and planning documents. *Journal of Sustainable Tourism, 22*(7), 1037–1051.

Preuss, H. (2015). A framework for identifying the legacies of a mega sport event. *Leisure Studies, 34*(6), 643–664.

Ponting, J., & O'Brien, D. (2014). Liberalizing Nirvana: An analysis of the consequences of common pool resource deregulation for the sustainability of Fiji's surf tourism industry. *Journal of Sustainable Tourism, 22*(3), 384–402.

Ruhanen, L. (2013). Local government: Facilitator or inhibitor of sustainable tourism development? *Journal of Sustainable Tourism, 21*(1), 80–98.

Ruhanen, L., Weiler, B., Moyle, B. D., & McLennan, C. L. J. (2015). Trends and patterns in sustainable tourism research: A 25-year bibliometric analysis. *Journal of Sustainable Tourism, 23*(4), 517–535.

Schianetz, K., & Kavanagh, L. (2008). Sustainability indicators for tourism destinations: A complex adaptive systems approach using systemic indicator systems. *Journal of Sustainable Tourism, 16*(6), 601–628.

Scherer, J., & Sam, M. P. (2008). Public consultation and stadium developments: Coercion and the polarization of debate. *Sociology of Sport Journal*, *25*(4), 443–61.

Schulenkorf, N. (2012). Sustainable community development through sport and events: A conceptual framework for Sport-for-Development projects. *Sport Management Review*, *15*(1), 1–12.

Shonk, D. J., & Chelladurai, P. (2008). Service quality, satisfaction, and intent to return in event sport tourism. *Journal of Sport Management*, *22*(5), 587–602.

Spaaij, R. (2009). The glue that holds the community together? Sport and sustainability in rural Australia. *Sport in Society*, *12*(9), 1132–1146.

Taks, M. (2013). Social sustainability of non-mega sport events in a global world. *EJSS. European Journal for Sport and Society*, *10*(2), 121.

Taks, M., Chalip, L., & Green, B. C. (2015). Impacts and strategic outcomes from non-mega sport events for local communities. *European Sport Management Quarterly*, *15*(1), 1–6.

Tassiopoulos, D., & Haydam, N. (2008). Golf tourists in South Africa: A demand-side study of a niche market in sports tourism. *Tourism Management*, *29*(5), 870–882.

Watts, J. (2016). Forced evictions in Rio favela for 2016 Olympics trigger violent clashes. Retrieved 10/9/16 from: https://www.theguardian.com/world/2015/jun/03/forced-evictions-vila-autodromo-rio-olympics-protests

Weed, M. (2005). Sports tourism theory and method—concepts, issues and epistemologies. *European Sport Management Quarterly*, *5*(3), 229–242.

Weed, M. (2006). Sports tourism research 2000–2004: A systematic review of knowledge and a meta-evaluation of methods. *Journal of Sport & Tourism*, *11*(1), 5–30.

Weed, M. E. (2008). *Olympic Tourism*. Oxford: Elsevier.

Weed, M., & Bull, C. (2012). *Sports tourism: Participants, policy and providers*. Oxford: Routledge.

Weed, M., Bull, C., Brown, M., Dowse, S., Lovell, J., Mansfield, L., & Wellard, I. (2014). A systematic review and meta-analyses of the potential local economic impact of tourism and leisure cycling and the development of an evidence-based market segmentation. *Tourism Review International*, *18*(1), 37–55.

Zimbalist, A. (2016). *Circus maximus: The economic gamble behind hosting the Olympics and the World Cup*. Washington, DC: Brookings Institution Press.

The role of travel conditions in cycling tourism: implications for destination and event management

Richard J. Buning and Heather J. Gibson

ABSTRACT
The purpose of this study was to explore the influence of travel conditions on preferred destination, event, and travel characteristics in the context of Active-Sport-Event Travel Carers among cyclists who travel to take part in events. Travel conditions are circumstances surrounding a trip such as travel with family or the length of travel. A sample of cyclists that travel to participate in events ($N = 1452$) was collected via online survey through cycling organizations and websites. Data analysis consisted of a series of repeated measures ANOVAs and paired sample t-tests. The results indicated an individual's event, destination, and travel-style preferences are dependent on whether he or she was traveling with a non-cyclist (e.g. family member) and the distance traveled. Prior research has suggested that for active sport tourists event criteria are more important than destination characteristics and travel preferences remain relatively stagnant with career progression. In contrast, the findings here suggest travel preferences vary based on travel conditions and that attractive destinations only become advantageous if event participants are traveling with non-cyclists or on trips involving longer distances. For instance when non-participant travel companions are included, the entertainment, attractions, and activities available in the destination become much more important to active event tourists. Communities seeking to attract sport tourists as a form of sustainable tourism development would be advised to organize events incorporating these preferences and to consider the influence of travel conditions.

The number of participatory sport events hosted by communities has grown significantly over the past 10–15 years (Physical Activity Council, 2015; Running USA, 2015). In particular, events oriented toward individual endurance sports such as running, cycling, and triathlons have grown in popularity as people seek opportunities to engage in physical activity while socializing amongst a group of likeminded individuals (e.g. Bull, 2006; Lamont, Kennelly, & Wilson, 2012; Shipway & Jones, 2008). With the growth in the number of events, competition among communities seeking to host these events has intensified as event and destination managers have realized the tourism benefits associated with the out-of-town active sport tourists attracted to these events (Gibson, Kaplanidou, & Kang, 2012). Kaplanidou and Gibson (2010) categorized this form of sport tourism as *event active sport tourism*, which they described as traveling to an event as a sports participant, rather than the a priori conceptualization of event sport tourism as spectator based (Gibson, 1998).

In conjunction with the growing numbers of participatory sports events, academics have focused increasingly on various aspects associated with taking part in these events from identity (Shipway & Jones, 2008), motivations (Gillett & Kelly, 2006), involvement (McGehee, Yoon, & Cardenas, 2003), social world membership (Getz & Patterson, 2013), and benefits sought (Gibson & Chang, 2012), among others. There are also a few studies that have focused on the role of the destination in an event active sport tourist's decisions to take part in participatory sport events, and more importantly to return to an event in the future. In one of the earliest of such studies, Chalip and McGuirty (2004) segmented marathoners by their running style and their preferences for different attractions in the host destination. The authors recommended that destinations offer bundled services based on the different preferences of the different runner segments. In a study of cycle tour participants, Kaplanidou and Vogt (2007) focused on the concepts of destination and event image and assessed the impact of this relationship of the participants' intentions to return to the destination and to take part in the event in the future. Adopting a similar focus, Kaplanidou and Gibson (2010) investigated senior games' athletes' intentions to return to participate again based not only on their image of the host community, but their satisfaction with the execution of the event. More recently, Kulczycki and Halpenny (2014) examined how a destination and the host venue for an event can influence cyclists' decisions and experiences associated with taking part in an event. Thus, while the focus on understanding the event participant- destination connection is growing, as communities view these participatory sports events as a form of sustainable tourism development (Gibson et al., 2012), there is a need to develop further work on the hosting of these events from a destination management perspective.

In an attempt to conceptualize the entirety of the intricacies involved in event travel and participation Getz (2008) proposed the concept of the *event travel career* (ETC) to help scholars organize their understanding of motives and travel behaviors and the integral relationship between an event active sport tourist's personal characteristics and those of the event and the destination (Getz & Andersson, 2010; Getz & McConnell, 2011). Getz (2008) suggested ETCs are characterized by an evolution in motivations and preferences for event participation and associated patterns of travel. Developing this idea further, Buning and Gibson (2015) established the term *active-sport-event travel careers* (ASETC) in the context of cycling events which they described through a six-stage grounded theory model beginning with initiation and concluding with maturity. Through this study the authors discovered individual travel behavior was more dependent on travel conditions rather than career progression. The term *travel conditions* is defined as the circumstances surrounding a particular trip that lead to altered travel behavior such as traveling with family or the travel distance associated with a specific event or the destination characteristics of the community hosting the event.

Historically, attractive destinations are thought to have a comparative advantage in attracting tourists (Gunn, 1972). Research on active sport tourism has generally suggested the contrary as event criteria have been demonstrated to be paramount while destination criteria are relatively unimportant in influencing event travel and choosing to participate in a specific event (e.g. Buning & Gibson, 2015; Bull, 2006; Chalip & McGurity, 2004; Kulczycki & Haplenny, 2014; Snelgrove & Wood, 2010). However, prior research has tended not to acknowledge that travel behavior may be based on the variability associated with travel conditions that spur individuals to alter their preferences and behavior. The purpose of the current study was to explore the influence of travel conditions on preferred destination, event, and travel characteristics amongst event active sport tourists, particularly cyclists who travel to participate in events (see Figure 1).

Literature review

Event travel careers

The idea behind the ETC (Getz, 2008) was originally derived from an integration of ideas from two existing concepts: *serious leisure* (Stebbins, 1992) and *travel careers* (Pearce, 2005). Serious leisure is the idea that engagement in a leisure activity ranges from casual to serious as individuals adopt a lifestyle of participation. Stebbins divided serious leisure into three types: amateur, hobbyist, or volunteer. He suggested that to be construed as serious leisure an activity must be substantial and interesting and have the ability to develop into a career for the individual directed at the acquisition and expression of the skills and abilities associated with the activity (Stebbins, 1992). Six distinctive qualities delineate serious leisure: perseverance, career potential, significant personal effort, durable benefits, a unique ethos, and identification with the leisure pursuit (Stebbins, 1982). Of the three types of serious leisure the focus of the ETC is on amateurs, who are motivated by seriousness and commitment to the activity through structured practice, schedules, and organization. The complimentary concept of travel careers as

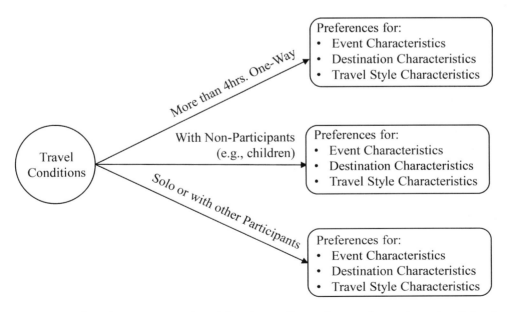

Figure 1. Travel conditions conceptual model: understanding preferences for sport event participants.

developed by Pearce (1988, 2005) is the view that tourists are motivated differently as they become more experienced travelers. Initially Pearce depicted this progression as the *travel career ladder* then later refined it as the *travel career pattern* (TCP). The TCP is described by Pearce (2005) as a dynamic concept based on identifiable stages that tourists experience throughout their travels that are influenced by their previous travel experiences, life stage, and/or contingency factors. Further, this pattern of motivation and career progress can be operationalized through travel experience, age, and life cycle.

Later, Getz expanded upon his original conception of the ETC through empirical research on cyclists and runners. Getz and Andersson (2010) investigated the tenets of the ETC through a study of runners at a Swedish half-marathon, while Getz and McConnell (2011) studied cyclists participating in a Canadian mountain bike event. Both of these studies focused on investigating six dimensions of the proposed ETC trajectory: motivation, travel style, temporal (i.e. frequency or travel and participation), spatial (i.e. distance traveled), event types, and destination criteria. This work was later followed up by Getz and Patterson's (2013) netnography of runners, mountain bikers, food lovers, and ballroom dancers and Patterson, Getz, and Gubb's (2016) investigation into the ETCs of yoga participants, which both argue the concept of social worlds provides a framework for the investigation of ETCs. Social worlds is a form a social organization based on the idea that individuals develop and maintain subcultures around a primary activity and is defined by Unruh (1980) as '… amorphous and diffuse constellations of actors, organizations, events, and practices which have coalesced into spheres of interest and involvement for a participant' (p. 277).

Active sport event travel career

In developing the ETC concept further and to demarcate the active sport tourist, Buning and Gibson (2015) defined the ASETC as 'a career like pattern of involvement and commitment to event-related travel and participation in physically active sport events, which leads to progression through time with regard to motivations, preferences, and modified behavior' (p. 555). Through a grounded theory study Buning and Gibson (2015) proposed ASETCs are illustrated through six stages beginning with initiation, which is described as the driving force behind his or her initial involvement in the sport and his/her first event. The second stage, introduction, is portrayed through little to no social connection to other cyclists, minimalistic travel style, and negligible event, travel, and destination knowledge. Next, expansion is the phase when individuals begin to increase their travel frequency, social connection to others, develop opinions on event evaluation, reduce the importance of superfluous event attributes (e.g. t-shirts and giveaways), and become willing to try new cycling disciplines. Buning and Gibson (2015) note that frequency of event participation is largely dependent on location, event availability, and seasonality. The fourth stage, peak threshold, is a pivotal moment for individuals pursing an ASETC as they reach an upper limit to their involvement and participation in the activity due to constraints. At this point they choose to maintain involvement, reduce involvement, or take a sabbatical.

The fifth stage, maintenance, occurs as individuals maintain their travel frequency, often disconnect from non-career cyclists, and are strongly motivated to maintain a healthy lifestyle and social connections. Maturity, the final stage, corresponds with advanced life stage and occurs as individuals reduce travel frequency, intensify their evaluation of event and destination characteristics, and increase their willingness to volunteer and mentor new cyclists. A follow-up study aimed at testing many of these suppositions quantitatively was performed by Buning and Gibson (2016) through a broad based international survey of cyclists. The results suggest motivation related to exploring/learning, social connection, mastery competence, giving back and competition against others escalated along with career progression. Further, Buning and Gibson (2016) found preferences for events characteristics also evolved with career progression, but preferences related to destinations and style of travel were mostly constant with career progression.

Destination, event, and travel characteristics

A growing body of literature has focused on understanding the preferred travel behavior of both event and non-event active sport tourists using a range of techniques and often in the context of cycling. For instance, Ritchie, Tkaczynski, and Faulks (2010) investigated the motivation and travel behavior of Australian cycling club members through involvement profiles. The results demonstrated that using involvement as a clustering variable creates segments of cycle tourists that differ based on gender, age, skill, experience, cycle frequency, and regularity of travel. Gibson and Chang (2012) also found that benefits sought from taking part in an organized cycle tour varied by involvement level, gender, and life stage with middle-aged participants emphasizing the relaxation associated with participating, whereas later life participants focused on the opportunities to experience new things and socializing. An earlier study by Ritchie (1998), which is often considered one of the first academic papers on cycling tourism, investigated touring cyclists in New Zealand. Of relevance to the current study, Ritchie found campgrounds and hostels were the most desirable accommodations; respondents were highly motivated to use alternate routes to avoid traffic and experience the environment; and road safety, weather, scenery, quality of driving, traffic, and signage were the most important factors to touring cyclists. Kaplanidou and Vogt's (2007) study of touring cyclists revealed destination image did not significantly influence sport event image. Further, satisfaction with the event did not influence revisit intentions, whereas destination satisfaction and past experience with the destination did indeed influence revisit intentions.

Moving to a different segment of the cycling tourism market Bull (2006) investigated the travel behavior of road racing cyclists in the UK. He found the majority of the racing cyclists took part in events requiring a day trip and trips requiring an overnight stay, only a fifth of the sample indicated they incorporate vacations into cycling trips and about half reported the destination was not important factor for cycling trips. Still, about half of the racing cyclists indicated they prefer an attractive environment/surroundings for cycling events. Another study into road racing cyclists by Kulczycki and Halpenny (2014) revealed cycling competition and event infrastructure (e.g. parking and bathrooms) were more important than destination elements such as scenery and tourism infrastructure (e.g. shopping and accommodations). Using conjoint analysis Larson and Won (2012) found road racing cyclists' preferred event characteristics differed based on level of recreational specialization. Specifically, the highly specialized ranked as prize purse the second most important characteristic whereas the least specialized group ranked point series as second. Regardless of specialization level travel distance was ranked as the most important event factor. Investigating mountain bike racers, Getz and McConnell (2011), discovered the highest rated event preferences were organization, a challenging course, scenery, and an informative easy to use website, while cost, prizes, size, and exclusivity were not important. Regarding destination importance, Getz and McConnell state the following:

> These factors were of lesser importance. It is quite possible that the TransRockies Challenge is so unique, even iconic in the mountain-biking world that the location and destination area is not particularly relevant. Or it might be that cross-country mountain biking is so dependent on rugged terrain that the traditional concept of a destination does not apply, only the site and route features matter. (p. 334)

Another segment of cycling tourism, charity events, was the focus of Snelgrove and Wood's (2010) study into the identity and motives of first time and repeat participants and confirms this same idea. The authors discovered learning about the destination was relatively unimportant compared to the physical, social, and cycling identity aspects of the event. A subsequent study on charity cycling events found the unique theme of overcoming the fear and anxiety related to cycling with traffic were powerful push factors to participate in an event (Coghlan, 2012).

Focusing specifically on cycling routes Downward and Lumsdon (2001) investigated the factors important to recreational cycle tourists in the UK. The findings revealed the cyclists strongly preferred quality scenery, a good network of cycling routes, quiet roads, and signed traffic-free routes. A similar study by Chen and Chen (2013) using a non-tourist sample of Taiwanese recreational cyclists found that individuals with higher levels of recreational specialization preferred more challenging routes and varied experiences compared to those reporting low recreational specialization. In general, the cyclists preferred cycling routes that had nearby attractions, cycling facilities (i.e. toilets and bike repair equipment), information centers, and bike-specific paths. Lamont and Jenkins (2013) used recreational specialization to segment participants of an Australian cycling event into intermediate and expert groups which revealed they preferred different course lengths and had varying opinions on event timing. Another study from Taiwan conducted by Lee and Huang (2014) using a Delphi study of experienced cycle tourists investigated the factors that attract cycle tourists revealing weather, bike facilities separated from vehicles, and road surface quality were the most important determinants of destination attractiveness. Lee, Chen, and Huang (2014) reported similar findings from a small sample of experienced Taiwanese touring and racing cyclists with the addition of grocery/convenience stores and lodging as important attributes of destination attractiveness.

Additionally, a wide range of facilitators to bicycle tourism have been revealed through the gray literature including: alternative routes, clean/smooth roads, low traffic, driver education, route safety, restaurants/stores nearby, maps/signage, lodging/camping, diverse scenery, bike-friendly businesses, length of ride, attractions, route variety, public transport, tour operators, and storage facilities (Cumberland County, 2000; Faulks, Ritchie, & Fluker, 2007; Nickerson et al., 2013; Parks & Trails New York, 2010). Conversely, Lamont and Buultjens (2011) explored the impediments to cycling tourism with an Australian sample and found perceptions of road safety, poor infrastructure (e.g. road quality, amenities, and services), and complications with the transportation of bicycles on public transport (i.e. air, train, and bus). However, researchers have yet to examine the role of travel conditions on preferred event, destination, and travel characteristics. Thus, three research questions were posed to guide the study:

- RQ1: Do *event-related* preferences differ based upon the travel conditions of traveling solo/with other cyclists, traveling with non-cyclists, and non-regional travel?
- RQ2: Do *destination* preferences differ based upon the travel conditions of traveling solo/with other cyclists, traveling with non-cyclists, and non-regional travel?
- RQ3: Do *travel-style* preferences differ based upon the travel conditions of traveling solo/with other cyclists and traveling with non-cyclists?

Method

Data collection

A quantitative approach was used to investigate the role of travel conditions in destination, event, and travel preferences. Amateur cyclists who were actively engaged, beginning, or have culminated active sport event travel served as the context of the study. Typically, data collection on this topic has focused on a single event; however, this approach is limited as the unit of analysis should be the individual and not limited to a specific event (Buning & Gibson, 2015; Getz & McConnell, 2011). However, data collection outside of an actual event eliminates the ability to use a sampling frame such as a registration database. Thus, the participant sample was recruited via partnerships created with cycling organizations (i.e. local cycling clubs), social networks, and industry groups (i.e. event promoters and cycling websites), an approach advanced by previous work on travel careers (i.e. Buning & Gibson, 2015; Getz & McConnell, 2011). In order to qualify for the study, potential respondents were asked two screening questions based on Lamont's (2009) definition of cycling tourism. If potential respondents had not traveled to participate in a cycling event that met the following criteria and/or were under the age of 18 they were excluded from the study. As adapted from Lamont (2009) the purpose of the travel must have been to actively participate in a cycling event that required a 50-mile, one-way trip or an overnight stay, defined as being away from home for a 24-hour period. Relying on Dillman, Smyth, and Christian's (2009) recommendations, a three-contact survey strategy (initial invitation and two follow-up invitations) was utilized to encourage responses.

Instrumentation

As part of a larger national study on active event travel, the questionnaire for the current study consisted of items identified in earlier research about active sport event travel (i.e. Buning & Gibson, 2015; Getz & McConnell, 2011) measuring preferences for event characteristics (22-items), destination characteristics (10-items), and travel-style characteristics (12-items). The 22 items measuring event preferences assessed characteristics such as size, safety, website quality, scenery, entry fees, sponsors, prestige, support, and course difficulty. The 10 items measuring destination preferences assessed characteristics including weather, local entertainment, scenery, terrain, and family activities. Lastly, the 12 travel-style items assessed characteristics related to costs, accommodations, mode of transportation, trip duration, and the opportunity to visit with friends/family or combine with a vacation. All preference items were measured using a 5-point Likert-type scale ranging from 1 (*not at all important*) to 5 (*very important*).

Based on previous research on travel careers (Buning & Gibson, 2015), the event and destination preference items were replicated on the questionnaire within the context of three travel conditions: traveling to an event solo or with other cyclists (TS/OC), event travel with non-cycling travel companions (Tw/NC), and non-regional travel defined as travel to events that required more than 4 h of travel one-way ($T > 4$ h). The travel-style items were measured across two travel conditions: TS/OC and Tw/NC. Qualifying questions paired with skip logic were utilized to prevent respondents from answering questions that did not apply to their travel patterns. Participants were also asked about the number of events they had completed within the past year and average time spent cycling in a week in hours. Lastly, demographic items were included consisting of: gender, age, employment status, ethnicity, education, marital status, household income, and location. The questionnaire was then pretested through cognitive interviews with five prospective participants to reduce measurement error (Willis, 2005). The cognitive interviewing procedure improved questionnaire design through a think-aloud process that identified problematic questions and misunderstandings (Drennan, 2003). After the cognitive interview process, final revisions to the questionnaire were completed and it was distributed online for data collection through the aforementioned partnerships.

Sample characteristics

The online data collection procedure procured $N = 1452$ total usable responses. The sample was predominantly male (74.7%), married (35.8%), college educated (88.8%), not a first-generation immigrant (95.8%), and white/Caucasian (91.1%). The majority of the sample reported annual household income between US $30,000 and $129,000 (62.7%) with a median between US $90,000 and $109,000 (14.3%). Participants ranged in age from 18 to 85 years old ($M = 52.03$, $SD = 13.45$). Regarding cycling characteristics, the sample reported having 1 month to 60 years of active cycling event travel experience ($M = 12.42$, $SD = 9.97$), a mean of 9.17 hrs. spent cycling during an average week ($SD = 5.71$ hrs.), and attended 0 to 55 ($M = 4.29$, $SD = 5.85$) events in the previous year. The overall highest rated event, destination, and travel-style preference items respectively were 'event is well organized' ($M = 4.38$, $SD = .75$), 'destination is a safe place to stay and visit' ($M = 3.98$, $SD = .99$), and 'I can drive there' ($M = 3.81$, $SD = 1.12$). The overall lowest rated event, destination, and travel-style items were 'prize money is awarded' ($M = 1.34$, $SD = .825$), 'event is in a world-class destination' ($M = 1.86$, $SD = 1.10$), and 'expensive/luxury accommodations' ($M = 1.43$, $SD = .79$). To ensure sampling error was not a significant threat to the generalizability of the study the characteristics of the sample were compared to the data from the United States national governing body for cycling (i.e. USA Cycling, Larson, 2013) and other studies on cycling tourism (e.g. Bull, 2006; Getz & McConnell, 2011; Lamont & Jenkins, 2013) revealing similarities between samples.

Data analysis

Data analysis consisted of four steps and was conducted via SPSS 22.00 statistics software. First, descriptive statistics were calculated to gain an overall understanding of the sample and investigate coding errors, skewness, and kurtosis concerns. Second, to answer RQ1 a series of repeated measures one-way ANOVAs were conducted to compare the preferred event characteristics (22-items) across the three travel conditions (i.e. TS/OC, Tw/NC, and $T > 4$ h). Third, to address RQ2 a series of repeated measures one-way ANOVAs were conducted to compare the preferred destination characteristics (10-items) across the three travel conditions (i.e. TS/OC, Tw/NC, and $T > 4$ h). Post hoc tests were performed at the $p < .05$ level of significance in conjunction with the ANOVAs using Bonferroni correction, a technique used with multiple comparisons to ensure the overall confidence level is sufficiently high (Agresti & Finlay, 2009). Lastly to answer RQ3, a paired samples t-test was conducted to assess the differences in preferred travel-style characteristics across the TS/OC and Tw/NC travel conditions. Initially, an exploratory factor analysis for the event, destination, and travel-style characteristics was conducted, but no factor structure emerged that was statistically or conceptually adequate; thus the items were analyzed individually which provides more actionable implications.

Results

Event preferences

In response to RQ1, the results indicated preferred event characteristics are dependent on three travel conditions: TS/OC, Tw/NC, and $T > 4$ h. The series of ANOVAs revealed statistically significant differences between the three travel conditions for 21 of the 22 event items (Table 1). The item 'small and intimate (few participants)' was the only non-significant event-related characteristic ($F (1, 648) = 1.78$, $p > .05$). The complete results for the repeated measures ANOVAs and the pairwise comparisons of the main effects are provided in Table 1. Of the 22 items, 18 event preferences were significantly rated less important when traveling with non-cyclists compared to travel solo or with other cyclists ($M_{TS/OC} = 1.61_{min}$ to 4.38_{max}; $M_{Tw/NC} = 1.39_{min}-4.05_{max}$). Only the item 'a recommendation to attend the event from someone I trust' was higher when traveling with non-cyclists ($M_{TS/OC} = 2.57$; $M_{Tw/NC} = 2.93$). Further, this item was rated as the most important with travel of more than 4 h ($M_{T > 4h} = 3.28$).

Indeed, five items were significantly greater with the $T > 4$ h condition compared to the TS/OC condition: 'recommendation to attend from someone I trust' ($M_{TS/OC} = 2.57$; $M_{T > 4h} = 3.28$), 'event website is use friendly' ($M_{TS/OC} = 3.65$; $M_{T > 4 h} = 3.93$), 'everything I need is on the website/social media' ($M_{TS/OC} = 3.70$; $M_{T > 4 h} = 3.92$), 'neutral support, SAG stops, aid stations' ($M_{TS/OC} = 3.53$; $M_{T > 4 h} = 3.76$), 'event and course safety' ($M_{TS/OC} = 4.03$; $M_{T > 4 h} = 4.19$). Three items were significantly more important when traveling more than 4 h one-way and the least important in travel with non-cyclists: 'everything I need to know is on the website/social media' ($M_{TS/OC} = 3.70$; $M_{Tw/NC} = 3.54$; $M_{T > 4 h} = 3.92$), 'event has neutral support' ($M_{TS/OC} = 3.53$; $M_{Tw/NC} = 3.36$; $M_{T > 4 h} = 3.76$), and 'event and course safety' ($M_{TS/OC} = 4.03$; $M_{Tw/NC} = 3.90$; $M_{T > 4 h} = 4.19$). Three items were significantly higher when traveling solo or with other cyclists than with non-cyclists and or on trips more than 4 h one-way: 'I want a new experience every time' ($M_{TS/OC} = 3.17$; $M_{Tw/NC} = 2.29$; $M_{T > 4 h} = 2.70$), 'a scenic and interesting course' ($M_{TS/OC} = 4.12$; $M_{Tw/NC} = 3.62$; $M_{T > 4 h} = 3.97$), and 'I prefer to go back to the same event(s)' ($M_{TS/OC} = 2.87$; $M_{Tw/NC} = 2.51$; $M_{T > 4 h} = 2.60$).

Table 1. Event preferences repeated measures ANOVA results.

	Solo or w/cyclists M	SE	w/Non-cyclists M	SE	More than 4 h M	SE	$F(1, 648)$	Post hoc
Event item								
Prize money is awarded	1.37	.03	1.33	.03	1.41	.04	12.38**	2 < 3**
A low entry fee	3.07	.04	2.88	.04	2.98	.05	16.75**	1 > 2**, 2 < 3*
It is a challenging course	3.23	.05	2.82	.05	3.21	.05	73.26**	1 > 2**, 2 < 3**
The larger the better (many participants)	2.29	.05	2.07	.05	2.32	.05	53.03**	1 > 2**, 2 < 3**
The event is well organized	4.38	.03	4.05	.04	4.37	.04	73.73**	1 > 2**, 2 < 3**
Participants receive gifts (shirts and medals)	2.12	.04	1.95	.05	2.13	.05	45.83**	1 > 2**, 2 < 3**
A course that makes it easy to get a good result	1.91	.04	1.76	.04	1.91	.05	22.81**	1 > 2**, 2 < 3**
Event is exclusive	1.61	.04	1.39	.03	1.64	.04	79.29**	1 > 2**, 2 < 3**
Involvement of a major corporate sponsor	1.63	.04	1.46	.33	1.59	.04	41.23**	1 > 2**, 2 < 3**
I want a new event experience every time	3.17	.04	2.29	.05	2.70	.05	257.00**	1 > 2**, 1 > 3**, 2 < 3**
Recommendation to attend from someone I trust	2.57	.05	2.93	.05	3.28	.05	133.25**	1 < 2**, 1 < 3**, 2 < 3**
The event gets media coverage	1.63	.04	1.53	.04	1.66	.04	17.815**	1 > 2**, 2 < 3**
A scenic and interesting course	4.12	.04	3.62	.05	3.97	.04	114.61**	1 > 2**, 1 > 3**, 2 < 3**
Small and intimate (few participants)	1.83	.04	1.78	.04	1.80	.04	1.78	–
A party atmosphere surrounding the event	2.62	.05	2.55	.05	2.64	.05	5.27*	2 < 3*
I prefer to go back to the same event(s)	2.87	.04	2.51	.04	2.60	.04	56.68**	1 > 2**, 1 > 3**, 2 < 3*
Event website is user-friendly	3.65	.04	3.59	.05	3.93	.04	70.06**	1 < 3**, 2 < 3**
Everything I need is on the website/social media	3.70	.05	3.54	.05	3.92	.05	53.15**	1 > 2**, 1 < 3**, 2 < 3**
Reputation and prestige of the event	2.64	.05	2.34	.05	2.72	.05	82.07**	1 > 2**, 2 < 3**
Neutral support, SAG stops, aid stations, etc.	3.53	.05	3.36	.05	3.76	.05	53.90**	1 > 2*, 1 < 3**, 2 < 3**
Event has a professional cycling component	1.71	.04	1.60	.04	1.70	.04	13.63**	1 > 2*, 2 < 3**
Event and course safety	4.03	.04	3.90	.05	4.19	.04	35.17**	1 > 2*, 1 < 3**, 2 < 3**

Note: All items measured from 1 (*not at all important*) to 5 (*very important*). Pairwise comparisons performed using Bonferroni correction. 1 = solo or with cyclists, 2 = traveling with non-cyclists, and 3 = traveling more than 4 h one-way.
*$p < .05$.
**$p < .001$.

Destination preferences

In response to RQ2, a series of repeated measures ANOVAs revealed statistically significant differences in preferred destination characteristics based on the three travel conditions for 9 of the 10 items. Only the single item 'the destination is scenic' was non-significant ($F(1, 622) = 2.79, p > .05$). The complete results for the repeated measures ANOVAs for destination characteristics are located in Table 2. The pairwise comparisons revealed four items were significantly more important when traveling with non-cyclists than the other travel conditions: 'entertainment is available in the area' ($M_{TS/OC} = 2.47$; $M_{Tw/NC} = 3.07$; $M_{T>4h} = 2.86$), 'there are things to do in the area besides the event' ($M_{TS/OC} = 2.98$; $M_{Tw/NC} = 3.46$; $M_{T>4h} = 3.21$), 'area has activities for families' ($M_{TS/OC} = 2.20$; $M_{Tw/NC} = 2.92$; $M_{T>4h} = 2.53$) and 'destination is of historical significance' ($M_{TS/OC} = 2.30$; $M_{Tw/NC} = 2.58$; $M_{T>4h} = 2.46$). Five items were rated as significantly more important with the $T > 4$ h condition than the TS/OC condition: 'expected weather conditions are favorable' ($M_{TS/OC} = 3.62$; $M_{T>4h} = 3.84$), 'event is a world-class destination' ($M_{TS/OC} = 1.91$; $M_{T>4h} = 2.19$), 'destination is iconic' ($M_{TS/OC} = 2.56$; $M_{T>4h} = 2.68$), 'destination is of historical significance' ($M_{TS/OC} = 2.30$; $M_{T>4h} = 2.46$) and 'destination is a safe place to stay and visit' ($M_{TS/OC} = 3.98$; $M_{T>4h} = 4.10$). Only one item the 'destination has attractive terrain' was more important with the $T > 4$ h condition and the least important with the Tw/NC condition ($M_{TS/OC} = 3.76$; $M_{Tw/NC} = 3.59$; $M_{T>4h} = 3.82$). This was also the only item where the TS/OC condition was significantly greater than the Tw/NC condition ($p < .001$).

Table 2. Destination preferences repeated measures ANOVA results.

	Travel condition							
	Solo or w/ cyclists		w/Non-cyclists		More than 4 h			
Destination item	M	SE	M	SE	M	SE	$F(1, 622)$	Post hoc
Expected weather conditions are favorable	3.62	.04	3.80	.05	3.84	.04	48.55**	1 < 2**, 1 < 3**
The event is in a world-class destination	1.91	.04	2.10	.05	2.19	.05	46.96**	1 < 2**, 1 < 3**
Entertainment is available in the area	2.47	.04	3.07	.04	2.86	.05	110.53**	1 < 2**, 1 < 3**, 2 > 3**
Things to do in the area besides the event	2.98	.05	3.46	.05	3.21	.05	67.07**	1 < 2**, 1 < 3**, 2 > 3**
Area has activities for families	2.20	.05	2.92	.06	2.53	.05	177.16**	1 < 2**, 1 < 3**, 2 > 3**
Destination is iconic/unique/famous	2.56	.04	2.68	.05	2.68	.05	7.29*	1 < 2*, 1 < 3*
Destination is of historical significance	2.30	.05	2.58	.05	2.46	.05	29.72**	1 < 2**, 1 < 3**, 2 > 3*
Destination is scenic	3.74	.04	3.72	.05	3.79	.04	2.79	–
Destination has attractive terrain	3.76	.04	3.59	.04	3.82	.04	35.00**	1 > 2**, 2 < 3**
Destination is a safe place to stay and visit	3.98	.04	4.02	.05	4.10	.04	15.44**	1 < 3**

Note: All items measured from 1 (*not at all important*) to 5 (*very important*). Estimated marginal means and standard errors reported. Pairwise comparisons performed using Bonferroni correction. 1 = solo or with cyclists, 2 = traveling with non-cyclists, and 3 = traveling more than 4 h one-way.
*$p < .05$.
**$p < .001$.

Travel-style preferences

Lastly to answer RQ3, a paired samples t-test revealed a statistically significant difference between the two travel conditions for 10 of the 12 travel-style items. The two non-significant items were 'keeping my overall costs low' ($t = 1.36, p > .05$) and 'the ability to travel to the cycling event and return home without staying overnight' ($t = -1.66, p > .05$). The complete paired samples t-test results are located in Table 3. Six items were rated as more important when traveling with non-cyclists compared to traveling solo or with other cyclists: 'my spouse or family wants to go there' ($M_{TS/OC} = 2.80; M_{Tw/NC} = 3.46$), 'special travel accommodation packages are available' ($M_{TS/OC} = 2.39; M_{Tw/NC} = 2.56$), 'availability of staying with friends or family instead of a hotel' ($M_{TS/OC} = 2.09; M_{Tw/NC} = 2.32$), 'expensive/luxury accommodations' ($M_{TS/OC} = 1.44; M_{Tw/NC} = 3.63$), and 'I can visit family or friends in the area' ($M_{TS/OC} = 2.18; M_{Tw/NC} = 3.16$). Conversely, four items were significantly greater when traveling solo or with other cyclists compared to traveling with non-cyclists: 'my friends are also going' ($M_{TS/OC} = 3.00; M_{Tw/NC} = 2.79$), 'economical/budget accommodations' ($M_{TS/OC} = 3.24; M_{Tw/NC} = 3.14$), 'I can drive there' ($M_{TS/OC} = 3.81; M_{Tw/NC} = 2.52$), and 'opportunity of combining the trip with a vacation' ($M_{TS/OC} = 2.90; M_{Tw/NC} = 1.61$).

Discussion

Previously, research indicated that travel behavior evolved as a result of progression through an ASETC, that attractive destinations have a comparative advantage (Getz, 2008; Getz & McConnell, 2011), and destination characteristics were relatively unimportant compared to event characteristics (Buning & Gibson, 2015; Bull, 2006; Chalip & Kulczycki & Haplenny, 2014; McGurity, 2004; Snelgrove & Wood, 2010). However, the current study found travel preferences are more so an outcome related to the travel conditions surrounding a trip. The results indicated an individual's event, destination, and travel-style preferences are dependent on whether he or she was traveling solo or with other cyclists, with a non-cyclist (e.g. family member), and/or the distance traveled (i.e. local vs regional).

Table 3. Travel-style preferences paired samples *t*-test results.

	Travel condition					
	Solo or w/ cyclists		w/Non-cyclists			
Travel-style item	M	SD	M	SD	df	t
Keeping my overall costs low	3.34	1.09	3.30	1.22	745	1.36
My friends are also going	3.00	1.17	2.79	1.22	747	5.39**
My spouse or family wants to go there	2.80	1.32	3.46	1.29	745	−14.10**
Special travel and accommodation packages are provided	2.39	1.18	2.56	1.27	750	−4.55**
Reducing my total travel time, from leaving home to returning	2.77	1.11	2.85	1.20	751	−1.97*
Availability of staying with friends or family instead of a hotel	2.09	1.19	2.32	1.25	751	−6.18**
Economical/budget accommodations	3.24	1.10	3.14	1.23	740	2.62*
Expensive/luxury accommodations	1.44	0.79	3.63	1.17	752	−41.97**
I can drive there	3.81	1.09	2.52	1.24	753	22.00**
I can visit family or friends in the area	2.18	1.12	3.16	1.26	746	−18.84**
Opportunity of combining the trip with a vacation	2.90	1.19	1.61	.93	626	23.66*
Ability to travel to the cycling event and return home without staying overnight	2.25	1.18	2.31	1.22	637	−1.66

Note: All items measured from 1 (*not at all important*) to 5 (*very important*).
*p < .05.
**p < .001.

Regarding the first research question, most event-related preferences were less important when traveling with non-cyclists and conversely more important when traveling to an event solo or with other cyclists. The one exception to this was the item incorporating a word-of-mouth (WOM) recommendation about the event from a trusted source. This was also important when traveling to an event more than 4 h from home with other family members. In the world of tourism generally, WOM recommendations are known to be powerful determinants of decision-making behavior (Chen & Tasi, 2007; Chi & Qu, 2008). In the context of a sport event, this also makes sense as a sport tourist making a decision about whether to bring his or her family to the event is likely to seek out more information about the suitability of the event for family members and similar to other tourism-related decisions would put trust in the opinions of others who have attended the event previously, more so than a website or other information source. This is consistent with Kaplanidou and Gibson's (2010) investigation of Senior Games participants' intentions to participate in an event again in the future. They postulated that the power of the athlete social world (Unruh, 1980) to evaluate the 'worth' of an event should be considered by event managers and future research should examine WOM among sport tourists. The results of this study seem to suggest that especially when traveling with non-competitors and trips of more than 4 h from home that WOM is more influential than official event-related sources such as websites.

Conversely, when participants were traveling solo or with other cyclists, event-related preferences such as low entry fees, a challenging/scenic course, and taking part in the same event again were rated as more important. These findings are also consistent with what we know about 'pure' sport tourists, that is where sport is the main purpose of the trip (Robinson & Gammon, 2004). For example, existing studies on event active sport tourists show that sport-related criteria are important for the satisfaction of the athletes (Ryan & Lockyer, 2002) and is linked to their intentions to take part in an event again (Kaplanidou & Gibson, 2010). If active sport tourists are investing their time and money in an event, especially one that is further away from home then event attributes and new experiences and challenging courses are likely to act as motives alongside sport-specific motives to participate in a particular event (Buning & Gibson, 2015; Bull, 2006; Robinson & Gammon, 2004). Certainly, these findings extend Buning and Gibson (2015) suppositions, as individuals tend to diminish the importance of several event attributes when traveling with non-cyclists, but they become more critical of these event attributes when traveling further away from home.

In answer to the second research question about destination characteristics, when traveling with non-cycling companions, destination attributes such as the availability of entertainment in the area, things to do besides the event, availability of activities for children, and historical attractions were more important. These findings support our suppositions above about the need to put more consideration on non-cycling travel companions and family when considering a particular event, but this time in the context of the destination. Moreover, when traveling more than 4 h away from home, several destination preferences were rated as more important including favorable weather, image of the destination as 'world-class' and iconic, has historic qualities, and has a reputation for being safe. These results are consistent with preferences noted in other forms of tourism as it is well-known in tourism for example that the presence and the age of children are very influential on travel choices in terms of accommodation, style of trip, and mode of transportation (e.g. Lawson, 1991; Ryan & Glendon, 1998; Schanzel & Yeoman, 2014).

Crompton (1979) in his classic study on tourist motivation noted that when traveling with children, parents are often more conscious about the educational nature of a trip, which might link here to the finding about the importance of history in the destination preferences. The issue of safety is also becoming more important in tourism as the issue of perceived risk has been linked to choice of destination and whether individuals will travel or not (Lepp & Gibson, 2008). Thus, again when traveling with non-cycling companions, especially events that are further from home, the evaluation of a destination as safe, which can include risk of crime, food, health, or the bigger risk factors such as terrorism or natural disasters, becomes more important to travel decision-making (Lepp & Gibson, 2003). Not surprisingly, perception of risk has been a growing consideration for the planners of mega sporting events (Qi, Gibson, & Zhang, 2009) and is beginning to filter down to the participatory events especially after the incidents at the Boston Marathon in 2013 (Seelye, 2014).

Similar to the results about event preferences, attractive terrain was the only destination item that was reported to be less important when traveling with non-cyclists and more important with travel more than 4 h. Scenery was the solitary destination preference that seems to be more universally important regardless of travel party composition when traveling further from home. Indeed, traveling longer distances leads to increased expenditure in the destination in total and per day (e.g. Cobb & Olberding, 2010; Tang & Turco, 2001; Weed et al., 2014). Conceivably, when active sport tourists choose to invest financially and temporally in a trip and include non-event participants the more emphasis they put on enjoying and experiencing the destination (Buning & Gibson, 2015). However, active sport tourists traveling less than 4 h by themselves or with other event participants perceive the destination to be relatively unimportant.

Travel style was also largely dependent on travel conditions as participants altered their preferred travel style to accommodate the interests of non-event participant(s). If participants were traveling solo/with other cyclists, they preferred traveling with friends, keeping costs low, budget lodging, driving, and combining the trip with a vacation. However, once a non-cyclist companion was introduced, the participants shifted their travel style toward luxury/special accommodations, spouse/family desires, travel packages, reduced travel time, and staying with and or visiting with friends or family in the area. However, the desire to decrease travel costs and accommodation costs was important regardless of travel condition, but differed in the way it was manifested. For the solo or cyclists traveling with other cyclists budget accommodations were sought. However, for trips with non-cyclists, comfortable and may be even luxurious accommodations were sought, but with the availability of special accommodation packages to allay the costs. Surprisingly, the opportunity of combining a cycling event trip with a vacation was more important when traveling solo or with other cyclists. In some ways this finding conflicts with our other results about the importance of family-friendly activities and more comfortable accommodations when traveling with non-cyclists.

Perhaps the participants' conceptions as to what constitutes a family vacation are important in explaining these preferences. Schanzel and Yeoman (2014) suggest there is a need to consider all family members' preferences when looking at family vacations including those of the children, the desire for relief from parental expectations especially for mothers, and even the inclusion of grandparents in such trips. Thus, travel to a cycling event is likely not to be considered as a family vacation, but may be perceived a short break. Certainly this finding seems to suggest that cyclists may prefer to distinguish traditional family style vacations from cycling-related vacations possibly as part of a tradeoff between competing life priorities that amateur athletes make in an attempt to negotiate constraints (Lamont & Kennelly, 2011; Lamont et al., 2012). At face value, this finding appears to contradict the proposition advanced by Getz and McConnell (2011) that there should be an increase in the combination of event-specific and mixed motive trips with career progression. Perhaps career progression needs to be put into the context of family dynamics as suggested by the results of this study and Lamont and Kennelly's (2011) work on competing priorities. Certainly, our results seem to suggest that travel style is more likely dependent on the presence of non-participant travel companions and not necessarily based on an inherent desire to not travel with other cyclists as suggested by Bull (2006) who found only a small proportion of the racing cyclists he studied traveled with other cycling club members.

Conclusion

Prior research into active sport tourism has tended to overlook the concept of travel conditions and has adopted the position that event active tourists primarily focus on event criteria as they make travel decisions (e.g. Getz & McConnell, 2011). In contrast, the results of this study seem to suggest that event, destination, and travel preferences vary based on travel conditions, particularly the presence of non-event participants or events that require longer travel distances. As a result, communities that have identified events as part of their economic development plan would be advised to strategically address not only the planning and execution of the event, but also attractions and facilities for travel companions. This is where community partnerships involving both sporting bodies such as events rights holder and sports commissions and destination management organizations (i.e. convention and visitor bureaus) should be working in unison as each stakeholder has knowledge in management, marketing, and logistics to create participatory sports events that attract and satisfy the active sport tourist and their companions. Weed (2003) called for cross-sectoral leveraging of events to bridge the divide between sporting and tourism agencies. Almost 15 years later, as communities around the world have embraced sports events, particularly the smaller-scale participatory variety, there are many examples of successful community partnerships where the hosting of smaller-scale events has become a sustainable form of tourism development (Gibson et al., 2012).

However, some challenges still exist such as the need to focus on not only the event participants, but their travel companions as suggested by the current study. Still, few scholars have examined the concept of flow-on tourism associated with hosting these events (Taks, Chalip, Green, Kesenne, & Martyn, 2009). Taks et al. defined flow-on tourism as 'tourism activities beyond the event but around the time of the event' (p. 121) and identified four segments of event attendees of whom first timers were more likely to take part in other tourism activities, as were those who engaged in searching for additional information about the destination before their trip. Yet, still the results of our current study seem to confirm those of Ritchie, Mosedale, and King (2002) and Gibson, Willming, and Holdnak (2003) that the avid or pure sport tourists are less likely to take part in flow-on activities, whereas the more casual participant, or in the case of the current study, those active sport tourists who are accompanied by non-participants and especially those on trips further from home appear to be the visitors who can be encouraged to take part in the wider tourism offerings of a destination. Furthermore, as Chalip and McGuirty (2004) suggested these event active sport tourists with non-sport traveling companions may also be the ideal markets for the bundling of event experiences within wider offerings of a destination.

Destination and event managers seeking to expand the travel distance of their potential participants are advised to focus on destination characteristics such as scenery and historical qualities that promote this behavior. Certainly, we are not suggesting that event organizers ignore the fine details of event planning, a sentiment supported by Kaplanidou, Kerwin, and Karadakis (2013) who found both event participants and providers perceive the effective management of event characteristics as an important factor for success. However, as Bull (2006) found, the majority of the racing cyclists he studied preferred to race locally, considered traveling far as not important, and when they decided to travel it was because racing events were not available locally. Considering most cyclists prefer to stay overnight in a destination only if the travel is more than 2 h one-way (Buning & Gibson, 2015) destinations and events need to entice individuals into traveling further and staying overnight by matching event offerings to the travel preferences of their target markets. Many small-scale participant sport events have problems with longevity as success that is sustainable over several years can be quite difficult especially if the event is not organized in an optimal manner and/or properly bundled with the destination (Chalip & McGuirty, 2004). If events and destinations are organized toward their current and past participants only and not the overall market then they are likely discouraging many individuals from attending and as a result event sustainability will become a serious problem (Taks et al., 2009). Freeman and Thomlinson (2014) argue a similar point, claiming that sustainable community-based mountain bike tourism is contingent on community partnerships, physical geography (i.e. trails access and design), legislation (i.e. land access and liability insurance), and funding sources.

For instance, if an event/destination is not offering activities for non-participants (e.g. family members and significant others), but the overall market prefers to travel with non-participants a large group of potential participants will not attend regardless of whether event or destination has desirable characteristics. Further, destination and event managers seeking to increase the economic impact of an event should organize and market to individuals traveling with non-participants (e.g. family members) as they are more likely to spend more in the host community and seek a more luxurious experience as reported by the participants in this study. Indeed, the research findings of Downward, Lumsdon, and Weston (2009) along with Sato, Jordan, Kaplanidou, and Funk (2014) confirm that group size is a determinant of visitor expenditure for active sport tourists as larger groups tend to spend more. For individuals traveling with non-cyclists, attractive destination criteria are often more important than event characteristics so events should be not only organized around the participants, but also their travel companions.

While this study has opened the discussion to focus on the travel companions and the distance traveled by event active sport tourists, there are more avenues to investigate. For example, our results hinted at concepts from the wider body of literature on tourism about WOM, information search behavior, and family travel decision-making that might be directions for future research on the travel associated with these participatory sports events. While the sample for the current study was tested for representativeness among the competitive US cycling population, to what extent do US sport travel behaviors generalize to other countries where concepts of travel distance, event offerings or tourism infrastructure might be different? Moreover, this study was focused on the cycling community. How similar or different are other sporting social worlds in running or triathlons or indeed team sports such as rugby or hockey?

In reflecting more broadly on the participatory event world, what appears to be apparent is the growing popularity of these participatory sports events, the diversity of sport offerings (marathons to obstacle races), the growth in travel to participate in these events, and the number of communities who have busy event portfolios to cater to this demand. For destinations going forward the challenges appear to be maintaining their competitive edge and off-setting both participant and host community fatigue in a sea of ever-increasing event offerings.

ORCID

Richard J. Buning http://orcid.org/0000-0002-0089-3967
Heather J. Gibsonb http://orcid.org/0000-0003-0014-6379

References

Agresti, A., & Finlay, B. (2009). *Statistical methods for the social sciences* (4th ed.). Upper Saddle River, NJ: Prentice Hall.
Buning, R. J. & Gibson, H. J. (2015). The evolution of active sport event travel careers. *Journal of Sport Management*, 29(5), 555–569. doi:10.1123/jsm.2014-0215.
Buning, R. J. & Gibson, H. J. (2016). The trajectory of active sport event travel careers: A social worlds perspective. *Journal of Sport Management*. Advance online publication. doi:10.1123/jsm.2015-0213.
Bull, C. J. (2006). Racing cyclists as sports tourists: The experiences and behaviours of a case study group of cyclists in East Kent, England. *Journal of Sport & Tourism, 11*, 259–274.

Chalip, L., & McGuirty, J. (2004). Bundling sport events with the host destination. *Journal of Sport & Tourism, 9*, 267–282.

Chen, C., & Chen, P. (2013). Estimating recreational cyclists' preferences for bicycle routes – Evidence from Taiwan. *Transport Policy, 26*, 23–30.

Chen, C. F., & Tsai, D. C. (2007). How destination image and evaluative factors affect behavioral intentions? *Tourism Management, 28*(4), 1115–1122.

Chi, C. G. Q., & Qu, H. (2008). Examining the structural relationships of destination image, tourist satisfaction and destination loyalty: An integrated approach. *Tourism Management, 29*(4), 624–636.

Cobb, S., & Olberding, D. J. (2010). Shipping the runners to the race: A sport tourism interpretation of the Alchian-Allen theorem. *International Journal of Sport Finance, 5*, 268–279.

Coghlan, A. (2012). An autoethnographic account of a cycling charity challenge event: Exploring manifest and latent aspects of the experience. *Journal of Sport & Tourism, 17*(2), 105–124.

Crompton, J. L. (1979). Motivations for pleasure vacation. *Annals of Tourism Research, 6*(1), 408–424.

Cumberland County. (2000). *Cumberland county bike trail study*. Retrieved from the South Jersey Transportation Planning Origination website. http://www.sjtpo.org/Documents/Studies/CumbCoBikeStudy_Dec2000.pdf

Dillman, D. A., Smyth, J. D., & Christian, L. M. (2009). *Internet, mail, and mixed-mode surveys: The tailored design method* (3rd ed.). Hoboken, NJ: John Wiley & Sons.

Downward, P., & Lumsdon, L. (2001). The development of recreational cycle routes: An evaluation of user needs. *Managing Leisure, 6*, 50–60.

Downward, P., Lumsdon, L., & Weston, R. (2009). Visitor expenditure: The case of cycle recreation and tourism. *Journal of Sport & Tourism, 14*(1), 25–42.

Drennan, J. (2003). Cognitive interviewing: Verbal data in the design and pretesting of questionnaires. *Journal of Advanced Nursing, 42*(1), 57–63.

Faulks, P., Ritchie, B., & Fluker, M. (2007). *Cycle tourism in Australia: An investigation into its size and scope*. Retrieved from the Sustainable Tourism Cooperative Research Centre website. http://www.crctourism.com.au/BookShop/BookDetail.aspx?d=500

Freeman, R., & Thomlinson, E. (2014). Mountain bike tourism and community development in British Columbia: Critical success factors for the future. *Tourism Review International, 18*, 9–22.

Getz, D. (2008). Event tourism: Definition, evolution, and research. *Tourism Management, 29*, 403–428.

Getz, D., & Andersson, T. D. (2010). The event-tourist career trajectory: A study of high-involvement amateur distance runners. *Scandinavian Journal of Hospitality and Tourism, 10*, 468–491.

Getz, D., & McConnell, A. (2011). Serious sport tourism and event travel careers. *Journal of Sport Management, 25*, 326–338.

Getz, D., & Patterson, I. (2013). Social worlds as a framework for event and travel careers. *Tourism Analysis, 18*, 485–501.

Gibson, H., Willming, C., & Holdnak, A. (2003). Small-scale event sport tourism: Fans as tourists. *Tourism Management, 24*, 181–190.

Gibson, H. J. (1998). Sport tourism: A critical analysis of research. *Sport Management Review, 1*(1), 45–76.

Gibson, H. J., & Chang, S. (2012). Cycling in mid and later life: Involvement and benefits sought from a bicycle tour. *Journal of Leisure Research, 44*(1), 23–51.

Gibson, H. J., Kaplanidou, K., & Kang, S. J. (2012). Small-scale event sport tourism: A case study in sustainable tourism. *Sport Management Review, 15*(2), 160–170.

Gillett, P., & Kelly, S. (2006). 'Non-local' masters games participants: An investigation of competitive active sport tourist motives. *Journal of Sport Tourism, 11*(3–4), 239–257.

Gunn, C. (1972). *Vacationscape: Designing tourist regions*. Austin: Bureau of Business Research, University of Texas.

Kaplanidou, K., & Gibson, H. J. (2010). Predicting behavioral intentions of active event sport tourists: The case of a small-scale recurring sports event. *Journal of Sport & Tourism, 15*(2), 163–179.

Kaplanidou, K., Kerwin, S., & Karadakis, K. (2013). Understanding sport event success: Exploring perceptions of sport event consumers and event providers. *Journal of Sport & Tourism, 18*(3), 137–159.

Kaplanidou, K., & Vogt, C. (2007). The interrelationship between sport event and destination image and sport tourists' behaviours. *Journal of Sport & Tourism, 12*(3–4), 183–206.

Kulczycki, C., & Halpenny, E. (2014). Sport cycling tourists' setting preferences, appraisals, and attachments. *Journal of Sport & Tourism, 19*(2), 169–197.

Lamont, M. (2009). Reinventing the wheel: A definitional discussion of bicycle tourism. *Journal of Sport & Tourism, 14*(1), 5–23.

Lamont, M., & Buultjens, J. (2011). Putting the brakes on: Impediments to the development of independent cycle tourism in Australia. *Current Issues in Tourism, 14*(1), 57–78.

Lamont, M., & Jenkins, J. (2013). Segmentation of cycling event participants: A two-step cluster method utilizing recreation specialization. *Event Management, 17,* 391–407.

Lamont, M., & Kennelly, M. (2011). I can't do everything! Competing priorities as constraints in triathlon event travel careers. *Tourism Review International, 14*(2), 85–97.

Lamont, M., Kennelly, M., & Wilson, E. (2012). Competing priorities as constraints in event travel careers. *Tourism Management, 33,* 1068–1079.

Larson, D. J. (2013). *Membership survey and analysis.* Retrieved from USA Cycling Inc website: https://s3.amazonaws.com/USACWeb/forms/encyc/2013-USAC-Membership-Survey-Report.pdf

Larson, D. J., & Won, D. (2012). Road cycling event preferences for racing cyclists. *International Journal of Sports Marketing and Sponsorship, 13*(2), 27–42.

Lawson, R. (1991). Patterns of tourist expenditures and types of vacation across the family life cycle. *Journal of Travel Research, 29*(4), 12–18.

Lee, C., Chen, P., & Huang, H. (2014). Attributes of destination attractiveness in Taiwanese bicycle tourism: The perspective of active experienced bicycle tourists. *International Journal of Hospitality & Tourism Administration, 15,* 275–297.

Lee, C., & Huang, H. (2014). The attractiveness of Taiwan as a bicycle tourism destination: A supply-side approach. *Asia Pacific Journal of Tourism Research, 19*(3), 273–299.

Lepp, A., & Gibson, H. (2003). Tourist roles, perceived risk and international tourism. *Annals of Tourism Research, 30*(3), 606–624.

Lepp, A., & Gibson, H. (2008). Sensation seeking and tourism: Tourist role, perception of risk and destination choice. *Tourism Management, 29*(4), 740–750.

McGehee, N., Yoon, Y., & Cardenas, D. (2003). Involvement and travel for recreational runners in North Carolina. *Journal of Sport Management, 17,* 305–324.

Nickerson, N. P., Jorgenson, J., Berry, M., Kwenye, J., Kozel, D., & Schutz, J. (2013). *Analysis of touring cyclists: Impacts, needs and opportunities for Montana.* Retrieved from the Institute for Tourism Recreation Research website. http://scholarworks.umt.edu/itrr_pubs/226/

Parks & Trails New York. (2010). *Bicyclists bring business: A guide for attracting bicyclists to New York's canal communities.* Retrieved from the Parks & Trails New York website. http://www.ptny.org/application/files/8514/3387/5238/Bicyclists_bring_business.pdf

Patterson, I., Getz, D., & Gubb, K. (2015). The social world and event travel career of the serious yoga devotee. *Leisure Studies, 23,* 1–18.

Patterson, I., Getz, D., & Gubb, K. (2016). The social world and event travel career of the serious yoga devotee. *Leisure Studies, 35*(3), 296–316.

Pearce, P. L. (1988). *The Ulysses factor: Evaluating visitors in tourist settings.* New York, NY: Springer-Verlag New York.

Pearce, P. L. (2005). *Tourist behaviour: Themes and conceptual schemes.* Buffalo, NY: Channel View Publications.

Physical Activity Council. (2015). *2015 Participation report.* Retrieved from www.physicalactivitycouncil.com/pdfs/current.pdf

Qi, C. X., Gibson, H. J., & Zhang, J. J. (2009). Perceptions of risk and travel intentions: The case of China and the Beijing Olympic Games. *Journal of Sport & Tourism, 14*(1), 43–67.

Ritchie, B., Mosedale, L., & King, J. (2002). Profiling sport tourists: The case of Super 12 Rugby Union in the Australian Capital Territory, Australia. *Current Issues in Tourism, 5*(1), 33–44.

Ritchie, B. W. (1998). Bicycle tourism in the South Island of New Zealand: Planning and management issues. *Tourism Management, 19*(6), 567–582.

Ritchie, B. W., Tkaczynski, A., & Faulks, P. (2010). Understanding the motivation and travel behavior of cycle tourists using involvement profiles. *Journal of Travel & Tourism Marketing, 27*(4), 409–425.

Robinson, T., & Gammon, S. (2004). A question of primary and secondary motives: Revisiting and applying the sport tourism framework. *Journal of Sport & Tourism, 9*(3), 221–233.

Running USA. (2015). *National running survey*. Retrieved from http://www.runningusa.org/statistics

Ryan, C., & Glendon, I. (1998). Application of leisure motivation scale to tourism. *Annals of Tourism Research, 25*(1), 169–184.

Ryan, C., & Lockyer, T. (2002). Masters' games – The nature of competitors' involvement and requirements. *Event Management, 7*(4), 259–270.

Sato, M., Jordan, J. S., Kaplanidou, K., & Funk, D. C. (2014). Determinants of tourists' expenditure at mass participant sport events: A five-year analysis. *Current Issues in Tourism, 17*(9), 763–771.

Schanzel, H. A., & Yeoman, I. (2014). The future of family tourism. *Tourism Recreation Research, 39*(3), 343–360.

Seelye, K. (2014). *Boston plans to tighten security at marathon*. Retrieved from http://www.nytimes.com/2014/03/11/us/boston-marathon-to-get-new-security-measures.html?_r=0

Shipway, R., & Jones, I. (2008). The great suburban Everest: An 'insiders' perspective on experiences at the 2007 Flora London Marathon. *Journal of Sport & Tourism, 13*(1), 61–77.

Snelgrove, R., & Wood, L. (2010). Attracting and leveraging visitors at a charity cycling event. *Journal of Sport & Tourism, 15*(4), 269–285.

Stebbins, R. A. (1982). Serious leisure: A conceptual statement. *The Pacific Sociological Review, 25*, 251–272.

Stebbins, R. A. (1992). *Amateurs, professionals, and serious leisure*. Buffalo, NY: McGill-Queen's University Press.

Taks, M., Chalip, L., Green, B. C., Kesenne, S., & Martyn, S. (2009). Factors affecting repeat visitation and flow-on tourism as sources of event strategy sustainability. *Journal of Sport & Tourism, 14*(2–3), 121–142.

Tang, Q., & Turco, D. M. (2001). Spending behaviors of event tourists. *Journal of Convention & Exhibition Management, 3*(2), 33–40.

Unruh, D. R. (1980). The nature of social worlds. *The Pacific Sociological Review, 23*(3), 271–296.

Weed, M. (2003). Why the two won't tango! Explaining the lack of integrated policies for sport and tourism in the UK. *Journal of Sport Management, 17*, 258–283.

Weed, M., Bull, C., Brown, M., Dowse, S., Lovell, J., Mansfield, L., & Wellard, I. (2014). A systematic review and meta-analyses of the potential local economic impact of tourism and leisure cycling and the development of an evidence-based market segmentation. *Tourism Review International, 18*, 37–55.

Willis, G. B. (2005). *Cognitive interviewing: A tool for improving questionnaire design*. Thousand Oaks, CA: Sage Publications.

Surf localism in Costa Rica: exploring territoriality among Costa Rican and foreign resident surfers

Lindsay E. Usher and Edwin Gómez

ABSTRACT
This study examines the phenomenon of surf localism among local Costa Rican and foreign resident surfers in Pavones, Costa Rica, a well-known surf break considered the second longest left-breaking wave in the world. A multidisciplinary territoriality framework is used to explore the ways in which surfers expressed ownership, defined boundaries and regulated behavior in the surf break. Using an ethnographic approach, the first author engaged in participant observation in the surf and the community. She also conducted interviews with Costa Rican residents, resident foreigners and tourists. The findings indicate a number of differences between Costa Rican surfers and resident foreigners with regard to ownership, boundary definition and regulating behavior. Costa Rican surfers felt a greater sense of ownership for the surf break, but were less likely to start verbal or physical conflicts with other surfers than resident foreigners. Resident foreigners indicated feeling a right to the surf break, more so than ownership, and were more likely to verbally confront tourists who were not following surf etiquette. There was also evidence of a cyclical pattern of localism. Many participants blamed conflicts between surfers on increased crowding. The results also highlight the importance of constant destination monitoring in order to ensure a positive surfing experience for Costa Ricans, foreigners and tourists in a community highly reliant on surf tourism income.

Host communities in sport tourism destinations experience a variety of positive and negative economic, social and environmental impacts (Fredline, 2005; Hritz & Ross, 2010). However, many sport researchers have focused on the challenges and opportunities of hosting sporting events within the destinations (Fredline, 2005; Han, Nelson, & Kim, 2015; Hinch & Ramshaw, 2014; Kaiser, Alfs, Beech, & Kaspar, 2013; Waller, Trendafilova, & Daniell, 2014). Less attention has been devoted to destinations that regularly attract tourists due to environmental features, which enable the practice of nature-based sports (Müller, Peters, & Blanco, 2010). However, surf tourism destinations have received an increased amount of attention in the past decade (Ponting & O'Brien, 2014; Towner, 2016).

Surf tourists' desires to avoid crowded surf breaks in their home countries and find the perfect wave have propelled them to the far corners of the developing world (Ponting,

2009; Ponting & O'Brien, 2015). The communities near world-class surf breaks have experienced significant positive and negative changes with the arrival of surf tourists (Krause, 2013; O'Brien & Ponting, 2013; Usher & Kerstetter, 2014). Researchers have focused considerable attention on the sustainability of surf tourism destinations (Martin & Assenov, 2015; Ponting & O'Brien, 2015). While surf tourism provides residents with access to a new sport and increased economic opportunities, foreign dominance of the industry, inflated land prices, increased levels of crime and drugs, prostitution and environmental degradation are some of the negative impacts observed in surf tourism destinations (Krause, 2013; Tantamjarik, 2004; Towner, 2016). Crowding and exceeding carrying capacity are other factors that threaten the sustainability of surf tourism destinations because a primary motivator of surf travel is crowd avoidance (Ponting & O'Brien, 2015).

One phenomenon, which some believe is the result of increasingly crowded surf breaks, is localism (Booth, 2013; Scott, 2003). Localism is the territorial behavior of resident surfers over surf breaks (Alessi, 2009; Usher & Kerstetter, 2015a). Kaffine (2009) noted that localism may manifest differently in each surf destination because of local environmental (i.e., type of surf break) and social factors (i.e., characteristics of the local community). Any form of localism has implications for the sustainability of surf destinations. If surf tourists feel unwelcome at a surf break, they may travel to other destinations with a better 'vibe', diverting needed economic income away from the local community (Ponting & O'Brien, 2015; Usher & Kerstetter, 2015a).

Localism is a type of human territoriality. Territoriality encompasses three aspects: (a) feelings of ownership, (b) the setting of boundaries and (c) the regulation of behavior within those boundaries (Altman, 1975; Sack, 1986; Usher & Kerstetter, 2015a). Given the implications of the claiming and regulating of leisure space, it is surprising territoriality has not received more attention in the sport, recreation and tourism literature. Researchers have used the concept of territoriality to examine localism (Comley & Thoman, 2011; Dorset, 2009; Usher & Kerstetter, 2015a). However, the research has primarily focused on local surfers as a single group. Some destinations in developing countries have at least two groups of 'local surfers' due to the presence of resident foreigners (Usher & Kerstetter, 2015b). Costa Rica is a country where the population of resident foreign surfers has greatly increased in the past decade (Krause, 2013; Noorloos, 2011).

Costa Rica gained popularity as a surf destination in the mid-1990s (Krause, 2013). Offering a multitude of world-class warm water surf breaks, Costa Rica is a quick, cheap flight from the United States and a relatively safe destination (Krause, 2013). According to the Instituto Costarricense de Turismo, surfing contributes approximately $800 million to Costa Rica's economy each year (Blanco, 2013). In a 2014 survey of tourists traveling through the Juan Santamaría International Airport, 16.6% said the main activity they engaged in was surfing (Instituto Costarricense de Turismo, 2014). Some of the surfers who visited Costa Rica have relocated to the country to live near high-quality surf breaks or start surf businesses (Krause, 2013). Increasing numbers of surfers in Costa Rica have created crowded surf breaks and a higher likelihood of conflict between all three groups of surfers: tourists, resident foreigners and Costa Ricans (Krause, 2013; Tantamjarik, 2004). In early 2012, Pavones, Costa Rica received negative attention when a video was posted online of a Costa Rican attacking a foreign stand-up paddleboarder (SUP) with a machete, suggesting localism could be a problem (Levin, 2012). Using Usher and Kerstetter's (2015a) territoriality framework for localism, this study explored the extent to which localism manifested among Costa Rican and resident foreigner surfers in Pavones.

Literature review

Territoriality

Human territoriality has been conceptualized differently by a wide variety of disciplines (Delaney, 2005). Territoriality is a social construction of boundaries around a space and is deeply rooted in notions of power (Delaney, 2005; Sack, 1986; Storey, 2001). Whoever controls the space can exert power by regulating what happens within the space and dictating who can enter and exit the territory. Territoriality has been studied at a variety of different scales: from homes, offices, beaches, neighborhoods and bars, to oceans and within and among nation-states (Altman, 1975; Brown, Lawrence, & Robinson, 2005; Malmberg, 1984; Storey, 2001).

Geographers were significantly influenced by Sack's (1986) work on territoriality, in which he defined territoriality as an attempt to control people or relationships by delimiting a certain space through classification, communication and enforcement of boundaries (Delaney, 2005). However, recent critics of Sack call for a more in-depth theorization of territoriality, which builds on current spatial theory, whereby space is constructed through interactions with people and the environment (Delaney, 2005; Murphy, 2012). Influenced by Lefebvre's work, Raffestin defined territoriality as a system of relationships, assisted by mediators (e.g., money or values), which people maintain within their physical and social environments in order to increase their autonomy over resources (Murphy, 2012; Raffestin, 2012). Delaney (2005) indicated the importance of incorporating critical perspectives into the study of territoriality, such as post-colonialism and identity politics. Taking this into consideration, territoriality is defined in the current study as the setting of *boundaries* around a space a person or group feels *ownership* toward, and their *regulation* of behavior within that space (Usher & Kerstetter, 2015a). This conceptualization of territoriality does not preclude the analysis of territoriality from a critical lens. The three dimensions of ownership, boundaries and regulation draw from Altman's and Sack's definitions of territoriality and are found within other researchers' definitions (Altman, 1975; Brown et al., 2005; Sack, 1986; Taylor, 1988).

Ownership. Feelings of ownership drive the creation of boundaries and regulation or defense of the space. Organizational psychologists have defined territoriality as the behavioral expression of psychological ownership (Brown et al., 2005). A worker might feel a sense of ownership over a work space or project, which he or she would indicate through personal objects on his or her desk, or by communicating their control over the work space/project in an email (Brown et al., 2005). Purrington and Zinn (2011) studied the ways in which mountain bikers' sense of ownership over trails could affect how they respond to the potential loss or addition of trails. A similar concept to the ownership dimension is place attachment. Place attachment, which has been extensively studied in the recreation and tourism literature but will not be discussed in detail here, is the positive emotional bond people feel toward a particular place (Lewicka, 2011).

Boundaries. Urban studies and community researchers have focused on physical boundaries, defining territoriality as the defense markers around the home, such as walls, fences or signs, which make residents feel safer (Johnson-Lawrence, Schulz, Zenk, Israel, & Rowe, 2015). Geographers have studied political boundaries, such as those of nation states or national parks (Sletto, 2009; Storey, 2001). However, others have examined less concrete boundaries. Examples range from the constantly changing water territories of fishermen to the boundaries created by social movements, such as Occupy London, which challenged traditional hierarchies (Halvorsen, 2015; Malmberg, 1984).

Regulation. Regulation includes the defense of a space from the entry of outsiders, but also the regulation of behavior within a space. According to Storey (2001), certain spaces have been restricted to others on the basis of class, race, religion and gender. Official policies and laws, such as segregation in the United States and apartheid in South Africa, created Black and White spaces, which still persist years after the dissolution of the laws (Storey, 2001). O'Brien, Gordon, and Baldwin (2014) examined how territorial feelings of one's neighborhood motivate residents to place maintenance calls to the city in an attempt to regulate their neighborhood. However, they found that social and physical attachment to the neighborhood, rather than control, motivated people's desires to request maintenance. Defense and regulation of space convey the ownership people feel for a space and delineate the boundaries of that space.

Localism

Surfing has become a popular sport throughout the world. In 2013, the number of surfers worldwide was estimated to be 35 million (O'Brien & Eddie, 2013). Prior to the 1950s, surfers did not have to worry about competing for waves. However, due to mass commercialization of the sport through surf movies and music in the 1950s and 1960s, surfing became mainstreamed (Booth, 2013; Ormrod, 2005). Surfing has remained popular in the twenty-first century. The proliferation of surf schools has made the sport accessible to more people and created increasingly crowded surf breaks in Hawaii, Australia and the East and West Coast of the contiguous United States (Stranger, 2011). Several scholars claim the commercialization of the sport and increasingly crowded surf line-ups have driven the formation of localism (Booth, 2013; Scott, 2003). As surf breaks became more crowded, local surfers who grew up next to surf breaks, and learned to surf there, had to defend 'their' waves from outsiders eager to try the exciting new sport (Scheibel, 1995).

Localism exists on a continuum from mild to heavy (Nazer, 2004). Mild localism occurs when local surfers allow visiting surfers into the surf break and expect to receive respect, may violate surf etiquette (the informal rules of surfing – discussed further below) or give visitors dirty looks. Mild localism is the most common form of localism and can be observed at many surf breaks (Beaumont & Brown, 2014; Dorset, 2009; Usher & Kerstetter, 2015a). Moderate localism comprises much of the same behavior, but also includes verbal warnings or abuse. Heavy localism occurs in one of two forms: (a) not allowing visiting surfers access to the surf or (b) allowing access to the surf, but inflicting heavy punishment for breaking surfing rules. In both instances, local surfers would enforce access or surfing rules through physical violence or property damage.

While localism is often acknowledged in the surfing and surf tourism literature, there have been few studies that included localism as the primary focus of the research. Daskalos (2007) examined a group of 'old school' surfers in Southern California, who discussed the ways in which surfing has changed over the years and how they tried to protect their wave resource from the newcomers who they felt had no respect for older surfers or their way of life in the surf. In Central California, Khachadoorian (2015) explored San Luis Obispo surfers' maintenance of their own local identity and their use of fear to repel outsider surfers. Kaffine (2009) analyzed California surf breaks on the Surfline website, which rates different aspects of surf breaks, such as wave quality, paddling difficulty, crowding and localism. He found that the level of localism was positively related to the level of wave quality.

Waitt and colleagues (Waitt, 2008; Waitt & Frazer, 2012; Waitt & Warren, 2008) found localism to be related to the deeply entrenched masculinity in surf culture and the close bonds male surfers form with one another. Beaumont and Brown (2014) found a mild form of localism (exacerbated by crowded conditions) in several beaches in England where local surfers expected visitors to give them respect, but also felt that, as locals, they were entitled to violate surf etiquette.

Localism as territoriality

Few studies have examined localism as a form of territoriality (Comley & Thoman, 2011; Dorset, 2009; Usher & Kerstetter, 2015a). Although Dorset's (2009) study combined place attachment and territoriality to examine localism, it lacked a theoretical framework. Localism was measured by whether it was present or not, and Dorset found a mild form of localism in New Zealand. Comley and Thoman (2011) found that surfers' perceptions of territoriality predicted surf-related negative affect (e.g., getting angry over waves). While these are the primary studies which utilized the concept of territoriality, there is considerable evidence of the ways in which surfers express ownership, define boundaries and regulate the surf break.

The enactment of localism is often rooted in the strong sense of ownership surfers feel for the local surf break (Young, 2000). As previously mentioned, this is similar to the notion of place attachment. Anderson (2014) and Dorset (2009) discussed the deep attachment surfers feel for a surf break because of the amount of time spent surfing and learning the wave at a particular surf break. Lawson-Remer and Valderrama (2010) argued that surfers' attachment to a surf break motivated them to protect the break through environmental activism if the break was threatened by coastal development. The origins of localism were surfers in California who felt threatened by people from the valley coming to the coast to surf 'their' waves (Scheibel, 1995). This sense of ownership compelled them to attempt to exclude people from their surf breaks.

The exclusion of visiting surfers from surf breaks through heavy localism (i.e., physical violence or property damage) is one of the ways in which surfers set boundaries around surf breaks (Nazer, 2004). It is their way of marking the space as theirs and not someone else's. The boundary is set around the surf break. However, the boundary line is not always drawn in order to exclude visiting surfers. In one Australian beach, shortboarders would attempt to exclude longboarders from certain surf breaks (Waitt & Frazer, 2012). They considered the surf break inappropriate for longboarders and did not want them surfing there. Surfers can also communicate the boundaries of the surf break through surf etiquette.

The creation of universal surfing rules (i.e., surf etiquette), which all surfers learn as they become socialized into the sport, originated from the need to create some system of order once surf breaks became more crowded (Lawson-Remer & Valderrama, 2010; Nazer, 2004;

Stranger, 2011). Surf etiquette includes not 'dropping in' on (catching the wave and surfing in front of) the surfer closest to the peak of the wave, waiting until everyone catches a wave before taking another one, maintaining control of one's board and giving incoming surfers the right-of-way when paddling out (Nazer, 2004). Much of the time, local surfers at a surf break are the ones who enforce these rules.

However, some local surfers believe there are additional rules that visiting surfers must follow (Stranger, 2011). Examples of these rules include respecting local surfers, waiting for waves on the shoulder instead of at the peak and local surfers having priority in the waves. Therefore, locals are not only supposed to get the best waves, but if a visiting surfer is competing with a local for a wave, the visiting surfer should let the local have it (Lawson-Remer & Valderrama, 2010; Usher & Kerstetter, 2015a). Locals will also violate surf etiquette because they believe they have priority or want to show dominance (Preston-Whyte, 2002). Local surfers' enforcement, or violation, of surf etiquette is how they regulate the break and delineate the space as theirs.

It is important to note that the majority of studies on localism have been in developed countries. With the spread of surfing into communities in the developing world, it is important to examine localism in developing countries as well (Usher & Kerstetter, 2015a). Usher and Kerstetter (2015a) proposed a territoriality framework with the dimensions of ownership, boundaries and regulation in order to examine localism of Nicaraguan surfers at Popoyo Reef. They found that Nicaraguan surfers felt a great sense of ownership, but wanted to share the break with other surfers. Nicaraguans thought of their boundaries as the surf break in the community and others thought of it as all of Nicaragua. The boundaries of the surf break also shifted with the tide and surf conditions. Nicaraguan surfers regulated the surf break by reminding tourists of surfing rules or providing helpful advice, but occasionally asserted dominance through violations of surf etiquette or working to catch waves as a group.

The study also found that resident foreigners in Nicaragua seemed to be responsible for instances of heavy localism (Usher & Kerstetter, 2015a). Krause (2013) had similar findings among resident foreigners in Costa Rica. Given this evidence, it was important to factor resident foreigners into the localism equation and treat them as a different group of 'local surfers' (Usher & Kerstetter, 2015b). Costa Rica has a large population of resident foreigners, and surfers have been traveling there since the 1970s, unlike Nicaragua, which has only gained traction as a surf destination in the past 15 years (Evans, 2015; Noorloos, 2011; Usher & Kerstetter, 2015a). Therefore, the current study extends Usher and Kerstetter's (2015a) previous work by using their territoriality framework to examine localism among two groups of resident surfers in Pavones, Costa Rica.

Methods

The researchers both consider themselves to be pragmatists. Pragmatists do not subscribe to any one philosophy or reality because reality is constantly changing through people's interactions (Bryant & Charmaz, 2007; Corbin & Strauss, 2008; Creswell, 2013). In line with a pragmatic approach, we wanted to use the most practical methods that would allow us to answer our research questions (Corbin & Strauss, 2008). Localism is considered a phenomenon of surf culture and therefore ethnography, which involves the study of cultural patterns and practices, was considered the best approach (Scheibel, 1995; Schensul, Schensul,

& LeCompte, 1999). Ethnography involves the immersion of the researcher in the culture and the researcher acts as the primary data collection instrument (Creswell, 2013; Schensul et al., 1999). The first author immersed herself in the local surf culture of Pavones in order to learn more about how Costa Ricans and resident foreigners expressed localism. To clarify terminology, local Costa Rican surfers are referred to as 'Ticos' (a name Costa Ricans call themselves), resident foreigner surfers will be referred to as 'foreigners' and surfers visiting the destination for a short time will be referred to as 'tourists'. Pseudonyms are also used to protect confidentiality. Several of the surf breaks are also not named in order to protect their location.

This study was conducted from May to July of 2014, and three weeks from July through August of 2015, in Pavones, Costa Rica. The first author lived with a Tico family in Pavones. During the second study period, she stayed in a small building with several other tourists in a *cabina* (Costa Rican word meaning guest rooms – combination of 'cabin' and 'cabaña'). She engaged in participant observation, which is a hallmark of ethnographic research (Bogdewic, 1999; Schensul et al., 1999). The primary way in which participant observation is documented is through field notes. The researcher's field notes included observations, interpretations and reflections of her time surfing (she surfed during approximately 25 of the days in the first fieldwork period, and 13 days in the second period, from 1 to 4 hours). She also kept a journal of her time there in order to document daily life so that she could achieve a rich description of the community and study site (Bogdewic, 1999). She took photos and videos of the community and surfing, which also contributed to the achievement of a detailed description of the culture, a key aspect of ethnography (Jones, 2010). These data sources provided additional confirmation of what the first researcher documented in her field notes and journal.

During the first period of field work, the first author conducted in-depth interviews with 24 current and former Tico surfers, 31 foreign surfers and brief interviews with 35 tourists. She used snowball sampling, which is a recognized method of sampling in qualitative inquiry, in order to find participants who could contribute rich information to the study (Kuzel, 1999). Her host family and community leaders introduced her to Tico and foreign surfers, who referred her to other surfers whom she could interview. Some surfers she saw regularly when she was out surfing and asked if they would like to participate. Two Tico surfers she saw frequently in the surf declined to be interviewed; however, she documented her observations of them in the surf. Data analysis occurs throughout the process of data collection in ethnographic research (LeCompte & Schensul, 1999). Therefore, as certain themes developed throughout her interviews and observations, the first author sought out participants who could provide disconfirming viewpoints or provide more information about what she had observed. Seeking out exceptions is part of achieving representative viewpoints in qualitative inquiry (Kuzel, 1999).

The interviews were digitally recorded and transcribed into the speaker's native language (English or Spanish). The first author used Nvivo to code the interview transcripts, field notes from surfing and her daily journal. Utilizing multiple sources of data in the analysis is known as data triangulation and contributes to the trustworthiness of the findings (Maxwell, 2005). While she coded the data within the territoriality framework (using a priori themes of 'ownership', 'boundaries' and 'regulation') she also remained alert to other emergent themes within the data. She used Nvivo queries in order to categorize participants' responses to particular questions in order to compare the groups to one another. The second author, who is a native Spanish speaker, read and coded half the Spanish transcripts of interviews with Tico surfers in order to challenge or affirm the primary researcher's findings through the process of peer debriefing (Creswell & Miller, 2000). They each coded independently and then discussed their interpretations to see if they agreed or disagreed.

The following research questions guided this study: (1) How do local (Tico and foreign) surfers express ownership over the surf break? (2) What are the boundaries of local (Tico and foreign) surfers' surfing space? (3) How do local (Tico and foreign) surfers regulate the surf space?

Positioning the researchers

In ethnographic research, it is important for the researchers to reflect on their identity and the ways in which it may have affected the study findings (Agar, 1996; May & Perry, 2011). Paying attention to biases is another way of ensuring validity in ethnographic inquiry (Schensul et al., 1999). Ethnographers are no longer thought of as objective observers; they influence, are influenced by, and are often part of, the communities they research (Agar, 1996). The first author has three years of experience living, working and conducting research in Central America. As a Peace Corps volunteer, she had learned how to work in a cross-cultural environment and abide by Central American cultural norms. This previous experience enabled her to adapt quickly to the local culture. Her Spanish-speaking ability and cultural insights enabled her to generate a rapport with Tico surfers and community residents. She is also a surfer; therefore she shared many commonalities with the participants as an insider to surf culture. She was able to understand the terminology, situations and experiences described by surfers. The first author is American, which also made it easier to gain access to foreigners, because she was one.

While the first researcher's identity as a surfer was important for the study of a surf culture phenomenon like localism, Pavlidis and Olive (2014) found the importance of having both an insider and outsider perspective for sport cultural studies. The second researcher is a Latino and therefore provided an important cultural perspective during the course of analysis. However, as a non-surfer, he also provided a different perspective on the data than the first author, who was coming from an insider perspective. Having researchers who provided two different perspectives on the data also contributes to the trustworthiness of the findings.

Study site: Pavones, Costa Rica

Costa Rica's reputation as a safe country is highly appealing to many tourists (Tantamjarik, 2004). The country declared permanent neutrality in 1993. There is no army and no recent history of armed political conflicts similar to other countries in Central America (Evans, 2015; Tantamjarik, 2004). American and European arrivals to Costa Rica began to increase in the 1980s (Tantamjarik, 2004). The country began focusing on the development of ecotourism in the late 1980s, and Costa Rica is now a well-known ecotourism destination (Hunt, Durham, Driscoll, & Honey, 2015; Tantamjarik, 2004). Many foreigners who visited Costa Rica decided to move to the country. Costa Rica encouraged the movement of retirees and other residential tourists due to the amount of foreign investment they generated

(Noorloos, 2011). In 2010, there were an estimated 50,000 residential tourists living in Costa Rica (Noorloos, 2011).

Costa Rica was featured in *The Endless Summer II* in 1994, which positioned it as a must-visit destination for surfers (Krause, 2013). The combination of Pacific Ocean swell, variety of high quality surf breaks and warm water make Costa Rica a popular surf destination. However, a study in 2003 found beaches on the central Pacific Coast were experiencing significant negative impacts due to surf tourism development (Tantamjarik, 2004). A more recent study by Krause (2013) indicated similar findings. The impacts included crowding in the water, pollution, environmental degradation, drugs, crime and Costa Ricans being priced out of land ownership (Krause, 2013; Tantamjarik, 2004). Krause (2013) also found that foreign resident surfers dealt with crowding by enacting localism against surf tourists, since they considered the surf breaks their own.

Pavones is known among surfers as the second longest left point break in the world (Surfline, 2013; World Surfing Collective, 2012). The community of Pavones, Costa Rica, is located in the municipality of Golfito, in the province of Puntarenas, near the border with Panama (see Figure 1). Several communities exist within the area known as Pavones, but the central one is Río Claro de Pavones. Local leaders estimate the population of Río Claro to be around 400 people. The community infrastructure includes a primary school, an evangelical church, a police post and two grocery stores. The Río Claro (Clear River) runs into Golfo Dulce (Sweet Gulf), which empties into the Pacific Ocean, forming the famous surf break. The town is roughly two hours by bus from Paso Canoas, the border town with Panama. It is 1.5–2 hours by bus from Golfito, much of which is on unpaved, gravel road. The difficulty in getting to Pavones is part of what contributes to its remoteness.

There is little scholarly information on Pavones, but the following is based on a recently published non-fiction book written about the community, as well as information obtained from interviews during the first author's field work. At least one foreign surfer had visited Pavones before the early 1970s and the Ticos had started making balsa surfboards in the 1970s. However, the first movement toward tourism began when American surfer Danny Fowlie came to Pavones in the 1970s and bought 3700 acres of land in the area (Evans, 2015). He brought professional surfers there from Hawaii to surf the wave. The Esquina

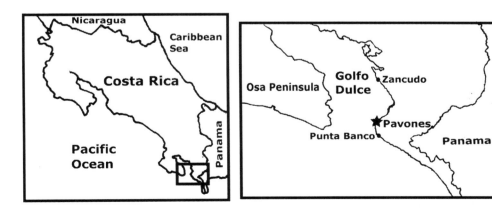

Figure 1. Map of Pavones, Costa Rica.

del Mar (known as 'the cantina'), which Fowlie built, and a locally owned Tico family hotel were the only formal lodging options in Pavones in the 1980s. Other Ticos would open their homes to surfers who came through and rent them rooms.

However, Fowlie had to abruptly leave Pavones in the middle of the night in 1985 because he was wanted in California for drug trafficking (Evans, 2015). The years following Fowlie's exit from Pavones and his 1987 arrest on drug charges were characterized by violent conflict over land between Costa Rican communist squatters and foreigners (Evans, 2015; Goodier, 2005). In the early 1990s, several foreigners started surf camps. Surfers were still coming despite the US State Department's warning to avoid the area (Evans, 2015). Part of the appeal for surfers was believing it would not be crowded with tourists because of the warnings. Presently, the town has some small lodging establishments, cafes, restaurants, *cabinas* and shops, some of which are foreign owned, and others locally owned or managed. Most foreigners came for the surf and a different lifestyle. Some foreigners have started tourism businesses, but others are retired or earn income through other means. Some Ticos work as fishermen, but surf tourism is the main economic driver. Many families work in, or run, *cabinas*, restaurants, hostels or other tourist services. The internet video which surfaced in 2012 of a man attacking a SUP seemed to suggest localism might be an issue in the area and did not portray a welcoming image of Pavones.

Findings

The findings are organized around Usher and Kerstetter's (2015a) framework. First, we report Ticos' and foreigners' perceptions of ownership toward the Pavones wave. Consequently, the findings are then reported for how stakeholders delineated surf boundaries and regulated the surf break. It is important to note that there is overlap among the three primary themes. Following the reporting of ownership, boundaries and regulations, we present our findings on three additional themes that emerged from the data analysis: (a) conflicts, (b) respect and (c) crowding. These three additional themes cut across the three primary themes of ownership, boundaries and regulation, which is why they are treated as separate themes. Tourists also factored into those themes more than the primary ones.

Ownership

Ticos. Several Tico surfers said they considered themselves to be owners of the wave. Some of them had family members who founded the community. They were born and raised in the community, learned how to surf and spent much of their lives surfing at Pavones. Eduardo characterized it as such, 'Obviously, because of the environment, it's like … something divine, it's like a divine inheritance … ' However, they did not believe this entitled them to yell at other surfers or tell them what to do. Many Ticos said the owner of the wave was the person that caught it first. Some clarified that it was not necessarily ownership, but they felt they had more rights than other surfers because they belonged to the community. Juan said, 'Yes, we have a right … because we know [the wave], we're from this place, we're the locals.'

Foreigners. Foreigners also did not like to characterize their attachment or connection to the wave as ownership. Several called Pavones their 'home break'. Others thought they had more rights than other tourists because of the time that they had lived and worked in Pavones. These rights were earned through the amount of time spent surfing Pavones and learning the wave. Eric described this feeling: 'So, I don't consider ownership out there, I consider it a respectful stewardship out there. And that's what I think I'm entitled to.' Several believed they had priority and should be respected, even by Ticos, because of their age and experience as surfers. Clara expressed the following, regarding other foreigners: '[Because] a lot of them feel like when they bought their land ... they bought the surf break as well and act accordingly.' Many Ticos also said foreigners thought they owned the wave.

Boundaries

Ticos. Many of the Ticos considered the nearby coastal area as their surfing territory: from Punta Banco to Zancudo (see Figure 1). Some mentioned that Río Claro was the best wave in the area, but they surfed all the waves on the coast. In Río Claro de Pavones, The Point and an area just on the other side of the river mouth from The Point (the middle section of Pavones) were the areas Ticos favored at the Pavones break. There was another wave near Pavones (Secret Break) where the first author had seen Ana (a Tica) while out surfing, and she discussed it in the interview, 'Before, that place was like a secret, so when the wave was big here, the people went there, but almost only locals or a few people because almost no one knew about it.' She was annoyed that Ticos had not guarded the secret break more closely. However, several Tico surfers readily volunteered information about the break to the first author in casual settings (not during interviews), even before she had developed friendships with them.

One Tico said that there were waves, which tended to be dangerous to surf, that only Ticos knew about and they would not allow anyone else to surf there. However, several foreigners mentioned that they surfed those waves as well, which challenged the Tico's claim. Ticos also demarcated boundaries by describing which surfers were supposed to surf in certain areas of Pavones; advanced surfers at the point and beginners at the bottom of the wave. If they saw inexperienced surfers at The Point, Marcos said they would tell them: 'It is better that you surf below because this is much faster, more dangerous, and below it's softer, more calm.' Telling surfers this was not only a form of regulation, but it established a boundary around The Point as well. Some Ticos also felt that longboards and SUPs were not appropriate for The Point.

Foreigners. Some foreigners preferred to surf The Point, but due to the increased crowd at Pavones, some preferred Point Two or smaller breaks in the area. Pete, who had grown up there, said, 'Me and a lot of the local kids surf on this side of the river mouth.' Several discussed how Point Two had been a secret and the different ways in which they tried to keep tourists away from it. They called it different code names and spread rumors about what would happen to a person's car if they parked and tried to surf there. Foreigners also agreed with Ticos in that The Point at Pavones was for more experienced surfers and the bottom of the wave was for beginners and would also offer this advice to tourists.

Regulation

Ticos. Many Ticos said that Pavones was free of regulation. Carlos said, 'You can surf calmly, you can catch your wave, no one bothers you.' Ticos said they did not tell other surfers they could not surf there, unlike some places in Costa Rica, where locals were more hostile. Several foreigners said that Ticos would not regulate the surf break and enforce order. However, some of the Ticos said that sometimes they had to tell tourists that they should respect other people and other people's waves, and not to fight. Ticos said that other times, they had to tell tourists to get off the wave if the tourists dropped in front of them while they were riding a wave. Many Ticos said they also offered help and advice to tourists.

With regard to surf etiquette, Ticos thought it disrespectful when someone dropped in on someone else's wave. However, if a wave broke on a surfer, another surfer could go in front of that person, because most likely the other surfer would fall. Another rule was not stealing turns. Once someone caught a wave, they had to go back out and wait in the line-up. However, the first author routinely saw Tico surfers violating these rules during both periods of field work. Most tourists and foreigners thought that the Ticos knew surf etiquette if they were experienced, but as some foreigners pointed out, that did not mean they would not violate it. Foreigners, tourists and some of the Ticos said that certain Ticos would drop in on people's waves all the time. Tim (a foreigner) said, 'The Ticos kinda put their blinkers on, they don't do a lot of shouting and calling anyone out in the water, they just drop in on you.' Several foreigners commented on the fact that Ticos could get away with violating surf etiquette because the break was so big.

Foreigners. Some of the foreigners believed that there was no order in the waves. Sarah noted, 'Yeah, people tell me when they watch surf in Pavones, it's just more of a circus than anywhere they've ever seen.' She also noted that the break was too long and there were too many people for any type of localism to work. Foreigners said they regulated the surf zone by reminding people of surf etiquette or calling them out for not following it. In the interviews, they accused tourists of being selfish and greedy and explained that was why they had to say something to them. They said Ticos would not regulate the break, so foreigners felt they had to do it. Several said they would just drop in on tourists who kept dropping in on, or paddling around, others. They thought clueless beginners placed all surfers at risk for injury. Brad said, 'Everybody that knows how to surf is threatened by the people that don't know how to surf because they are dangerous.' A few foreigners (including two who owned tourist accommodations) thought that tourists should start out on the shoulder of the wave and advance to surfing at The Point, or wait until the locals were gone. Some believed there was a local hierarchy and the surfers who lived there were at the top and deserved to get the best position and waves at The Point.

Some foreigners said they would not drop in on Ticos or girls and women. Several said they always gave women the right of way and confronted tourists if they dropped in on, or bothered, female surfers. The majority of the tourists thought that foreigners knew surf etiquette if they were experienced surfers. However, one foreigner said that a few long-time foreigners still would not follow the rules. The first author, during both periods of fieldwork, observed foreigners and tourists dropping in on other surfers on a regular basis when she went surfing. All three groups were guilty of this violation.

Conflicts

In terms of conflicts between surfers, many of the Ticos and approximately 10 of the foreigners said that there were not many problems at Pavones. Tourists also said they experienced positive interactions in the surf at Pavones. Foreigners said if there were plenty of waves, there were no problems. Foreigners and Ticos said that other places in Costa Rica, and the world, had much heavier localism (i.e., locals picking physical fights). Ana, the same Tica quoted above, noted, '[In] other places in Costa Rica ... it's different, there are many places where they don't let foreigners get in, only locals.' Ticos and foreigners blamed aggressive tourists for some conflicts. Brazilians and Israelis were the worst offenders. Foreigners, tourists and some Ticos said that Ticos would not argue and fight with tourists, they were 'tranquilo' (tranquil or laid back). However, there was one long-time Tico surfer, who several Ticos and resident foreigners pointed out, who would get angry and yell at surfers. All three groups agreed foreigners were much more aggressive and caused more problems in the water for tourists than Ticos did: foreigners had a greater tendency to get angry and yell at tourists. Daniela, a foreigner, noted, '[The] people that I've seen fighting the most is the foreigners that have moved in here and then they are the ones that kinda get a little more aggressive in the water ... '

Most fights Ticos and foreigners said they had seen were verbal confrontations. However, members of both groups admitted to having been in physical or verbal fights with other surfers. Participants said fights originated in repeated surf etiquette violations or surfers insulting others. Incidents with violence or property damage included 'Hawaiian styling' people's fins (breaking the fins off the board while they are still screwed in), knocking people off boards or holding them under the water. Most of these incidents happened years ago and Ticos and foreigners said that things had calmed down significantly. Maria, a Tica, recounted, 'There were aggressive locals, not now because they have families or they left ... but before, yes they were aggressive, rocks to the cars and physical fights, but not now.' The first author learned that the machete incident posted online between the SUP (who was a resident foreigner) and the Tico had actually not occurred at the main break in Río Claro but at Point Two. One of the study participants witnessed the incident and described it as having more to do with substance abuse and mental health than territoriality.

During the first fieldwork period, a physical fight did occur between a foreigner and a Tico. The foreigner said that he was tired of the local kids being disrespectful toward him, doing things like dropping in on and paddling around him, and that was why he started the fight. Several participants noted that conflict was a male problem. Gloria (a Tica) said, 'That always happens with the men, because I always see it with the men, I don't think between the women. We are calmer than the men.'

Respect

Respect was a major theme that came up with Ticos, foreigners and tourists. Everyone noted that as long as you were respectful to other surfers, they would respect you. This demonstrated how respect had obvious ties to regulation of the surf break, but was connected to ownership as well. Amaro, a Tico, described respect for local surfers as a worldwide tradition in surfing, 'So, it's the same in every point of, of the locals, in every point.

You have to have a respect.' Respect is an important principle in Latin culture and several Ticos emphasized how offensive it was if someone was disrespectful. A surfer verbally insulting another surfer or their family member was unacceptable. Foreigners also thought tourists should respect everyone who lived there because of the time they had dedicated to the wave and the town. Some of the foreigners had been surfing for decades and thought that the respect level had decreased dramatically in surfing. They had grown up surfing and learning to respect older surfers, but the new generation did not respect them. Bill, an older foreigner, spoke about the lack of respect at Pavones, '[Where] here there's absolutely none and I don't – from the Ticos to most of the stinking gringo tourists, and surfing has changed, not just in Hawaii, but surfing has changed for the worse in that respect too.' Several foreigners also mentioned that they thought young Tico surfers would have more respect if they traveled outside of Pavones and had to surf somewhere as a non-local. They thought they would not drop in on others as much once they had that experience.

Crowding

Recent technological advances have changed the flow of surf tourists to Pavones. Instead of flying down and waiting for a swell for weeks, surfers could check the swell forecast and fly in the day before a swell. Once the swell was gone, the tourists were gone. This meant there were many people in the water at the same time. During the second period of fieldwork, a tourist who visited Pavones regularly said that he had counted 157 people in the water several days after a swell in May of 2015. Robert, a foreigner, remarked that the Pavones wave could hold a large number of people due to its size. However, with 100–150 people, even a kilometer-long point break becomes a difficult place to have a worthwhile surfing experience. A number of surfers blamed the tensions in the water on crowding. Brad noted, 'Because it's just too many people, it's like you put a bunch of rats in a cage and they chew at each other, it's just out of control … ' The first author spoke with several older Tico surfers and they said when they first started surfing (1970s and 1980s), there were no fights between surfers because there were not many surfers.

During the largest swell in the first fieldwork period, the first author counted a maximum of 40 people in the water; however, during an earlier smaller swell, there had been up to 80. She spoke with a long-time foreigner, Steve, about this who said it was common to see more people during a smaller swell than a larger swell because it naturally weeded out the less skilled surfers. However, during several days of the large swell, the first author surfed Secret Break, where the waves were manageable during a big swell. There were many people there (30) because the large swell at Pavones was beyond the skill level of most tourists. Now that Secret Break was no longer a secret, crowding became a problem there during the big swells because it was a much smaller point and could not hold as many surfers.

Discussion

There are some similarities and differences in the ways Ticos and foreigners enact localism at Pavones. In terms of ownership, both felt an attachment to the wave, but for different reasons. Both groups felt the same attachment many surfers feel for a wave they have spent long periods of time surfing and learning (Anderson, 2014). However, part of Ticos' connection involved their deep social ties to the community. Foreigners' attachment was more connected to their surfing experience. This was similar to findings that showed social ties were more important for community residents, and environmental qualities were more important for newer residents, in developing place attachment (Lewicka, 2011). Most Tico surfers also seemed to agree with the Nicaraguan surfers from Usher and Kerstetter's (2015a) study that however much ownership or right they felt, that did not entitle them to prohibit other people from surfing or being aggressive.

The boundaries of resident foreigners and Ticos were similar. Both had tried to defend nearby surf breaks more than they did Pavones because they thought of those as off limits to tourists. Some of these methods included using code names or claiming they would remove tourists if they tried to surf certain places. This finding coincides with MacCannell's (1999) theory of frontstage and backstage in a tourism destination. His concept of staged authenticity, drawn from Goffman's (1959) work, primarily focuses on cultural tourism experiences. Tourists are presented with a frontstage by hosts, but they want to experience the authentic backstage of a destination, where the set-up of the tourism site and daily life of the community occurs. Hosts sometimes attempt to present a backstage area to tourists, but it is still a staged version. The final stage on MacCannell's continuum of front to backstage is a backstage which is not staged for tourists; it is what is really happening in the community. This concept plays out differently when the front- and backstages are the natural environment.

Pavones was the frontstage of the tourism destination. Tourists knew about, and wanted to surf, the famous wave there. Much like the tourist beaches where surf instructors taught classes in Tantamjarik's (2004) study on the central Pacific coast, Pavones was accepted as a place where there was going to be a crowd. It was not something the host community had to 'stage' for tourists, it drew tourists because it was a naturally formed, high-quality, long wave. The lesser known surf breaks in the area had become residents' backstage, places where they could surf on their own and tourists would not intrude. The breaks were not places where locals set up the front stage, just places where they could surf among other locals, in social solidarity (MacCannell, 1999). As participants mentioned, these boundaries were getting crossed more frequently as more tourists found out about the other breaks. Many surf breaks are now frontstage and resident surfers have few places to escape from tourists. Unlike cultural tourism, there were no surf breaks resident surfers could 'present' as backstage to tourists. Tourists could walk down the beach, or look on a map and judge the quality of these waves for themselves.

The designation of The Point as a space not for beginners, longboarders or SUPs was similar to Waitt and Frazer's (2012) findings in Australia, which indicated that shortboarders would try to designate a space as off limits to longboarders. These ways in which resident surfers set boundaries recall Raffestin's (2012) theory of territoriality. Surfers communicated their values (which dictated where beginners, advanced surfers and tourists should be) to other surfers in order to maintain a system of relationships (advanced surfers at The Point, tourists away from nearby surf breaks) and increase their autonomy over the waves. By keeping the number of surfers low at The Point, and at other surf breaks, resident surfers acquired more waves.

The changeable aspects of water territories altered the boundaries for surfers (Malmberg, 1984; Usher & Kerstetter, 2015a). A large swell created conditions at Pavones that were off limits to all but highly skilled surfers and lowered the crowds. Resident surfers no longer had to regulate the boundaries by advising beginners, the surf conditions did it for them. Similarly, Kaffine (2009) found that the higher the paddling difficulty of a surf break, the lower the level of localism because it naturally limited the number of surfers. However, a large swell also meant visitors would search out nearby breaks for more manageable surf conditions, thereby increasing the crowds at those breaks and the need for more regulation. A smaller swell at Pavones meant fewer waves, but also more surfers in the water (and many inexperienced ones), which meant fewer waves for each surfer. As many participants mentioned, this created frustration, tensions and increased the need for regulation. In Nicaragua, Usher and Kerstetter (2015a) similarly found that the changeable nature of surf breaks meant that the territorial boundaries were never the same and the regulation of it could change as well.

The biggest difference between Ticos and foreigners was the way in which they regulated the surf space. Ticos used more covert means of expressing dominance, such as dropping in on tourists. Several foreigners would drop in too, instead of arguing or fighting with tourists. This illustrates a key aspect of localism, which has been observed at other surf breaks, locals will violate surf etiquette because they believe they have priority or want to show dominance (Dorset, 2009; Preston-Whyte, 2002; Usher & Kerstetter, 2015a). Some foreigners used more overt means of expressing dominance, such as confronting tourists or yelling at them. They felt the time they had dedicated to surfing Pavones entitled them to this and they had to do it because the Ticos would not; it was their way of demonstrating their power and status to tourists (Delaney, 2005). This was similar to findings from other studies, which have shown that resident foreigners enact heavier localism than native residents (Krause, 2013; Usher & Kerstetter, 2015a). However, men from both groups regulated the break more often than women, especially Tica women, which corroborates Waitt and Warren's (Waitt, 2008; Waitt & Warren, 2008) findings in Australia that found localism to be a demonstration of masculinity.

Localism at Pavones did differ between Ticos and foreigners; however, it appeared to be mild to moderate at the time of the study (Nazer, 2004). The destination seemed to have gone through a period of heavier localism 10–15 years prior. This 'cycle' of localism is a new contribution, which has not been found or discussed in previous studies. Even though crowding had increased and created problems, the severity of localism and the hierarchy associated with it, overall, had decreased. This conflicts with previous findings, which blamed the formation of localism on increasing crowds (Booth, 2013). The older Ticos' mention of the lack of conflict in the 1970s indicated localism was not present. However, as tourist numbers increased in the 1990s to early 2000s, resident surfers (Tico and foreign) felt the need to regulate surfers' behaviors through physical violence and property damage, because it was a manageable number of surfers to regulate. Once surf forecasting improved throughout the 2000s, the number of tourists grew much larger and might have overwhelmed the resident surfers' ability to regulate the surf break. As Sarah, one of the foreigners, pointed out, it is impossible for residents to regulate such a large number of surfers. This decrease in localism might have been due to the exit of some of the aggressive surfers from the surf, as one participant mentioned, but the crowd may have factored in as well. At least one surfer who subscribed to the idea of a hierarchy was one of the people who said he would go and surf other breaks because he could not deal with the crowd. This finding also disagrees with Nazer's (2004) continuum of mild to heavy localism; localism may fluctuate from mild to heavy and back to mild again as the hosts respond to the number of visitors over time.

Even though Ticos and foreigners differed with regard to regulation, respect was one aspect that was the same for both groups. Other studies have indicated local surfers' expectation of respect from outsiders, whereby respect guarantees a more manageable interaction with local surfers (Beaumont & Brown, 2014; Dorset, 2009; Usher & Kerstetter, 2015a). The older foreigners, who spoke about the decreased respect level in surfing, expressed sentiments similar to the 'old school' surfers in Daskalos' (2007) study. The older surfers in both studies lamented the new and younger surfers who were not brought up in the same surf culture they were, where elders and hierarchies were respected. While some foreigners placed greater importance on the age of a surfer, some Ticos seemed to believe the amount of respect someone should get was determined by their native status. Foreigners also echoed UK surfers, who discussed learning the importance of surf etiquette through the humbling experience of traveling and being a non-local surfer (Beaumont & Brown, 2014). According to foreigners, if Ticos could have that same experience, they would have more respect and follow surf etiquette. However, unlike foreigners, many Ticos could not afford to travel to surf, even to other parts of Costa Rica.

Our findings agreed with Tantamjarik's (2004) study on sustainability in Costa Rica's surf tourism industry; crowding had become an issue, which annoyed locals, caused tensions and created dangerous situations. Similar to what Beaumont and Brown (2014) found in the UK, crowding at Pavones exacerbated even mild expressions of localism. Ponting and O'Brien (2014, 2015) have analyzed surf breaks as common pool resources. They noted that as long as everyone follows surf etiquette so that all surfers are able to catch waves, it does not seem as crowded. However, this did not seem to occur in the 'circus' of Pavones, in which tourists, Ticos and foreigners all violate surf etiquette for a variety of reasons (lack of knowledge, show of dominance, necessity because others are doing it, etc.). Therefore, the crowded conditions of predicted swells were exacerbated by the amount of surf etiquette violations. Surf rage, which is aggressive behavior from any surfer (regardless of local or outsider status) due to the frustrations of crowding or experiencing violations of surf etiquette, could become a much bigger problem than localism (Stranger, 2011; Young, 2000). Surfers travel in order to avoid crowds (Alessi, 2009), and the 'flash crowds' generated by increasingly accurate swell predictions threaten the sustainability of the destination. Despite the high quality of the wave, if surfers cannot catch enough waves because there are too many people in the water, there are plenty of uncrowded quality waves to which they could travel.

Conclusion

Tico and foreign surfers showed similarities and differences in the ways they territorialize the waves. While they both expressed attachment to the wave and the natural environment through the time they had spent surfing and living there, Ticos had stronger social ties to the community than foreigners. Ticos and foreigners had similar boundaries and both communicated these boundaries to tourists. Spaces, which some had tried to guard from tourists, were no longer secret and pressured by increasing crowds. Ticos used more covert methods to regulate the surf break, such as dropping in on tourists and foreigners, but would offer tourists certain rules, etiquette or advice. Foreigners were more likely to be more aggressive when addressing tourists and regulating the surf break. Despite the one incident, physical confrontations were rare and verbal confrontations occurred with more frequency. The cycle of localism had gone from heavy back down to mild or moderate with increasing crowds. Respect was important to Ticos, foreigners and tourists, but it was not always observed by all groups. Crowding is a problem, which exacerbates tensions and annoys foreigners and Ticos.

This study has filled a gap in the sport tourism destination literature. It contributes to the growing body of literature on surf destinations and highlights the importance of studying localism at different surf breaks due to the nuances of local social and environmental conditions (Kaffine, 2009). It extends Usher and Kerstetter's (2015a) work, and other studies (Beaumont & Brown, 2014), which have found that localism is much more complex than the blatant physical violence which surfers often associate with the term. Conceptually, this study contributes the notion of localism being cyclical, which could be explored in future studies. It also highlights the importance of acknowledging the heterogeneity of local surfing communities, especially in destinations with large expatriate contingents. The study contributes a much needed perspective on localism in developing countries to a body of literature primarily focused on localism in developed surf destinations. More of these remote destinations should be examined in order to learn the ways in which localism manifests and if it is a threat to further tourism development.

There were some limitations to this study. The combined time of the fieldwork was approximately three months; therefore, a longer study period might have produced different results. However, the tourist season in Pavones is only 5 months; therefore 3 months, over the course of two different seasons, may have been an adequate period of time. Findings from interviews with surfers who had lived there all of their lives, or long periods of time, seemed to agree with the first author's observations during both periods of fieldwork. Future studies could be conducted during different parts of the tourist season and for longer periods of time. An attempt could have been made to interview more Tico surfers; however, the first author requested interviews with the majority of the Tico surfers she saw surfing on a regular basis. She also tried to ensure she had representation from female Tica surfers, who often had valuable insight on male surfers, since they were out there with them and might not have had the same experiences.

This study has important implications for the management of surf destinations. Swell forecasts are beginning to affect many surf destinations because of their increased accuracy. Crowding, more than localism, appears to be a threat to Pavones. Surf destinations such as Pavones should be monitored for crowding, in order to ensure the carrying capacity is not being exceeded and tourists are not repelled. Surf tourists are motivated by crowd avoidance; therefore bigger crowds will not make the destination more appealing (Ponting & O'Brien, 2015). In the future, local officials in Pavones may have to set limits on use of the surf break in order to mitigate conflict. Marketing campaigns, which counter inaccurate media representations, could also be utilized when issues such as the internet video arise. Resident foreigners need to be aware of their role as outsiders, even though some feel like part of the community, and realize how their behavior could affect tourists' experiences. Resident foreigners and local communities should keep lines of communication open and work together to ensure the sustainability of surf destinations like Pavones.

Acknowledgement

The authors would like to thank Samantha Calhoun for her contributions to the study. We would also like to express our appreciation to Kurt Williamson for his assistance with the map.

Funding

This research was supported by a grant from the Old Dominion University Summer Research Fellowship Program.

Disclosure statement

No potential conflict of interest was reported by the authors.

References

Agar, M. H. (1996). *The professional stranger: An informal introduction to ethnography*. San Diego, CA: Academic Press.

Alessi, M. D. (2009). The customs and culture of surfing, and an opportunity for a new territorialism? *Reef Journal, 1*(1), 85–92.

Altman, I. (1975). *The environment and social behavior: Privacy, personal space, territory, crowding*. Monterey: Brooks/Cole.

Anderson, J. (2014). Surfing between the local and the global: Identifying spatial divisions in surfing practice. *Transactions of the Institute of British Geographers, 39*, 237–249.

Beaumont, E., & Brown, D. (2014). 'It's not something I'm proud of but it's … just how I feel': Local surfer perspectives of localism. *Leisure Studies*, 1–18. doi:10.1080/02614367.2014.962586

Blanco, C. (2013, January 5). Surf deja a Costa Rica mas de ₡400 mil millones al año, *La Prensa Libre*.

Bogdewic, S. P. (1999). Participant observation. In B. F. Crabtree & W. L. Miller (Eds.), *Doing qualitative research* (2nd ed., pp. 47–69). Thousand Oaks, CA: Sage.

Booth, D. (2013). History, culture, surfing: Exploring historiographical relationships. *Journal of Sport History, 40*(1), 3–20.

Brown, G., Lawrence, T. B., & Robinson, S. L. (2005). Territoriality in organizations. *Academy of Management Review, 30*(3), 577–594.

Bryant, A., & Charmaz, K. (Eds.). (2007). *The Sage handbook of grounded theory*. Los Angeles, CA: Sage.

Comley, C., & Thoman, D. (2011). *Fall in line: How surfers' perceptions of localism, territoriality and waves as limited resources influence surf-related aggression*. Paper presented at the 91st Annual Convention of the Western Psychological Association, Los Angeles, CA.

Corbin, J., & Strauss, A. L. (2008). *Basics of qualitative research: Techniques and procedures for developing grounded theory* (3rd ed.). Los Angeles, CA: Sage.

Creswell, J. W. (2013). *Qualitative inquiry & research design: Choosing among five approaches* (3rd ed.). Los Angeles, CA: Sage.

Creswell, J. W., & Miller, D. L. (2000). Determining the validity in qualitative inquiry. *Theory into Practice, 39*(3), 124–130.

Daskalos, C. T. (2007). Locals only! The impact of modernity on a local surfing context. *Sociological Perspectives, 50*(1), 155–173.

Delaney, D. (2005). *Territory: A short introduction*. Malden, MA: Blackwell.

Dorset, W. (2009). *Surfing localism and attachment to beach space: A Christchurch, New Zealand, perspective*. Christchurch: University of Canterbury (BA).

Evans, J. (2015). *The battle for paradise: Surfing, tuna, and one town's quest to save a wave*. Lincoln: University of Nebraska Press.

Fredline, E. (2005). Host and guest relations and sport tourism. *Sport in Society, 8*(2), 263–279.

Goffman, E. (1959). *The presentation of self in everyday life*. Garden City, NY: Doubleday.

Goodier, R. (2005). Ex-convict returns to claim property, *The Tico Times*. Retrieved from http://www.ticotimes.net/2005/06/10/ex-convict-returns-to-claim-property

Halvorsen, S. (2015). Encountering occupy London: Boundary making and the territoriality of urban activism. *Environment and Planning D: Society and Space, 33*, 314–330.

Han, J. H., Nelson, C. M., & Kim, C. (2015). Pro-environmental behavior in sport event tourism: Roles of event attendees and destinations. *Tourism Geographies, 17*(5), 719–737.

Hinch, T., & Ramshaw, G. (2014). Heritage sport tourism in Canada. *Tourism Geographies, 16*(2), 237–251. doi:10.1080/14616688.2013.823234

Hritz, N. M., & Ross, C. (2010). The perceived impacts of sport tourism: An urban host community perspective. *Journal of Sport Management, 24*, 119–138.

Hunt, C. A., Durham, W. H., Driscoll, L., & Honey, M. (2015). Can ecotourism deliver real economic, social, and environmental benefits? A study of the Osa Peninsula, Costa Rica. *Journal of Sustainable Tourism, 23*(2), 339–357.

Instituto Costarricense de Turismo. (2014). *Encuesta aérea de no residentes, Aeropuerto Internacional Juan Santamaría*. San Jose: Author.

Johnson-Lawrence, V., Schulz, A. J., Zenk, S. N., Israel, B. A., & Rowe, Z. (2015). Does territoriality modify the relationship between perceived neighborhood challenges and physical activity? A multilevel analysis. *Annals of Epidemiology, 25*, 107–112.

Jones, J. S. (2010). Introductions. In J. S. Jones & S. Watt (Eds.), *Ethnography in social science practice* (pp. 3–12). New York: Routledge.

Kaffine, D. T. (2009). Quality and the commons: The surf gangs of California. *The Journal of Law and Economics, 52*(4), 727–743.

Kaiser, S., Alfs, C., Beech, J., & Kaspar, R. (2013). Challenges of tourism development in winter sports destinations and for post-event tourism marketing: The cases of the Ramsau Nordic Ski World Championships 1999 and the St Anton Alpine Ski World Championships 2001. *Journal of Sport & Tourism, 18*(1), 33–48.

Khachadoorian, M. A. (2015). *Locals only! Understanding localism in San Luis Obispo surfing*. San Luis Obispo: California Polytechnic State University (BA).

Krause, S. (2013). Pilgrammage to the playas: Surf tourism in Costa Rica. *Anthropology in Action, 19*(3), 37–48.

Kuzel, A. J. (1999). Sampling in qualitative inquiry. In B. F. Crabtree & W. L. Miller (Eds.), *Doing qualitative research* (2nd ed., pp. 33–45). Thousand Oaks, CA: Sage.

Lawson-Remer, T., & Valderrama, A. (2010). *Collective action and the rules of surfing*. Retrieved from http://ssrn.com/abstract=1420122

LeCompte, M. D., & Schensul, J. J. (1999). *Analyzing and interpreting ethnographic data*. Walnut Creek, CA: AltaMira Press.

Levin, M. (2012). Man accused of attacking U.S. surfers with machete in Pavones. *The Tico Times*. Retrieved from http://www.ticotimes.net/2012/01/19/man-accused-of-attacking-u-s-surfers-with-machete-in-pavones

Lewicka, M. (2011). Place attachment: How far have we come in the last 40 years? *Journal of Environmental Psychology, 31*, 207–230.

MacCannell, D. (1999). *The tourist: A new theory of the leisure class*. Berkeley: University of California Press.

Malmberg, T. (1984). Water rhythm and territoriality. *Geografiska Annaler. Series B, Human Geography, 66*(2), 73–89.

Martin, S. A., & Assenov, I. (2015). Measuring the conservation aptitude of surf beaches in Phuket, Thailand: An application of the Surf Resource Sustainability Index. *International Journal of Tourism Research, 17*, 105–117.

Maxwell, J. A. (2005). *Qualitative research design: An interactive approach* (2nd ed. Vol. 41). Thousand Oaks, CA: Sage.

May, T., & Perry, B. (2011). *Social research & reflexivity: Content, consequence and context*. Los Angeles, CA: Sage.

Müller, S., Peters, M., & Blanco, E. (2010). Rejuvenation strategies: A comparison of winter sport destinations in Alpine regions. *Tourism, 58*(1), 19–36.

Murphy, A. B. (2012). Entente territorial: Sack and Raffestin on territoriality. *Environment and Planning D: Society and Space, 30*(Theme issue: Claude Raffestin), 159–172.

Nazer, D. (2004). The tragicomedy of the surfers' commons. *Deakin Law Review, 9*(2), 655–713.

Noorloos, F. V. (2011). Residential tourism causing land privatization and alienation: New pressures on Costa Rica's coasts. *Development, 54*(1), 85–90.

O'Brien, D., & Eddie, I. (2013). *Benchmarking global best practice: Innovation and leadership in surf city tourism and industry development*. Paper presented at the Global Surf Cities Conference, Kirra Community and Cultural Centre.

O'Brien, D., & Ponting, J. (2013). Sustainable surf tourism: A community centered approach in Papua New Guinea. *Journal of Sport Management, 27*, 158–172.

O'Brien, D. T., Gordon, E., & Baldwin, J. (2014). Caring about the community, counteracting disorder: 311 reports of public issues as expressions of territoriality. *Journal of Environmental Psychology, 40*, 320–330.

Ormrod, J. (2005). Endless summer (1964): Consuming waves and surfing the frontier. *Film & History, 35*(1), 39–52.

Pavlidis, A., & Olive, R. (2014). On the track/in the bleachers: Authenticity and feminist ethnographic research in sport and physical cultural studies. *Sport in Society, 17*(2), 218–232.

Ponting, J. (2009). Projecting paradise: The surf media and the hermeneutic circle in surfing tourism. *Tourism Analysis, 14*(2), 175–185.

Ponting, J., & O'Brien, D. (2014). Liberalizing Nirvana: An analysis of the consequences of common pool resource deregulation for the sustainability of Fiji's surf tourism industry. *Journal of Sustainable Tourism, 22*(3), 384–402.

Ponting, J., & O'Brien, D. (2015). Regulating 'Nirvana': Sustainable surf tourism in a climate of increasing regulation. *Sport Management Review, 18*(1), 99–110.

Preston-Whyte, R. (2002). Constructions of surfing space at Durban, South Africa. *Tourism Geographies, 4*(3), 307–328.

Purrington, A., & Zinn, H. (2011). The influence of loss aversion on mountain bikers' behavioral intentions. *Environmental Management, 48*, 547–557.

Raffestin, C. (2012). Space, territory, and territoriality. *Environment and Planning D: Society and Space, 30*(Theme issue: Claude Raffestin), 121–141.

Sack, R. D. (1986). *Human territoriality: Its theory and history*. Cambridge: Cambridge University Press.

Scheibel, D. (1995). 'Making waves' with Burke: Surf Nazi culture and the rhetoric of localism. *Western Journal of Communication, 59*(4), 253–269.

Schensul, S. L., Schensul, J. J., & LeCompte, M. D. (1999). *Essential ethnographic methods: Observations, interviews, and questionnaires*. Walnut Creek, CA: AltaMira Press.

Scott, P. (2003). 'We shall fight on the seas and the oceans ... we shall': Commodification, localism and violence. *M/C: A Journal of Media and Culture, 6*(1). http://www.media-culture.org.au/0302/05-weshallfight.html

Sletto, B. (2009). 'Indigenous people don't have boundaries': Reborderings, fire managment and productions of authenticities in indigenous landscapes. *Cultural Geographies, 16*(2), 253–277.

Storey, D. (2001). *Territory: The claiming of space*. Harlow: Prentice Hall.

Stranger, M. (2011). *Surfing life: Surface, substructure and the commodification of the sublime*. Surrey: Ashgate.

Surfline. (2013). *Pavones travel info*. Retrieved from http://www.surfline.com/surf-report/pavones-costa-rica_5796/travel/

Tantamjarik, P. A. (2004). *Sustainability issues facing the Costa Rica surf tourism industry*. Honolulu: University of Hawai'i (Master of Science).

Taylor, R. B. (1988). *Human territorial functioning: An empirical, evolutionary perspective on individual and small group territorial cognitions, behaviors, and consequences*. Cambridge: Cambridge University Press.

Towner, N. (2016). How to manage the perfect wave: Surfing tourism management in the Mentawai Islands, Indonesia. *Ocean & Coastal Management, 119*, 217–226.

Usher, L. E., & Kerstetter, D. (2014). Residents' perceptions of quality of life in a surf tourism destination: A case study of Las Salinas, Nicaragua. *Progress in Development Studies, 14*(4), 321–333.

Usher, L. E., & Kerstetter, D. (2015a). Re-defining localism: An ethnography of human territoriality in the surf. *International Journal of Tourism Anthropology, 4*(3), 286–302.

Usher, L. E., & Kerstetter, D. (2015b). 'Surfistas locales': Transnationalism and the construction of surfer identity in Nicaragua. *Journal of Sport and Social Issues, 39*(6), 455–479.

Waitt, G. (2008). 'Killing waves': Surfing, space and gender. *Social & Cultural Geography, 9*(1), 75–94.

Waitt, G., & Frazer, R. (2012). 'The vibe' and 'the glide': Surfing through the voices of longboarders. *Journal of Australian Studies, 36*(3), 327–343.

Waitt, G., & Warren, A. (2008). 'Talking shit over a brew after a good session with your mates': Surfing, space and masculinity. *Australian Geographer, 39*(3), 353–365.

Waller, S., Trendafilova, S., & Daniell, R. (2014). Did the 2012 World series positively impact the image of Detroit? Sport as a transformative agent in changing images of tourism destinations. *Journal of Sport & Tourism, 19*(1), 79–100.

World Surfing Collective. (2012). *World wave guide: Pavones, Costa Rica*. Retrieved from http://worldwaveguide.com/pavones-costa-rica.html

Young, N. (Ed.). (2000). *Surf rage: A surfer's guide to turning negatives into positives*. Angourie, NSW: Nymboida Press.

Local identities in a global game: the social production of football space in Liverpool

Daniel Evans and Glen Norcliffe

ABSTRACT

This paper explores the tensions between local identities and the globalization of the English Premier League by presenting a case study of football fandom in Liverpool. Our findings are based on participant observation and numerous interviews in Liverpool, UK. We examine the tensions resulting from reliance on, and resistance to, tourist-based consumption of the game. We use a Lefebvrian theoretical framework that analyses how football spaces in Liverpool are socially and economically produced, and how the supporters' groups of different teams in the city work to both globalize and glocalize the football culture of the city. We also look at how supporters are attempting to reshape their relationship with football's current economic and cultural space. As Liverpool increasingly relies on a tourist-based economy with sport as its focus, the relationships between local and distant supporters, their clubs, and other fans are altered.

Introduction

Standing outside Liverpool FC's Anfield Stadium, following the 'Merseyside derby' between Liverpool FC and local rivals Everton FC, one of the authors was greeted with chants from the marching Evertonians, 'You're not from here, you're not from here, go back to Norway, you're not from here.' His puzzlement at the hostility clearly directed at a passive spectator watching the visiting fans move up the road to their pubs was replaced by surprise when the man standing next to him serendipitously turned and asked 'How did they know I was from Norway?'[1] In this paper we seek to situate such reactions to the globalization of the Premier League and its consequences for football fandom in Liverpool, looking at both the reliance on and resistance to a tourist-based consumption of the game, and performance at the game by local and other fans.

Sport as a cultural practice has a long history of globalization, and football has experienced this more so than most other forms of sport (Giulianotti, 2000). Liverpool through its association as one of the original centres of football and its prominence through the twentieth century places the city as one of the cores of the sport, and even here at one of the sport's centres there are local consequences to that process of globalization (Williams, 2011). Growing reliance of Liverpool's economy on the performance of football and the performativity of supporter culture intersect with Lefebvre's (1991) theorization of the production of space. Fans contribute to the very economic model that underpins the consumption of their sport, yet simultaneously use these same representations of space – Anfield or Goodison Park – as stages to agitate for a new economic paradigm for their cultural production (Kennedy, 2012). Performances of identity and territoriality give cultural significance to these football spaces. The stands are given particular meaning through how they are lived in and how they are symbolically represented. Furthermore, the valorization of specific places related to consumption of the sport is tied into how the space itself is conceived: the architecture of the stadium, its location, and surrounding amenities all play a part in this (Bale, 1993). This in turn relates to the spatial practices of the wider city and society that have shaped Liverpool's history, and contributed to the creation of a football culture and economy.

The issue faced by many commodified sports in recent decades concerns the tension between the globalization of the sport financially and in player recruitment, and the unalterable fact that a team's identity is local, as are many of the most engaged supporters. Financial survival depends upon winning, and winning depends upon having the, best players, the best trainers and managers, the best sales staff, the best stadium all of which require that the geographical scale of operations grow from the original local scale up to the global. The need for success is driven by both fans who want their team to win and owners who want to recover the financial outlay invested in the players. In so doing many football clubs have developed connections with wealthy owners who are prepared to invest on a scale that exceeds local resources either by seeking them out, or by being 'found' by predatory entrepreneurs. Clubs are provided with their needed capital while the owners are compensated with the prestige of owning such a luxury asset and, occasionally, a return on their investment. Without the ticket-purchasing crowd drawn largely from the local area yet supplemented with tourists, and the television revenues generated elsewhere, a club would face the financial difficulties comparable to Leeds United in 2002, going from competing at the highest level of Europe before crashing down to the third tier of England. Globalization is then dependent on success within the local hierarchical structure of the football leagues.

In undertaking this study of Liverpool and the fans of its two major football clubs (Liverpool FC and Everton FC) we are looking to conceptualize the organization and production of football space in this city. This study will serve as an example of how the globalization of sport affects local spectator culture and how that culture is expressed in relationship to the teams and other fans, as both teams have had different experiences in a global football environment. An examination of how fans interact and participate in the production of their club culture illustrates how the differential globalization of football clubs in Liverpool has affected their fans' relationships not just with the club, but with each other. Tension between different groups of fans and between the fans and the clubs has a spatial manifestation. We explore how the commercial success of the Premier League has manifested itself in Liverpool (Sondaal, 2013), and how football in the stadia, which form the heart of the sport, has impacted the surrounding neighbourhood, city, and region.

Theorizing football

Globalization works to compress both space and time in the movement of capital, ideas, people, and commodities around the world (Harvey, 1990), thereby accelerating the diffusion of dominant cultures such as football. But the scale at which these processes operate is not a binary of global versus local: it operates in complex ways at a multitude of scalar levels (Brenner, 2001). There is a constant tension between forces of *globalization* – often seen as homogenizing and suppressing things local ideas, cultures, and products in favour of a dominant universal versus forces of localization. These forces are fused by a process of *glocalization* where global ideas, products, and services are socially re-constructed and adapted to suit local particularities (Andrews & Ritzer, 2007). In this understanding, the global and the local are 'inextricably and irreversibly bound together through a dynamic relationship' (Urry, 2002, p. 84). The ability of events to jump scale from micro to meso to macro, or vice versa, creates a potential for the global to be felt at intensely personal levels and, conversely, for personal responses to trigger much larger events (Marston, Jones , & Woodward, 2005). Tourism, likewise, is also a process of glocalization as the interactions between local and global continually reshape the site of tourism and its local relations (Salazar, 2005).

O'Brien and Leichenko (2003) demonstrate that not all places benefit equally from the concentration of power in world cities (Massey, 2011): peripheral locations may become marginalized by places of economic, political, social, and cultural power. Some cities have successfully responded to such globalizing forces by rebranding themselves by capitalizing on local assets (Boland, 2010). Thus the increasing importance of football to Liverpool's economy results from a footballing city taking advantage of the sport as a globalized cultural commodity (Giulianotti, 2000). The sport illustrates several key dimensions of globalization: it is almost universally played around the world; it remains a *people's sport* requiring little more than a ball and a pair of boots to participate; the sport itself is overseen by a problematic supra-national governing body (la Fédération Internationale de Football Association or FIFA) that regulates the game and the global labour market of the sport; and the movement of teams, players, broadcasts, and merchandise creates a global flow of products, labour, and capital. Yet despite all these elements of late-capitalist globalization, there is a distinct glocalization of the sport working not just in territories that have adopted the game, but also at the historical heart of the game in England (Andrews & Ritzer, 2007).

Although space forms an integral part of the fans' experience at games, sociological studies of the sport predominate (Benkwitz & Molnar, 2012). Yet for both of Liverpool's teams, space is crucial to understanding their long history at their current sites and the place attachment of the community (Williams, 2011). The football spaces of Liverpool are constantly being refashioned by local, regional, and global forces. For example, plans for Liverpool FC to build a new stadium in Stanley Park or Everton to move to nearby Walton Hall Park or a possible move out of the neighbourhood entirely have stirred up heated protests. The importance of the current locations to supporters of both clubs reflects the symbolic value of the current built environment.

Henri Lefebvre's writings on the social production of space are foundational to an understanding of geographic space as a social construct that structures not just how people conceive and perceive space, but also shapes relationships to power (Lefebvre, 1991; Merrifield, 2006). His framework has been widely used by others in urban studies, development studies, and gender studies (Harvey, 1989; Knopp, 1992; Smith, 1984). This study seeks to illuminate the impacts of globalization on Liverpool's two football clubs through an analysis of how they exist in and also create a socially constructed football space. When the clubs were formed in the late nineteenth century, Liverpool was Britain's premier Atlantic port and a major industrial and financial centre. The late twentieth century has seen social and economic forces produce an entirely different City of Liverpool, as British trade has been re-oriented from the Atlantic to Europe, as Britain has seen massive de-industrialization, and as London has risen as a global financial centre. Liverpool's resulting decline led to a search for ways to re-invent the city and develop new practices to sustain an alternative social model for Liverpool. In Lefebvre's frame (1991, p. 53): 'Capitalism and neocapitalism have produced abstract space, which includes the "world of commodities", its "logic" and its worldwide strategies, as well as the power of money and that of the political state ... Within this space ... , the town has disintegrated.' By embracing the global commodification of football, Liverpool has entered a new larger space in which to re-invent itself. Lefebvre (1991, p. 33) proposes a conceptual triad designed to capture the ways in which spaces – such as Liverpool's contemporary football society – are produced:

- spatial practice taking the form of social actions that produce and reproduce spaces characterized by social formations and maintained through performance, notably at the football games themselves, thereby creating social cohesion;
- representation of space via a semiotic ordering of spatial relations using signs and codes, such as the colour coding of supporters and players and the identification of pubs with particular teams; and
- representational spaces embody complex and sometimes clandestine symbolisms through art, music, chants etc. that reflect other aspects of social life, including performances in Liverpool's kop stand where outsiders are criticized for unfamiliarity with supporters' rehearsed rituals.

These three elements influence the production of football space in Liverpool. Spatial practice is, of course, not restricted to the world of football. It operates at many scales by producing and reproducing social relations, often as part of everyday praxis. The concentration of neo-liberal Britain's financial sector in London has created a sense of alienation in the poorer northern provinces, notably in Liverpool. The City has turned increasingly to cultural production, from Merseybeat, to football pools, to the Albert Docks, to Tate North, to the extension of Liverpool football culture to a global audience.

Appadurai (1996) discusses the -*scapes* that shape the cultural dimensions of globalization, another version of spatial practice. Ethnoscapes, financescapes, mediascapes, ideoscapes, and technoscapes serve as frameworks for different global cultural flows. As Appadurai states, 'the suffix –*scape* indicate[s] that these are not objectively given relations that look the same from every angle of vision but, rather, they are deeply perspectival constructs' (1996, p. 33). Much like Lefebvre's spatial practice, Appadurai's -*scapes* shape our perceptions of our world and its connectedness. Football and its role in Liverpool are shaped by the perceptions of not just the sport, but how it fits into the wider cultural and economic frame of the city. The centrality of football to Liverpudlian culture is due to the way that the technology, media, finance, and identity frame the sport.

The representation of space, often by performative actions with semiotic meanings, is an on-going process for fans, which crests during and after games through the production and contestation of space, a constant process on match days. There are contested spaces around and within the stadium as groupings of fans attempt to establish and assert their own dominance. Production of these spaces is largely governed by the different performances of the fans from passive observation to physical confrontation. This phenomenon is not simply restricted to the contestation of space between supporters of the two clubs, but also to different groups and types of fans supporting the same team who differentiate themselves according to what can be construed as acceptable behaviou. What constitutes 'acceptable behaviour' is somewhat contextual, requiring conformity with the conduct of surrounding fans, the context of the game, and a standard set of rules accepted as part of the entrance to the stadium (Wagg, 1995). There is, then, a socialized aspect of crowd control, where standards of behaviour and the power of enforcement of that behaviour are diffused not just through security, but through the fans themselves, a self-policing of acceptable behaviour, and manifestation of spatial practice (Dixon, 2014). Groups with different behaviours spatially differentiate themselves from others in their representation of spaces.

Clubs have also been accused of using rising ticket prices to displace 'undesirable' fans out of the stadium (Pearson, 2012), leading to concerns over the gentrification of the English football experience (Giulianotti, 2000; King, 1998). Within the stadium are representational spaces organized mainly by class as wealthier supporters and tourists infiltrate what was formerly a working class sport: the cheapest seats at the ends propagating one form of class performance, while expensive midfield seats engender a different class performance. The football club identifiers are normally linked to race, religion, ethnicity, or neighbourhood, which are not very evident in the Merseyside clubs (Giulianotti, 2000). Football spectatorship has long been considered a working class activity – indeed it is one of the definitive activities of the British working class (Savage, Bagnall, & Longhurst, 2005). Class here is not simply an economic category, but also a social performance, an 'interweaving of cultural, ideological and material processes' (Bondi & Christie, 2000, p. 339) to create a class practice. Authenticity as judged through such a performance is always contextual, as the heterogeneous crowd at a match will come with multiple definitions of what is authentic (Dixon, 2014). This paper is not seeking to evaluate the validity of what is 'authentic' as we take that as discursively negotiated through repeated interactions between individuals and groups of supporters. Such claims to authenticity mainly serve as the basis for forming collective identity and associations through the exclusion of others.

Regardless of the intentionality of these associations, fans create social systems and social orders that have important implications for others (Malesevic & Haugaard, 2002). These social orders, such as support for a particular team or membership in a particular supporters' group, create boundaries that differentiate one group from 'others.' While these boundaries may not necessarily originate as spatial boundaries, a spatial differentiation of these social groups is often formed or at the very least implied by the behaviour of these social groups. Members of a supporters' group find common cause in the expression of their support for the club and their expectations from that same club. Thus a member of *LFC Supporters in Toronto* has different expectations and expressions of support for the club than a member of *Keep Flags Scouse*, even if they share a common interest in supporting Liverpool FC.

Fans are often conceived of as a unified whole as in Anderson's (1991) 'imagined community' such that, even without face-to-face interaction, they are viewed as sharing a common sense of belonging and purpose (Benkwitz & Molnar, 2012; Conner, 2014). In practice, a far more complex series of fan motivations operate and at times work at cross-purposes. A typical match is, therefore, far from being a binary of two opposing teams and their fans. There may be conflict between different groups of supporters who, while unified in their opposition against the other team, differ in their approaches to that opposition. Thus buried within the spatial practice of the football game are sub-spaces using various symbols and codes to represent different sub-groups. Pearson (2012) found that some supporters prefer to attend away games that minimize conflicts, while Rookwood and Millward (2011) found contrasting perceptions of Liverpool-born players when comparing local and international fans. Both studies demonstrate that supporters do not form monolithic groups.

Research methodology

Returning to the overarching frame that this paper seeks to use to understand football space, we theorize such a space as the interaction of the globalized sport, economics of the city and its teams, and the cultural significance of the sport to tourists and residents. The methods dictated by the study require direct observation of the case in question, understanding of others' perceptions of the event, and larger contextual information about the role of football in the local culture and economy. The empirical sections of this article that follow are based primarily on participant observation that provided a first-hand understanding of many of the fan dynamics. The observations were supplemented by interviews conducted with supporters' groups, fans, and city and police authorities that are more fully explored in a companion paper.

Match day participant observation of four Liverpool-area football matches in May 2013 followed pre-match activities from central Liverpool to the stadium neighbourhood, local pubs, fan zones, merchandise stalls, and into the stadium. Match observation focused primarily on the crowd, noting reactions of the crowd in particular sections to events on the field or elsewhere in the stand. Some of the sport and its spectatorship is about ritual, and so while standing in the midst of thousands of individuals, certain points of the performance are set to a schedule of the fans' repertoires. Even the movement of people into, out of, and through the stadium has a particularly set pattern that police and stewards rely on in their marshalling of resources and anticipation or reaction to potential problems (O'Neill, 2005). Moments of song or other signals (signs and banners) as markers of space created by supporters were the particular focus of observations. Following matches, observations were focused on the streets outside the stadium and in local pubs before returning to the downtown. The movement of observed locations followed the migrations of other match attendees as best as possible. Participant observation was also conducted during a stadium tour, and at two local meetings of concerned football supporters. Observations were recorded on smartphones when possible, or recounted later that day in a journal. Methods for observation were based on ethnographies of football by Pearson (2012) and O'Neill (2005).

Additionally, a total of 10 such semi-structured interviews were completed, using a varying protocol according to the expertise of the interviewee. Senior club and police managers declined being interviewed so that secondary sources had to be used to gauge their perspectives on globalization and local reactions. Further research utilizing libraries, newspapers, and other sources of documentation (including the web) were exhaustively searched. With the combination of field notes, interview transcripts, and additional documents we were able to find recurrent themes of how football space was conceptualized and represented by the clubs and their fans.

Building a football environment

Football is an integral part of the economic and cultural fabric of Liverpool. Betting shops everywhere advertise game odds, buskers perform acts of streetball juggling, pubs announce game times – any televised game, and vendors sell team merchandise. The decline of industry and the port, and the associated de-urbanization of Liverpool through the last half of the twentieth century had a profound impact not just on the socio-economic conditions of the city, but the culture of Merseyside. In reinventing itself, Liverpool has focused on cultural production as a means of securing its future. And within culture, sport – specifically football – has become the key product of this new economy. This dominance of the landscape extends beyond the immediate vicinity of the Anfield-Everton neighbourhood of the two stadia, to include a number of businesses in Central Liverpool. Beyond the official merchandise shops at their home stadium, Liverpool FC has two merchandise stores in the downtown core, while Everton FC has a store in Liverpool One Mall. Street vendors and unofficial merchandise stalls are found in any shopping centre and many non-sporting stores include an appropriate selection of team-related merchandise.

To quantify the importance of the clubs to the UK economy, Liverpool FC had a turnover of £206 million in 2012–2013, and Everton FC a turnover of £86 million for the same year (Conn, 2014). Revenue breakdowns for both clubs (Table 1) show that match day income accounts for significantly less of total club turnover than television revenues, and this was for the 2012–2013 season, the final year before a new, more lucrative TV deal boosted television revenues to £97.5 million for Liverpool and £85 million for Everton in the 2013–2014 season (Sporting Intelligence, 2014). The other category of commercial activity, consisting of merchandising and sponsorship deals, demonstrates the power of a global fan base: Liverpool's large following produced a turnover of £98 million, while Everton's more local support could only manage a meagre £14 million of commercial activities.

With tourism increasingly important to the Liverpool economy, contributing approximately £1.9 billion or 10.1% of the local GDP (England's North West Research Service [ENWRS], 2011, p. 5), football-related tourism is increasingly part of the tourism planning for the city. In 2011, the City of Liverpool had 30 million visitors, of which 1.9 million had an overnight stay (ENWRS, 2011). One-third of all weekend stays in Liverpool's four-star hotels are football related; additionally, one-quarter of all budget hotel stays in the region are

Table 1. 2012–2013 Club revenues.

	Broadcasting	Gate & Matchday income	Commercial activities	Total revenues
Everton FC	£56 million	£17 million	£14 million	£86 million
Liverpool FC	£64 million	£45 million	£98 million	£206 million

football related (Regeneris, 2011). Football is the most important generator of overnight stays in Liverpool, and the most important attraction for visitors, with Liverpool FC season attendances totalling 1,037,092 and Everton FC 888,905 (ENWRS, 2011). Liverpool FC's Museum and Anfield Tour add a further 143,122 visits per year on non-match days, which is itself the fifth best attended attraction in Liverpool (ENWRS, 2011). In addition to local tourists, the two football clubs have an international following of invisible tourists who follow their clubs' fortunes in bars and clubs and at home by satellite. This growing international viewership accounts for part of the substantial payments the two clubs receive for television rights.

Despite the importance of football to the tourism economy of Liverpool, the actual distribution of economic benefits is strongly tilted against the Anfield-Everton neighbourhood. Despite having two football stadia that draw thousands of visitors each weekend, the neighbourhood is in fact one of the poorest in Liverpool, and the UK. Over 80% of the neighbourhood is considered in the highest quintile of the UK's index of deprivation – a national measure of income, housing, crime, health, and education (Anon, 2014).

As a means to address this, the City of Liverpool released its vision for the Anfield Project in June 2013, which would see a revitalization of the Anfield neighbourhood. Beyond bulldozing a street of houses to allow for the expansion of the Main Stand, the Anfield Project would reconfigure the neighbourhood to encourage development of a number of tourist-related businesses that would benefit from their proximity to the refurbished and expanded stadium. The intention is that the neighbourhood as a whole benefits from football (Anon, 2014), thereby furthering the reorientation and production of the built environment of the city and this neighbourhood in particular around football.

Inside the stadium space has been transformed too. Along with the growth of television spectators, the audience of the Premier League has shifted over the last two decades. An oft-cited reason for the decline of hooliganism is the gentrification of the English football crowd via mandatory seating at all top-flight grounds (see Giulianotti, 2000; King, 1998). While the change from standing to seating reduced crowding and movement, it also reduced potential club revenues and required massive redesigns or retrofits to the stadia (King, 1998). Some of the cost recovery for this has been borne through higher ticket prices that have gone up 751% since the foundation of the Premier League in 1992 (Conn, 2011; Spirit of Shankly, n.d.). In fact the rise in ticket prices was probably inevitable with the changed product on the field. The creation of the Premier League, which replaced the old First Division of the Football League, changed the national and global consumption of the game through satellite broadcasts and increased revenue used to purchase elite players from around the world, creating an increased demand for English top-flight football.

In the case of Liverpool, the change in crowd is partially due to the influx of tourists taking in games at Anfield, and to a lesser extent at Goodison Park. The presence of so many football fans in Liverpool for match day has created a seller's market for tickets, as demand far outstrips supply. It is further exacerbated through the nature of the visiting fans – if you have just paid several hundred dollars in airfare, hundreds of pounds in accommodation and food, you are not going to not pay to go to the game. It is not just the touted tickets that have driven up the costs of attending the game, but the basic price offered by the club has also risen drastically. As Conn (2011) noted, between 1990 and 2011 British cumulative inflation came to 77.1%, yet football ticket prices rose 1108% at Anfield.

Everton's place in Liverpool

For Everton FC to compete with other Premier League clubs it has long been thought that its 35,000-seat stadium is too small for the regular spatial practice of football, and they too have explored options for redevelopment or relocation, that is, ways to produce a new performative space. The redevelopment option is even more difficult at Goodison than Anfield because Everton does not own any of the adjacent properties, and would have to figure the cost of expropriation into any redevelopment; its location closer to a local business centre would make the costs significantly higher. Instead the club focused on the potential of relocating the stadium either outside of the neighbourhood or to nearby Walton Hall Gardens. In 2006 Everton FC turned their attention to the nearby town of Kirkby, just outside Liverpool, where they would create a 55,000-seat stadium combined with a retail location (Fitzpatrick, 2013). Against this were a number of active Everton fans, who formed their own group, Keep Everton in our City (KEIOC). The organization played a vocal role during the assessment phase of the Kirkby proposal that was eventually rejected (Fitzpatrick, 2013). Despite the work of KEIOC in the development of a Football Quarter proposal that would see both Anfield and Goodison Park as the nexus of a Anfield-Breckfield regeneration plan, Everton is conspicuously absent in the latest Anfield Project Framework. Members of KEIOC fear that this unique co-production of space through local club rivalry may be lost (Fitzpatrick, 2013).

In a city long organized and divided around football, the sport is taking an increasingly prominent role in the culture and economy of the city. The production of Lefebvrian space with a quarter mile separating Anfield from Goodison Park feeds a historical rivalry in the shadow of two cathedrals of football. For both Liverpool clubs, the formation of organized supporters' groups is a response to actions taken by the Football Clubs themselves. The local supporters' clubs vary in purpose and construct their spaces in different ways, but all were founded by fans feeling threatened by the direction that their club and sport was headed in.

The city is ours: claiming football space

Lefebvre's representational space is manifest in the symbols, images, and songs of each club, curated not just by the club, but through its fans. Each football club in Liverpool has created its own distinct identity; and within that, each supporters group also has an identity distinct from the football club. Football space is a heterotopic space, with meanings contested by its various groups. From the original split of Everton FC and Liverpool FC, there has been a formation of collective identities for each group that has a spatial element, even if these particular clubs do not have the clear territorial division of support that is found at other locations. The club's reputations reflect what it means to be a Liverpool or Everton fan.

Everton FC: 'If you know your history ... '

Everton FC is, as their song goes, 'A grand old team to support' by virtue of being the oldest club in the city. While Everton FC has seen its own share of successes, its smaller international profile and support has had an effect on the psyche of Everton supporters and how they relate to Liverpool and foreign fans. The identity of the Everton fan was summed up by one fan as, 'We've got history. We were here first.' It is a common theme in the fans' chants and the songs of the club (Armstrong & Young, 2000). Everton fans are intensely focused on the local, and especially their local rivals.

In observing Everton fans at matches, their primary concern is Liverpool FC: their identity as a set of supporters hinges deeply on their othering of Liverpool FC. At the Merseyside derby, Everton fans maximized their presence at the game through a number of strategies common to visiting fans in football (Pearson, 2012). In the vignette that opened the paper, the use of Norway by Evertonians departing Anfield seemed almost incidental to the meaning of the chant: that Evertonians are 'local' and Liverpool fans are 'foreign' and Norway could have stood in for any other nation. The chant had two audiences, one was the listening Liverpool fans who were directly targeted and even pointed at in an act of isolation and exclusion implying their support was less 'true' than that of the Evertonians. The other audience was the listening Evertonian fans, who are then further incorporated into the spaces of Everton through their identification with or performance of a chant against the Liverpool fans, reaffirming their localness.

An observation of the match experience at Goodison Park demonstrated that the rivalry remains fixed on Liverpool FC. When playing West Ham FC at home, visiting fans played the expected role of seeking to disrupt Evertonians through their chants, but this was largely ignored by Everton fans who instead continued to direct their chants against Liverpool FC (that weekend playing in London). Even public address (PA) club itself joins in, representing Evertonian space by playing of *It's a Grand Old Team* over the PA system. Two lines stick out as particularly focused on the local rivalry 'and if you know your history …' as a reference to both past successes and their being *the* original team; and the line 'We don't care what the red side say,'[2] where the meaning is a clear enough reference to Liverpool FC. The paramount rivalry is between the two clubs, and the 'othering' of Liverpool FC is the tie that binds Evertonians, defining themselves by excluding what they are not.

The great irony of Everton is that while their rivalry is intensely local, and it is almost singularly directed against Liverpool FC, the fans themselves are more accepting and welcoming of tourists because they still are not present in significant enough numbers to threaten access or atmosphere at games. Instead, tourist fans are almost welcomed for their choice of supporting Everton FC. Conversations with Everton fans were often more relaxed as there was less obvious judging of fan authenticity, neutrality was tolerated, and there was optimism that neutrals could be persuaded to join the Everton diaspora. Two Americans observed attending the Everton-West Ham game were readily accepted by Everton fans in a pub adjacent to the stadium prior to the match. In that case, the American fans' non-local identity actually enhanced their status among Evertonians in the pub. Everton's smaller international following does not have a critical mass needed to alter the habitus of local fans (Bourdieu, 1990), and so posed little existential threat to the Everton identity. Supporters of Everton see the 'localness' of the support base as a virtue, yet welcome any additional support from interlopers.

Evertonians would appear to be engaged in the glocalization of the club identity as a way of preserving its economic competitiveness in relation to teams that have managed to secure much larger international followings. Liverpool FC can claim millions of fans around the world, and so the smaller club instead seeks to chip away at the local support from the larger club by constantly reasserting its localness. An innate quality of being local and Evertonian demonstrates the supposed authenticity and superiority of being an Everton supporter, as the fans at the beginning of the article demonstrated. This is not to say that all Everton supporters reject or exclude potential fans from taking up their team, but that there is a dissonance between how different fans perform being Evertonian and how others engage with non-local individuals. Everton FC requires more global supporters for the continued economic health and success of the club, but despite the club's claim to being 'the Peoples' Club' some fans place a premium on representing localness.

Liverpool FC: never walking alone

Liverpool FC draws its identity from its history as well but, unlike Everton's focus on the deep local history of the team, theirs is based on the more recent national and international success of the team: Liverpool's spatial practices have gone global. It is a taunt to their less successful neighbours, and a drawing point for fans near and far. But Liverpool FC is far more than its trophies: its stadium, Anfield, is home to the famous Kop,[3] which is in itself one of the spectacles of the football world, and the site for renditions of the team's anthem *You'll Never Walk Alone* (Williams, 2012). This is a space where the culture of Liverpool FC is reproduced game after game: maintaining support for that culture is a major concern for Liverpool supporters.

Seat location is critical to the performance of Liverpool fandom, with Main Stand tickets more generally available to tourists. Their behaviour is dominated by the tourist persona: video recording but not participating in the songs. And while most of the fans in that section avoided wearing jerseys, many who were not recording held aloft a half and half scarf during the singing of *You'll Never Walk Alone* (a sure sign of a tourist).

There is a generally acknowledged spatial hierarchy in the stands at Anfield, with a clearly segregated section along the Anfield Road end stand reserved by the club for the away fans, opposite the loudest and most passionate home fans on the Kop end. The Main and Centenary Stands – along the sidelines – contain a less noisy, but still clearly partisan local crowd that often follows the lead of the Kop, rather than instigating chants themselves. So while the Kop does not have the most expensive tickets, there is a prestige accorded to those occupying a place in the Kop that reflects its cultural importance to the fans.

It is not surprising that the battles among Liverpool FC fans are largely over who should have access to Anfield and to the Kop (Millward, 2012). Some supporters argue that the influx of tourists is so great that it threatens the atmosphere in the stadium. Already there are complaints about the number of fans who come simply to watch *You'll Never Walk Alone* and stand there taking a video of the crowd singing rather than participating (i.e. actively representing the space) (Williams, 2012). Significantly, during games attended there was a number of spectators who began to applaud *You'll Never Walk Alone* after the chorus, but before the rest of the crowd sang the final reprise of the chorus, indicating that a number of visitors were familiar with the song, but not how it was to be sung. The mistimed clapping, seen by 'authentic' fans as a failure to understand the most basic traditions of Anfield, fosters resentment of 'inauthentic' fans.

Locals resent fans who do not play their part in the Kop. Indeed the tribalism of some fans manifests itself in a territoriality by claiming the Kop as 'their' space (Millward, 2012). Several years ago, one such group called 'Keep Flags Scouse' was organized to self-police visual displays in the Kop, educating fans that Union Jacks and St. George's Crosses were not appropriate (Wells, 2007). This expectation of conformity was also displayed by a supporter sitting in the Kop for the final game of the season who twice loudly declared the purpose of those in the Kop by shouting, 'If you're not singing, go sit in the Main Stand,' and 'If I'd wanted it this quiet, I would have sat in the Main Stand.' Certain sets of behaviour are appropriate for certain spaces at the stadium. A number of semiotic cues, particularly clothing and behaviour, indicate whether a fan is a tourist or a diehard (Dixon, 2014). Such tribalism leads some of the local members of the Kop to practice social exclusion of these visiting fans because they do not participate in the habitus of the Kop. By discouraging visitors, or requesting them to behave according to Kop rules, Kop residents are enforcing boundaries both of behaviour and space amongst Liverpool supporters.

The self-surveillance of supporters and enforcement of unwritten behavioural codes is a troubling aspect of group behaviour. The definition of what constitutes a Kop supporter can be arbitrary and contradictory depending on the individuals asserting authority among the group. Tourists interviewed assert that the ticket that they paid for entitles them to sit in the indicated section and that the club itself often allocates Kop tickets to out-of-town fan groups; Liverpool fans argue that it is the Kop that is what makes Anfield what it is, and should therefore be reserved for those most prepared to participate in its activity. Lateral surveillance works for both daytrippers and Kopites; wherever one or the other dominates, there is a tendency for the general behaviour of that group to reinforce its own behavioural code in that space.

Other conflicts emerge between fans over how players are valued. For locals, the local-born players are held up as heroes because they are home-grown boys who made the team, whereas for international fans, they are not seen as critical to the team's success. Rookwood and Millward (2011) discuss the importance of locally born Jamie Carragher to Liverpool FC's local standing, and how that perception shifts between local and international fans. Just as FC Barcelona plays a role in Catalan nationalism, so both Liverpool FC and Everton FC play an important role in affirming the Scouse identity. At the matches observed, songs sung for local players Jamie Carragher and Steven Gerrard used Beatles tunes (Yellow Submarine and Let it Be, respectively), further emphasizing their connection to the city.

Discussion and conclusion

The restructuring of English football and its commercialization on an unprecedented global scale have encouraged particular markets – especially Liverpool – to increasingly orient local economic development around football. The changing nature of consumption has made television revenues a key priority (Deloitte, 2014; Gibson, 2012). But live consumption remains an essential component in the production of the Premier League cultural experience by engaging in the practices that produce these fabled spaces of football. Overseas supporters benefit teams through merchandise sales, by increasing television ratings, and sometimes making a pilgrimage as a football-tourist to watch the team in person, and taking part in the rituals they have witnessed from afar (Edensor & Millington, 2008). Though their visits are of short-term duration, expenditures are relatively high, therefore valuable to the local club and city. Meanwhile, local fans remain enthusiastic supporters because there is no viable alternative; they are emotionally invested in a club that has come to be part of their own identity.

As Lefebvre anticipated, the practices of fans have a particular spatial structure. Local supporters both love and loathe other fans of their team. On the one hand, a large and passionate international fan base can affect results on the field and provide a team with the financial resources to secure the talent necessary to compete at the highest level of the game. On the other hand, tourists are not very active in representing the club spaces and unfamiliar with many of the symbols and songs. Everton FC's fans pride themselves on their 'localness' and mock Liverpool FC's tourist fans although they are quite willing to accept non-locals into their own fold. But growing a legion of foreign fans directly threatens regular supporters' access to matches (Kerr & Emery, 2011). Through noise and visual display, local fans have an affective influence on other fans and the club. Self-awareness of their own agency is encouraging some supporter groups to increasingly organize and regulate their own actions. Informal surveillance and self-policing in the stands encourages particular modes of behaviour by supporters in different sections of the stands (Dixon, 2014). How fans shape and occupy football space is not the only dimension of how that space is socially produced. In Liverpool, this organizing of football space is becoming critical because the sport is no longer just an amusing pastime, but a key plank of the City's economic base; it is a city building itself for football. The importance of football then creates its own space where, in Lefebvre's (1991) framework, football is perceived, conceived, and represented as vital to the city.

Liverpool is building a football space created and shaped by the clubs and their many supporters. Fans are able to participate in the cultural event by attending a match or forming part of the audience who watch the televised event. Clubs reinforce their brand both through the active use of their marketing as part of the event, or through the less direct use of branded fans and supporters, who also form a part of the clubs' revenue streams through the merchandising of various paraphernalia (Kerr & Emery, 2011). In Liverpool it is clear that this is a dynamic process with a constant mediation between the groups of fans and the clubs. But there is a distinct spatial element to this negotiation of club identity. It embraces what is considered home, what territory belongs to the club and its adherents, and how a network of fans and supporters is diffused through the rest of the football world. In a world where club reputation is judged by the size of the trophy room foreign supporters may re-assess their loyalty following poor results. Groups in Liverpool – and elsewhere – have sought to intervene in the cultural production of football in their city by giving their sport a glocalized version of the product, one that is recognized worldwide for its particular performance of fandom. The local fans of both clubs have to negotiate how it is they deal with an influx of global fans. The local cannot be separate from the global, since it is the local identity of clubs that fascinates foreign audiences (Salazar, 2005). Would Liverpool FC or Everton FC be as popular if they were exactly the same as all the other teams? No. It is the specific football space created in Merseyside that has contributed to the global following of those teams. The football space of Liverpool is a social and cultural space that extends beyond its economic value. The contestation of this space by locals is an attempt to control the production of football space and assert that the global game can have a Liverpool-specific and even a club-specific inflection that is, in their view, best managed by the hands of the locals that created it.

Notes

1. Liverpool FC's large Scandinavian support has long been a joke amongst Everton FC supporters (see Nash, 2000).
2. Also sung by Everton fans as 'We don't care what the red shite say ... '
3. The Kop, or Spion Kop, the name for the west end stand of Anfield derives its name as a memorial to the Battle of Spion Kop during the Boer War, many terraces around England were so named for their resemblance to the Kop, or hill, that formed the site of the battle (Williams, 2011).

Disclosure statement

No potential conflict of interest was reported by the authors.

References

Anderson, B. (1991). *Imagined communities: Reflections on the origin and spread of nationalism*. New York: Verso.
Andrews, D., & Ritzer, G. (2007). The grobal in the sporting glocal. *Global Networks, 7*(2), 113–153.
Anon. (2014). *Anfield spatial regeneration framework (draft)*. Liverpool: Liverpool City Council.
Appadurai, A. (1996). *Modernity at large: Cultural dimensions of globalization*. Minneapolis, MN: University of Minnesota Press.
Armstrong, G., & Young, M. (2000). Fanatical football chants: Creating and controlling the carnival. In G. Finn & R. Giulianotti (Eds.), *Football culture: Local contests, global visions* (pp. 173–211). London: Frank Cass.
Bale, J. (1993). *Sport, space, and the city*. London: Routledge.
Benkwitz, A., & Molnar, G. (2012). Interpreting and exploring football fan rivalries: An overview. *Soccer and Society, 13*(4), 479–494.
Boland, P. (2010). 'Capital of culture – you must be having a laugh!' Challenging the official rhetoric of Liverpool as the 2008 European cultural capital. *Social and Cultural Geography, 11*(7), 627–645.
Bondi, L., & Christie, H. (2000). The best of times for some and the worst of times for others? Gender and class divisions in urban Britain today. *Geoforum, 31*, 329–343.
Bourdieu, P. (1990). *The logic of practice*. London: Polity Press.
Brenner, N. (2001). The limits to scale? Methodological reflections on scalar structuration. *Progress in Human Geography, 25*(4), 591–614.
Conn, D. (2011). The Premier League has priced out fans, young and old. *The Guardian*. Retrieved from http://www.theguardian.com/sport/david-conn-inside-sport-blog/2011/aug/16/premier-league-football-ticket-prices
Conn, D. (2014). Premier League finances: The full club-by-club breakdown and verdict. *The Guardian*. Retrieved from https://www.theguardian.com/football/2014/may/01/premier-league-accounts-club-by-club-david-conn
Conner, N. (2014). Global cultural flows and the routes of identity: The imagined worlds of Celtic FC. *Social and Cultural Geography, 15*(5), 525–546.
Deloitte. (2014). *All to play for: Global money league*. Manchester: Author.
Dixon, K. (2014). The role of lateral surveillance in the construction of authentic football fandom practice. *Surveillance & Society, 11*(4), 424–438.
Edensor, T., & Millington, S. (2008). 'This is our city': Branding football and local embeddedness. *Global Networks-a Journal of Transnational Affairs, 8*(2), 172–193.

England's North West Research Service. (2011). *Digest of tourism statistics*. Liverpool: Liverpool Local Enterprise Partnership.

Fitzpatrick, C. (2013). The struggle for grassroots involvement in football club governance: Experiences of a supporter-activist. *Soccer & Society, 14*(2), 201–214.

Gibson, O. (2012). Premier League lands £3bn TV rights bonanza from Sky and BT. *The Guardian*. Retrieved from http://www.theguardian.com/media/2012/jun/13/premier-league-tv-rights-3-billion-sky-bt

Giulianotti, R. (2000). *Football: A sociology of the global game*. London: Polity Press.

Harvey, D. (1989). *The urban experience*. Baltimore: Johns Hopkins University Press.

Harvey, D. (1990). Between space and time – reflections on the geographical imagination. *Annals of the Association of American Geographers, 80*(3), 418–434.

Kennedy, D. (2012). Football stadium relocation and the commodification of football: The case of Everton supporters and their adoption of the language of commerce. *Soccer & Society, 13*(3), 341–358.

Kerr, A. K., & Emery, P. R. (2011). Foreign fandom and the Liverpool FC: A cyber-mediated romance. *Soccer and Society, 12*(6), 880–896.

King, A. (1998). *The end of the terraces: The transformation of English football in the 1990s*. London: Leicester University Press.

Knopp, L. (1992). Sexuality and the spatial dynamics of capitalism. *Environment and Planning D: Society and Space, 10*(6), 651–669.

Lefebvre, H. (1991). *The production of space*. (Donald Nicholson-Smith, Trans.). Oxford: Blackwell (originally published 1974).

Malesevic, S., & Haugaard, M. (2002). *Making sense of collectivity, ethnicity, nationalism and globalization*. London: Pluto Press.

Marston, S., Jones III, J., & Woodward, K. (2005). Human geography without scale. *Transactions of the Institute of British Geographers, 30*, 416–436.

Massey, D. (2011). *World city*. London: Wiley.

Merrifield, A. (2006). *Henri Lefebvre: A critical introduction*. London: Routledge.

Millward, P. (2012). Reclaiming the kop? Analysing Liverpool supporters' 21st century mobilizations. *Sociology – the Journal of the British Sociological Association, 46*(4), 633–648.

Nash, R. (2000). Globalized football fandom: Scandinavian Liverpool FC supporters. *Football Studies, 3*(2), 5–24.

O'Brien, K., & Leichenko, R. (2003). Winners and losers in the context of global change. *Annals of the Association of American Geographers, 93*(1), 89–103.

O'Neill, M. (2005). *Policing football: Social interaction and negotiated disorder*. New York, NY: Palgrave MacMillan.

Pearson, G. (2012). *An ethnography of English football fans: Cans, cops and carnivals*. Manchester: Manchester University Press.

Regeneris Consulting Ltd. (2011). *New stadium for Liverpool football club: Stanley Park, Liverpool – economic impact assessment*. Altrincham: Author.

Rookwood, J., & Millward, P. (2011). 'We all dream of a team of carraghers': Comparing 'local' and Texan Liverpool fans' talk. *Sport in Society, 14*(1), 37–52.

Salazar, N. (2005). Tourism and glocalization: 'local' tour guiding. *Annals of Tourism Research, 32*(3), 628–646.

Savage, M., Bagnall, G., & Longhurst, B. (2005). *Globalization and belonging*. London: Sage.

Smith, N. (1984). *Uneven development: Nature, capital, and the production of space*. Athens: University of Georgia Press.

Sondaal, T. (2013). Football's grobalization or globalization? The lessons of Liverpool football club's evolution in the premier league era. *Soccer and Society, 14*(4), 485–501.

Spirit of Shankly. (n.d.). *Spirit of Shankly homepage*. Retrieved from http://www.spiritofshankly.com

Sporting Intelligence. (2014). *Where the money went: Liverpool top premier league prize cash in 2013–2014*. Retrieved from http://www.sportingintelligence.com/2014/05/14/where-the-money-went-liverpool-top-premier-league-prize-cash-in-2013-14-140501/

Urry, J. (2002). *The tourist gaze*. London: Sage.

Wagg, S. (1995). *Giving the game away: Football, politics, and culture on five continents.* New York, NY: St. Marten's Press.

Wells, S. (2007). Dissent and we'll fatwa you. What do you think this is, a free country? *The Guardian.* Retrieved from http://www.theguardian.com/football/2007/feb/28/sport.comment

Williams, J. (2011). *Red men: Liverpool football club, the biography.* London: Mainstream Publishing.

Williams, J. (2012). Walking alone together the Liverpool way: Fan culture and 'clueless' yanks. *Soccer and Society, 13*(3), 426–442.

Factors effecting destination and event loyalty: examining the sustainability of a recurrent small-scale running event at Banff National Park

Elizabeth A. Halpenny, Cory Kulczycki and Farhad Moghimehfar

ABSTRACT

An important form of economic sustainability for tourism businesses is customer loyalty. Using a sample of 387 active sport tourists, factors that influence destination and event tourism loyalty are reported on in this paper. Thirty-six per cent of destination loyalty's variance was explained – operationalized as intentions of active sport tourists to revisit and recommend Banff National Park (NP). Thirty-one per cent of event loyalty's variance was explained – operationalized as participation in future offerings of an annual small-scale running race, Melissa's Road Race, located in the park. Destination loyalty was directly and positively predicted by park attachment and indirectly influenced by event attachment, followed by nature-related travel motives, frequency of visits to the park and history of engagement in the race. Event loyalty was directly and positively predicted by event attachment and racers' views regarding the appropriateness of Banff NP as a race context and indirectly by history of race participation. Running travel motives, perceived value of park entry and event fees failed to predict loyalty intentions. Two models were used to explore the 'correct' conceptualization of relationships between event attachment and park attachment. The model that depicted event attachment as an antecedent to park attachment demonstrated better fit with the data, and thus suggests support for the proposition that attachments which develop for special events may in turn support the development of destination attachment.

Introduction

An important way for destinations and special events to be sustainable is to foster loyalty among their visitors. Loyalty manifests through repeat visitation, recommendation of the event or destination to others, the recounting of positive stories via Word of Mouth (WoM), volunteering, financial support and willingness to pay. Loyalty promotion is desirable because retaining existing clients can cost much less than attracting new ones (Gursoy, McCleary, & Lepsito, 2003, 2007). Further, studies suggest 'that a small decrease in customer retention cost is likely to cause a significant increase in profits' (Reichheld & Sasser, 1990, cited in Gursoy, Chen, & Chi, 2014, p. 810). Tourism researchers realize the importance of retaining existing clients and have devoted much effort to examining factors that affect tourists' destination loyalty. McKercher, Denizci-Guillet, and Ng (2012) and Gursoy et al. (2014) provide good overviews of these factors which can include perceived value, satisfaction, place attachment, destination image, service quality perception, pervious experience, activity and destination involvement, and familiarity. Understanding of the intensity of effect produced by these factors and their relationship with each other is still developing. Additionally, specific types of destinations and tourists remain understudied.

Loyalty drivers for active sport tourists and sporting events have received little attention. Sport tourism is 'travel away from home to play sport, watch sport, or to visit a sport attraction including both competitive and non-competitive activities' (Deply, 1998, p. 23). Active sport tourists, the main source of data for this study, are individuals who travel to participate in a chosen sporting activity (Gibson, 1998). Higham (1999) and Gibson, Kaplanidou, and Kang (2012) agree that small-scale sport tourism is compatible with many host destinations and is congruent with the main principles of sustainable tourism. In our case study, Swarbrooke's (1999, cited in Saarinen, 2006) definition of sustainable tourism is used: 'which is economically viable but does not destroy the resources on which the future of tourism will depend, notably the physical environment and the social fabric of the host community' (p. 1124). This definition prioritizes economic sustainability of tourism activities; an examination of factors effecting event and destination loyalty supports advancement of economically sustainable tourism.

Kaplanidou and Vogt (2007) were two of the first researchers to study sport tourists' intentions and actual engagement in repeat visitation of a destination for active sport tourism. Taks, Chalip, Green, Kesenne, and Martyn (2009) explicitly linked sustainability and repeat visitation of sport tourists in their exploration of factors that affect repeat visitation. More recently, though not necessarily a tourist-dominated sample, Filo, Funk, and O'Brien's (2010) investigation of sport charity event participants revealed that motives, sponsor image and event attachment appeared to encourage future event participation.

Destination loyalty associated with parks has received more attention (see Moore, Rodger, & Taplin 2015 for review); these studies range from protected areas with high levels of long-haul tourists (Halpenny, 2007; Kil, Holland, Stein, & Ko, 2012; Weaver & Lawton, 2011) to parks that are characterized by a blend of tourists and local recreationists (Lee, 2009; Lee & Shen, 2013; López-Mosquera & Sánchez, 2013). Many of these studies are less focused on profit-making and more interested in generating long-term supporters of parks and conservation, in addition to recurrent park visitation as desired outcomes.

This paper explores the factors that promote destination and event sustainability – specifically visitors' intention to re-visit and recommend a destination and sport tourism event. The destination, Banff National Park (NP), hosts a recurring small-scale running event each year, Melissa's Road Race. The paper focuses on the factors that appear to encourage active sport tourists' loyalty to the park and race event. In addition to advancing understanding of factors that promote destination and event loyalty, the study addresses Kaplanidou and Gibson's (2010) call for more research that focuses on small-scale sport tourism events.

Literature review

Re-visitation and positive recommendations as sustainable tourism indicators

After participating in a sport tourism event, intentions to revisit a destination or recommend it to others as a travel destination can arise; here these behaviours are used as indicators of sustainable tourism. Many factors can inspire visitation to and recommendation of a destination. In this study, motivations for trip, frequency of travel to the destination, perceived value, place attachment and perceived appropriateness of the event taking place in the destination were examined. Gursoy et al.'s (2014) theoretical review of destination loyalty formation supports the selection of these indicators.

Motivations are factors that drive individuals to engage in tourism; they represent tourists' reasons for actions, desires and needs. Only a few studies have explored the motives of individuals who travel to engage in a running competition. Funk and Bruun (2007) conducted research on the 2005 Gold Coast Airport Marathon with a focus on international participants' motives for participation and culture education. They found that participants' motives were influenced by 'running involvement and desire to participate in running events' (p. 815). Furthermore, while participants were motivated by physical fitness, the international participants who were not of a similar culture were interested in learning about Australian culture. Shipway and Jones (2007) researched the Cyprus International Four-day Challenge using the theory of serious leisure. They noted that participants associated their personal identity with running and in the period up to the completion of the event displayed running capital (e.g. t-shirts and stories) from previous events. They suggested that 'the very act of travelling allowed the running identity to become more salient' (p. 378) and 'This in itself seems to provide an attraction for such events' (p. 378). For their participants visiting places was a motivation for travel. Participants 'valued social identities … unique ethos of the group, the perseverance of its members … personal effort, the careers of the runners and the subsequent durable benefits' (p. 382). Similar results were presented by Shipway and Jones's (2008) study of 2007 Flora London Marathon participants.

A broader examination of the tourism literature reveals that travel motives and destinations' ability to address these motives can result in return visitation and recommendation of the destination to others (e.g. Baloglu, 2000; Yoon & Uysal, 2005). These studies theorize that individuals seek to fulfil specific needs through travel to specific sites. For example, in a study of Chinese heritage tourists, Wang and Leou (2015) found that travel motives were positive predictors of destination loyalty. Lee and Hsu's (2013) study of Aboriginal festival attendees reported that motivation indirectly affected event loyalty; its effects were fully mediated by event satisfaction.

If the destination satisfactorily addresses individuals' needs, then attachments can form through repeated interactions and the satiation of needs. Kyle, Mowen, and Tarrant's (2004) study of Cleveland park visitors examined this and found that nature-based motivations were weak positive predictors of affective and social bonding park attachment sub-dimensions, but not cognitive or conative sub-dimensions. Filo et al. (2010) found that recreation motives were predictive of attachment to a sport charity event, and indirectly influenced future participation in the event.

The desire to be physically challenged, emotionally fulfilled by achieving a personal best race time, spending time with friends and family, or a myriad of other desired outcome can drive recreation and travel. If a destination or event satisfies desires, attachment may follow. Based on these observations, the following hypotheses are proposed:

H1. Running Travel Motives will positively predict Event Attachment.
H2. Running Travel Motives will positively predict Event Sustainability.
H3. Running Travel Motives will positively predict Frequency of Event participation.
H4. Running Travel Motives will positively predict Perceived Value of Event Entry Fee.
H5. Nature Travel Motives will positively predict Frequency of Park Visitation.
H6. Nature Travel Motives will positively predict Park Attachment.
H7. Nature Travel Motives will positively predict Park Visitation Sustainability.
H8. Nature Travel Motives will positively predict Perceived Value of Park Entry Fee.

Value for money paid can be another factor that influences travel intentions. For example, in a study of international tourists at Bangkok's airport, Rittichainuwat, Qu, and Leong (2003) found that good value for food and accommodation was strongly linked with destination loyalty. Chen and Chen (2010) observed that quality of experience, perceived value and satisfaction combined to predict Taiwan heritage site tourists' return visitation. In a study of Chinese tourists to Hainan Island, Sun, Chi, and Xu (2013) revealed that perceived value's positive effect on destination loyalty was mediated by tourist satisfaction. Finally, Forgas-Coll, Palau-Saumell, Sánchez-García, and Callarisa-Fiol (2012) reported that the effect of perceived value on conative (behavioural) loyalty was mediated by satisfaction and affective attitude among American and Italian tourists visiting Barcelona. Hypotheses arising from these observations are

H9. Perceived value of race entry fee will positively predict Event Sustainability.
H10. Perceived value of park entry fee will positively predict Park Visitation Sustainability.

Destination loyalty has also been predicted by frequency of prior visitation. For example, in a study of European sun holiday tourists Alegre and Cladera (2006) found that repeat visitors are more likely to make a further visit to a destination. However in contrast, Halpenny (2007) reported that frequency of visitation and length of affiliation were not predictive of return visitation and instead intensity of attachment to the destination expressed by visitors was significantly and positivity predictive. Further modelling that explored the effects of mediation by Halpenny in her study of park visitors may have revealed the mediation of visitation frequency's effect on return visitation by attachment, as other studies suggest frequency of visitation is associated and potentially a predictor of place attachment (Bricker & Kerstetter, 2000; Moore & Graefe, 1994; Williams, Patterson, Roggenbuck, & Watson, 1992). In comparison with first-time visitors, repeat visitors are more likely to be more satisfied, have stronger intentions to return and more likely to give positive WoM recommendations (Kim, Hallab, & Kim, 2012; Li, Cheng, Kim, & Petrick, 2008). Based on these previous empirical observations, the following hypotheses are proposed:

H11. Times participated in Melissa's Road Race will be a positive predictor of Event Attachment.
H12. Times participated in Melissa's Road Race will be a positive predictor of Event Sustainability.

H13. Times participated in Melissa's Road Race will be a positive predictor of Park Attachment.

H14. Times participated in Melissa's Road Race will be a positive predictor of Park Visitation Sustainability.

H15. Days visited Banff NP in the last 12 months will be a positive predictor of Park Attachment.

H16. Days visited Banff NP in the last 12 months will be a positive predictor of Park Visitation Sustainability.

Halpenny (2007) highlighted the importance of place attachment as a potential predictor of plans to return and recommend a destination. Other studies have observed similar results. For example, in a study of festival of patrons, Lee, Kyle, and Scott (2012) found that satisfied visitors who expressed moderate levels of emotional attachment to the festival host destination would become loyal to that destination. Lee and Shen (2013) reported that place attachment was a strong positive predictor of destination loyalty among dog walkers. Cognitive and affective attachments expressed by holiday-makers travelling to Turkey were found to be positive predictors of destination loyalty (Yuksel, Yuksel, & Bilim, 2010). López-Mosquera and Sánchez (2013) observed that Spanish suburban park users' affective and functional park attachments, but not cognitive attachment, were positive predictors of repeat use and recommendation of a park to others. Kaplanidou, Jordan, Funk, and Ridinger (2012) noted that place attachment has not been extensively examined in sport tourism settings. They along with Kirkup and Sutherland (2015) recommend an examination of place and place-attachment in sport event tourism research. Based on these studies, the following hypotheses are proposed:

H17. Event attachment will be a positive predictor of Event Sustainability.

H18. Event attachment will be a positive predictor of Park Attachment.

H19. Event attachment will be a positive predictor of Park Visiting Sustainability.

H20. Park attachment will be a positive predictor of Event attachment.

H21. Park attachment will be a positive predictor of Event Sustainability.

H22. Park attachment will be a positive predictor of Park Visitation Sustainability.

Finally, the activities that occur in that destination must align with the tourist's perceptions of what is appropriate for that context. A harmonious and appealing image of the destination exists if this is achieved. When a destination hosts activities that create cognitive dissonance (Festinger, 1957) for the potential tourist, a tourist may choose to travel elsewhere. Cognitive dissonance can be described as 'anxiety that results from simultaneously holding contradictory or otherwise incompatible attitudes, beliefs, etc.' (Dictionary.com, n.d.). Researchers have attempted to examine tourists' attitudes towards specific activities in distinct settings. A study that provides an example of this is Deng, Walker, and Swinnerton's (2006) comparison of Chinese and Canadian park tourists' perceptions of the appropriateness of specific park activities; however, a specific focus on sport activities was not reported. In short, if a visitor perceives the races are an inappropriate activity in a national park, she/he may choose not to return.

Additionally, tourists will only return to a destination if they feel the activities and attributes of that destination will help them achieve their trip goals. While few studies have examined the 'appropriateness' of a destination for sporting activities, many studies have examined the relationship between a destination or events' ability to supply particular benefits or possess particular characteristics that can facilitate satisfaction of

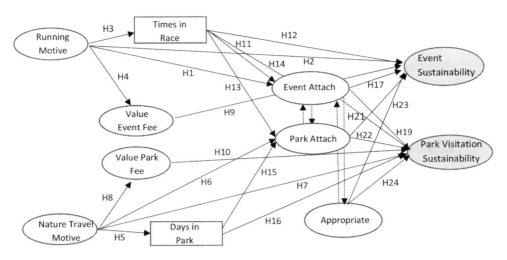

Figure 1. Theoretical model – predicting Event Sustainability (Event Loyalty) and Park Visitation Sustainability (Destination Loyalty). Note: All paths are positive, except for the relationship between Appropriate and Event Sustainability and Park Visitation Sustainability.

individuals' needs (e.g. Lee & Hsu, 2013; López-Mosquera & Sánchez, 2013; Wang & Leou, 2015; Yoon & Uysal, 2005). The appropriateness of Banff NP as a location for a competitive running race may be assessed by racers based on the location's ability to provide elements essential to a running event, such as fun social atmosphere, routes that facilitate personal challenge or personal best running times, memorable race routes, ease of access, affordability and so on. Grounded in previous studies' examination of a destinations' ability to supply specific attributes necessary for a fulfilling visitor experience and association with destination loyalty, the following hypotheses are proposed:

> *H23.* Perceived appropriateness of Banff NP as a venue for Melissa's Road Race will be a positive predictor of Event Sustainability.
>
> *H24.* Perceived appropriateness of Banff NP as a venue for Melissa's Road Race will be a positive predictor of Park Visitation Sustainability.

Figure 1 summarizes the proposed relationships between variables and efforts to predict intentions to return and recommend to Banff NP and Melissa's Road Race. The one-time measurement of intentions and related study variables do not permit us to claim the causal effects of these variables on one another, but merely suggest that a predictive relationship may exist. Solid lines in Figure 1 propose potential relationships and the direction of influence. Dotted lines indicate the inconclusive nature of associations between variables due to a lack of theoretical and empirical studies devoted to investigating these relationships.

Methodology

Event and setting

Data were collected as part of a larger study that explored the hosting of special events within Banff NP, Canada. One of these special events was Melissa's Road Race; in its

28th year, this event featured a 10-kilometre and 22-kilometre race, dinner, pre- and post-run entertainment, and participant prizes. The annual event is held during the fall tourism shoulder season. Banff NP, located in Canada's Rocky Mountains, was the first national park in Canada and established primarily for its tourism and resource potential (Draper, 2000; McNamee, 2009). In 2014–2015, the park attracted 3,609,639 visitors (Parks Canada, 2015) demonstrating the importance and popularity of the mountain parks (Jones & Scott, 2006). Data collection was conducted for Parks Canada, the management agency for the park, which was interested in documenting the impacts of the race on resident and visitor experience.

Sampling

On the days prior to the start of the event a total of 1200 self-completion paper-based questionnaires were distributed at registration to the 3500 potential recipients. The study was explained to every third participant and they were asked to complete the survey and return it once they returned home. Three hundred and ninety-four surveys were returned resulting in a response rate of 33%. Racers were incentivized to participate in the survey through the entry of their names in a draw to win annual park passes and hot springs passes.

Instrumentation

Design of the survey instrument was informed by previous resident attitude surveys and studies of competitive running events (Gibson, Willming, & Holdnak, 2003; Green, Costa, & Fitzgerald, 2003; Kaplanidou & Vogt, 2007). The survey documented race participants' socio-demographic characteristics, tourist and race activities within Banff NP, familiarity with the destination and the race, travel party characteristics, perceived value for fees paid to race and enter the park, and stewardship activities related to the park. Motivations for travel were documented using 25 items modified from Driver's (1983) master list of recreation experience motivations. These have been used extensively in previous recreation and tourism studies and have shown good validity and reliability (Manfredo, Driver, & Tarrant, 1996). Attachment to the park and the event was measured using items drawn from outdoor recreation, tourism and park management studies (Kyle, Graefe, Manning, & Bacon, 2003; Williams et al., 1992). Validity and reliability of these place attachment scales, designed to measure social bonding, identity attachment, affective attachment and place dependence was previously assessed in studies by Halpenny (2006, 2010), Raymond, Brown, and Weber (2010), Williams and Roggenbuck (1989), Williams and Vaske (2003) and many others. The final survey instrument was reviewed for clarity and contextual appropriateness by park staff ($n = 4$) and competitive runners ($n = 5$).

Analysis

Numerical data were inputted into a database and analysed using SPSS 23.0 and AMOS 23.0. Data were first checked for errors and assessed for normality, outliers and multicollinearity. The distributions of all variables used in the behavioural modelling portion of the analysis demonstrated non-normal distribution (i.e. non-significant Kolmogorov–Smirnov statistic). This was unconcerning for two reasons: first, this is very common in large samples (Pallant, 2005), and second an examination of histograms, Detrended Normal Q-Q plots, skewness and kurtosis values suggested that the results were a reasonable reflection of what the constructs being measured would likely reveal. For example, the variable 'Times participated in the Race' was characterized by a high kurtosis and positive skewness confirming that most respondents had run the race between 1 and 3 times and few had run 10 or more. In other words, the data appeared to reflect what was expected. An examination of outliers revealed one variable of concern; the 'Number of days in Banff NP in the last 12 months' had two respondents reporting visitation to the park totalling 100 days or more. These two respondents were eliminated from further analysis. Multicollinearity was assessed and correlations between the main behavioural model variables were within a preferred range (i.e. above .3 and below .7) (Pallant, 2005; Tabachnick & Fidell, 2007). Missing data were examined and determined to be a non-issue with all main variables being characterized by less than 5% missing data (Tabachnick & Fidell, 2007).

In preparation for behavioural modelling of race participants' intention to return to the race and park and recommend the race and park to others, further refinement of variables was conducted. First, SPSS 23.0 was used to infill the missing data prior to structural equation modelling. To accomplish this, Little's (1998) Missing Completely at Random test was conducted; results from this test suggested that data were missing completely at random (How2stats.com, 2011), and therefore it was reasonable to continue engage in missing value estimation. Multiple imputation method was then used to estimate missing values; this along with maximum likelihood methods are considered strong approaches for dealing with missing values (Horton & Kleinman, 2007). Multiple imputation method's advantage is that it considers variability due to sampling as well as the imputation process when finalizing replacement values (Allison, 2001; Enders, 2010; Rubin, 1987).

Next, a principal components factor analysis (PCA) was conducted with both sets of attachment items. The 14 Park Attachment items PCA revealed two factors; however, examination of explained variance and a scree plot suggested elimination of one item, 'My friends would be disappointed if I stopped visiting Banff NP' due to low correlations with other Park Attachment items and the selection of just one factor. A second PCA that asked for the extraction of just one factor revealed 52.1% explained Park Attachment variance. A PCA of the 14 Event Attachment items revealed three factors and recommended the removal of two social bonding items, 'I will (do) bring family and friends to the Race' and 'I have pleasant memories of spending time with friends at the Race' and one identity item 'When I run in the Race others see me the way I want them to see me' due to low correlations with other Event Attachment items (i.e. <.280) and a review of the scree plot. The remaining 11 items were resubmitted to a PCA and a single factor that explained 53.9% of variance was achieved. To confirm internal consistency of these two scales, Cronbach's alpha coefficients were generated. Good scale reliability (i.e. above .7 for Cronbach's alpha scores; Nunnally, 1978) was observed with the 13-item Park Attachment scale (.92) and the 11-item Event Attachment scale (.91).

From a 25-item trip motivation scale, 2 running-oriented motive items and 3 nature-oriented items (Table 1) were used to create 2 measurement models and inserted into a larger structural regression model (SRM). These measurement models were used to

Table 1. Motivations.

	Mean	SD	Aggregate mean	Aggregate SD	Scale reliability
Travel motive					
(a) To experience a Canadian Rocky Mountain park	3.62	1.076			
(b) To enjoy scenery	4.57	0.687			
(c) To be close to nature	4.21	0.878			
Nature motives			4.12	0.730	0.737 (3 items)
(a) To develop my knowledge of running	2.97	1.074			
(b) To participate in competition	3.78	1.056			
(c) To expand my running portfolio/record	3.42	1.208			
Running/competition motives			3.39	0.835	0.606 (3 items)

Note: Measured with a scale where 1 = Very unimportant and 5 = Very important. The PCA, conducted on each set of motives, revealed the presence of one component explaining 55.96% of the Running Motive variance and 68.5% of nature motive variance.

generate the following factors: Running Travel Motives and Nature Visitation Motives. A factor representing participants' views of Banff NP as an appropriate venue for Melissa's Road Race was also created and tested; three items (Table 2) were used to create a measurement model and placed in the SRM.

Finally, race participants' intention to return to the race and park and recommend the race and park to others these items were collapsed into combined sustainability indicators, Park Visitation Sustainability, and Event Sustainability. These were modelled as observed variables in the SRM. Prior to producing aggregate scores for these two variables, inter-item correlation was used to assess the internal consistency of each set of items (Table 6). Internal consistency was assessed, and found to be good (i.e. between .2 and .4 for inter-item correlations; Briggs & Cheek, 1986). Two other sets of observed variables completed the path model portion of the SRM: perceived value of the event and park entry fees, and frequencies of visitation to Banff NP and participation in Melissa's Road Race.

Details regarding the re-specification of this model to fit the sample data are outlined in the findings section. In summary, measurement models were assessed for their prediction of their respective factors and non-significant paths were trimmed, along with variables that did not appear to explain the dependent variables' variance. Modification indices were consulted to further adjust the fit of the model with the date; however, adjustments were engaged in only when they were assessed to be theoretically sound (Kline, 2011). Desirable statistical power was calculated based on Cohen's (1988, 1992) and Westland's (2010) guidelines using Soper's (2016) a priori sample size calculator for structural equation modeling. The final model of the study included 12 observed and 2 latent variables. With a small anticipated

Table 2. Appropriateness of race in Banff National Park.

Appropriateness items	M	SD	Scale reliability
Physical landscape of Banff makes it an appropriate setting for a race	4.56	0.670	
Socio-cultural atmosphere of Banff makes it an appropriate setting for a race	4.26	0.715	
Race is appropriate for Banff NP	4.47	0.625	
Race in a variety of locations in Banff is appropriate	2.51	1.090	
Appropriateness	0.737 (3 items)	0.737 (3 items)	0.737 (3 items)

Note: 'Race in a variety of locations is appropriate' was excluded from the creation of the aggregate variable. Appropriate Race based on its lack of correlation with the other appropriateness items and scale reliability assessment.

effect size ($.10 < f^2 < .30$; Cohen, 1988), the sample of this study ($n = 387$) provided a desirable statistical power of above .90 at the 5% probability level. An analysis arising from the descriptive statistical analysis is presented next, with an emphasis on sample description followed by consideration of behavioural modelling using PCA, scale reliability assessment, Pearson's correlation coefficient analysis and structural equation modelling.

Findings

Participant characteristics

Of the 394 survey questionnaires returned, data from 5 residents of Banff and 2 respondents who had visited the park 100 days or more during the last 12 months were removed. Day visitors represented 37% of the final sample ($n = 387$), while 62.7% were overnight visitors. A higher proportion (67.6%) of respondents were female. The average age of respondents was 41 years ($SD = 10.58$). The most commonly reported level of completed education was a university bachelor's degree (46.3%) followed by a college diploma (26.2%). Income levels fell in line with provincial norms, with the largest number of respondents reporting household incomes of over CND 140,000 or more ($\geq$USD 139,800). Respondents travelled an average of 372.11 km ($SD = 418.02$) to participate in the event, with 50.8% travelling 150 km or more. The majority (96.6%) arrived by car.

Thirty-three per cent of respondents were first-time participants in Melissa's Road Race. Including the survey race year, respondents had participated in the race 3.3 ($SD = 3.13$) times. Thirty-five per cent ran in the 22 km race and 64.5% ran in the 10 km race. Less than 2% of visitors had not been to Banff NP prior to competing in the race, and 12 months prior to the race respondents averaged 8.13 ($SD = 12.15$) days visiting Banff NP.

In terms of engagement in competitive running, participants competed in 3.73 ($SD = 3.97$) races in the last 12 months and spent an average of CND 652.69 ($SD = \$1107.30$) on overnight trips to observe and/or participate in running races in the last 12 months. Racers were asked about their travel motives relating to running and engaging in competition (Table 1). Respondents indicated on a scale of 1 (Very unimportant) to 5 (Very important) moderate agreement with running-related motives ($M = 3.39$, $SD = 0.835$).

When asked about motives related to visiting a Rocky Mountain park setting and experiencing nature, respondents expressed slightly higher levels of agreement ($M = 4.124$, $SD = 0.731$) (Table 1). Interest in travelling to visit nature is unsurprising as more than 72% of survey respondents indicated that they had 'visited a park several times per year' or 'at least once per month in the last year'.

Only 6.9% of respondents reported that they travelled to the race on their own. For the remaining respondents, 35.6% travelled with one other individual and 61% of respondents travelled with 3 people or more. We did not ask participants to differentiate race participants and non-participants in their travel party, but we did ask what portion were children. Eighty-two per cent of respondents travelled without children, while 8% travelled with 1 child and 10% travelled with 2 or more. A majority of travellers stayed in hotels or campgrounds (56.5%), while 3.7% stayed with friends and family, and 32.4% did not use accommodations. Race participants who stayed overnight stayed an average of 2.4 days ($SD = 1.07$) in the park, while day visitors stayed 5.5 hours ($SD = 2.43$) in the park.

Sustainable tourism indicators

Several questions were included in the survey instrument that served as indicators of event and tourism sustainability. Respondents were asked to comment on the appropriateness of Melissa's Road Race in Banff NP (Table 2). On a scale where 1 equated 'Strongly disagree' to 5 equated 'Strongly agree,' respondents indicated strong agreement that the 'Physical landscape of Banff NP makes it an appropriate site for the Race' ($M = 4.56$, $SD = 0.670$), 'Social cultural atmosphere of Banff NP & town site makes it an appropriate site for the Race' ($M = 4.26$, $SD = 0.715$) and 'Melissa's Road Race is appropriate for Banff NP' ($M = 4.47$, $SD = 0.625$). Respondents were very mixed in their reaction to, and somewhat unsupportive of, the statement 'Melissa's Road Race should be located in a variety of locations within Banff NP' ($M = 2.51$, $SD = 1.09$).

As a second indicator of sustainability, respondents were also asked about their attachment to the race and the destination. On a scale where 1 indicated low levels of attachment and 5 indicated high levels of attachment, respondents expressed moderate levels of attachment to Banff NP ($M = 3.45$, $SD = 0.644$) and Melissa's Road Race ($M = 3.48$, $SD = 0.627$). Related to this, when asked about the importance of Banff NP in racers' decision to engage in the Melissa's Road Race-related trip, an average score of 6.09 ($SD = 2.85$) was documented using a scale where 0 was equal to 'No influence' and 10 was equivalent to 'Entire influence.' It appears that the race was the main motivating force for the trip. However, using a similar scale, respondents stated the race was made much more appealing ($M = 8.18$, $SD = 1.922$) because it was held in Banff NP (Table 3).

Table 3. Attachment to Banff National Park and Melissa's Road Race.

Attachment item	Race Mean	SD	α	Park Mean	SD	α
(a) I feel like Park/Race is part of me[a]	3.15	0.973		3.21	1.056	
(b) Park/Race is the best park/race for what I like to do[b]	3.35	0.938		3.26	0.874	
(c) I have a special connection to Park/Race and the people I spend time with there[c]	3.65	0.967		3.46	1.005	
(d) I identify strongly with Park/Race[a]	3.35	0.992		3.36	1.000	
(e) I would not substitute any other park/race for doing the visiting/running I do at Park/Race[b]	3.30	1.093		3.05	1.077	
(f) I have strong positive feelings for Park/Race[d]	3.98	0.705		4.02	0.802	
(g) I have pleasant memories of spending time with friends in Park/Race[c]	4.29	0.691		4.42	0.623	
(h) Visiting/Participating in Park/Race says a lot about who I am[a]	3.34	0.914		3.23	0.978	
(i) I get more satisfaction out of visiting/participating in Park/Race than any other race[b]	3.10	1.063		2.87	0.988	
(j) I feel happiest when I am at Park/Race[d]	2.77	0.884		2.82	0.879	
(k) When I visit/run in Park/Race others see me the way I want them to see me[a]	2.97	0.961		2.77	0.925	
(l) I will (do) bring my family and friends to Park/Race[c]	4.08	0.685		4.25	0.647	
(m) I am fond of Park/Race[d]	4.23	0.581		4.32	0.641	
(n) My friends/family would be disappointed if I stopped attending Park/Race[c]	3.21	1.117		3.31	1.089	
Banff NP Attachment (13 items)*				3.46	0.644	.920
Melissa's Race Attachment (11 items)*	3.49	0.654	0.910			

Note: Two separate sets of 14 items were used to measure Park Attachment and Race Attachment. Responses were measured with a scale where 1 = Strongly disagree and 5 = Strongly agree. Sub-dimensions represented include a = Place identity, b = Place dependence, c = Social Bonding and d = Place affect.
*Exploratory factor analysis identified 1 Event Attachment factor (53.9% explained variance; 11 items) and 1 Park Attachment factor (52.1% explained variance; 13 items). Scale reliability was assessed using Cronbach's alpha statistic; good internal consistency was observed (Event Attachment α = .910 (11 items), Banff Attachment α = .920 (13 items)).

Table 4. Park and event associations (N = 386).

Association item	Mean	SD
When I think of Banff NP I immediately associate it with Melissa's Road Race	2.89	1.111
When I think of the Town of Banff I immediately associate it with Melissa's Road Race	2.92	1.131
When I think of Melissa's Road Race I immediately associate it with Banff NP	4.41	0.995

Note: Measured with a scale where 1 = Strongly disagree and 5 = Strongly agree.

Table 5. Plans to return and recommend Melissa's Road Race and Banff National Park.

Return and recommend item	Mean	SD	Scale reliability
(a) Plans to return to Park	4.22	0.774	
(b) Recommend Park to others	4.49	0.569	
Park Visitation Sustainability	**4.35**	**0.613**	**0.762 (2 items)**
(a) Plans to run race again	4.47	0.637	
(b) Recommend race to others	4.51	0.578	
Race sustainability	**4.48**	**0.566**	**0.847 (2 items)**

Note: Each set of items was checked for scale reliability prior to combining and averaging. Inter-item correlations suggested adequate fit (i.e. between .2 and .4; Briggs & Cheek, 1986).

Image of a sport event or destination is also an important indicator of sustainability. Melissa's Road Race participants were asked how the event and destination were associated with each other (Table 4). Overall, Banff NP appeared to have a stronger image, less associated with Melissa's Road Race ($M = 2.89$, $SD = 1.11$), whereas the race was strongly associated with Banff NP ($M = 4.14$, $SD = 0.995$). Participants were also asked to comment on their perceived value for the price paid to visit the park, and compete in the race. On a scale where 0 equalled 'Very poor value' and 10 indicated 'Very good value,' the value of the fee to visit Banff NP ($M = 6.39$, $SD = 2.556$) was much lower than the perceived value of the fee to race in Melissa's Road Race ($M = 8.09$, $SD = 1.752$).

Our final indicator of sustainability was respondents' responses to questions about plans to revisit and recommend that others visit Banff NP and participate in Melissa's Road Race (Table 5). On a scale where 1 equalled 'Strongly disagree' and 5 equalled 'Strongly agree,' responses were very similar and positive regarding return visitation to the park ($M = 4.22$, $SD = 0.774$), recommending the park to others ($M = 4.49$, $SD = 0.569$), returning to run in the race ($M = 4.47$, $SD = 0.637$) and recommending the race to others ($M = 4.51$, $SD = 0.578$). As reported in the Methodology, due to the importance of plans to return and recommend the destination and race as indicators of sustainability, these variables were then converted to aggregate scores, and used as dependent variables to explore factors that affect these behavioural intentions (Table 5).

Model specification

Measurement models representing participants' views regarding the appropriateness of Banff NP as a race location, as well as nature and running-related travel motives were inserted into a larger SRM designed to explain Event Sustainability and Park Visitation Sustainability (i.e. intentions to recommend and revisit/re-participate). Measurement models were first examined for fit with the data. Fit indices used to assess model fit with data included the chi-square goodness of fit, Normed Fit Index (NFI), Comparative Fit Index (CFI) and root-mean-square error of approximation (RMSEA). The latter two measures should be characterized by values higher than .90, whereas RMSEA values between .5 and .8 and chi-square goodness-of-fit values of .3 or under are desirable (Hu & Bentler, 1999; Jöreskog & Sörbom, 1996; McDonald & Ho, 2002). Satisfactory fit was achieved after the removal of one of the three items from the Running Motives factor, 'To participate in competition,' due to low factor loading (i.e. .45).

Next, the confirmatory factor analysis found support for the retention of the Appropriateness and Running Travel Motives and Nature Travel Motives factors (Table 7). With the exception of the item relating to Banff NP being an appropriate context for the race (.483), most standard factors loadings were significant and above the .50 recommended threshold (Bagozzi, 1980; Bagozzi & Yi, 1998). Additionally, desirable average variance extracted (AVE) values (i.e. above 0.5) were observed for two of the three factors; and the third factor's AVE was near to 0.5 (Fornell & Larcker, 1981). The internal reliability of the scales were affirmed as the composite reliability indices, namely Cronbach's alpha and Dillon-Goldstein's rho, were higher than 0.6 (Bagozzi & Yi, 1988; Cortina, 1993) (Table 6). Because only two items were used for the Running Travel Motives construct, inter-item correlations was also examined, and found to be adequate, as a 0.4 correlation just fell within the recommend 0.2–0.4 threshold (Briggs & Cheek, 1986). In short, while Nature Travel Motive and Appropriateness constructs appeared to be robust representations of their concepts, the Running Travel Motives measure was less desirable. Finally, discriminant validity was examined for each construct and found to be satisfactory; namely correlations for any pair of latent variables were less than the square root of the AVE (Fornell & Larcker, 1981) (Table 7).

In examining the SRM, modification indices generated by AMOS 23 were consulted to achieve a desirable fit between the model and data. Two incremental re-specifications were undertaken: first, Event Sustainability and Park Visitation Sustainability were correlated. Theoretically this made sense as the variables were related to travel to the same context. Second, the Appropriateness of Banff NP as a venue for Melissa's Road Race was correlated with Event Attachment. A priori we had not considered a relationship between these two variables; upon reconsideration their association does appear to be theoretically sound, as they are both positive indicators of participants' relationship with the event. To enhance the parsimony of the model, non-significant paths were eliminated.

Table 6. Confirmatory factor analysis results: analysis of the dimensionality, reliability and validity of scales of measurement.

Latent variable	Manifest variable items	Standard factor loadings	Cronbach's alpha	Dillon-Goldstein rho	AVE
Appropriateness			.745	0.766	0.535
	Race context	.483			
	Physical setting	.864			
	Social setting	.792			
Nature Travel Motives			.737	0.788	0.565
	Scenery	.806			
	Mountain parks	.519			
	Nature	.874			
Running Travel Motives			.609[a]	0.630	0.467
	Running portfolio	.788			
	Learning to run	.560			

Note: $\chi^2(17) = 36.802$ ($p = .004$), $\chi^2/d.f. = 2.165$, CFI > .977; NFI > .958; RMSEA = .055.
[a]Inter-item correlation which was assessed to be .4.

Table 7. Discriminant validity of measurement model.

	Appropriateness	Nature Travel Motives	Running Travel Motives	AVE
Appropriateness	1	0.378	0.173	0.535
Nature Travel Motives		1	0.295	0.565
Running Travel Motives			1	0.467
Square root of AVE	0.731	0.752	0.684	

Running Travel Motives was removed from the model as no significant relationships with the dependent variables were observed.

Modest fit parameters (Table 8) were achieved for Model 1; however, two relationships were characterized by significance values between $p = .001$ and .05. The first of these was respondents' valuation of the fee paid to enter Banff NP and Park Sustainability ($\beta = .09$, $t = 2.467$, $p = .014$). Value of park entry fees was characterized by a positive relationship with Nature Travel Motivations ($\beta = .237$, $t = 4.356$, $p = .001$). The second was a relationship between frequency of park visitation in the last 12 months and Park Sustainability ($\beta = .087$, $t = 2.184$, $p = .029$). While these relationships were statistically significant, the overall contribution to explaining the two main dependent variables was minimal. To enhance parsimony of the model, the two paths characterized by significant values of $\geq .001$ were dropped, and the value of park entry fee variable was eliminated. This resulted in Model 2, which was characterized by superior fit with the data (Table 8).

A third model, similar to Model 2 was then designed and tested; the point of this model was to explore the role of Park Attachment versus Event Attachment in explaining the dependent variables. In Model 3 Park Attachment is proposed as a predictor of Event Attachment; it was hypothesized that those who love Banff would also love Melissa's Road Race and participate in the event because it was located in Banff NP. Model 3 was characterized by poor fit with the data and was abandoned in favour of Model 2 (Figure 2). Model 2 was characterized by adequate fit with the data: $\chi^2(51) = 157.462$ ($p = .000$), $\chi^2/\text{d.f.} = 3.087$; RMSEA $= .074$; CFI $= .931$; and NFI $= .901$. While the chi-square goodness-of-fit test should produce a value of 3 or less, results from this goodness-of-fit test can be elevated in studies with large samples (i.e. >300 respondents; Kline, 2011).

To assess mediation, Sobel's test was administered; all indirect paths were significant suggesting full mediation (Table 10). The Sobel test is a specialized t-test that provides a method to determine whether the reduction in the effect of the independent variable, after including the mediator in the model, is a significant reduction and therefore whether the mediation effect is statistically significant. A bootstrapping analysis is recommended in addition to the Sobel's test for mediation (MacKinnon, Lockwood, Hoffman, West, & Sheets, 2002). AMOS was instructed to perform 1000 bootstrap samples. Using repeated resampling of the data bootstrapping provides an estimate of the true indirect effect and its bias-corrected 95% confidence interval.

Table 8. Model fit indices.

		χ^2 (df)	NFI	CFI	RMSEA
Model 1	All significant paths ($p \leq .05$)	202.291	.879	.911	.078
Model 2	**Event attachment predicts place attachment**	**157.462**	**.901**	**.931**	**.074**
Model 3	Place attachment predicts Event Attachment	196.965	.877	.905	.086

Note: Model 2, in bold, was the final model used in the study.

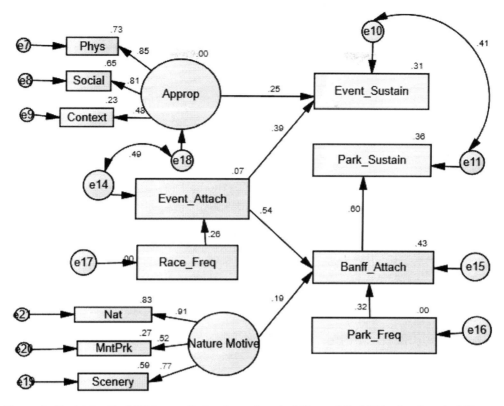

Figure 2. Model 2 – final SRM – predicting Event Sustainability and Park Visitation Sustainability.

In the study's final model, Model 2, approximately one-third of intentions to revisit and recommend Banff NP and re-participate in and recommend Melissa's Road Race was explained: 31% of Event Sustainability's variance and 36% of Park Visitation Sustainability variance. Direct effects are summarized in Table 9, while indirect effects and mediation analyses are reported in Table 10.

Attachment to Banff NP ($\beta = .60$, $t = 15.62$, $p < .001$) accounted for a large proportion of the variance in Park Visitation Sustainability (intentions to revisit and recommend Banff NP as a destination). Park Attachment appears to have mediated the more modest effects of other variables, including Event Attachment ($\beta = .324$, $t = 10.800$, $p < .001$), Days in the Park

Table 9. Model 2 – structural model analysis – direct effects.

Dependent variable	Independent variable	B	SE B	β	t-Value	R^2	Hypothesis supported (at $p < .001$)
Event Attachment	← Frequency of Race	.054	.009	.258	5.869	.067	H12 – Yes
Park Attachment	← Frequency of Park Visitation	.023	.003	.315	8.168	.430	H15 – Yes
Park Attachment	← Nature Motive	.227	.050	.192	4.542		H6 – Yes
Park Attachment	← Event Attachment	.520	.037	.542	14.050		H18 – Yes
Event Sustainment	← Appropriate	.439	.099	.247	4.423	.310	H23 – Yes
Event Sustainment	← Event Attachment	.345	.041	.395	8.466		H17 – Yes
Park Sustainment	← Park Attachment	.580	.037	.598	15.619	.367	H22 – Yes

Note: $p < .001$.

Table 10. Model 2 – structural model analysis – indirect effects and mediation analysis.

Dependent variable	Mediator	Independent variable	Bootstrap analysis							Sobel test			Hypothesis supported
			Indirect effects			Mediation confidence interval						
			B	SE B	β	Lower	Upper	p	Z-values	p	
Park Sustainability	Park Attachment	Nature Motive	.131	.046	.115	.054	.185	.001	4.361	.000	H7 – Yes
Park Sustainability	Park Attachment	Frequency of Park Visitation	.016	.002	.188	.135	.243	.001	6.887	.000	H16 – Yes
Park Sustainability	Park Attachment	Event Attachment	.301	.033	.324	.270	.387	.001	10.464	.000	H19 – Yes
Park Sustainability	Event Attachment + Park Attachment	Race Frequency	.013	.003	.084	.058	.114	.001	–	.000	H13 + H4 – Yes[a]
Event Sustainability	Event Attachment	Race Frequency	.019	.005	.102	.065	.147	.001	4.885	.000	H12 – Yes
Park Attachment	Event Attachment	Race Frequency	.028	.006	.140	.097	.187	.001	5.518	.000	H13 – Yes

Note: Using AMOS bootstrapping (set to 1000 bootstrap and 95% confidence interval) to determine confidence interval and the Sobel test for mediation.
[a]Kline (2011) cites Cohen and Cohen's (1983) rule of thumb which suggests that if all unstandardized path coefficients are statistically significant at the same level of significance then the whole indirect effect can be taken as statistically significant to the same level of significance.

($\beta = .188$, $t = 6.962$, $p = .001$) and Nature Travel Motives ($\beta = .115$, $t = 3.484$, $p = .001$). The small indirect effects of Times in the Race were mediated by Event Attachment ($\beta = .140$, $t = 6.086$, $p = .001$) and Park Attachment ($\beta = .084$, $t = 6.000$, $p = .001$). Event Attachment ($\beta = .395$, $t = 8.466$, $p = .001$) explained a large portion of Event Sustainability and shared a positive association with Appropriateness of Banff NP as the event location ($r = .492$, $t = 30.750$, $p = .001$). It mediated the small indirect effect of Times participated in the Race (NP ($\beta = .102$, $t = 4.857$, $p = .001$). Respondents' views regarding the Appropriateness of Banff NP as a location for Melissa's Road Race ($\beta = .347$, $t = 4.423$, $p = .001$) accounted for a moderate proportion of Event Sustainability.

Further, we observed a number of non-significant relationships between proposed antecedent variables and the dependent variables. No significant relationships were observed between Running Travel Motives, the Value of Event Fee and the other variables (H1 thru H4 and H9 were rejected). While the Value of the Park Entry Fee did directly explain variance of Park Sustainability in Model; 1 after re-specification and a tightening of model fit standards, and statistical significance parameters to $p < .001$, its contribution was eliminated (H10 was rejected). Nature Travel Motives failed to explain variance in Frequency of Park Visitation (H5 was rejected) and Times in Race failed to explain respondents' Park Attachment or Park Visitation Sustainability (H13 and H14 were rejected).

It was hypothesized that perceived Appropriateness of a running event in a national park might negatively impact individuals' future visits and intentions to recommend the park as a destination if cognitive dissonance was inspired by concerns about the event in a national park. Alternatively, it could also inspire more visitation as enhanced recreational offerings may make the park more attractive to tourists. Neither proposal appears to be have been supported, as no significant relationship was observed (H24 was rejected). Finally, and perhaps most interestingly, poor model fit with the sample data resulting from Park Attachment being proposed as an antecedent of Event Attachment, suggested a rejection of this proposed relationship (H20 and H21were rejected). Instead it appears that Event Attachment, at least with this sample of active sport tourists, is more correctly theorized as an antecedent to Park Attachment and subsequent positive intentions towards Banff NP and Melissa's Road Race in the form of re-visitation and recommendation.

Discussion

In summary, Event Sustainability – defined as intentions to re-participate in Melissa's Road Race and recommend participation to others – was significantly and positively predicted by Event Attachment and participants' views regarding the Appropriateness of Banff NP as the race location. The indirect effects of previous participation in the event appeared to be fully mediated by Event Attachment. Banff Visitation Sustainability – defined as intentions to re-visit Banff NP and recommend the destination to others – was significantly and positively predicted by Attachment to Banff NP. Attachment to Banff NP also mediated the positive indirect effects of Attachment to Melissa's Road Race, followed by weaker indirect effects transmitted by Nature Travel Motives, number of times the respondent has visited the park in the last 12 months and previous participation in the event.

Park and event attachment

A key theoretical implication arising from this study is the importance of place and event attachment as predictors of event and destination loyalty. This agrees with previously published theoretical (Gursoy et al., 2014) and empirical papers (e.g. Alexandris, Kouthouris, & Meligdis, 2006; Kil et al., 2012; Prayag & Ryan, 2012; Tsai, 2012; Yuksel et al., 2010). The inclusion of two foci of attachment, the event and the context, begins to address calls for an examination of 'multiple points of attachment' (Kirkup & Sutherland, 2015, p. 3). Additionally, it reinforces the importance of exploring the role of place (Kirkup & Sutherland, 2014) and attachment in sport tourism and sport events (Kaplanidou et al., 2012).

In this study, Park Attachment was the strongest predictor of intentions to return and recommend the destination, and mediated the effects of several other key predictive factors. This is congruent with previous studies that found attachment can be a strong, positive predictor of re-visitation to destinations (Halpenny, 2007; Lee et al., 2012; Yuksel et al., 2010) and re-engagement in preferred recreational activities (Anderson & Fulton, 2008; Hailu, Boxall, & McFarlane, 2005). Additionally, the conceptual positioning of Event Attachment as an antecedent to Park Attachment appears to support the proposition that through participation in meaningful experiences such as a competitive sport race, attachments for the event contexts, namely the park may be created and fostered. A lack of model of fit with the data derived from active sport tourist survey participants resulted in a rejection of the theory that Park Attachment is more accurately portrayed as a precursor to Event Attachment. While attachments to particular destinations may drive participation in festivals and other types of events in destinations, in this study, stronger support for the event as a predictor of destination attachment and ultimately intentions to revisit and recommend the destination were observed.

Interestingly respondents expressed only moderate levels of attachment to the park. This is puzzling given the frequent visitation to and long-term relationship with the park that many participants reported. The behaviour model, which depicts Event Attachment as an antecedent to Park Attachment, and eventually destination loyalty appears to align with Kaplanidou et al.'s (2012) suggestion that the intensity of the sport experience in a landscape can enhance visitors' attachment (Tuan, 1977). Additionally, other researchers have identified that landscapes, which can supply unique settings for specific recreational activities, may foster attachment (e.g. Bricker & Kerstetter, 2000). Banff NP is a unique context for a recreational road race, but unlike the set of unique rapids necessary for paddling enthusiasts as Kerstetter and Bricker observed, a road race is not dependent upon the attributes that Banff's landscape offers.

Event Attachment was the strongest direct predictor of intentions to recommend and re-participate in Melissa's Road Race and mediated the small indirect effect of previous race participation. Like Park Attachment, the accumulation of experiences derived through repeated participation in the event appeared to build attachment to the race. Event and Park Attachment were characterized by modest, positive attachment scores; however, affect and social bonding items had the highest values, suggesting the respondents' positive feelings and emotions for the park and race as well as the social bonding opportunities the two contexts afford may be important drivers of event and destination loyalty. Future analysis that explores the distinct contributions of place and event attachment sub-dimensions would enhance understanding. The role of place identity and place affect appears to be especially promising in predicting tourist behaviour (Halpenny, 2010).

Previous experience

Gursoy et al. (2014) theorized that previous experience with a destination would be the 'most influential driver' of destination loyalty (p. 809). Support for this proposition is documented in at least one sport tourism paper: Kaplanidou and Vogt's (2007) study of sport cycling event tourists observed the direct influence of previous visits to the destination for sport tourism activity engagement on intentions to return to the same destination to engage in sport or recreation activity. Kaplanidou and Vogt did not include event or place attachment as a predictive variable, potentially because the event moved annually to different locations. Gursoy et al. also proposed previous experience as a predictor of place attachment in their Figure 1 (p. 819) but failed to suggest this as a written proposition in their paper. Studies from outdoor recreation and tourism (Bricker & Kerstetter, 2000; Moore & Graefe, 1994; Williams et al., 1992) suggest that this is an appropriate conceptualization of the relationship of these two variables. In this current study of Melissa's Road Race, the effects of previous park visitation and participation in Melissa's Road Race on intentions to return, re-participate and recommend to others appeared to be fully mediated by attachment. The impact of other factors on repeat visitation and participation such as distance to the destination/race context (Bull, 2006; Nyaupane & Graefe, 2008) and the effect of habit and routine (Oppermann, 1999) could perhaps help explain the lesser role of previous experience in explaining destination and event loyalty. The positive indirect effect of Days in Banff NP within the 12 months preceding the race and intention to engage in event and destination loyalty makes sense, as frequency of visitation can denote proximity of residence and ease of access to the park (Tiefenbacher, Day, & Walton, 2000), therefore repeat visitation will likely be easy to accomplish in the future.

Motives

Motives have been confirmed in other studies as direct and indirect predictors of attachment to events (Filo, Groza, & Fairley, 2012; Filo et al., 2010), parks (Kil et al., 2012; Kyle et al., 2004) and destinations (Wang & Leou, 2015). In this study, while natured-based travel motives were small but significant positive predictors of Park Attachment and indirectly Park Visitation Sustainability, they did not predict Event Attachment or intentions to re-participate or recommend Melissa's Road Race to others. It seems other motives may be playing a role in respondents' decision to engage in the event. Running Travel Motives failed to explain runners' engagement in the event. Insignificant relations between these motives and Event Sustainability and Event Attachment may be due to the content of the running motive items used for measurement. They were very wide ranging in scope (i.e. learn to run, improve my running portfolio, engage in physical challenge and competition). A tighter focus, such as a cluster of items designed to measure motives related to learning to run, social running motives, physical challenge and running motives, may have performed better to explain the impact of active sport tourists' motivations' on Event Attachment and Event Sustainability.

Perceived appropriateness

Race respondents appeared to agree that Banff NP's socio-cultural atmosphere and physical landscape made the park an appropriate location for the race. The importance of setting characteristics in supporting the development of destination and event loyalty has been demonstrated by other studies (Alegre & Juaneda, 2006; Lee et al., 2012). Kaplanidou et al.'s (2012) study of Miami marathon tourists valued the destination atmosphere and event characteristics. These variables, which align well with items used in this current study to measure participants' assessment of Banff as an appropriate location for the race, were predictive of intentions to return to the Miami marathon.

A caution should be expressed here regarding the items used to measure appropriateness. Respondents could interpret questions about appropriateness in at least two distinct ways. First, they could assess the race setting as a venue for achieving their running competition goals. Alternatively they could assess the impact (e.g. environment, social/crowding) of the race on the destination, a national park. We cannot claim which interpretation each respondent embraced, however by choosing to compete in Melissa's Road Race, respondents likely felt that it was an appropriate activity. However, when asked if running the race in a variety of locations throughout Banff was appropriate, a majority disagreed. One reading of this high level of disagreement is that race participants may have understood the race's potential negative impact on cultural and natural heritage located in the park's more sensitive areas. Alternatively, they may have felt that certain areas were not conducive to successful racing (Kulczycki & Halpenny, 2014).

Overall, respondents' appeared to possess positive views about Banff NP being an appropriate setting for a recurrent running race, and thus their continued patronage and positive WoM of the event are likely. It also appears that they are accepting sport tourism in a national park and thus concerns about cognitive dissonance being experienced due to a misalignment of what should be allowed in Banff NP did not appear to be an issue – this should not negatively impact decisions to revisit the park, and perhaps even promote more visitation, with a new appreciation of the diverse activities available in the protected area.

Finally, in the behavioural model, Appropriateness was strongly and positively co-related to Event Attachment. It was also a direct positive predictor of respondents' intentions to re-participate and recommend the event to others. The positive views of Banff's appropriateness as a venue to Melissa's Road Race aligns well with observations from such studies as Kaplanidou et al. (2012) and Brown, Smith, and Assaker (2016). The correlation between Event Attachment and event re-participation and recommendation suggests that further investigation of this relationship is required as insufficient empirical and theoretical background was available to suggest which may impact the other.

Perceived value

The level of perceived value of the fee to visit Banff NP was much lower than the value of the fee to race in Melissa's Road Race. While perceived park fee value was a significant ($p < .05$) yet weak positive predictor of Park Sustainability in Model 1, the move to a more parsimonious model with better fit and a higher standard for assessing significant relationships between variables (i.e. $p < .001$) eliminated perceived park fee value as a significant predictor of either Event Sustainability or Park Visitation Sustainability. This is in contrast to previous empirical studies that suggest value can be a moderate to strong predictor of destination loyalty (Chen & Chen, 2010; Forgas-Coll et al., 2012; Rittichainuwat et al., 2003; Sun et al., 2013; Wang & Leou, 2015), often mediated by satisfaction.

Other variables -- sustainable tourism to Banff NP

In addition to investigating plans to return and revisit Banff NP and Melissa's Road Race, other observations documented in this study contribute to knowledge of the sustainability of participation in Melissa's Road Race and visitation to Banff NP.

First, the race encourages park visitation, enhancing recreation opportunities for visitors, either as active sport tourists or providing entertainment for spectators. However, it appears that the race does not encourage new visitors to Banff NP, as only 2% of respondents reported that they had not been to the park previously, therefore encouraging visitation from new markets does not appear to be an added value for park managers who wish to expand the park's market share. There is a debate in the conservation community about the desirability of attracting additional visitors to parks (Shultis & More, 2011), however, a majority of park proponents see the merit in pursuing new markets as an important means of expanding conservation supporters (Jager & Halpenny, 2012; Wright & Matthews, 2014).

As with other studies of active sport tourists, these tourists tend to travel with friends and family members (Agrusa, Tanner, & Lema, 2005). These travel companions also utilize destination resources; however, they can multiply the economic returns experienced by tourism entrepreneurs and park coffers. Respondents who stayed overnight stayed an average of 2.4 days. This extended stay, what Taks et al. (2009) would call flow-on effect, extends economic and ecological impacts. It also enables tourists time to engage, enjoy and potentially learn about the park's cultural and natural heritage.

In addition to the behavioural intension modelling, an examination of other participant responses reveals additional insights into the sustainability of Melissa's Road Race and park visitation. As two-thirds of respondents were repeat racers, this demonstrated a strong pattern of loyalty to the event. This has been observed in other sport tourism papers, those that document the travels of passive sport tourists such as team or event groupies (Kulczycki & Hyatt, 2005) and those that document active sport tourists (Agrusa et al., 2005). Similarly, the higher rates of repeat park tourists, with over 8 days of visitation in the 12 months prior to the race suggests ongoing robust park visitation. Perceived value for the race fee was strongly supported by respondents, however, less support was observed for park fees. Park managers should take note of unhappiness with park fees. Park fees, which cost approximately $10 a day or $140 annually were frozen from 2008 to 2013, but fee hikes were proposed for 2015 (Derworiz, 2013) amidst concerns about affordable access to parks.

Unlike findings reported by Kaplanidou and Vogt (2007), the race's image appeared to be strongly tied to Banff NP, conversely the park's image appeared to be strong and less associated with Melissa's Road Race. This bodes well for Banff NP, as this confirms its iconic, unique status; however, it appears that the identity and appeal of Melissa's Road Race is partly reliant on its location in Banff NP. Race organizers must strive to ensure its continued contextualization in the park to sustain interest. The timing of the event in the shoulder season contributes to sustainable tourism in Banff overall, as it extends revenue opportunities (Connell, Page, & Meyer, 2015). Melissa's Road Race's recurrent character is also supportive of sustainable tourism, as it has built a strong base of fans and regional awareness – thereby fostering annual interest.

Practical implications

Practical implications can be identified for Banff NP and but also for other natural areas globally that host sport tourism events. In Canada's Rocky Mountain parks, there has been considerable discussion in recent years regarding the commercialization of the parks. Banff NP's former superintendent has stated that 'Parks Canada is trying to solve the wrong problem by catering to largescale events rather than improving what's established the park as a Canadian icon: its natural areas' (Derworiz, 2014, p. 1). He suggested that crowding and premium hotel prices result from these large events. A Gran Fondo bike race, a marathon and other built developments are examples of recent additions. However, Melissa's Road Race is arguably a different kind of event. Its small-scale, recurrent well-rehearsed repurposing of Banff streetscapes appears to have few negative impacts. Additionally, its timing outside of the peak summer months helps ease congestion. Even with all these minimal impacts, it is unclear how the event actually contributes the park's sustainability. With the exception of its enhancement of recreational opportunities in the park, the event appears to fail to attract new visitors to the park, who could be encouraged to build attachments to the park and potentially support its conservation efforts. In contrast, Event Attachment, modelled in this study as an antecedent to Place Attachment, may play a role in fostering attachment to Banff NP, and long-term loyalty to the park.

While the debate continues to rage in Canada's mountain parks about what level of development and frequency of special events is appropriate, Parks Canada has made efforts to assess the impacts of new recreation uses and special events. Recommendations are outlined in the 2011 document titled *Provisional guidelines for new recreational activities in Banff National Park* (Parks Canada, 2011). These, combined with lessons from other parks that describe best practice in managing and planning for tourism in a sustainable way need to be consulted and implemented collaboratively by park practitioners and event organizers (Halpenny & Salenieks, in press; Leung, Spenceley, Hvenegaard, & Buckley, in press; Manning & Anderson, 2012).

Event organizers, park managers and tourism entrepreneurs in the Banff NP region should be cautioned. A repeat customer is not necessarily a loyal customer. The organizers of Melissa's Road Race and Parks Canada, Banff NP's management agency must focus on customer relationship management (CRM) to convert recurrent visitors to loyal patrons. This involves a focused analysis of visitor needs, valuation of their opinions, treating them as individuals, emphasizing after visit communications and direct communications, and a number of other CRM best practices (McGarry, 1995). Further, Banff NP and Melissa's Road Race must strive to understand what elements of their offerings foster positive affective bonds between their destination or event and active sport tourists. Kaplanidou et al. (2012) suggested that the quality of the tourist experience, attractions, destination atmosphere and event characteristics assist in fostering event attachment. Filo et al. (2012) identified the importance of motives as well as belief in 'making a difference' among the factors affecting attachment to a charitable sporting event. Studies that identify other factors that contribute to successful small-scale sport events include Kaplanidou, Kerwin, and Karadakis (2013) and Theodorakis, Kaplanidou, and Karabaxoglou (2015). The special elements of the Banff NP context, such as mountains, extensive tourism amenities, and a vibrant social atmosphere serve as pull factors initially. Enhancement of these offerings and others will serve to build attachments through a holistic tourist experience (Tsai, 2012). Eventually these attachments serve as push factors – driving visitors to re-visit Banff NP and re-patronize Melissa's Road Race. As Harrison-Hill and Chalip (2005) suggested 'cross-leveraging of sport and destinations is facilitated when vertical and horizontal alliances are formed among sport and tourism providers' (p. 302). They call for additional exploration of the social and psychological characteristics of sport tourists to facilitate effective destination and event synergy, and ultimately sustainability.

Limitations and recommendations for improvements

In drawing conclusions from this study, one must be aware of several limitations. First, responses to questions regarding the appropriateness of the park as a race location were difficult to interpret. Respondents likely had a positive bias towards the race and its enactment in Banff NP. Concerns regarding the approval of specific recreational activities in the park may exist, but were undocumented by the appropriateness items used in this study. Second, measurement of behaviours rather than behavioural intentions would be more desirable, as intentions are not always an accurate predictor of visitors' future behaviours (Caneen, 2003; McKercher & Tony, 2012). Follow-up email or telephone interviews with study participants 12 months after the event would have enabled the documentation of actual behaviour. Third, an unusually high portion of respondents were female, however how this may have impacted responses is unknown. Fourth, the Banff NP's iconic status as a 'world-class' tourism destination may affect results, especially those related to the strength of Banff NP's image versus Melissa's Road Race. This was unlike Kaplanidou and Vogt's (2007) study that found that the event's image was stronger than the destination's image and more likely to encourage visitation.

Future research

Several variables, not measured in this study, show promise as predictors of destination and event loyalty. Service quality (Hadi, Abdullah, & Sentosa, 2016), destination attributes and image (Kaplanidou et al., 2012; Kaplanidou & Vogt, 2007; Lee et al., 2012; Taks et al., 2009), activity and destination involvement (Lee & Shen, 2013; Prayag & Ryan, 2012) and satisfaction (Brown et al., 2016; Prayag & Ryan, 2012) appear to be promising indicators of destination loyalty (Moore et al., 2015; Weaver & Lawton, 2011), and should be included in future research efforts that explore the role of previous experience, attachment, motivations/pursuit of benefits and perceived value to explain destination and event loyalty.

A more nuanced examination of the effect of travel motives could also be enacted. In this study, clusters of nature and running motives were developed, and other motivations were ignored, in part to preserve statistical power to complete behavioural modelling. More sport-specific motivational items could be utilized to improve understanding of active sport tourists' behaviours; alternatively motivations could be parcelled into push and pull factors to improve parsimony (Gavcar & Gursoy, 2002; Prebensen et al., 2013).

As with this study, Prayag and Ryan (2012) and Chen and Phou (2013) used a unidimensional representation of attachment in their models to successfully predict destination loyalty. However, several recent papers have explored the impact of place attachment sub-dimensions in predicting destination loyalty variables, identifying very mixed results regarding the impacts of attachment sub-dimensions on destination loyalty (Lee et al., 2012; López-Mosquera & Sánchez, 2013; Yuksel et al., 2010). A more refined analysis of the impact of specific attachment sub-dimensions (i.e. affect, cognitive, social, conative) may generate greater insight into what aspects of attachment may more strongly affect destination loyalty.

Conclusion

This paper reported survey responses from active sport tourists who participated in a recurrent small-scale sport tourism event in a mountain national park. We addressed calls by Kaplanidou et al. (2012) and Kirkup and Sutherland (2015) to examine the role of place and place-attachment in sport event tourism research. While this has been advanced by Halpenny and Kulczycki (2012), Tsai (2012), Weed and Bull (2004), among others, the current paper verifies the key role of attachment in fostering destination and event loyalty, and the potential role event attachment may play in advancing destination attachment. This latter observation addressed a recommendation for research on sport tourists' attachment to more than one 'point' of attachment (Kirkup & Southerland, 2015; Robinson & Trail, 2005) – namely an iconic national park and a recurrent local running race. A more nuanced examination of attachment to the event and park would be a natural next step. Questions that compare differences in attachment to these two phenomena might include: Are active sport tourists more affectively attached to the event due to nostalgia and less functionally attached (dependent) to the event because other available races? For the same sample, do social bonding attachments play a lesser role in explaining destination loyalty than identity (cognitive-based) attachment?

We identified the role that several factors appeared to play in influencing intentions to revisit and recommend a small-scale sport tourism event and a mountain park. These included place attachment, event attachment, previous race participation and park visitation, travel motives relating to nature and active sport tourists' perceptions of the appropriateness of Banff NP as a location for the race. Perceived value of the park fee (at a $p < .001$ significance level) and event fee were not meaningful predictors of event and destination loyalty. Travel motives relating to running and competition also failed to predict revisitation and recommendation intentions.

The study also contributed to greater understanding of small-scale recurrent sport events (Kaplanidou & Gibson's, 2010), enhancing understanding of small sport event participants, and revealing the importance of attachment as a tool for event organizers to capitalize on as they direct their scarce resources towards building meaningful client relations.

In closing, attachment to place and the event were overwhelmingly the most important explanatory factors in predicting intentions to revisit and recommend a destination, Banff NP and a recurring small-scale sport tourism event, Melissa's Road Race. Efforts to further unpack how attachments form and affect tourists' travel decisions appears warranted if managers are to gain valuable insights relevant for sustaining visitation to tourist attractions, events and destinations.

Disclosure statement

No potential conflict of interest was reported by the authors.

Funding

This work was supported by Parks Canada.

References

Agrusa, J., Tanner, J., & Lema, D. (2005). Japanese runners in the Honolulu Marathon and their economic benefits to Hawaii. *Tourism Review International*, 9(3), 261–270.

Alegre, J., & Cladera, M. (2006). Repeat visitation in mature sun and sand holiday destinations. *Journal of Travel Research*, 44(3), 288–297.

Alegre, J., & Juaneda, C. (2006). Destination loyalty: Consumers' economic behavior. *Annals of Tourism Research*, 33(3), 684–706.

Alexandris, K., Kouthouris, C., & Meligdis, A. (2006). Increasing customers' loyalty in a skiing resort: The contribution of place attachment and service quality. *International Journal of Contemporary Hospitality Management*, 18(5), 414–425.

Allison, P. D. (2001). *Missing data. Sage university papers series on quantitative applications in the social sciences*. Thousand Oaks, CA: Sage.

Anderson, D. H., & Fulton, D. C. (2008). Experience preferences as mediators of the wildlife related recreation participation: Place attachment relationship. *Human Dimensions of Wildlife*, 13(2), 73–88.

Bagozzi, R. P. (1980). *Causal models in marketing*. New York, NY: Wiley.

Bagozzi, R. P., & Yi, Y. (1988). On the evaluation of structural equation models. *Journal of the Academy of Marketing Science*, 16(1), 74–94.

Baloglu, S. (2000). A path analytic model of visitation intention involving information sources, sociopsychological motivations, and destination image. *Journal of Travel & Tourism Marketing*, 8(3), 81–90.

Bricker, K. S., & Kerstetter, D. L. (2000). Level of specialization and place attachment: An exploratory study of whitewater recreationists. *Leisure Sciences*, 22(4), 233–257.

Briggs, S. R., & Cheek, J. M. (1986). The role of factor analysis in the development and evaluation of personality scales. *Journal of Personality*, 54(1), 106–148.

Brown, G., Smith, A., & Assaker, G. (2016). Revisiting the host city: An empirical examination of sport involvement, place attachment, event satisfaction and spectator intentions at the London Olympics. *Tourism Management*, 55, 160–172.

Bull, C. J. (2006). Racing cyclists as sport tourists: The experiences and behaviours of a case study group of cyclists in East Kent, England. *Journal of Sport & Tourism*, 11(3 & 4), 259–274.

Caneen, J. M. (2003). Cultural determinants of tourist intention to return. *Tourism Analysis*, 8(2), 237–242.

Chen, C. F., & Chen, F. S. (2010). Experience quality, perceived value, satisfaction and behavioral intentions for heritage tourists. *Tourism Management*, 31(1), 29–35.

Chen, C. F., & Phou, S. (2013). A closer look at destination: Image, personality, relationship and loyalty. *Tourism Management*, 36, 269–278.

Cohen, J. (1988). *Statistical power analysis for the behavioral sciences* (2nd ed.). Hillsdale, NJ: Lawrence Earlbaum Associates.

Cohen, J. (1992). A power primer. *Psychological Bulletin*, 112, 155–159.

Connell, J., Page, S. J., & Meyer, D. (2015). Visitor attractions and events: Responding to seasonality. *Tourism Management, 46*, 283–298.

Cortina, J. M. (1993). What is coefficient alpha? An examination of theory and applications. *Journal of Applied Psychology, 78*(1), 98–104.

Deng, J., Walker, G. J., & Swinnerton, G. S. (2006). A comparison of attitudes toward appropriate use of national parks between Chinese in Canada and Anglo-Canadians. *World Leisure Journal, 47*(3), 28–41.

Deply, L. (1998). An overview of sport tourism: Building towards a dimensional framework. *Journal of Vacation Marketing, 4*(1), 23–38.

Derworiz, C. (2013). Parks Canada proposes user fee hikes. *Calgary Herald*. Retrieved January 6, 2016, from http://www.calgaryherald.com/parks+canada+proposes+user+hikes/7829949/story.html

Derworiz, C. (2014). Former superintendent raises concerns about commercialization in Banff National Park. *Calgary Herald*. Retrieved January 6, 2016, from http://calgaryherald.com/news/local-news/1125-banff-commercialization

Dictionary.com. (n.d.). Cognitive dissonance. *Dictionary.com Unabridged*. Retrieved June 22, 2016, from http://www.dictionary.com/browse/cognitive-dissonance

Draper, D. (2000). Toward sustainable mountain communities: Balancing tourism development and environmental protection in Banff and Banff National Park, Canada. *AMBIO: A Journal of the Human Environment, 29*(7), 408–415.

Driver, B. L. (1983). *Master list of items for recreation experience preference scales and domains* (Unpublished document). USDA Forest Service, Rocky Mountain Forest and Range Experiment Station, Ft. Collins, CO.

Enders, C. (2010). *Applied missing data analysis*. New York, NY: Guilford Press.

Festinger, L. (1957). *A theory of cognitive dissonance*. Stanford, CA: Stanford University Press.

Filo, K., Funk, D., & O'Brien, D. (2010). The antecedents and outcomes of attachment and sponsor image within charity sport events. *Journal of Sport Management, 24*(6), 623–648.

Filo, K., Groza, M. D., & Fairley, S. (2012). The role of belief in making a difference in enhancing attachment to a charity sport event. *Journal of Nonprofit & Public Sector Marketing, 24*(2), 123–140.

Forgas-Coll, S., Palau-Saumell, R., Sánchez-García, J., & Callarisa-Fiol, L. J. (2012). Urban destination loyalty drivers and cross-national moderator effects: The case of Barcelona. *Tourism Management, 33*(6), 1309–1320.

Fornell, C., & Larcker, D. F. (1981). Structural equation models with unobservable variables and measurement error: Algebra and statistics. *Journal of Marketing Research, 18*(1), 382–388.

Funk, D. C., & Bruun, T. J. (2007). The role of socio-psychological and culture-education motives in marketing international sport tourism: A cross-cultural perspective. *Tourism Management, 28*, 806–819.

Gavcar, E., & Gursoy, D. (2002). Research note: An examination of destination-originated (pull) factors. *Tourism Analysis, 7*(1), 75–81.

Gibson, H. J. (1998). The wide world of sport tourism. *Parks and Recreation, 33*(9), 7–11.

Gibson, H. J., Kaplanidou, K., & Kang, S. J. (2012). Small-scale event sport tourism: A case study in sustainable tourism. *Sport Management Review, 15*, 160–170.

Gibson, H. J., Willming, C., & Holdnak, A. (2003). Small-scale event sport tourism: Fans as tourists. *Tourism Management, 24*(2), 181–190.

Green, B. C., Costa, C., & Fitzgerald, M. (2003). Marketing the host city: Analyzing exposure generated by a sport event. *International Journal of Sports Marketing & Sponsorship, 4*(4), 48–66.

Gursoy, D., McCleary, K. W., & Lepsito, L. R. (2003). Segmenting dissatisfied restaurant customers based on their complaining response styles. *Journal of Foodservice Business Research, 6*(1), 25–44.

Gursoy, D., McCleary, K. W., & Lepsito, L. R. (2007). Propensity to complain: Effects of personality and behavioral factors. *Journal of Hospitality & Tourism Research, 31*(3), 358–386.

Gursoy, D. S., Chen, J., & Chi, C. (2014). Theoretical examination of destination loyalty formation. *International Journal of Contemporary Hospitality Management, 26*(5), 809–827.

Hadi, N. U., Abdullah, N., & Sentosa, I. (2016). Making sense of mediating analysis: A marketing perspective. *Review of Integrative Business & Economics Research, 5*(1), 62–76.

Hailu, G., Boxall, P. C., & McFarlane, B. L. (2005). The influence of place attachment on recreation demand. *Journal of Economic Psychology, 26*(4), 581–598.

Halpenny, E. A. (2006). *Environmental behaviour, place attachment and park visitation: A case study of visitors to Point Pelee National Park* (Unpublished doctoral dissertation). University of Waterloo, Waterloo.

Halpenny, E. A. (2007, May). Fostering return visitation to nature-based destinations: The role of place attachment, length of affiliation, frequency of visitation and distance between residence and destination. In *Tourism and Travel Research Association (TTRA) international 35th annual conference proceedings, Montreal, Quebec* (pp. 18–22).

Halpenny, E. A. (2010). Pro-environmental behaviours and park visitors: The effect of place attachment. *Journal of Environmental Psychology, 30*(4), 409–421.

Halpenny, E. A., & Kulczycki, C. (2012). Sport fan and non-sport fans' perceptions about hosting a bicycle sporting event in a mountain park. *Tourism Today, 12*, 25–33.

Halpenny, E. A., & Salenieks, T. (in press). Visitor management tools. In Y.-F. Leung, A. Spenceley, G. Hvenegaard, & R. Buckley (Eds.), *IUCN best practice guidelines for sustainable tourism in protected areas* (3rd ed.). Gland: IUCN.

Harrison-Hill, T., & Chalip, L. (2005). Marketing sport tourism: Creating synergy between sport and destination. *Sport in Society, 8*(2), 302–320.

Higham, J. (1999). Commentary – sport as an avenue of tourism development: An analysis of the positive and negative impacts of sport tourism. *Current Issues in Tourism, 2*(1), 82–90.

Horton, N. J., & Kleinman, K. P. (2007). Much ado about nothing. *The American Statistician, 61*(1), 79–90.

How2stats.com. (2011). Little's Missing Completely at Random (MCAR) test – SPSS. Retrieved June 22, 2015, from https://www.youtube.com/watch?v=22aR9ruSig4

Hu, L. T., & Bentler, P. M. (1999). Cutoff criteria for fit indexes in covariance structure analysis: Conventional criteria versus new alternatives. *Structural Equation Modeling: A Multidisciplinary Journal, 6*(1), 1–55.

Jager, E., & Halpenny, E. A. (2012). Supporting the CBD Aichi biodiversity conservation targets through park tourism: A case study of parks Canada's visitor experience programme. *PARKS, 18*(2), 79–92.

Jones, B., & Scott, D. (2006). Climate change, seasonality and visitation to Canada's national parks. *Journal of Park and Recreation Administration, 24*(2), 42–62.

Jöreskog, K. G., & Sörbom, D. (1996). *PRELIS 2 User's reference guide: A program for multivariate data screening and data summarization: A preprocessor for LISREL*. Lincolnwood, IL: Scientific Software International.

Kaplanidou, K., & Gibson, H. (2010). Predicting behavioral intentions of active event sport tourists: The case of a small-scale recurring sports event. *Journal of Sport and Tourism, 15*(2), 163–179.

Kaplanidou, K., Jordan, J. S., Funk, D., & Ridinger, L. L. (2012). Recurring sport events and destination image perceptions: Impact on active sport tourist behavioral intentions and place attachment. *Journal of Sport Management, 26*, 237–248.

Kaplanidou, K., Kerwin, S., & Karadakis, K. (2013). Understanding sport event success: Exploring perceptions of sport event consumers and event providers. *Journal of Sport & Tourism, 18*(3), 137–159.

Kaplanidou, K., & Vogt, C. (2007). The interrelationship between sport event and destination image and sport tourists' behaviours. *Journal of Sport & Tourism, 12*(3), 183–206.

Kil, N., Holland, S. M., Stein, T. V., & Ko, Y. J. (2012). Place attachment as a mediator of the relationship between nature-based recreation benefits and future visit intentions. *Journal of Sustainable Tourism, 20*(4), 603–626.

Kim, K., Hallab, Z., & Kim, J. N. (2012). The moderating effect of travel experience in a destination on the relationship between the destination image and the intention to revisit. *Journal of Hospitality Marketing & Management, 21*(5), 486–505.

Kirkup, N., & Sutherland, M. (2014). *An investigation into the role of place attachment within extreme sport tourism*. Retrieved May 28, 2016, from http://nrl.northumbria.ac.uk/17361/

Kirkup, N., & Sutherland, M. (2015). Exploring the relationships between motivation, attachment and loyalty within sport event tourism. *Current Issues in Tourism*, 1–8. doi:10.1080/13683500.2015.1046819

Kline, R. B. (2011). *Principles and practice of structural equation modeling*. New York, NY: Guilford Press.

Kulczycki, C., & Halpenny, E. A. (2014). Sport cycling tourists' setting preferences, appraisals and attachments. *Journal of Sport & Tourism*, *19*(2), 169–197.

Kulczycki, C., & Hyatt, C. (2005). Expanding the conceptualization of nostalgia sport tourism: Lessons learned from fans left behind after sport franchise relocation. *Journal of Sport Tourism*, *10*(4), 273–293.

Kyle, G., Graefe, A., Manning, R., & Bacon, J. (2003). An examination of the relationship between leisure activity involvement and place attachment among hikers along the Appalachian Trail. *Journal of Leisure Research*, *35*(3), 249–273.

Kyle, G., Mowen, A. J., & Tarrant, M. (2004). Linking place preferences with place meaning: An examination of the relationship between place motivation and place attachment. *Journal of Environmental Psychology*, *24*, 439–454.

Lee, J. J., Kyle, G., & Scott, D. (2012). The mediating effect of place attachment on the relationship between festival satisfaction and loyalty to the festival hosting destination. *Journal of Travel Research*, *51*(6), 754–767.

Lee, T. H. (2009). A structural model to examine how destination image, attitude, and motivation affect the future behavior of tourists. *Leisure Sciences*, *31*(3), 215–236.

Lee, T. H., & Hsu, F. Y. (2013). Examining how attending motivation and satisfaction affects the loyalty for attendees at aboriginal festivals. *International Journal of Tourism Research*, *15*(1), 18–34.

Lee, T. H., & Shen, Y. L. (2013). The influence of leisure involvement and place attachment on destination loyalty: Evidence from recreationists walking their dogs in urban parks. *Journal of Environmental Psychology*, *33*, 76–85.

Leung, Y., Spenceley, A., Hvenegaard, G., & Buckley, R. (in press). *IUCN best practice guidelines for sustainable tourism in protected areas* (3rd ed.). Gland: IUCN.

Li, X. R., Cheng, C. K., Kim, H., & Petrick, J. F. (2008). A systematic comparison of first-time and repeat visitors via a two-phase online survey. *Tourism Management*, *29*(2), 278–293.

Little, R. J. A. (1988). A test of Missing Completely at Random for multivariate data with missing values. *Journal of the American Statistical Association*, *83*(404), 1198–1202.

López-Mosquera, N., & Sánchez, M. (2013). Direct and indirect effects of received benefits and place attachment in willingness to pay and loyalty in suburban natural areas. *Journal of Environmental Psychology*, *34*, 27–35.

MacKinnon, D. P., Lockwood, C. M., Hoffman, J. M., West, S. G., & Sheets, V. (2002). A comparison of methods to test mediation and other intervening variable effects. *Psychological Methods*, *7*(1), 83–104.

Manfredo, M. J., Driver, B. L., & Tarrant, M. A. (1996). Measuring leisure motivation: A meta-analysis of the recreation experience preference scales. *Journal of Leisure Research*, *28*(3), 188–213.

Manning, R. E., & Anderson, L. E. (2012). *Managing outdoor recreation: Case studies in the national parks*. Cambridge, MA: CABI.

McDonald, R. P., & Ho, M. H. R. (2002). Principles and practice in reporting structural equation analyses. *Psychological Methods*, *7*(1), 64–82.

McGarry, D. (1995). The road to customer loyalty. *Canadian Business Review*, *22*(1), 35–36.

McKercher, B., Denizci-Guillet, B., & Ng, E. (2012). Rethinking loyalty. *Annals of Tourism Research*, *39*(2), 708–734.

McKercher, B., & Tony, S. M. (2012). Is intention to return a valid proxy for actual repeat visitation? *Journal of Travel Research*, *51*(6), 671–686.

McNamee, K. (2009). From wild places to endangered spaces: A history of Canada's national parks. In P. Dearden & R. Rollins (eds.), *Parks and protected areas in Canada* (pp. 24–55). Don Mills: Oxford University Press.

Moore, R. L., & Graefe, A. R. (1994). Attachments to recreations settings: The case of rail-trail users. *Leisure Sciences*, *16*(1), 17–31.

Moore, S. A., Rodger, K., & Taplin, R. (2015). Moving beyond visitor satisfaction to loyalty in nature-based tourism: A review and research agenda. *Current Issues in Tourism, 18*(7), 667–683.

Nunnally, J. C. (1978). *Psychometric theory* (2nd ed.). New York, NY: McGraw-Hill.

Nyaupane, G. P., & Graefe, A. R. (2008). Travel distance: A tool for nature-based tourism market segmentation. *Journal of Travel & Tourism Marketing, 25*(3–4), 355–366.

Oppermann, M. (1999). Predicting destination choice – a discussion of destination loyalty. *Journal of Vacation Marketing, 5*(1), 51–65.

Pallant, J. (2005). *SPSSB survival manual: A step guide to data analysis using SPSS*. Chicago, IL: Open University Press.

Parks Canada. (2011, June). *Provisional guidelines for new recreational activities in Banff National Park*. Parks Canada. Retrieved January 6, 2016, from http://highlineonline.ca/wp-content/uploads/2011/05/Provisional-Guidelines-for-New-Recreational-Activities-in-Banff-National-Park.pdf

Parks Canada. (2015). *Parks Canada attendance 2010–11 to 2014–15 national parks, park reserves, & marine conservation areas*. Retrieved from www.pc.gc.ca/eng/docs/pc/attend/table3.aspx

Prayag, G., & Ryan, C. (2012). Antecedents of tourists' loyalty to Mauritius the role and influence of destination image, place attachment, personal involvement, and satisfaction. *Journal of Travel Research, 51*(3), 342–356.

Prebensen, N. K., Woo, E., Chen, J. S., & Uysal, M. (2013). Motivation and involvement as antecedents of the perceived value of the destination experience. *Journal of Travel Research, 52*(2), 253–264. doi:10.1177/0047287512461181

Raymond, C. M., Brown, G., & Weber, D. (2010). The measurement of place attachment: Personal, community, and environmental connections. *Journal of Environmental Psychology, 30*(4), 422–434.

Rittichainuwat, B. N., Qu, H., & Leong, J. K. (2003). The collective impacts of a bundle of travel determinants on repeat visitation. *Journal of Hospitality & Tourism Research, 27*(2), 217–236.

Robinson, M. J., & Trail, G. T. (2005). Relationships among spectator gender, motives, points of attachment, and sport preference. *Journal of Sport management, 19*(1), 58–80.

Rubin, D. B. (1987). *Multiple imputation for nonresponse in surveys*. New York, NY: Wiley.

Saarinen, J. (2006). Traditions of sustainability in tourism studies. Annals of Tourism Research, *33*(4), 1121–1140. doi:10.1016/j.annals.2006.06.007

Shipway, R., & Jones, I. (2007). Running away from home: Understanding visitor experiences and behaviour at sport tourism events. *International Journal of Tourism Research, 9*, 373–383.

Shipway, R., & Jones, I. (2008). The great suburban Everest: An 'insiders' perspective on experiences at the 2007 Flora London Marathon. *Journal of Sport and Tourism, 13*(1), 61–77.

Shultis, J., & More, T. (2011). American and Canadian national park agency responses to declining visitation. *Journal of Leisure Research, 43*(1), 110–132.

Soper, D. S. (2016). *A-priori sample size calculator for structural equation models* [Software]. Retrieved from http://www.danielsoper.com/statcalc

Sun, X., Chi, C. G. Q., & Xu, H. (2013). Developing destination loyalty: The case of Hainan Island. *Annals of Tourism Research, 43*, 547–577.

Tabachnick, B. G., & Fidell, L. S. (2007). *Using multivariate statistics* (5th ed.). Needham Height, MA: Allyn & Bacon.

Taks, M., Chalip, L., Green, B. C., Kesenne, S., & Martyn, S. (2009). Factors affecting repeat visitation and flow-on tourism as sources of event strategy sustainability. *Journal of Sport & Tourism, 14*(2–3), 121–142.

Theodorakis, N. D., Kaplanidou, K., & Karabaxoglou, I. (2015). Effect of event service quality and satisfaction on happiness among runners of a recurring sport event. *Leisure Sciences, 37*(1), 87–107.

Tiefenbacher, J. P., Day, F. A., & Walton, J. A. (2000). Attributes of repeat visitors to small tourist-oriented communities. *The Social Science Journal, 37*(2), 299–308.

Tsai, S. P. (2012). Place attachment and tourism marketing: Investigating international tourists in Singapore. *International Journal of Tourism Research, 14*(2), 139–152.

Tuan, Y. F. (1977). *Space and place: The perspective of experience*. Minneapolis: University of Minnesota Press.

Wang, X., & Leou, C. H. (2015). A study of tourism motivation, perceived value and destination loyalty for Macao cultural and heritage tourists. *International Journal of Marketing Studies, 7*(6), 83–91.

Weaver, D. B., & Lawton, L. J. (2011). Visitor loyalty at a private South Carolina protected area. *Journal of Travel Research, 50*(3), 335–346.

Weed, M., & Bull, C. (2004). *Sport tourism: Participants, policies and providers*. Oxford: Elsevier Butterworth.

Westland, J. C. (2010). Lower bounds on sample size in structural equation modeling. *Electronic Commerce Research and Applications, 9*(6), 476–487.

Williams, D. R., Patterson, M. E., Roggenbuck, J. W., & Watson, A. E. (1992). Beyond the commodity metaphor: Examining emotional and symbolic attachment to place. *Leisure Sciences, 14*, 29–46.

Williams, D. R., & Roggenbuck, J. W. (1989, October). Measuring place attachment: Some preliminary results. In *NRPA symposium on leisure research* (Vol. 9). San Antonio, TX.

Williams, D. R., & Vaske, J. J. (2003). The measurement of place attachment: Validity and generalizability of a psychometric approach. *Forest Science, 49*(6), 830–840.

Wright, P. & Matthews, C. (2014). *Building a culture of conservation: State of knowledge report on connecting people to nature in parks*. Canadian Parks and Wilderness Society and University of Northern British Columbia. Retrieved January 6, 2016, from http://cpaws.org/uploads/buildingacultureofconservation-web.pdf

Yoon, Y., & Uysal, M. (2005). An examination of the effects of motivation and satisfaction on destination loyalty: a structural model. *Tourism Management, 26*(1), 45–56.

Yuksel, A., Yuksel, F., & Bilim, Y. (2010). Destination attachment: Effects on customer satisfaction and cognitive, affective and conative loyalty. *Tourism Management, 31*(2), 274–284.

Leveraging sport heritage to promote tourism destinations: the case of the Tour of Flanders Cyclo event

Inge Derom and Gregory Ramshaw

ABSTRACT
The conceptual framework of event leverage has been applied to cases of event sport tourism, but it has been under-examined in cases of heritage-based active sport tourism. Using the framework of event leverage, the purpose of this paper is to explore the strategic opportunities for tourism destination development associated with hosting heritage-based active sport tourism events. Quantitative and qualitative survey data were collected from participants ($N = 1091$) at the 2013 edition of the Tour of Flanders Cyclo event. This annual active sport tourism event has gained world-wide popularity through explicit associations with Flanders' cycling heritage. The findings reveal significant differences between national and international event participants in terms of their socio-demographic profiles, cycling behaviours, and event motivations. Active sport tourists who travelled internationally to take part in the event were more committed to experiencing and pursuing the event's heritage, as active participants as well as passive spectators. While sport tourism events are commonly identified as the key resource in the event leveraging literature, this paper highlights the leveraging potential of other event and destination-related resources, including event heritage, route, and atmosphere. The findings contribute to the conceptual framing of event leverage by identifying active sport heritage as an important resource to promote participation among sport tourists. This study suggests a broader conceptualisation of sport heritage as an active and embodied process. Event stakeholders are advised to create temporary and permanent transformations that can enhance the connection between the facets of the event and the context of the host to attract domestic and international participants all year round.

Introduction

Sport is an attractive tool for destinations to develop and market their tourism product (Ziakas & Boukas, 2012). Cycling as a sport tourism activity, in particular, has received considerable attention because of its potential to create economic, social, and environmental benefits for both the host region and participants (Dickinson & Robbins, 2009). Because of the variety of potential benefits, cities have been competitive in seeking to host major cycling events such as the Tour de France, Giro d'Italia, and Vuelta Ciclista a España. These sport events are now commonly used as a resource that can be actively and strategically leveraged, or more specifically, a financial asset that provides opportunities for economic growth by attracting potential investors and tourists to the host city and region (Chalip, 2004). Hosting the Tour de France Grand Départ – the official start of the race – has been argued to boost the local economy, promote the city as a tourist destination, and attract investors and developers, but also promote cycling among host residents (e.g. Balduck, Maes, & Buelens, 2011; Berridge, 2012; Bull & Lovell, 2007; van Bedaf, 2012).

Using Gibson's (1998) typology of sport tourism, most scholars have examined event leverage in cases of 'event sport tourism' where thousands of spectators travel internationally to watch a major sport event and benefit the host's tourism industry financially (e.g. Grix, 2012; Sant, Mason, & Hinch, 2013; Smith & Stevenson, 2009). The investments associated with hosting major cycling events illustrate that cities are willing to pay significant sums of public money to leverage an ever-widening spectrum of benefits.[1] Encouraged by the achievement of potential economic impacts related to place promotion and tourism development, cities showcase their most valuable assets to an international audience of spectators. These assets can include a particular historical or natural backdrop to the event, a collective social enthusiasm for the event, and an available event-related heritage (Derom & VanWynsberghe, 2015). The financial risks as well as the socially disruptive character of these major events, however, have promoted a research agenda to better understand the true value – economic as well as social – of leveraging smaller events that are more likely to build on existing resources of a city, benefit local people and companies, and occur more frequently in the same locality (Smith, 2009; Taks, 2013). Therefore, there is a need for current research to advance our understanding of event leverage in cases of 'active sport tourism' where participants travel to actively take part in sport events (e.g. Snelgrove & Wood, 2010) and 'heritage sport tourism' which includes visits to sports museums and famous sports venues (e.g. Ramshaw & Gammon, 2005). This need extends to whether and how these types of events can be leveraged to benefit the host region financially. Active sport tourism events such as marathons and cycling events are frequently organised in many countries across the world, without large-scale investments in sport and urban infrastructure, making it a relevant case to further examine.

This paper reports on data collected from the Tour of Flanders Cyclo, an annual active sport tourism event which has gained world-wide popularity by making explicit associations to Flanders' cycling heritage. Similar to other cycling events for active sport tourists, the region of the Flemish Ardennes in Belgium where the cycling event takes place is an iconic destination with a unique physical landscape and enjoyable scenery, which has proven to be a successful attribute in attracting event participants (Kulczycki & Halpenny, 2014). When regions seek to capitalise upon active sport tourism as an economic development tool, it is important to understand that different sport tourists may have different interests and expectations when visiting a particular destination and relatedly, different strategies must be put in place to attract them (Roche, Spake, & Joseph, 2013). Using the conceptual framework of event leverage (Chalip, 2004), the purpose of this paper is to explore the strategic opportunities for tourism development associated with hosting heritage-based active sport tourism events. The 2013 edition of the Tour of Flanders Cyclo presented an opportunity to elaborate upon a sample of active sport tourists who visited the region of the Flemish Ardennes to take part in the event. The following questions have guided this research: (1) What are the socio-demographic profiles and cycling behaviours of active sport tourists who take part in the Tour of Flanders Cyclo? (2) What elements of the event and the destination motivate these individuals to take part in the Tour of Flanders Cyclo? And (3) how do these differ between the national and international event participants? This paper makes a unique contribution to the literature by considering whether and how heritage, and in particular 'active' sport heritage, can be employed as a resource in broader tourism development initiatives associated with active sport tourism events.

Event leverage and active sport tourism

Chalip (2004) introduced the concept of event leverage to the sport mega-event literature to describe the strategies used by event stakeholders to maximise immediate and long-term economic benefits from hosting events. The event itself – or, when applicable, a portfolio of several events throughout the year – has been conceived to be a resource that can be leveraged or, more specifically, a financial asset that provides opportunities for economic growth. The main assumption that underpins the event leveraging framework is that hosting creates a window of opportunity for event stakeholders to strategically use the event to plan for additional economic outcomes. The leveraging process includes a series of actions for achieving a particular objective, while converting the available resources within the community into initiatives that will benefit the host (Chelladurai, 2009). Event owners, public sector agencies responsible for economic and tourism development, and commercial organisations have been identified as leaders in initiating and conducting the leverage (O'Brien, 2006). According to the conceptual framework, immediate increases in economic activity come from tourists who consume at local business during their stay, whereas long-term sources of economic activity come from heightened international media exposure during the event, which in turn can enhance the host destination's image and promote imminent tourism following the event (Chalip, 2004).

The economic benefits that are possible in the case of sport mega-events are relatively circumscribed in that venues, infrastructure, and accommodations have to be built or hosting the event and the (inter)national tourists may be impossible. The prospect of welcoming thousands of additional tourists is often one of the main rationales for cities to bid for a sport mega-event (Horne, 2007). Researchers, however, have increased scepticism and critique with respect to leveraging sport mega-events and the promise of future legacies (e.g. Smith, 2014; Ziakas, 2015). Because sport mega-events are unsustainable and unattainable for the majority of cities around the world, the authors of this paper aim to encourage event stakeholders to explore opportunities associated with leveraging smaller active sport tourism events. These events can also generate substantial economic impacts by drawing on the thousands of annual event participants, without large-scale investments in sport and urban infrastructure (Coleman & Ramchandani, 2010). Furthermore, leveraging can help to transform the landscapes where these active sport tourism events are held into other '-scapes' that work in conjunction with one another in the context of the event, including a heritagescape (Garden, 2006), a sportscape (Bale, 2003), and an eventscape (Brown, Lee, King, & Shipway, 2015).

By applying the concept of eventscape to leveraging active sport tourism events, such as cycling events where competitors move through a particular landscape, the event itself is no longer the only potential leverageable resource within the host community. The available resources that can influence the event impact can include the route and scenic backdrop to the event, temporary and permanent transformations, symbolic resources (such as reference to the event's heritage), spectator behaviour and participant experiences, and destination brands (Brown et al., 2015). Given the long history and tradition of the Tour of Flanders, many locations have been transformed by the event, for example by the construction of the permanent Tour of Flanders cycling network in and around the arrival host city of Oudenaarde. Through permanent eventscapes, cities are able to maintain a distinctive and managed 'look' beyond the duration of the event, providing a long-term connection between the event and the specific locality (Brown et al., 2015, p. 523). It is important to further explore how these event and destination-related resources can be leveraged for additional benefits, by focusing on increases in economic activity coming from additional spectators as well as additional participants visiting the host region.

Sport heritage and tourism development

The relationship between sport and heritage is significant. Sport has played a role in many cultures and societies for thousands of years and, as such, the artefacts, places, and events associated with the sporting past are frequently recognised and protected because of their heritage value (Timothy, 2011). Furthermore, the significance of sport in contemporary societies means that various sporting heritages have been created and consumed for a variety of social, economic, and political purposes, from creating a sense of shared identity to the development of public works projects like sports stadia (Ramshaw & Gammon, 2015). Experiencing heritage is also a significant part of tourists' motivation to travel internationally (Alzua, O'Leary, & Morrison, 1998; Timothy, 2011). Given that sporting attractions can be positioned as both an authentic form of local culture (Hinch & Higham, 2005) as well as symbols of local and national heritages (Gammon, 2011; Wright, 2012), sport heritage can be an effective tool in attracting international visitors. The manifestations of sport-based heritage are also multifaceted. Ramshaw and Gammon (2005) proposed a permeable typology, arguing that sport heritage may be tangible-immovable (e.g. sports stadia), tangible-movable (e.g. sports memorabilia), intangible (e.g. chants, cheers, and rituals), or consumable goods and services with a heritage component (e.g. retro sports apparel). While this sport heritage typology is useful, particularly in understanding sport heritage as a tourism resource, it primarily understands heritage as an extrinsic object or practice and not necessarily an embodied process.

Current thinking in both sport studies and heritage studies see sport as well as heritage as intrinsically active processes. Hinch and Higham (2011) see a sense of play as being essential to an understanding of sport, while Watson and Waterton (2015) view heritage as an active, and often physical, performative process. Although sport heritage has been readily linked to spectator consumption sporting events (e.g. Gammon, Ramshaw, & Waterton, 2013; Hinch & Ramshaw, 2014; Storey, 2012), the notion of participants actively constructing their own sport heritage, or being motivated to participate because of an event's sport heritage associations, has received nominal attention. Joseph's (2011) exploration of Caribbean-Canadian cricketers returning to the West Indies to both play the sport and reconnect with their cultural heritage is one of the few studies to consider a kind-of 'active' sport heritage, where heritage connections are created and maintained through physical participation in sport. Here, the act of travel is essential in creating the sport heritage, as there is – to borrow from Rickly-Boyd (2013) – a crucial connection between place and the construction of existential heritages. Given the predominance of active sport tourism events, the links between participatory sport events and how participants use these events to construct either personal heritage or nostalgia narratives, or attach their participation to broader regional or national sport heritages, requires exploration. Similarly, as Ramshaw and Bottelberghe (2014) argued, 'though both heritage and sport tourism individually are understood as significant components in tourism development, there is relatively little understanding as to how these areas together contribute to tourism development initiatives' (p. 24). As such, an exploration of the relationship between active and heritage sport tourism would not only shed light on how these two sport tourism types interact, but would also contribute to our understanding of how sport heritage might contribute to broader sport tourism development initiatives.

The Tour of Flanders Cyclo event presented an opportunity to further explore this relationship as sport tourists actively engage with the event's heritage. Although the route of the Tour of Flanders has changed at various points since its establishment in 1913, the cobblestone hills – which make riding the race exceptionally difficult, particularly in wet weather – are legendary among cycling enthusiasts. Twenty-five of the cobblestone stretches in the Tour of Flanders are officially recognised and protected as national monuments (Douchy, 2010). These cobblestones not only attract elite cyclists and their teams for training purposes but also cyclists from across the world who take on the challenge of physically experiencing elements of Flanders' cycling heritage along the Tour of Flanders cycling network. Since 2003, the city of Oudenaarde is home to the Tour of Flanders Visitor Centre where tourists can relive and experience the unique atmosphere and history of the race, while focusing on extra-ordinary winners, difficult cobblestone hills, and harsh weather conditions (Ramshaw & Bottelberghe, 2014). To further exploit the international tourism potential of the Tour of Flanders, different levels of government continue to use the event as a resource to promote the Flemish Ardennes as the exclusive location and unique décor where cycling enthusiasts from across the world can experience the world-famous cycling race (Derom, 2014). These efforts resulted in the inauguration of the Tour of Flanders Street in 2016, which includes a monument of Karel Van Wijnendaele (one of the founders of the Tour of Flanders), a mosaic out of cobblestones with the portraits of all the previous winners, and a hall of fame of the most legendary Tour of Flanders' heroes (Tourism Flanders, 2016). Although the race is more than a century old, it remains an important asset for tourism development in Flanders.

Method

Data were collected from participants at the 2013 edition of the Tour of Flanders Cyclo event, using a single (embedded) case study design (Yin, 2009). The Tour of Flanders Cyclo is known as a *cyclosportive* in the European context or *gran fondo* in the North American context. It is a single-day participatory cycling event that covers a long distance and requires great endurance. The event includes three routes that differ in length, intensity, and difficulty (83, 133, and 259 km) and these currently start and/or arrive in Bruges and Oudenaarde. The backdrop to this physically demanding sport event is formed by the many cobblestone hills of the Flemish Ardennes. The Tour of Flanders Cyclo is inextricably linked to, and leverages benefits from, the Tour of Flanders elite cycling race by using the same timing and route (Smith, 2014). The fact that participants can ride their own Tour of Flanders on the day before the elite cyclists – while, depending on the length of the route, completely or partially copying the route of the elites – makes it a unique participatory cycling event. Although the Tour of Flanders Cyclo event is not a competition because participants do not start simultaneously, it definitely includes competitive elements such as the physical challenge of the distance, speed, cobblestones, and hills that are covered on a race bike. A total of 16,000 active sport tourists take part in the Tour of Flanders Cyclo annually since 2013. Within this population, the percentage of international event participants has continued to increase from 40% of all participants in 2013 to 55% in 2016 (Chris Vannoppen, personal communication, March 30, 2016).

Data collection

Data from event participants were collected through an online and self-completed survey. Based on the international attendance at the event and the bilingualism in Belgium, the survey was developed in Dutch, English, and French. There were a total of 16,000 participants, of which 15,700 registered online and 300 in person. The online registrants received an e-mail from the event organiser 10 days prior to the event and this e-mail included information about their participation and an invitation to complete the survey. It was explained that participation was voluntary, confidential, and anonymous. The study procedures were approved by the Research Ethics Board of the University of British Columbia. A total of 1091 registrants completed the survey prior to their participation in the event (response rate = 6.95%), of which 441 were international respondents.[2] The survey tool showed that another 760 registrants accessed but abandoned the web link without completing the survey, which means that data from these individuals were not collected. The event organiser agreed to send out the invitation to the survey only once, whereas a follow-up reminder could have improved the response rate. Using the empirical data collected from a sample of event participants, this paper describes (1) the socio-demographic profiles and cycling behaviours of the active sport tourists and (2) the event and the destination-related elements that motivate the active sport tourists to take part in the Tour of Flanders Cyclo, by elaborating upon the differences between national and international event participants.

Survey respondents

In the Tour of Flanders Cyclo sample (*N* = 1091), just over 95% of the respondents were male and approximately 62% were in their thirties or forties (*M* age = 40.75; SD = 10.76). About 68% completed tertiary education and more than 88% were employed. Only 2% of the respondents reported having limited discretionary income. The most popular event distance was the 133 km, followed by the 259 and the 83 km distances. Using a Pearson chi-square test, statistically significant differences were found between the national and international respondents in terms of age, education, professional status, subjective income status, and event distance (Table 1). The international sample was

Table 1. Socio-demographic profile of survey respondents, in percentages.

	Respondent sample (N = 1091)	National sample (N = 650)	International sample (N = 441)
Gender ($\chi^2(1) = 0.03$; not significant)			
Male	95.3	95.2	95.5
Female	4.7	4.8	4.5
Age ($\chi^2(4) = 57.12$; $p < .001$)			
Twenties	15.8	**21.5**	**7.3**
Thirties	30.8	31.2	30.2
Forties	31.3	29.7	33.8
Fifties	17.2	**14.9**	**20.6**
Sixties	4.9	**2.6**	**8.2**
Education ($\chi^2(2) = 49.79$; $p < .001$)			
Primary	8.4	9.7	6.6
Secondary	23.1	**29.8**	**13.2**
Tertiary	68.5	**60.5**	**80.3**
Professional status ($\chi^2(3) = 12.31$; $p < .01$)			
Employed	88.5	89.5	86.8
Student	5.1	6.0	3.9
No paid employment	2.5	1.8	3.4
Retired	3.9	**2.6**	**5.9**
Subjective income status ($\chi^2(2) = 7.31$; $p < .05$)			
(Very) easy to make ends meet	49.3	50.5	47.6
In between	48.5	48.3	48.8
(Very) difficult to make ends meet	2.2	**1.2**	**3.6**
Event distance ($\chi^2(2) = 25.98$; $p < .001$)			
83 km	17.3	**19.2**	**14.5**
133 km	56.1	**49.8**	**65.3**
259 km	26.6	**30.9**	**20.2**

Note: The values in bold are the ones that are significantly different.

significantly older and included a higher percentage of individuals in their fifties and sixties, which also explains the higher percentage of retired participants. Far fewer individuals who were in their twenties travelled internationally to take part in the event. The international participants were also more highly educated compared to the national participants, although the former sample revealed having less discretionary income compared to the latter sample. Lastly, the 133 km event distance was significantly more popular among the international sample when compared to the national one. The survey data revealed that the 2013 edition of the Tour of Flanders Cyclo attracted active sport tourists from various countries across the world, including Canada, Brazil, and South Africa. However, the majority of the international respondents travelled from Belgium's neighbouring countries, including the Netherlands (50%), Great Britain[3] (20%), France (13%), and Germany (4%). Other more distant countries that were somewhat represented were Spain, Switzerland, Italy, Denmark, and Sweden.

Survey instrument

A survey was designed to examine socio-demographic characteristics, cycling behaviours, and event motivations among a sample of national and international event participants. Five university researchers who are experts in event impact research reviewed the content validity of the survey questions. Subsequently, a pre-test of the questions was conducted among doctoral researchers at the University of British Columbia and the KU Leuven, which resulted in minor changes regarding the wording of some questions.

Data on socio-demographic variables including gender, age, education, professional status, and subjective income status were collected. Individual behaviours in terms of active participation in the Tour of Flanders Cyclo and passive spectating of the Tour of Flanders were measured as follows. Respondents were asked whether they had previously participated in the Tour of Flanders Cyclo and whether they would participate in other participatory cycling events in addition to the Tour of Flanders Cyclo (in the 2013 cycling season). The survey asked whether and how they would watch the Tour of Flanders (more than one option could be selected) and how many professional cycling races they had attended during the past 12 months. In order to understand respondents' cycling orientation, they were asked to identify themselves as being competitive (i.e. I cycle to improve my distance, time, and/or performance and may do this through a competition), recreational (i.e. I cycle to relax, socialise, improve my health), and/or functional cyclists (i.e. I cycle to get to work, to the store, to school). More than one option could be selected.

Twelve items measured the importance of specific event and destination-related elements in motivating respondents to take part in the Tour of Flanders Cyclo event, and these are presented in Table 2. Five of the items have been previously used by Ramchandani and Coleman (2012) in a study that examined the levers that might cause spectators at major sport events in the United Kingdom to act on the inspiration effect and become more active in sport. The other items were developed based on the event features of the Tour of Flanders. The response range was a five-point Likert scale ranging from 0 (*not important at all*) to 4 (*very important*) (e.g. the tradition of the Tour of Flanders motivates me to participate, riding an event with legendary hills motivates me to participate, and the skill and ability of current elite cyclists motivate me to participate). To test the assumption that elements of the event and the destination can be significant resources in leveraging the Tour of Flanders and attracting event participants, it was necessary to ask participants themselves why they participated in the Tour of Flanders Cyclo. Therefore, one open-ended question was included in the online survey. Respondents were invited to provide a short answer to the following question: Why do you participate in the Tour of Flanders Cyclo? Answering this question, contrary to the quantitative questions, was not mandatory to submit the survey responses. Less than 2% of the respondents provided no answer to this question or provided an answer that did not reflect the question, which were subsequently omitted from further analyses.

Table 2. Descriptive analyses of event and destination-related items.

	M	SD
Riding an event with legendary hills such as the 'Koppenberg'	3.39	0.97
Riding a classic event such as the Tour of Flanders	3.28	0.98
The pride that comes with finishing the Tour of Flanders	3.20	1.10
Riding the same route as the elite cyclists the following day	3.17	1.07
Whole atmosphere around the Tour of Flanders (spectacle, crowd, excitement)	3.14	1.07
The tradition of the Tour of Flanders	3.08	1.11
Riding the Tour of Flanders on the day before the elite cyclists	2.67	1.22
Skill and ability of current elite cyclists	2.19	1.16
Accomplishments of past 'Flandriens'	2.10	1.26
Quality of the competition among current elite cyclists	2.08	1.14
Performance of the elite cyclist I am supporting	1.88	1.22
Activities that have been organised around the Tour of Flanders	1.83	1.05

Note: Measured using a five-point Likert scale ranging from 0 (*not important at all*) to 4 (*very important*). $N = 1091$.

Data analysis

All statistical analyses were performed in SPSS (Version 20). To examine the socio-demographic profiles and cycling behaviours of the active sport tourists, the variables were analysed descriptively using means, percentages, standard deviations, Pearson chi-square tests, and correlations. Descriptive analyses were also used to examine event motivations among the active sport tourists. To examine differences between international and national event participants in terms of event motivations, the Welch *t* test for independent samples was used as the observations were independent from one another and the samples followed a normal distribution. Because the Levene's test noted that the assumption of the homogeneity of variance was violated on some items, the Welch *t* test corrected this problem as this test does not assume equal population variances or equal sample sizes (Field, 2013). To enhance our understanding about event motivations, one open-ended question was analysed using a combination of deductive and inductive coding, assisted by the second version of the Exercise Motivations Inventory (Markland, 2007). When respondents provided multiple answers, only the first one was translated and coded, which is identified as a limitation to the study. This was done in particular to facilitate the translations from three different languages and to assist in the data analysis with a workable data set. Adapted from the Exercise Motivations Inventory were motivations such as enjoyment (e.g. because I enjoy cycling), challenge (e.g. to test my own physical abilities), affiliation (e.g. to be together with friends), strength and endurance (e.g. to prepare myself for the Mont Ventoux in France), and positive health (e.g. because this challenge motivates me to stay fit). Other motivations that were self-developed were heritage (e.g. to experience the iconic cobblestones up-close) and charity (e.g. to raise money for health research). A binary logistical regression analysis was performed to explore the relationships between the characteristics of active sport tourists who are motivated to actively experience Flanders' cycling heritage in association with the event (Field, 2013). This regression, which can be justified because the dependent variable is categorical, can predict which individuals might be more responsive to the use of heritage as a leverageable resource and this has implications to promote Flanders as a tourism destination.

Findings

Cycling behaviours

To understand active sport tourists' cycling behaviours, respondents were asked about their active participation in the Tour of Flanders Cyclo and other participatory cycling events, as well as their passive spectating of the Tour of Flanders and other elite cycling races. The percentages and Pearson chi-square tests comparing the national and international sample of event participants are presented in Table 3. In terms of active participation, national respondents had significantly more experience with the Tour of Flanders Cyclo, as well as other participatory cycling events. International respondents were more likely to be first-time participants at the Tour of Flanders Cyclo. They were also more likely to only take part in the Tour of Flanders Cyclo and not in other participatory cycling events throughout the season, not even in their home country. This finding provides support for the assumption that the Tour of Flanders Cyclo is an attractive and popular 'bucket-list'

Table 3. Cycling behaviour of survey respondents, in percentages.

	Respondent sample ($N = 1091$)	National sample ($N = 650$)	International sample ($N = 441$)
Previous participation in Tour of Flanders Cyclo			
No, 2013 was first time	46.2	**37.2**	**59.4**
Yes, once	17.2	16.5	18.4
Yes, twice	10.3	**13.5**	**5.4**
Yes, three times	7.6	8.5	6.3
Yes, four times	6.4	**8.0**	**4.1**
Yes, five times	3.1	**4.2**	**1.6**
Yes, more than five times	9.2	**12.2**	**4.8**
($\chi^2(6) = 74.35; p < .001$)			
Participation in other participatory cycling events			
No, only Tour of Flanders Cyclo	47.8	**34.8**	**66.9**
Yes, also other events	52.2	**65.2**	**33.1**
($\chi^2(1) = 108.67; p < .001$)			
Watching Tour of Flanders elite race			
No ($\chi^2(1) = 4.93; p < .05$)	2.4	**1.5**	**3.6**
Yes, live along the route ($\chi^2(1) = 46.20; p < .001$)	25.2	**17.8**	**36.1**
Yes, at start in Bruges	8.5	7.8	9.5
Yes, at finish in Oudenaarde ($\chi^2(1) = 27.93; p < .001$)	5.9	**2.8**	**10.4**
Yes, on television/internet ($\chi^2(1) = 124.30; p < .001$)	72.9	**85.2**	**54.6**
Watching other elite cycling races			
Never	29.0	30.0	27.4
Once	21.2	**18.6**	**24.9**
2–3 times	29.7	29.8	29.5
4–6 times	10.5	11.2	9.5
7–12 times	3.6	**4.6**	**2.0**
More than 12 times	6.0	5.7	6.6
($\chi^2(5) = 11.51; p < .05$)			
Competitive cyclist			
Yes	39.1	**28.8**	**54.4**
($\chi^2(1) = 72.58; p < .001$)			
Recreational cyclist			
Yes	69.6	**77.7**	**58.5**
($\chi^2(1) = 46.01; p < .001$)			
Functional cyclist			
Yes	23.6	23.4	24.0
($\chi^2(1) = .06; p = .80$)			

Note: The values in bold are the ones that are significantly different.

event for international active sport tourists. In terms of passive spectating, international respondents were more likely to watch the Tour of Flanders elite cycling race live along the route or in the arrival host city of Oudenaarde, whereas national respondents were more likely to watch the race live on television. Both samples were comparable in terms of watching other elite cycling races (which can be live along the route or live on television), with approximately 70% of all event participants watching at least one other cycling race during the 12 months prior to the Tour of Flanders.

In terms of cycling orientation, there were significantly more competitive cyclists among the international sample and more recreational cyclists among the national sample. No differences with regard to functional cycling, which was the least popular cycling orientation based on participant percentages, were reported. The correlations among the binary cycling behaviour variables that are presented in Table 4 show that the strongest correlation was the one found between respondents' competitive and recreational cycling orientation ($r = -.74; p < .001$), indicating that an increase in competitiveness is associated with a decrease recreationally and vice versa. The results also suggested

Table 4. Correlations among cycling behaviour variables.

	1	2	3	4	5	6	7
1. Previous participation in Tour of Flanders Cyclo	-	.26***	−.04	.06*	−.09**	.09**	−.02
2. Participation in other cycling events		-	−.08**	.07*	−.04	.06*	−.06*
3. Watching Tour of Flanders elite race			-	−.12***	−.05	.02	.04
4. Watching other elite cycling races				-	.09**	−.06	−.01
5. Competitive cyclist					-	−.74***	−.07*
6. Recreational cyclist						-	.13***
7. Functional cyclist							-

Note: $N = 1091$.
*** $p < .001$; ** $p < .01$; * $p < .05$; two-tailed.

that a competitive and recreational cycling orientation correlate differently with a functional cycling orientation, the former negatively and the latter positively. In terms of active participation, participating in the Tour of Flanders Cyclo was positively correlated with participating in other participatory cycling events ($r = .26$; $p < .001$), whereas in terms of passive spectating, watching the Tour of Flanders was negatively correlated with watching other elite cycling races ($r = −.12$; $p < .001$).

Motives for event participation

The mean scores and standard deviations for the specific event and destination-related resources, which were measured using a five-point Likert scale, are presented in Table 2. These scores represent the importance of each item in motivating the respondents to take part in the Tour of Flanders Cyclo. Event participants assigned great importance to legendary and traditional elements of the Tour of Flanders. Riding the iconic cobblestone hills was ranked the highest and event participants agreed on the importance of this item, as reflected in the lowest standard deviation among all the items. In terms of the event route, participants agreed that it is important to ride the same route as the elite cyclists who compete the following day. The event route is known to be physically challenging, which provides participants with a desirable sense of pride when finishing the Tour of Flanders Cyclo. Other important motivators were the tradition, history, and atmosphere of the event (all items had mean scores greater than 3 on a five-point scale). Event participants assigned less importance to the performances and abilities of current and past elite cyclists (mean scores ranged from 1.88 to 2.19 on a five-point scale). The activities that have been organised around the Tour of Flanders was ranked as the least important item in motivating the respondents to take part in the event.

The mean differences between national and international event respondents on these items are presented in Table 5. The results suggest that specific event and destination-related resources motivated both samples differently. The differences were consistent with the international sample assigning greater importance to the legendary and traditional elements of the Tour of Flanders in promoting event participation when compared to the national sample. This pertains to the route, history, tradition, and atmosphere of the Tour of Flanders, as well as the timing (day before elite cycling race) and other organised activities around the event. Again, this finding provides support for the assumption that the Tour of Flanders Cyclo is an attractive and popular event specifically for international active sport tourists based upon its unique characteristics.

Table 5. Comparing mean differences of event motivation among two samples of event participants.

	International sample (N = 441)	National sample (N = 650)	Welch statistic
	M (SD)	M (SD)	F (df1, df2)
Riding an event with legendary hills such as the 'Koppenberg'	**3.56 (0.86)**	**3.27 (1.03)**	25.17 (1, 1041)***
Riding a classic event such as the Tour of Flanders	**3.45 (0.92)**	**3.17 (1.01)**	22.52 (1, 1089)***
The pride that comes with finishing the Tour of Flanders	3.12 (1.12)	3.24 (1.09)	3.03 (1, 1089) NS
Riding the same route as the elite cyclists the following day	**3.37 (0.95)**	**3.04 (1.12)**	28.52 (1,1038)***
Whole atmosphere around the Tour of Flanders (spectacle, crowd, excitement)	**3.35 (0.95)**	**3.00 (1.12)**	29.20 (1, 1089)***
The tradition of the Tour of Flanders	**3.30 (1.04)**	**2.94 (1.13)**	29.33 (1, 1089)***
Riding the Tour of Flanders on the day before the elite cyclists	**2.95 (1.16)**	**2.48 (1.23)**	41.78 (1, 979)***
Skill and ability of current elite cyclists	2.20 (1.19)	2.17 (1.14)	0.15 (1, 1089) NS
Accomplishments of past 'Flandriens'	2.01 (1.31)	2.17 (1.22)	3.86 (1, 1089) NS
Quality of the competition among current elite cyclists	2.12 (1.18)	2.05 (1.11)	1.08 (1, 906) NS
Performance of the elite cyclist I am supporting	1.82 (1.22)	1.91 (1.23)	1.52 (1, 1089) NS
Activities that have been organised around the Tour of Flanders	**1.95 (1.06)**	**1.75 (1.03)**	10.22 (1, 1089)**

Note: The values that are highlighted in bold are the ones that are significantly different (Min = 0; Max = 4). NS = not significant.
** $p < .01$.
*** $p < .001$.

The analysis of the qualitative, open-ended question about why active sport tourists take part in the Tour of Flanders Cyclo revealed four important and commonly shared motives, which have been categorised as heritage, challenge, enjoyment, and strength and endurance. These were the most important motives among the international as well as the national respondents, only the ranking of heritage and challenge was different among the two samples ($\chi^2(10) = 34.32; p < .001$). On the one hand, more than 35% of the national respondents (compared to about 27% of the international respondents) argued that they took part in the Tour of Flanders Cyclo because the event provided a challenge to test one's personal and physical abilities (e.g. the event is a personal challenge for my 35th birthday; it is a challenge to successfully complete this event; cycling 260 km is a sporting challenge). On the other hand, more than 43% of international respondents (compared to about 27% of the national respondents) provided an answer that described the unique and attractive characteristics of the Tour of Flanders, including its cobblestone hills, history, and atmosphere (e.g. I want to ride in one of the Spring Classics; I always wanted to experience the cobbled climbs; it is a legendary race; I want to cycle on hallowed ground; I participate for its history and heroism; I want to ride the cobbles of Flanders just like I have watched the professional cyclists do for years). Respondents implied that the Tour of Flanders was an event that you have to ride at least once when you consider yourself to be a real cycling enthusiast, again referring to the 'bucket-list' popularity of the event among international active sport tourists.

Less important, but still relevant for about 17% of the respondents, was the motive of enjoyment (with no significant differences between national and international respondents). Individuals participated for fun and pleasure and because they were passionate about cycling, with the event being one opportunity to cultivate that passion. Also noteworthy was the motive of strength and endurance, as about 7% of the respondents indicated that the Tour of Flanders Cyclo was one element in their long-term training plans (again, with no significant differences among international and national respondents). It should be noted that the Tour of Flanders is organised as one of the first cycling events of the season. Therefore, cyclists identified training for and participating in the Tour of Flanders Cyclo as an important step in building physical fitness for the remainder of the season, which for many (mostly Belgian) respondents included participation in other participatory sport events.

Predicting heritage motivation

Using a binary logistic regression analysis, the variables that determine whether individuals were motivated to experience the event's heritage when participating in the Tour of Flanders Cyclo have been examined and the results are presented in Table 6. Gender was the only socio-demographic variable that significantly determined individuals' heritage motivation. Men had more than twice the probability of being motivated by the heritage of the Tour of Flanders when compared to women. Home country significantly determined heritage motivation as individuals from Belgium and the Netherlands had more than 50% less probability of being motivated to experience the event's heritage when compared to active sport tourists from other countries. The event distance was also a significant variable, as those who completed the longest event distance of 259 km had almost 50% less probability of being motivated to experience the event's heritage when compared to those who completed the shortest event distance of 83 km. In terms of active participation, previous participation in the Tour of Flanders Cyclo significantly determined heritage motivation. Repeat participants had a greater probability of being motivated by the event's heritage when compared to first-time participants. In terms of passive spectating, those who watched other elite cycling races in the months leading-up to the Tour of Flanders had a greater probability of being motivated by the event's heritage when compared to those who did not watch any other elite cycling races.

Table 6. Results of the binary logistic regression analysis for heritage motives among event participants.

Variables and categories	Odds ratio	Wald statistic
Gender		
Male	2.38	5.08*
Female (ref. cat.)		
Age		
Twenties (ref. cat.)		
Thirties	0.83	0.60
Forties	0.86	0.38
Fifties	0.82	0.55
Sixties	0.74	0.42
Education		
Primary	0.78	0.86
Secondary	0.95	0.08
Tertiary (ref. cat.)		
Professional status		
Employed	0.65	0.94
Student	0.38	2.69
No paid employment	0.76	0.20
Retired (ref. cat.)		
Subjective income status		
(Very) easy to make ends meet (ref. cat.)		
In between	1.00	0.00
(Very) difficult to make ends meet	0.50	1.83

(Continued)

Table 6. Continued.

Variables and categories	Odds ratio	Wald statistic
Home country		
Belgium	0.25	16.86***
The Netherlands	0.39	7.77**
Great Britain	0.67	1.31
France	1.83	2.06
Germany	0.63	0.60
Other (ref.cat.)		
Event distance		
83 km (ref. cat.)		
133 km	0.85	0.71
259 km	0.57	6.36*
Repeat participation		
Yes	1.55	8.57**
No (ref. cat.)		
Other participatory cycling events		
Yes	1.24	1.85
No, only Tour of Flanders Cylco (ref. cat.)		
Recreational cyclist		
Yes	1.02	0.01
No (ref. cat.)		
Competitive cyclist		
Yes	1.03	0.01
No (ref. cat.)		
Functional cyclist		
Yes	0.89	0.53
No (ref. cat.)		
Tour of Flanders along route		
Yes	0.94	0.12
No (ref. cat.)		
Tour of Flanders on television		
Yes	1.11	0.31
No (ref. cat.)		
Tour of Flanders start in Bruges		
Yes	1.23	0.80
No (ref. cat.)		
Tour of Flanders arrival in Oudenaarde		
Yes	0.99	0.00
No (ref. cat.)		
Watching other elite cycling races		
Yes	1.62	8.78**
No (ref. cat.)		
Constant	0.66	0.34

Notes: $N = 1091$; Hosmer–Lemeshow $= .35$; Nagelkerke $R^2 = .12$; Cox and Snell $R^2 = .09$; Model $\chi^2(29) = 98.564$, $p < .001$.
* $p < .05$.
** $p < .01$.
*** $p < .001$.

Discussion

The findings in this paper add to our knowledge about the strategic opportunities for event leverage associated with hosting heritage-based active sport tourism events by reporting on case study data from the Tour of Flanders Cyclo. The discussion focuses on two elements of the event leveraging framework, namely the 'leveragees' (i.e. those who are recipients of leveraging efforts) (Tian & Johnston, 2008) and the 'leverageable resources' (i.e. the assets that can be aligned with newly developed initiatives) (Chalip, 2004; O'Brien, 2006; Smith, 2014). The leveragees are the active sport tourists who travelled to the region of the Flemish Ardennes to participate in the 2013 edition of the Tour of Flanders Cyclo. Using an online survey, data on socio-demographic variables, cycling behaviours, and event motives were collected from 1091 event participants. The data on socio-demographic variables and cycling behaviours are discussed to understand the leveragees, whereas the data on event motives are discussed to better understand how the available leverageable resources can be employed in broader tourism development initiatives.

Overall, active sport tourists were almost exclusively men in their thirties or forties, who were highly educated and employed. Although this socio-demographic profile resembles findings from other participatory cycling events in terms of gender, education, and professional status, other events succeeded in attracting participants who were slightly older (e.g. Bull, 2006; Dickson, Phelps, Schofield, & Funk, 2010; Lamont & Jenkins, 2013). This might, in part, be due to the fact that the many cobblestone hills in the Flemish Ardennes make the Tour of Flanders Cyclo a physically challenging event. Physical effort, endurance, and skill are desired to successfully take part. However, the significant older age of the international participants at the Tour of Flanders Cyclo suggests that the physical challenge of the event might be a greater barrier for those participating in their home country, in particular as they are competing against their much younger Belgian counterparts. National participants were more highly motivated by the challenge of the event, whereas heritage was the most important motivator among international participants. Nonetheless, international participants were more likely to identify themselves as competitive cyclists as opposed to national participants more as recreational cyclists. Therefore, the findings support the idea that travelling to take part in an active sport tourism event is a serious undertaking that requires a significant commitment of time and financial resources, resulting in a more competitive orientation (Getz & McConnell, 2011, 2014).

Particular resources of the event and the destination were rated as highly important in promoting event participation. This finding adds to our knowledge about using heritage in leveraging active sport tourism events, as well as developing, promoting, and showcasing eventscapes that better align a particular event within a particular destination. Furthermore, this finding also opposes the general belief about the inspiration or demonstration effect where the performances of elite athletes at major spectator events act as the main sources of inspiration for individuals to be or become active (e.g. Ramchandani & Coleman, 2012; Weed, Coren, & Fiore, 2009). In the case of the Tour of Flanders, the performances of elite athletes were less important than the event itself. International participants were motivated to personally and physically experience what it feels like to ride the cobblestones along the route that the elite cyclists complete the following day, even more so than the Belgian participants, who arguably have more opportunities to cycle in the region of the Flemish Ardennes all year round along the permanent Tour of Flanders cycling network. The heritage of the Tour of Flanders, nonetheless, has been identified as an important resource to leverage event participation among active sport tourists and relatedly, leverage future tourism development to further promote the destination.

The study findings showed significant differences in reasons for selecting a particular event, including the embodiment of 'active' sport heritage. Active sport tourists who travelled internationally to take part in the event were more committed to experiencing and pursuing the event's heritage, as active participants as well as passive spectators. However, given the high percentage of first-time participants among the international sample, it appears that involvement and engagement with the Tour of Flanders is associated with an active but possibly once-in-a-lifetime experience of sport heritage, without initiating a long-term career with the Tour of Flanders Cyclo similar to the national sample. Further exploiting sport heritage as an individual motivator could increase repeat participation in the future, focusing in particular on individuals outside of Belgium and the Netherlands.

The findings in this paper assert that organising a medium-sized, joint participatory and spectator sport event presents valuable leveraging opportunities for host communities, in particular when the event is hosted annually in and around the same cities. Strategic planning around annual sport events, more so than one-off events, can lead to cities becoming part of the eventscape (Brown et al., 2015). This connection between the event and the host, for example through the cultivation of sport heritage, can attract visitors outside the event-period which will benefit spending and other forms of investment in the region. Tourism leveraging in association with the Tour of Flanders, in particular, should mainly focus on international event participants who were more likely to engage in a complete weekend to experience Flanders' cycling heritage in the region of the Flemish Ardennes. Firstly, by actively participating in the Tour of Flanders Cyclo. Secondly, by passively spectating the elite cyclists live along the route of the Tour of Flanders the following day or in the arrival host city of Oudenaarde. National event participants, assumingly excluding those who live close to the route and watch the event live, were more likely to watch the race on television. Consequently, these participants did not spend any additional money in the host region of the Flemish Ardennes.

Theoretical implications

The prospect of generating economic benefits has inspired many cities to leverage major spectator events, aiming to attract event spectators as repeat visitors to the host destination. Previous research has examined the conceptual framework of event leverage in cases of event sport tourism, but the process has been under-examined in cases of active sport tourism and heritage sport tourism. This paper confirmed the applicability of event leverage to active sport tourism events by examining the case of the Tour of Flanders Cyclo. As opposed to attracting event spectators as repeat visitors, event leveraging in cases of active sport tourism can be used as a means to attracting event participants as repeat visitors to the host destination while offering additional event-related opportunities to be active. The findings contribute to the conceptual framework of event leverage by identifying elements of the eventscape that are embedded in the context of the host as important leverageable resources when leveraging active sport tourism events, as opposed to solely the event itself or a portfolio of events. In the case of the Tour of Flanders Cyclo which makes explicit associations to Flanders' cycling heritage, sport heritage and more specifically 'active' sport heritage has been identified as an important resource to promote participation among active sport tourists.

From a broader tourism development perspective, this study highlights the role an event's heritage plays as motivation for participation as well as the idea that sport heritage can be an 'active' pursuit. Heritage should be more prominently developed as part of an eventscape within a particular host region, as a pull factor based on the availability of community resources (e.g. route selection, natural backdrop, and permanent transformations) as well as a push factor based on the individual experiences of event participants (e.g. unique atmosphere and history of the event) (Apostolakis, 2003). The notion that experiencing heritage can motivate tourists is not new (Prentice, 1993). However, the idea that a sport event's heritage can motivate a very dedicated, rigorous, and committed form of participation is, to date, under-explored, and may have significant implications for sport tourism development. Many participatory sport events – not the least of which are marathons – have developed their own heritage or are associated with fairly significant and durable heritages (Faber, 2010). As Morley and Robins (1995) remind us, heritage is an essential ingredient in the race between places, and if sport events can highlight a specific heritage that separates their event from competing events, it appears that participants may have a greater incentive to register and compete in those events. Motivation to experience 'active' sport heritage appears to be more important among repeat event participants, which highlights that heritage in relation to annual events should be cultivated as an ongoing process to promote the sustainability of an event within a particular destination. Furthermore, this study highlights that sport heritage should be considered beyond its passive, consumptive, and artefact-based roots. Ramshaw (2014) argued that what might separate sport heritage from other forms of heritage is that 'it must continue to be made and remade through play and performance' (p. 194). As such, it is important that sport heritage research also considers many forms of active sport participation as a kind of heritage performance.

Managerial implications

It is recommended that public sector agencies work together with event owners and commercial organisations in conducting the event leverage to promote (inter)national tourism. Smaller active sport tourism events that are hosted annually in and around the same cities within a particular destination should be identified and developed as valuable resources in the leveraging process. This is important because the longevity of annual smaller events is sometimes overlooked and even taken for granted, as host cities are seeking benefits from hosting non-local and one-off major sport events within the destination. Local, provincial, and regional levels of government are advised to implement tactics and strategies to more strongly embed heritage-based elements of annual smaller sport events within the context of the host, to attract active sport tourists as well as to promote the host region as a tourism destination. A long-term connection between the event and the destination can be fostered through the development of permanent eventscapes, which in the case of the Tour of Flanders include a visitor centre and cycling network, among other things.

These permanent developments also have implications in terms of targeting domestic and international event participants when leveraging the available sport heritage for tourism development purposes. The case of the Tour of Flanders Cyclo highlighted that leveraging sport heritage to attract domestic event participants was less relevant. Although the event is organised only once every year, the temporal limitations associated with the event have been removed thanks to the development of a permanent Tour of Flanders cycling network in and around Oudenaarde. Interested individuals can explore the routes of the Tour of Flanders all year round by following the signposts in the area, buying a printed map, or downloading the route onto their satellite navigation system. It is very likely that this permanent cycling infrastructure created a domestic and international divide in the use of sport heritage to attract interested cycling enthusiasts, as international cyclists are more likely to travel to the region specifically for the event itself. Nonetheless, strategically linking permanent infrastructure to a popular sport event with an extensive local history can be an effective strategy to promote long-term usage and broad-based engagement among community members.

From a destination marketing perspective, event managers may wish to create a kind of 'Tour Village' along the route where all participants can come together as fans to watch the elite cycling race and relive their own event experience the day after. Preferably, given the heritage importance assigned to the route of races such as Tour of Flanders, this location should be a strategic one where spectators can watch their heroes battle infamous sections of the course, such as the cobblestones at the 'Koppenberg.' This social gathering can be complemented with other activities such as a presentation about new cycling equipment, training methods, or nutritional advice with a focus on challenge and competition to satisfy participants from the longest event distance. Event organisers may wish to also explicitly highlight the heritage and traditions of the race and route, such as through a video projection or the exhibition of displays and artefacts. These additional activities can create more meaningful connections between the different facets of the event (in the case of the Tour of Flanders, the public participatory race and the elite spectator race), as well as re-enforce the meanings associated with the event's location.

In terms of future research, a broader comparative study using other famous and heritage-based public cycling events may confirm that an event's heritage is a lure for visitors to engage in 'active' sport heritage. Cycling events selected for future research should include events that are hosted annually in and around the same cities, where the event and the sport heritage are embedded in the local context (e.g. Amstel Gold Race, Paris-Roubaix, Milan-San Remo), as well as one-off events, where there is only a short-term connection between the event and a specific host locality (e.g. Tour de France, Giro d'Italia, Vuelta Ciclista a España). Furthermore, this comparative study may also elucidate whether and how visitors build 'active' sport heritage careers when elaborating upon the reasons for selecting particular active sport tourism events. The understanding of this career trajectory would have several implications, including an understanding of the role heritage plays in active sport tourism decisions, the portfolio of heritage-based participatory events, as well as the geography of these events. Furthermore, it can help to clarify the intention to revisit events from the 'active' sport heritage career, perhaps to experience certain heritage components of the event again, to nostalgise past accomplishments at these sites, or to revisit the event at different life and career stages, which has implications for future tourism development in the region.

Conclusion

Using the conceptual framework of event leverage (Chalip, 2004), this study intended to explore the strategic opportunities for tourism development associated with hosting heritage-based active sport tourism events. Quantitative and qualitative data were collected through an online and self-completed survey from event participants at the Tour of Flanders Cyclo ($N = 1091$), an annual active sport tourism event which has gained world-wide popularity by making explicit connections to Flanders' cycling heritage. The following questions have guided this research: (1) What are the socio-demographic profiles and cycling behaviours of active sport tourists who take part in the Tour of Flanders Cyclo? (2) What elements of the event and the destination motivate these individuals to take part in the Tour of Flanders Cyclo? And (3) how do these differ between the national and international event participants? The study has demonstrated that the heritage of a sport event along with the region and landscape where the event is situated may motivate international active sport tourists to travel to a destination to participate in and watch an event. As a result, active sport tourism events may wish to overtly employ sport heritage as a resource to leverage future tourism development initiatives. To do so, greater attention should be given to the leveraging potential of available event and destination-related resources that can be permanently embedded within the tourism destination, including, for example, an event's heritage, route, and atmosphere. Ultimately, the sport event as well as the tourism destination may benefit financially from a meaningful and long-term connection.

Notes

1. In 2012, the province of Liège (Belgium) paid more than €2.5 million to the event organiser Amaury Sport Organisation to host the Tour de France Grand Départ. Combined with the costs related to promotion and safety, the total expenditures for the province exceeded €4 million (Het Nieuwsblad, 2012).
2. According to data received from the event organiser, the sample of respondents in this study was representative to the event population based upon the variables gender, event distance, and home country.
3. Participants from England ($n = 78$), Scotland ($n = 4$), Wales ($n = 2$), Isle of Man ($n = 1$), and Ireland ($n = 2$) have been included in this category (although Ireland is not officially part of Great Britain). This was done so to highlight the geographical distance from Belgium (travelling across the North Sea).

Disclosure statement

No potential conflict of interest was reported by the authors.

References

Alzua, A., O'Leary, J. T., & Morrison, A. M. (1998). Cultural and heritage tourism: Identifying niches for international travelers. *Journal of Tourism Studies, 9*(2), 2–13.
Apostolakis, A. (2003). The convergence process in heritage tourism. *Annals of Tourism Research, 30*(4), 795–812.
Balduck, A.-L., Maes, M., & Buelens, M. (2011). The social impact of the Tour de France: Comparisons of residents' pre- and post-event perceptions. *European Sport Management Quarterly, 11*(2), 91–113.
Bale, J. (2003). *Sports geographies* (2nd ed.). London: Routledge.
Berridge, G. (2012). The promotion of cycling in London: The impact of the 2007 Tour de France grand départ on the image and provision of cycling in the capital. *Journal of Sport & Tourism, 17*(1), 43–61.
Brown, G., Lee, I. S., King, K., & Shipway, R. (2015). Eventscapes and the creation of event legacies. *Annals of Tourism Research, 18*(4), 510–527.
Bull, C. J. (2006). Racing cyclists as sports tourists: The experiences and behaviours of a case study group of cyclists in East Kent, England. *Journal of Sport & Tourism, 11*(3/4), 259–274.
Bull, C., & Lovell, J. (2007). The impact of hosting major sporting events on local residents: An analysis of the views and perceptions of Canterbury residents in relation to the Tour de France 2007. *Journal of Sport & Tourism, 12*(3/4), 229–248.

Chalip, L. (2004). Beyond impact: A general model for sport event leverage. In B. W. Ritchie & D. Adair (Eds.), *Sport tourism: Interrelationships, impacts and issues* (pp. 236–262). Clevedon: Channel View Publications.

Chelladurai, P. (2009). *Managing organisations for sport and physical activity: A systems perspective* (3rd. ed.). Scottsdale, AZ: Holcomb Hathaway.

Coleman, R., & Ramchandani, G. M. (2010). The hidden benefits of non-elite mass participation sports events: An economic perspective. *International Journal of Sports Marketing & Sponsorship*, *12*(1), 24–36.

Derom, I. (2014). *Event leveraging and health promotion: The case of the Tour of Flanders* (Unpublished doctoral dissertation). The University of British Columbia, Vancouver, Canada.

Derom, I., & VanWynsberghe, R. (2015). Extending the benefits of leveraging cycling events: Evidence from the Tour of Flanders. *European Sport Management Quarterly*, *15*(1), 111–131.

Dickinson, J. E., & Robbins, D. (2009). 'Other people, other times and special places': A social representations perspective of cycling in a tourism destination. *Tourism and Hospitality Planning & Development*, *6*(1), 69–85.

Dickson, G., Phelps, S., Schofield, G., & Funk, D. (2010). *Participation events and sustained, increased levels of physical activity*. Retrieved August 30, 2014, from http://www.srknowledge.org.nz/research-completed/participation-events-and-sustained-increased-levels-of-physical-activity/

Douchy, V. (2010, April 6). Ronde van Vlaanderen binnenkort Werelderfgoed? *Het Nieuwsblad*. Retrieved October 4, 2012, from http://www.nieuwsblad.be/sportwereld/cnt/GVR2OGCCA

Faber, M. (2010). The 2,500-year-old man. *Sports Illustrated*, *113*(18), 64–70.

Field, A. (2013). *Discovering statistics using IBM SPSS statistics* (4th ed.). London: Sage.

Gammon, S. (2011). Sporting new attractions: The commodification of the sleeping stadium. In R. Sharpley & P. Stone (Eds.), *Tourism experiences: Contemporary perspectives* (pp. 115–126). London: Routledge.

Gammon, S., Ramshaw, G., & Waterton, E. (2013). Examining the Olympics: Heritage, identity and performance. *International Journal of Heritage Studies*, *19*(2), 119–124.

Garden, M. E. (2006). The heritagescape: Looking at landscapes of the past. *International Journal of Heritage Studies*, *12*(5), 394–411.

Getz, D., & McConnell, A. (2011). Serious sport tourism and event travel careers. *Journal of Sport Management*, *25*(4), 326–338.

Getz, D., & McConnell, A. (2014). Comparing trail runners and mountain bikers: Motivation, involvement, portfolios, and event-tourist careers. *Journal of Convention & Event Tourism*, *15*(1), 69–100.

Gibson, H. (1998). Sport tourism: A critical analysis of research. *Sport Management Review*, *1*(1), 45–76.

Grix, J. (2012). 'Image' leveraging and sports mega-events: Germany and the 2006 FIFA World Cup. *Journal of Sport & Tourism*, *17*(4), 289–312.

Het Nieuwsblad. (2012). *Provincie Luik betaalt meer dan 4 miljoen euro voor Tourstart*. Retrieved on August 26, 2014, from http://www.nieuwsblad.be/cnt/dmf20120628_00204779

Hinch, T., & Higham, J. (2005). Sport, tourism and authenticity. *European Sport Management Quarterly*, *5*(3), 243–256.

Hinch, T., & Higham, J. (2011). *Sport tourism development* (2nd ed.). Bristol: Channel View Publications.

Hinch, T., & Ramshaw, G. (2014). Heritage sport tourism in Canada. *Tourism Geographies*, *16*(2), 237–251.

Horne, J. (2007). The four 'knowns' of sports mega-events. *Leisure Studies*, *26*(1), 81–96.

Joseph, J. (2011). A diaspora approach to sport tourism. *Journal of Sport and Social Issues*, *35*(2), 146–167.

Kulczycki, C., & Halpenny, E. A. (2014). Sport cycling tourists' setting preferences, appraisals and attachments. *Journal of Sport & Tourism*, *19*(2), 169–197.

Lamont, M., & Jenkins, J. (2013). Segmentation of cycling event participants: A two-step cluster method utilizing recreation specialization. *Event Management*, *17*(4), 391–417.

Markland, D. (2007). *Exercise motivation measurement*. Retrieved August 31, 2014, from http://pages.bangor.ac.uk/~pes004/exercise_motivation/scales.htm

Morley, D., & Robins, K. (1995). *Spaces of identity: Global media, electronic landscapes and cultural boundaries*. London: Routledge.

O'Brien, D. (2006). Event business leveraging: The Sydney 2000 Olympic Games. *Annals of Tourism Research*, *33*(1), 240–261.

Prentice, R. (1993). *Tourism and heritage attractions*. London: Routledge.

Ramchandani, G. M., & Coleman, R. J. (2012). The inspirational effects of three major sport events. *International Journal of Event and Festival Management*, *3*(3), 257–271.

Ramshaw, G. (2014). Sport, heritage, and tourism. *Journal of Heritage Tourism*, *9*(3), 191–196.

Ramshaw, G., & Bottelberghe, T. (2014). Pedaling through the past: Sport heritage, tourism development, and the Tour of Flanders. *Tourism Review International*, *18*(1/2), 23–36.

Ramshaw, G., & Gammon, S. (2005). More than just nostalgia? Exploring the heritage/sport tourism nexus. *Journal of Sport & Tourism*, *10*(4), 229–241.

Ramshaw, G., & Gammon, S. (2015). Heritage and sport. In E. Waterton & S. Watson (Eds.), *The Palgrave companion of contemporary heritage research* (pp. 248–257). London: Palgrave Macmillan.

Rickly-Boyd, J. M. (2013). Existential authenticity: Place matters. *Tourism Geographies*, *15*(4), 680–686.

Roche, S., Spake, D. F., & Joseph, M. (2013). A model of sporting event tourism as economic development. *Sport, Business and Management: An International Journal*, 3(2), 147–157.

Sant, S.-L., Mason, D. S., & Hinch, T. D. (2013). Conceptualising Olympic tourism legacy: Destination marketing organisations and Vancouver 2010. *Journal of Sport & Tourism*, *18*(4), 287–312.

Smith, A. (2009). Theorising the relationship between major sport events and social sustainability. *Journal of Sport & Tourism*, *14*(2), 109–120.

Smith, A. (2014). Leveraging sport mega-events: New model or convenient justification? *Journal of Policy Research in Tourism, Leisure and Events*, *6*(1), 15–30.

Smith, A., & Stevenson, N. (2009). A review of tourism policy for the 2012 Olympics. *Cultural Trends*, *18*(1), 97–102.

Snelgrove, R., & Wood, L. (2010). Attracting and leveraging visitors at a charity cycling event. *Journal of Sport & Tourism*, *15*(4), 269–285.

Storey, D. (2012). Heritage, culture and identity: The case of the Gaelic Games. In J. Hill, K. Moore, & J. Wood (Eds.), *Sport, history, and heritage: Studies in public representation* (pp. 223–234). Suffolk: The Boydell Press.

Taks, M. (2013). Social sustainability of non-mega sport events in a global world. *European Journal for Sport and Society*, *10*(2), 121–141.

Tian, J., & Johnston, C. (2008). The 2008 Olympic Games: Leveraging a 'best ever' games to benefit Beijing. *Asian Social Science*, *4*(4), 22–47.

Timothy, D. J. (2011). *Cultural heritage and tourism: An introduction*. Bristol: Channel View Publications.

Tourism Flanders. (2016). *Vernieuwde Ronde van Vlaanderenstraat eert helden van de Ronde*. Retrieved on May 20, 2016, from http://www.toerismevlaanderen.be/nieuws/vernieuwde-ronde-van-vlaanderenstraat-eert-helden-van-de-ronde

van Bedaf, A. (2012). *Topsportevenementen als aanjager voor de sportparticipatie: Verkennend onderzoek naar de doelen, interventies, en effecten van Le Grand Départ 2010, het WK Tafeltennis 2011 en de World Open Squash 2011*. Utrecht: Mulier Instituut.

Watson, S., & Waterton, E. (2015). Themes, thoughts, reflections. In E. Waterton & S. Watson (Eds.), *The Palgrave companion of contemporary heritage research* (pp. 524–529). London: Palgrave Macmillan.

Weed, M., Coren, E., & Fiore, J. (2009). *A systematic review of the evidence base for developing a physical activity and health legacy from the London 2012 Olympic and Paralympic Games*. Canterbury: Department of Health and Sport, Physical Education and Activity Research.

Wright, R. K. (2012). Stadia, identity and belonging: Stirring the sleeping giants of sports tourism. In R. Shipway & A. Fyall (Eds.), *International sports events: Impacts, experiences and identities* (pp. 195–207). Oxon: Routledge.

Yin, R. K. (2009). *Case study research: Design and methods* (4th ed.). London: Sage.

Ziakas, V. (2015). For the benefit of all? Developing a critical perspective in mega-event leverage. *Leisure Studies*, *34*(6), 689–702.

Ziakas, V., & Boukas, N. (2012). A neglected legacy. *International Journal of Event and Festival Management*, *3*(3), 292–316.

Serious about leisure, serious about destinations: mountain bikers and destination attractiveness

Julie Moularde and Adam Weaver

ABSTRACT
Despite the relevance of the concept of serious leisure to the study of certain types of sports participants, little is known about the relevance of the serious leisure framework to the study of destination preferences. This paper outlines the findings of a qualitative study of "serious" mountain bikers in New Zealand. In-depth interviews were used to determine the attractiveness of certain destinations to mountain bikers whose devotion to the sport conforms to the notion of serious leisure. Travel to tourism destinations helps mountains bikers pursue serious participation in mountain biking. Reciprocally, destinations are assessed by serious mountain bikers on the basis of their ability to advance participants' degree of seriousness. Therefore, this study suggests that the serious leisure framework can enhance understanding of destination preferences in sport tourism as well as provide management and marketing professionals with insight regarding destination development and promotional strategies. Implications for practitioners are discussed. This paper aims to make a scholarly contribution by exploring specific connections amongst serious leisure, sport tourist behaviour and destination preference.

Introduction

The consumption of tourism and sport can embody symbols, convey meanings and provide a frame for identity making (Arnould & Thompson, 2005; Higham & Hinch, 2009; Humphreys, 2011). This paper examines the relationship between mountain bikers (in particular, those who are serious leisure participants) and the appeal of mountain biking destinations. It proposes that serious leisure and destination attractiveness are interwoven concepts: the characteristics of destinations facilitate the pursuit of serious leisure and, in turn, destination image is shaped by the capacity of destinations to strengthen the commitment of serious leisure participants. A two-way relationship is explored.

This study addresses research gaps in sport tourism and tourist behaviour, and it aims to advance understanding of active sport tourists. It also contributes to knowledge about mountain biking tourism, a small but growing market segment (TNZ, 2014) and provides a better understanding of mountain bikers' preferences. Sport tourism is considered a niche market but sports-related travel will continue to grow and diversify (Higham, 2005;

Higham & Hinch, 2009) and serve as a path to economic development (Green & Chalip, 1998; Hinch & Higham, 2011). Various sports-related activities – and the travel associated with them – reflect global consumer culture and have become a means to shape personal identity and obtain authentic experiences. Due in part to sport, place-based competition for visitors and events is intense in the global marketplace (Filo, Chen, King, & Funk, 2011; Higham & Hinch, 2009) and decision makers need to understand destination attractiveness and tourist involvement to achieve sustainable destination development.

In tourism studies, sustainable development is interpreted as economic, ecological and human sustainability while focusing on the long-term viability of tourism, namely competitiveness (Butler, 1999). It is development that preserves the capacity and quality of natural and human resources in a destination (Liu, 2003). Although sustainability is a complex concept, sustainable development is often reduced to environmental concerns (Butler, 1999) and "the sustainable tourism literature has overwhelmingly focused on the preservation and conservation of natural resources" (Liu, 2003, p. 463). While natural resources are at the core of mountain biking tourism, it is restrictive to limit the discussion of sustainability to environmental factors. In a competitive economic environment, maintaining tourism demand is critical to developing tourism sustainably (Liu, 2003). Thus, understanding sport consumer behaviour and preferences is essential to plan natural and human resource use, ensure economic viability and define appropriate policies.

Following this introduction, the paper is divided into four sections. The literature review introduces relevant definitions and discusses pertinent academic work. A brief methodology follows. The findings are organised around the bi-directional nature of this research, first showing the relevance of tourism destinations for mountain bikers as serious leisure participants and then describing the relevance of the serious leisure framework in understanding destination attractiveness. The conclusion includes recommendations for practitioners for sustaining the interest of a subculture with specific values and preferences.

Literature review

Mountain biking tourism

In special interest tourism, a particular activity is at the core of the decision-making process and travel experience (Weiler & Hall, 1992). Sport tourism is an example of special interest tourism (Higham, 2005) for which sports involvement is a primary travel purpose and a determining factor in destination choice (Gibson, 2006). Sport tourism research has mostly focused on events and spectatorship with limited attention given to active sport tourism (Weed, 2014), particularly recreational participation (Novelli, 2005). Cycling tourism has received growing attention as planners and policy-makers recognise its economic potential and develop supporting infrastructure (Kulczycki & Halpenny, 2014; Lamont, 2009). It encompasses any holiday where cycling is perceived as an integral part of the tourist experience (Douglas, Douglas, & Derrett, 2001). However, there is a broader heterogeneity within that group based on trip length, purpose, cycling activities and involvement with the sport (Douglas et al., 2001; Lamont, 2009).

Mountain biking is "the sport of riding durable bikes with special riding gear off-road, usually over rough terrain along narrow trails that wind through forests, mountains, deserts or fields" (Siderelis, Naber, & Leung, 2010, p. 574). It is a sport which requires technical skills and is sometimes practiced in remote, unfamiliar terrain (Davidson & Stebbins, 2011; Taylor, 2010). Based on the characteristics of cycling tourism (Lamont, 2009) and special interest tourism (Gibson, 2006), mountain bike tourism is defined in this study as:

> Trips of at least 24 hours away from a person's home environment for which active participation in mountain biking for recreational purposes is the primary motivation and determining factor in destination choice.

Since its origin in the 1970s, mountain biking has become one of the most popular sports worldwide. Over 8.5 million Americans participated in mountain biking in 2013 (Outdoor Foundation, 2014) and the industry contributed $26 billion to the US economy in 2008 (Taylor, 2010). Purpose-built mountain biking sites are increasing participation and travel (Taylor, 2010). Eighty percent of American mountain bikers take at least one overnight trip annually for the main purpose of mountain biking (People for Bikes, 2014). Over half of the visitors in Oregon cited mountain biking as their primary motivation and another quarter included it as one of their main motivations (Runyan, 2012). In Whistler, British Columbia, Canada, total visitor spending "attributable to mountain biking exceeded $34.3 million over the period June 4 to September 17, 2006" (MBTA, 2006). Mountain biking is, by many measures, a fast-growing and money-generating tourism niche.

A consumer behaviour focus

Most existing sport tourism research has focused on sport as a purpose rather than as a behaviour (Weed & Bull, 2012) and demonstrated "a tendency to examine the activity itself rather than the meanings, norms and values of the individual undertaking the activity" (Gibson, 2006, p. 33). Cycling tourism research is sparse and has mostly focused on cycle touring; it provides limited understanding of concepts such as motivation, involvement, behaviour and the destination preferences of niche segments such as mountain bikers.

Sport tourism researchers are being encouraged to move beyond models of participation versus non-participation and integrate concepts from wider fields of literature by investigating consumption patterns (Gibson, 2006; Green & Jones, 2005; Weed, 2014). The process of consumption in tourism involves needs, goals, motivations, evaluations, behavioural intentions, participation and post-purchase appraisals (Solomon, Russell-Bennett, & Previte, 2013). During the evaluation process, preferences emerge based on destination attractiveness. Destination attractiveness "reflects the feelings, beliefs and opinions that an individual has about a destination's perceived ability to provide satisfaction in relation to his or her special vacation needs" (Hu & Ritchie, 1993, p. 25). There is a synergy between destination and activity in sport tourism (Filo et al., 2011); destinations provide opportunities for the desired experiences to occur.

Serious leisure

Serious leisure has been used to study involvement in sports (Davidson & Stebbins, 2011; Higham & Hinch, 2009). Leisure, the pursuit of freely chosen interests, is often described as the direct opposite of work, and it is not always readily associated with "seriousness" (Green & Jones, 2005). However, for many individuals, leisure activities involve obligations, commitment and responsibilities (Gibson, 2006). The concept of serious leisure was developed by Robert Stebbins in the 1970s to further the understanding of "complex forms of leisure that are central to participants' identities and lifestyles" (Scott, 2012, p. 366).

On a continuum from casual to serious, six distinctive characteristics are used to identify serious leisure participants (Green & Jones, 2005):

1. Perseverance of participation in the face of constraints
2. Progression throughout a long-term career involving contingencies, turning points and achievements
3. Significant personal effort, such as skills and knowledge, is utilised to practice the activity and gained through long-term effort from specialised media, peers and tutors
4. Durable benefits for the participants such as self-esteem, self-actualisation and social interactions
5. A unique ethos exists within the activity; a subculture, a form of social organisation among individuals sharing common interests and identifiable through their norms, values, behaviour and language
6. Social identification with the activity linked to a sense of belonging

Mountain bikers fit the serious leisure profile with their "perseverance, personal effort, and a strong identification with mountain biking and its social scene" (Taylor, 2010, p. 263). However, only a few attempts have been made to integrate the concept of serious leisure into the study of tourism (Davidson & Stebbins, 2011; Green & Jones, 2005; Higham & Hinch, 2009). More specifically, reciprocal connections between the concepts of serious leisure and destination attractiveness have not been explored.

Serious leisure: tourism experiences and destinations

The serious leisure concept is helpful in conceptualising special interest tourism (Weiler & Hall, 1992) and sport tourism (Gibson, 2006). Serious leisure and travel to participate in serious leisure have been found to be mutually reinforcing; "serious leisure finds an outlet in sport tourism, whilst sport tourism encourages serious leisure" (Green & Jones, 2005, p. 43). Green and Jones (2005) also note that "tourism may become part of the unique ethos of the serious leisure participant" (p. 169). They believe that the extension of serious leisure to tourism helps "form stronger, more valued social identities for those individuals" (p. 169).

Furthermore, the tourism experience can be enhanced if it provides an opportunity to revel in a subculture (Green & Chalip, 1998). A key element of serious leisure is the interpersonal dimension of the activity through social identities and a shared ethos. Sport tourists are highly concerned with aligning themselves with the unique ethos of their sport, a normative system shared by individuals of a specific subculture (Gibson, 2006). Participants adhere to, and internalise, group norms and values (Weed & Bull, 2012) to set themselves apart from casual participants and non-participants (Hagen, 2013). It provides them with a sense of belonging, develops social connections and helps enhance self-esteem (Green & Jones, 2005). Indeed, many sports have a tradition of associated socialisation experiences such as the *après* when skiing and the nineteenth hole when golfing (Weed & Bull, 2012). Sports such as golf and skiing are individual by nature but were found to be highly influenced by subcultures (Humphreys, 2011) which provide knowledge about destinations and their attributes as well as shape preferences (Weed & Bull, 2012). Similarly, Hagen (2013) uncovers evidence of a mountain biking subculture, which influences mountain bikers' tourism consumption.

In sport tourism, travel decisions are made with the sport in mind (Weed & Bull, 2012); destinations are preferred for the experiences they enable (Filo et al., 2011). Higham (2005) explains that sport tourists evaluate destinations through specialised knowledge and information search. Humphreys (2011) acknowledges the existence of golf subcultures and their role in influencing golf destination selection; destinations are evaluated in the subculture and ascribed subcultural capital which can be transferred to individuals visiting these destinations. Acquired subcultural capital allows individuals to further their leisure career, obtain social recognition within the subculture and reinforce their commitment to the sport (Gibson, 2006; Humphreys, 2011). The influence of subcultures on destination preference is apparent when individuals collect places or plan to visit notable destinations and so-called "sport meccas" (Higham, 2005; Weed & Bull, 2012). The subcultural capital attached to destinations is thus a symbol of, and influences, their attractiveness to sport tourists (Filo et al., 2011).

This research aims to understand the relationship between the pursuit of serious leisure by mountain bikers and the attractiveness of mountain biking destinations. There is a two-way relationship between serious leisure participants and sport tourism destinations. Sport tourists look to further their serious leisure participant characteristics through tourism; in turn, sport tourism destination preferences are influenced by serious leisure. Thus, it is argued that the six characteristics of serious leisure can be used as a framework to understand sport tourism consumption as well as the attractiveness of sport tourism destinations.

Methodology

This study focuses on recreational mountain bikers who had previously travelled, and plan to do so again, for the primary purpose of mountain biking. They provided information-rich cases of sport-related travel and destination choices. Historically, tourism research has relied on quantitative methods (Jennings, 2010). However, qualitative approaches are gaining in popularity in tourism studies. Qualitative methods can provide greater insight into the cultural and social dimensions of tourism (Phillimore & Goodson, 2004) and offer an opportunity to explore personal meanings (Silverman, 2013). This research was grounded in interpretivism and looked to understand the emotional context of actions and experiences (Jennings, 2010). The goal was to investigate not only what is happening but also how and why social realities are produced and sustained through social processes (Silverman, 2013).

Semi-structured interviews permitted respondents to describe what was meaningful to them. The aim of the interviews was to encourage respondents to share their experiences of, and preferences for, destinations as well as the role mountain biking plays in their everyday life, travel motivations and destination evaluations. The interview guide included flexible open-ended questions, leaving the interviewer free to ask for clarification, additional details or pursue new issues as they arose in conversation (Jennings, 2010). A projective exercise using ten images of mountain bikers in various settings was used during the interviews; the locations depicted were not disclosed to the respondents. In this article, the numbered pictures (#1 to #10) refer to those used in the projective exercise. The interview guide was designed to access respondents' thoughts and feelings about mountain biking tourism, destinations and the sport in general and to understand underlying values and preferences.

Only active mountain bikers who had previously travelled for the main purpose of mountain biking were interviewed. Respondents were recruited through snowball sampling from formal and informal mountain biking groups and clubs in Wellington, New Zealand. Several were foreigners or had lived abroad for extended periods of time, adding an international dimension to the sample. A stratified strategy was used to capture variations as well as shared dimensions. Stratified purposeful sampling is recommended in qualitative research to maximise opportunities to compare and contrast findings within the sample (Patton, 2002). This means that, as the interviews unfolded, the researcher aimed to include male and female respondents from different age groups who varied in terms of their experience and skill level. A total of 25 interviews were completed.

The combination of projective techniques and open-ended questions encouraged respondents to evaluate and communicate their explicit and implicit perceptions. It was expected that the respondents' responses could be interpreted at both the literal and symbolic levels (Dann, 1996). During the analysis, important dimensions, constructs and attributes were extracted from the data (Jenkins, 1999). Later, through interpretation, patterns and themes were identified, inferences made and explanations offered (Patton, 2002).

The respondents

Respondents were interviewed between 4 June and 22 July 2014. Table 1 profiles the respondents and notes their gender, age, degree of experience and skill level in mountain biking, frequency of participation in the activity and frequency of travel for this purpose. The "seriousness" of each participant was confirmed by comparing each transcript back and forth with the aforementioned characteristics of serious leisure (Green & Jones, 2005). Pseudonyms are used in order to protect respondents' identities.

Findings

This research intends to demonstrate that serious leisure shapes travel decisions and destination preferences. This section systematically addresses each of the six characteristics of serious leisure (Green & Jones, 2005) as they relate to mountain bikers:

1. Perseverance of participation
2. Progression through a long-term career
3. Significant personal effort
4. Durable benefits
5. Unique ethos
6. Social identification

Table 1. Profile of respondents.

Name	Gender	Age	Years of experience	Skill level	Riding frequency (per week)	Mountain biking trips (per year)
James	M	42	21	Expert	Several times	More than 5
Celia	F	22	9	Advanced	Several times	More than 5
Laura	F	32	5	Intermediate	Several times	More than 5
Kim	F	39	14	Expert	At least once	More than 5
Kurt	M	34	11	Expert	Several times	3–5
Sam	M	40	21	Expert	Several times	3–5
Becca	F	31	10	Advanced	At least once	3–5
Tom	M	31	3.5	Advanced	Several times	3–5
Nate	M	40	23	Advanced	At least once	3–5
Olivia	F	38	9	Advanced	Several times	3–5
Megan	F	40	15	Intermediate	Several times	3–5
Lucy	F	36	5	Intermediate	At least once	3–5
Luca	M	24	13	Expert	Several times	1 or 2
Eli	M	20	5	Expert	At least once	1 or 2
Rosa	F	35	5	Advanced	Several times	More than 5
Nelson	M	31	0.5	Advanced	Several times	1 or 2
Phil	M	24	10	Advanced	At least once	3–5
Lenny	M	48	13	Expert	At least once	3–5
Abby	F	29	3	Intermediate	At least once	3–5
Kevin	M	40	16	Advanced	A few times per month	3–5
Colin	M	28	2	Advanced	Several times	3–5
Elise	F	45	17	Advanced	At least once	More than 5
Steve	M	23	3	Advanced	At least once	1 or 2
Alex	M	31	3	Advanced	A few times per month	1 or 2
Zoe	F	49	3	Intermediate	At least once	3–5

For each characteristic, two topics are addressed: (1) serious leisure can, for mountain bikers, be supported or enhanced by travel to mountain biking destinations and (2) destinations facilitating the pursuit of serious leisure are preferred by serious mountain bikers.

Perseverance of participation

Evidence of perseverance in the face of constraints can vary from finding the necessary time to overcoming injuries. In the case of sport tourists, perseverance can be demonstrated in the face of travel constraints (Green & Jones, 2005). The respondents feel pride and increased self-esteem when travelling for the purpose of mountain biking; it sets them apart from non-participants and casual participants.

> You're standing on some pass or some saddle and you're like "oh my goodness, here I am, and I'm riding with my bike and not like everyone else taking the gondola", you know, it's great. (Rosa)

Respondents' enthusiasm is not hindered by remoteness and adversity; they are willing to persevere through these constraints.

> I mean if the trails are good enough, ... particularly if I haven't ridden there before, like the distance or the inaccessibility is less relevant. (Kurt)

Respondents enjoyed travelling for the purpose of mountain biking and wanted to visit many different destinations. As serious mountains bikers, they confirm their perseverance through their ability and willingness to travel to participate in mountain biking.

When studying the destination preferences of respondents, it was apparent that the likelihood of having to persevere led to increased destination attractiveness. Less-than-perfect experiences did not deter respondents. They largely remained positive about most destinations, even when faced with adverse conditions. In the interviews, respondents related experiences that would typically be seen as unpleasant.

> [The Queen Charlotte Track] was good, but we had some pretty terrible weather.... And I don't really have good wet weather gear so half an hour into the second day I was like a drowned rat.... But it was really good fun, it was a cool trip. (Steve)

Similarly, negative word-of-mouth rarely appeared to diminish the attractiveness of destinations for the respondents. They often questioned the source or circumstances leading to negative feedback. In general, they seemed willing to take a chance and form their own opinion.

> I've got a terrible quality of thinking if someone doesn't like somewhere it's because they weren't good enough to ride it. (Eli)

In addition, some attributes were perceived as symbolic of perseverance. The concept of adventure is subjective but common themes emerged when the respondents explained wanting to step outside of their comfort zone and routine. They enjoy visiting unfamiliar destinations where they can partake in extraordinary experiences. At the core of destination attractiveness are "those challenges and those opportunities to do stuff that you don't get to do every day" (James). Remoteness, novelty and uniqueness of natural surroundings were valued as promises of adventure and extraordinary experiences. The respondents looked for "less chartered territories" (Megan) and often avoided "manufactured experiences" (Elise).

> I love mountain regions.... They kind of convey a sense of adventure. You know on a larger scale, like, you're kinda removed from civilisation.... You're out in the wild and, yeah, it's a real adventure. (Luca)

When travelling for the purpose of mountain biking, the respondents demonstrate their willingness to persevere through constraints and thus feel that they fulfil the requirements of being serious mountain bikers. Remoteness, challenges or adverse conditions do not diminish destination attractiveness; on the contrary, they are symbols of perseverance, sought for the sense of adventure they provide.

Progression through a long-term career

Serious leisure participants progress through long-term careers involving contingencies, turning points and achievements (Gibson, 2006). Practicing the activity in specific destinations, demonstrating particular skills or engaging in particular experiences while travelling can further serious leisure careers (Davidson & Stebbins, 2011; Green & Jones, 2005; Humphreys, 2011). Through mountain biking tourism, the respondents seek challenges; they want to advance their abilities and skills but also put themselves in novel and extraordinary situations and settings to experience "something that you haven't felt before" (James).

Nate's comments are particularly relevant and show how the respondents' mountain biking careers depend on, and are affected by, mountain biking tourism in specialised destinations.

> I got bored of riding ... then I bought a different style of bike. ... Because I went to Rotorua with some of my mates, half of them ex-downhillers, and rode some of the Sesame Street tracks ... and I ended up with a spoke through the derailleur and I was just like "this is not the right bike for this stuff!" [laughs] So I came home and I went "I just need a bike that I can ride that stuff, because that was really fun". ... So that was kind of the rationale for the change. And it's invigorated me to ride again. Because I was kinda just a bit bored with the cross-country thing. So it has changed my perception of riding. (Nate)

Similar to golf tourism (Humphreys, 2011), career stages can be attained through mountain biking tourism, and destinations provide respondents with evidence of career development, reinforcing their identity as serious mountain bikers.

Certain destinations can be preferred because they are identified as necessary steps in a serious mountain biker's career. Some destinations were identified as the "norm" for any respectable mountain biker, particularly Rotorua and Queenstown in New Zealand, British Columbia (predominantly Whistler), Moab (Utah) and the European Alps. Regardless of respondents' actual knowledge of their attributes, these destinations were deemed highly attractive.

> Places like Moab and Whistler mostly have really good mountain biking for whatever level you are. ... They're pretty well-known for mountain biking at least. (Zoe)

Novelty is also a factor that influences destination attractiveness. The respondents were interested in discovering new destinations, but also in revisiting destinations where they could attempt new trails, explore new areas and face different challenges. Destinations that cannot provide novelty were often dismissed because they did not provide career advancement.

> The Heaphy track, ... I've ticked it, I don't need to go back. (Megan)

Destination attractiveness is affected by the respondents' consumption of mountain biking tourism as a means to advance towards the next stage of their leisure career. Destinations that are perceived as offering career progression, particularly destinations that symbolise career stages or enable milestones, are preferred by serious leisure participants.

Significant personal effort

Serious leisure involves significant personal effort, acquiring specific skills or knowledge in order to participate in the activity. Sport tourists often need to undertake significant efforts to prepare for travel, access destinations and participate in the activity after arrival. For mountain bikers, these can include financial costs, training to develop skills or increase fitness, time spent away from family and acquiring knowledge about trails and destinations. Many respondents were aware that their commitment and efforts would be hard for outsiders to understand.

> A lot of the people I know who don't mountain bike would think it's crazy, how much money and time goes into [mountain biking trips]. (Luca)

Respondents demonstrate significant personal effort by travelling to various destinations, indicating their dedication and involvement. In return, mountain biking tourism allows serious mountain bikers to develop their skills and gain new experiences, representative of the significant personal effort made in the name of mountain biking. These opportunities to acquire skills and knowledge, as noted by Kurt, "motivate you as a rider".

> It's variety. And it's challenge. Constant challenging, because there's just no point being able to ride all the hardest trails here and ... then what? You can wait for a new one to be built? (Kim)

When discussing destination preferences, most respondents are driven by an intrinsic motivation to improve and seek challenges: "I look to get into situations where I'm feeling challenged" (James). Destinations are deemed attractive when they offer challenges about which the respondents feel enthusiastic.

> [The riding] is different, especially the North Shore [of British Columbia]. ... It was kinda nice because it was getting me out of my comfort zone. ... I rode down Clown Shoes and I got to the wooden drop at the end ... and it just looked so dodgy. ... I went to look at it and I thought "wow, it's a lot bigger than anything I've done before" ... and I just rode it. And it was fine. ... I really enjoyed [it] because it was more technical. I mean it [scared me] but the steep things and narrow things are quite fun. (James)

Mountain biking tourism, through the challenges and opportunities offered, is usually perceived as worth investing significant effort. However, some destinations appeared unworthy if they offered inadequate challenges or delivered limited rewards; they were deemed a "wasted opportunity" (Elise).

Alternatively, too much challenge reduced destination attractiveness. The respondents compared expectations regarding the destination with perceptions of their own abilities.

> [Picture #1]. Awesome location. Obviously looks like a [female] riding one of the bike, so it seems more appealing to me because ... it's definitely something I could do in terms of the section of track they're showing. (Abby)

Mountain biking tourism is a manifestation of personal effort dedicated to the sport, and experiences in destinations are symbols of mountain bikers' commitment to mountain biking. Destinations are preferred based on the perception that the effort invested is rewarded by increased mastery. Destination attractiveness relies on the skills required to ride there, the potential skills to be gained and the challenges promised or imagined. Required training and financial or time constraints do not negatively affect destination preferences as long as rewards are worth the effort.

Durable benefits

Serious leisure provides complex benefits to participants. Respondents perceive mountain biking as a holistic experience and associate it with a range of durable outcomes such as a physical health, self-expression, self-actualisation and sense of belonging that lead to general well-being; as Becca states "I get cross if I don't [ride]". The positive outcomes of mountain biking tourism were described as richer than those derived from a simple ride. It allows the respondents to focus on their passion, escape their routines and engage in enriching experiences.

> The sort of carrying all your gear, backpacking style of riding ... out in the middle of nowhere, with overnight gear, and that's something that I love doing. ... It's sort of once or twice a year having only one responsibility and that's just to keep yourself safe. And it's kind of absolute freedom. (Kevin)

Exploring new places, overcoming new challenges and – temporarily – living a more adventurous life symbolises respondents' authentic selves.

When discussing destination preferences, destinations were preferred for the journey they offered rather than solely for their tangible riding attributes, and their capacity to provide an exhilarating sense of accomplishment. The importance of being in the middle of nowhere was a recurring theme in the interviews. As Zoe states "scenery is sort of an integral part of mountain biking". In a mountain biking destination, nature is perceived as the indispensable stage on which the activity is performed. Beautiful and peaceful settings and natural-looking trails are associated with a sense of escape.

> [Picture #7] seems like a very raw mountain bike experience, you know. The isolation, the sort of implied self-sufficiency ... you're the only person up there. ... I think it's exciting because it's a little bit scary. Because you're on your own, you're relying on yourself, and it's a challenge, and overcoming that challenge, and making it out, back to your house in one piece, with that experience on your belt, it's quite rewarding I find. (Eli)

Moreover, social interactions are central to the respondents' involvement in mountain biking and tourism provides a context for extended contact with other serious leisure participants. Respondents prefer destinations based on overarching, durable benefits linked to their emotional well-being. When Eli describes his preference for Whistler, and strong desire to visit this destination again, he does not focus purely on tangible trails or facilities. Rather, he describes a sense of personal fulfilment, a valued experience, from the association he felt with the community.

> Thinking about being ... [in Whistler] makes me ecstatic. ... I was there for one and a half days of full riding ... [and] it really just builds a longing to just return to that place and experience that again. ... [Whistler] is a mountain bike village. In summer at least. Everything is devoted to mountain biking. ... It's just ideally suited to a mountain biker. It almost seems singly purposed towards it. The drawback is that it's quite expensive. ... But you pay for the quality of the experience that you receive. (Eli)

While practical details such as number, variety and difficulty of trails in the destination as well as accommodation and other facilities were considered by the respondents, they were not enough. Mountain biking tourism destinations are preferred on the basis of the complex benefits they enable – such as escapism, sense of adventure, social interactions, personal challenge, fun and sense of accomplishment.

Unique ethos

In serious leisure, a unique ethos permeates the activity. There is a subculture, a form of social organisation among individuals sharing common interests and identifiable through their norms, values, behaviour and language (Green & Jones, 2005). Throughout the interviews, the respondents indicated their awareness of sharing common traits with members of the mountain biking community in Wellington, but also nation-wide and internationally. The respondents acknowledge that mountain bikers are identifiable through their appearance, attitudes and behaviour:

> You can recognise [mountain bikers], can't you?! I think by the clothes they wear sometimes … These [on picture #1], not that I know these people, but they look like recreational mountain bikers. Whereas this chap [picture #10], looks like a hardy chap, looks like a mountain biker. So a mountain biker is characterised by their love of the outdoors. Their love of speed and challenge. (Eli)

Knowledge of equipment, trails, particular skills and specialised jargon form the mountain biking ethos – as well as knowledge of, and experiences in, mountain biking destinations. Serious leisure participants are able to connect with other members of the subculture through the ethos when they convey this knowledge in their actions and conversations. James refers to different types of mountain bikes, even specific models, and presumes others understand the outcomes of riding these different bikes in a specific destination, the French Alps (relevant keywords are italicised in the quotation). He does not think it necessary to explain that trails in that region are steep and technical, meaning that a full-suspension bike would provide a better experience for the rider. Such descriptions can evoke clear images in the mind of serious mountain bikers based on direct (riding) or indirect (watching videos, reading articles) experiences.

> I knew I was going to the *French Alps* and … I just thought that I would be taking my *cross-country bike* [but I bought a new bike]. It was my first *full suspension* bike. It was a *Santa Cruz Bullit*, so a *7-inch travel*, do-everything bike. So I went from a titanium *hardtail* to this. So I was planning on taking my hardtail, but I had so much more fun on the Bullit. (James)

In the interviews, the respondents relied heavily on destinations and experiences as part of the ethos; they have internalised the specialised knowledge related to mountain biking and expect other serious participants to have done the same. Mountain biking tourism provides experiences which increase serious leisure participants' subcultural capital. This knowledge is essential if they want to be able to understand others and make themselves understood. Tourism can thus confirm, maintain and reinforce serious participants' belonging to the mountain biking subculture.

Furthermore, the mountain biking ethos influences knowledge of, and preferences for, destinations. In this research, social interactions shaped by the unique ethos appeared to influence the respondents' awareness of destinations as well as their preference for certain destinations. This finding is consistent with previous studies reporting that "the most influential source of information for destination choice was interpersonal relationships" (Um & Crompton, 1990, p. 434). As Megan indicates, it is "90% word-of-mouth, from people who have been before". The respondents collected information from conversations with, and stories shared by, mountain bikers in their social circles.

> I think mountain biking is a very social sport. And you meet a lot of very like-minded people and you're just constantly sharing stories … "you should go do this, and you should ride this, you should travel here". (Steve)

As a result, awareness of new or up-and-coming destinations is high among serious mountain bikers.

> You kinda know most of what's going on, or you can easily find out through someone. (Lenny)

Sharing the mountain biking ethos means that the respondents know about destinations, their features and associated experiences. Through social interactions, specialised media and personal experiences, respondents have acquired and internalised beliefs about numerous destinations, even places they had never been. This was exemplified in the interviews when respondents were able to identify most of the locations in the photographs used in the projective exercise; as Luca stated, "I reckon I could probably tell you where every photo is from". In addition to recognising various destinations, the respondents associated these locations with specific trails, riding styles and tourism experiences. Elise and Sam identified the human-made riding features characteristic of the North Shore area in British Columbia depicted in pictures #6 and #8. Although they had divergent opinions, both had internalised associations between the location and the expected experience they might find at this destination. Sam likes picture #6 "because it looks like a bit of an adventure. It's the North Shore-y, kinda BC-like with the structure". Conversely, Elise is not attracted to picture #8 because "it kinda makes me think of North Shore style riding. And that's not really … my thing".

Feedback from peers based on direct experiences appeared to be the most trustworthy source of information and heavily influenced destination preferences. Phil explains: "I would definitely talk to people who have travelled there" because "people know secret places". Information is shared and consumed within the subculture with a high degree of trust beyond regions or even countries. Unknown mountain bikers can be trusted advisors as long as they are recognised as sharing the same ethos. Word-of-mouth was sometimes sufficient for the respondents to consider a destination attractive. As serious mountain bikers, the respondents feel confident that destinations that are commended within the subculture would be worth visiting.

> I don't actually know anything [laughs]. So I haven't done any particular research on any of [those destinations], it's just all people telling me and I'm like "OK, I'll believe that." (Becca)

Having access to localised subcultural capital is also central to destination attractiveness. The respondents truly felt part of the community of mountain bikers when they had access to specialised, regional information.

> There's nothing worse than coming back and hear[ing] "oh, did you ride that trail?" and "well, we couldnt find it". … We've been in situations where you're driving around a place, trying to find this carpark to this mythical trail. So yeah, [accurate information] is important. (Laura)

Mountain biking is a solo enterprise but has a rich social dimension; the fostering of community is central to the unique ethos of the sport. The sense of belonging to the mountain biking community is heightened through travelling when individuals have the chance to immerse themselves in the subculture. Respondents tended to favour destinations where they could experience a sense of community with other mountain bikers. Rotorua was often cited as an example of a destination facilitating social interaction. Eli calls it a "great community". Amenities facilitating social interactions influenced destination attractiveness for the respondents. They looked for a variety of trails to satisfy all group members and facilities that enabled socialising.

> I just like [picture #9] because it looks like you can just like go for a really nice relaxed ride and end up in a pub somewhere. ... That's a very appealing sort of mountain bike ride. ... It's kind of part of the whole experience. ... Especially if you're going with other people, having somewhere to chill out and ... look back at the day and chat about it. (Zoe)

Therefore, the mountain biking ethos is essential to destination awareness, the source of destination knowledge and the foundation of values and beliefs that shape destination preferences.

Social identification

Serious leisure provides participants with positive social identities that are voluntarily chosen, resulting in a strong personal investment in maintaining these identities (Green & Jones, 2005). Social identification with the sport is strongly interrelated with the unique ethos. As explained above, the respondents are aware of belonging to a group and of sharing characteristics with its members. The social importance of mountain biking for them, and the resulting social identity they derive from it, can be observed in the interviews.

> It's just who I am I guess, eh? [laughs] ... I think if you're really into mountain biking it becomes who you are. (Celia)

Travel stories are how individuals learn about destinations. Sharing travel stories appears to be at the core of the respondents' social identification with the activity as well as interactions within the subculture. Travelling allows participants to collect stories and experiences to increase their subcultural capital, helping them create and maintain their social identity. As Nelson indicates, mountain biking tourism is "another point of similarity that people can relate to and talk about". Discussions between mountain bikers about particular trips or destinations include inside banter, comparison of experiences and questions about trail status.

> Sharing stories and comparing stories is good. ... Like lots of people have been to Rotorua, and when you come back from Rotorua people are like "oh, how was that?" or if you've been somewhere new, people are always interested. (Lucy)

Tom explains: "I enjoy sharing the experience of those places with people"; these interactions reinforce his involvement in the sport and subculture. As storytellers, respondents confirm their identity and strengthen their membership in the mountain biking community.

> A lot of riders are kind of [interested in travel stories] because there is a possibility that they might one day go there as well. So they're interested to see what it might be like and ... what you thought of it, and they're keen to see pictures or look at maps. (Elise)

Tourism appears to be an essential part of the respondents' mountain biking identity on a personal and social level. Adventures in new and exciting destinations, along with the challenges conquered and new skills acquired, confirm their social identities as mountain bikers and reinforce their involvement with the sport. The capacity of a destination to provide a stage for stories worth sharing influences its perceived attractiveness to the respondents.

> People are interested in telling stories and that's how you get inspired. ... So you're always looking for that shot that is going to make everyone else jealous because you're in some place that looks amazing. ... [Picture #10] looks like it would be the one that I would be talking about the most afterwards. ... It terms of feeling like you got the most reward from it. It was the most challenging. (James)

Good stories, particularly from unique or unusual destinations, are regarded as important parts of mountain bikers' social identity. It allows respondents to express their individuality within the subculture. Destination attractiveness is therefore based on the potential stories to be told.

Conclusion

The serious leisure framework

Serious leisure and sport tourism are mutually reinforcing and a number of researchers have previously suggested that serious leisure could provide a framework to study special interest tourism (Weiler & Hall, 1992) and sport tourism (Davidson & Stebbins, 2011; Gibson, 2006; Higham & Hinch, 2009). This study corroborates the opinion of Green and Jones (2005) that special interest tourism facilitates and reinforces serious leisure participation. It also demonstrates that serious leisure, broken down into its defining characteristics, is helpful in understanding destination attractiveness among serious leisure participants when examining mountain biking destinations.

Tourism was perceived as offering increased opportunities to further respondents' involvement with the sport of mountain biking by providing immersion in the activity and subculture. This research demonstrates that mountain biking tourism is a source of subcultural capital and identity confirmation, and a space where participants can revel in the subculture, as noted in the sport tourism literature (Gibson, 2006; Green & Chalip, 1998). This notion was evident when considering the importance of sharing travel stories and the social milieu at destinations. Mountain biking is a solo endeavour that simultaneously offers a connection with a wider community. Except for work that has acknowledged the relatively short history of organised mountain biking events (Davidson & Stebbins, 2011), the social dimension of mountain biking has not been fully explored.

The respondents were found to ascribe value and meanings to destinations when evaluating them. Subcultural capital appears to be attributed to tourism experiences according to the serious leisure framework. Respondents often preferred mountain biking "meccas" and destinations they perceived as mandatory for authentic mountain bikers; they strived to collect places, sought variety and novelty with the goal of furthering their careers, thus testing and gaining skills. An outdoor pursuit such as mountain biking offers a means of confronting and overcoming the challenges presented by the activity itself as well as the environs (Davidson & Stebbins, 2011).

Visiting and discussing mountain biking tourism destinations also provides respondents with a sense of belonging and social connectedness. It confirms and strengthens their social identity and membership in the subculture, as seen in Humphreys (2011) and Weed and Bull (2012). The meanings and values ascribed to destinations according to the serious leisure characteristics convey the destination preferences of serious mountain bikers. In addition, destination attractiveness can be explained through the destination's ability to assist serious leisure participants in maintaining, demonstrating or increasing their level of involvement with the sport. Serious leisure can be seen as occurring within a self-sustaining system that is oriented around places and people. It is suggested that destinations targeting serious leisure participants should consider the serious leisure framework when planning development and marketing strategies.

Implications for destinations

As discussed in the introduction, maintaining adequate tourism demand is an essential, if often overlooked, aspect of achieving the sustainability of sport tourism destinations in a competitive market. As Liu (2003) suggests, demand management is critical in sustainable development to prevent unwanted and unexpected demand fluctuations. In this context, understanding "the motivations, preferences and perceptions of tourists" is crucial as they determine destinations' "relative value in the marketplace" (Liu, 2003, p. 463). In this study, the six characteristics that underpin the concept of serious leisure and their connection to the notion of destination attractiveness demonstrate that the sustainability of sport tourism destinations involves tapping into the desires and ambitions of serious leisure participants.

Addressing matters related to tourist demand could fortuitously direct needed attention towards the "main" pillars of sustainability. The strong predilection for beautiful scenery, untouched landscapes and raw trails would most likely lead mountain bikers to prefer, and therefore share more stories about, destinations in pristine natural settings. In addition, serious mountain bikers are attracted to destinations with a strong sense of community which could encourage a consideration of the more interpersonal dimensions of tourism development, especially those which relate to host communities. Some recommendations are provided for sport destinations targeting mountain bikers or possibly other types of serious leisure participants with similar behaviour.

Attributes of destinations are perceived according to the tourist experiences enabled. Since tourists are looking to reinforce their serious leisure characteristics, it is important to relate a destination's attributes to these characteristics and relevant personal values. This view is consistent with Ho, Liao, Huang, and Chen (2015) who recommend that product characteristics should be linked to end-states desired by tourists. Interpretation of destination attributes according to the serious leisure framework can help destination managers and marketers create sustainable destinations by creating, maintaining and promoting the attractiveness of the destination. For example, that serious mountain bikers strive for adventure and are willing to spend time and money accessing destinations should support the development of more remote destinations.

Therefore, it is suggested that serious leisure should be considered as a basis for market segmentation because personal involvement in an activity influences mountain bikers' motivations and preferences. Although skill level can be partially related to degree of seriousness, this study shows that individuals can be highly serious – thus more likely to travel frequently, for long periods of time to visit distant destinations – while not referring to themselves as experts or even advanced riders. This should be taken into consideration when creating advertising campaigns and targeted promotions. It confirms the suggestion from Ritchie, Tkaczynski, and Faulks (2010) that tourists should be segmented according to their enduring involvement and/or their travel motivations.

Involvement in the mountain biking subculture strongly influenced destination evaluation and preference (e.g. travel stories as information sources and destination characteristics facilitating valued social interactions) for all respondents. This finding is consistent with Novelli (2005) who suggests that social influence is paramount in special interest tourism. It also confirms that subcultures – through ethos and identities – generate strong social influence among serious sports participants, even in individual sports such as mountain biking (Bricker & Kerstetter, 2000; Humphreys, 2011; Weed & Bull, 2012).

Word-of-mouth, either face-to-face or through social media, either from friends or from members of formal or informal communities, remains the primary source of knowledge for serious mountain bikers. Attracting riders through festivals, trail opening ceremonies, races or other special events has the potential of getting the "buzz" started for new and emerging destinations. Moreover, content easily shared online, particularly photographs and videos, needs to be a priority for marketers. Social media are at the core of the ethos because they (1) enable on-going social interaction with members of the subculture, (2) facilitate the diffusion of word-of-mouth about destinations and (3) allow individuals to access and share third-party content (from marketers, journalists and professional riders).

Trails and riding opportunities are obviously at the core of mountain bikers' evaluations of destinations. With riders looking for diversity and the right challenge, managers and planners should develop a variety of trails and access points. Destinations can potentially offer a wide range of riding types and levels (e.g. Queenstown and Rotorua in New Zealand). However, if smaller destinations cannot provide such a range, collaborative marketing can help to promote and group a cluster of riding opportunities, therefore enhancing competitiveness vis-à-vis other regions (Freeman & Thomlinson, 2014). Mountain bikers also look for novelty and are interested in discovering new places and enjoying new experiences. In order to satisfy their desire to collect places while encouraging repeat visits, multiple access points should be developed where possible and continuous upgrades should be made to boost novelty and variety.

As indicated in the study, trails were not always the sole motivation of, or attributes sought by, respondents. Mountain bikers often live in areas where they are able to practice the sport close to home; therefore, the simple act of riding a bike is not the sole purpose of travelling. They are looking for intensive and extensive time riding, career stage development and immersion in the subculture; they seek identity-constructing experiences. Managers and planners should provide spaces to facilitate social interactions among mountain bikers. Trails and terrain are the foundation of destinations but there are opportunities to develop mountain biking destinations through the making and marketing of complementary experiences (Freeman & Thomlinson, 2014).

References

Arnould, E. J., & Thompson, C. J. (2005). Consumer culture theory (CCT): Twenty years of research. *Journal of Consumer Research*, *31*(4), 868–882.

Bricker, K. S., & Kerstetter, D. L. (2000). Level of specialization and place attachment: An exploratory study of whitewater recreationists. *Leisure Sciences*, *22*(4), 233–257.

Butler, R. W. (1999). Sustainable tourism: A state-of-the-art review. *Tourism Geographies*, *1*(1), 7–25.

Dann, G. M. (1996). Tourists' images of a destination: An alternative analysis. *Journal of Travel & Tourism Marketing, 5*(1–2), 41–55.

Davidson, L., & Stebbins, R. (2011). *Serious leisure and nature: Sustainable consumption in the outdoors.* New York: Palgrave Macmillan.

Douglas, N., Douglas, N., & Derrett, R. (Eds.). (2001). *Special interest tourism: Context and cases.* New York: John Wiley & Sons Australia.

Filo, K., Chen, N., King, C., & Funk, D. C. (2011). Sport tourists' involvement with a destination: A stage-based examination. *Journal of Hospitality & Tourism Research, 37*(1), 100–124.

Freeman, R., & Thomlinson, E. (2014). Mountain bike tourism and community development in British Columbia: Critical success factors for the future. *Tourism Review International, 18*(1), 9–22.

Gibson, H. J. (2006). *Sport tourism: Concepts and theories.* London: Routledge.

Green, B. C., & Chalip, L. (1998). Sport tourism as the celebration of subculture. *Annals of Tourism Research, 25*(2), 275–291.

Green, B. C., & Jones, I. (2005). Serious leisure, social identity and sport tourism. *Sport in Society, 8*(2), 164–181.

Hagen, S. (2013). *The downhill mountain bike subculture in New Zealand* (Unpublished Master's Thesis). University of Otago.

Higham, J. (Ed.). (2005). *Sport tourism destinations: Issues, opportunities and analysis.* Amsterdam: Butterworth-Heinemann.

Higham, J., & Hinch, T. (2009). *Sport and tourism: Globalization, mobility and identity.* Amsterdam: Butterworth-Heinemann.

Hinch, T., & Higham, J. (2011). *Sport tourism development* (2nd ed.). Bristol: Channel View Publications.

Ho, C. I., Liao, T. Y., Huang, S. C., & Chen, H. M. (2015). Beyond environmental concerns: Using means–end chains to explore the personal psychological values and motivations of leisure/recreational cyclists. *Journal of Sustainable Tourism, 23*(2), 234–254.

Hu, Y., & Ritchie, J. B. (1993). Measuring destination attractiveness: A contextual approach. *Journal of Travel Research, 32*(2), 25–34.

Humphreys, C. (2011). Who cares where I play? Linking reputation with the golfing capital and the implication for golf destinations. *Journal of Sport & Tourism, 16*(2), 105–128.

Jenkins, O. H. (1999). Understanding and measuring tourist destination images. *International Journal of Tourism Research, 1*(1), 1–15.

Jennings, G. (2010). *Tourism research* (2nd ed.). Milton, Queensland: John Wiley & Sons.

Kulczycki, C., & Halpenny, E. A. (2014). Sport cycling tourists' setting preferences, appraisals and attachments. *Journal of Sport & Tourism, 19*(2), 169–197.

Lamont, M. (2009). Reinventing the wheel: A definitional discussion of bicycle tourism. *Journal of Sport & Tourism, 14*(1), 5–23.

Liu, Z. (2003). Sustainable tourism development: A critique. *Journal of Sustainable Tourism, 11*(6), 459–475.

MBTA, Mountain Bike Tourism Association. (2006). *Sea-to-sky mountain biking economic impact study – Whistler report.* Vancouver, BC: Mountain Bike Tourism Association.

Novelli, M. (Ed.). (2005). *Niche tourism: contemporary issues, trends and cases.* Amsterdam: Butterworth-Heinemann.

Outdoor Foundation. (2014). *Outdoor recreation participation report 2014.* Washington, DC: Outdoor Foundation.

Patton, M. Q. (2002). *Qualitative research and evaluation methods.* Thousand Oaks, CA: Sage.

People for Bikes. (2014). *Economic benefits of the bicycling industry and tourism.* Retrieved July 15, 2014, from http://www.peopleforbikes.org/statistics/category/economic-statistics#economic-benefits-of-the-bicycling-industry-and-tourism

Phillimore, J., & Goodson, L. (Eds.). (2004). *Qualitative research in tourism: Ontologies, epistemologies and methodologies.* New York: Routledge.

Ritchie, B. W., Tkaczynski, A., & Faulks, P. (2010). Understanding the motivation and travel behavior of cycle tourists using involvement profiles. *Journal of Travel & Tourism Marketing, 27*(4), 409–425.

Runyan, D. (2012). *The economic significance of bicycle-related travel in Oregon.* Oregon: Travel Oregon.

Scott, D. (2012). Serious leisure and recreation specialization: An uneasy marriage. *Leisure Sciences, 34*(4), 366–371.

Siderelis, C., Naber, M., & Leung, Y.-F. (2010). The influence of site design and resource conditions on outdoor recreation demand: A mountain biking case study. *Journal of Leisure Research, 42*(4), 573–590.

Silverman, D. (2013). *Doing qualitative research: A practical handbook.* Thousand Oaks, CA: Sage.

Solomon, M. R., Russell-Bennett, R., & Previte, J. (2013). *Consumer behaviour: Buying, having, being.* Australia: Pearson Australia Group.

Taylor, S. (2010). 'Extending the dream machine': Understanding people's participation in mountain biking. *Annals of Leisure Research, 13*(1–2), 259–281.

TNZ, Tourism New Zealand (2014, July 1). Cycling and mountain biking – 'naturally breathtaking'. Retrieved September 24, 2014, from http://www.tourismnewzealand.com/sector-marketing/special-interest/cycling-and-mountain-biking/

Um, S., & Crompton, J. L. (1990). Attitude determinants in tourism destination choice. *Annals of Tourism Research, 17*(3), 432–448.

Weed, M. (2014). After 20 years, what are the big questions for sports tourism research? *Journal of Sport & Tourism, 19*(1), 1–4.

Weed, M., & Bull, C. (2012). *Sports tourism: Participants, policy and providers* (2nd ed.). Oxford: Elsevier.

Weiler, B., & Hall, C. M. (1992). *Special interest tourism.* New York: Belhaven Press.

Sports tourism development and destination sustainability: the case of the coastal area of the Aveiro region, Portugal

Maria João Carneiro, Zélia Breda and Catarina Cordeiro

ABSTRACT

There is increasing awareness of the importance of sustainability in sports tourism. Research in this field is nevertheless still limited and is mostly confined to specific areas such as mega-events. The adoption of sustainable management practices by companies offering sports tourism products has been widely neglected. This paper aims to extend previous research by analysing the adoption of sustainable management practices by small and medium enterprises offering sports tourism products, specifically across five sustainability dimensions – economic, sociocultural, environmental, policy, and technological. The methodological approach used in this study is qualitative in nature. A series of 15 face-to-face semi-structured interviews were conducted with company managers offering sports tourism activities in the coastal area of the Aveiro region in the centre of Portugal. The discourses were content-analysed and the findings reveal that these companies have already adopted certain sustainability management practices in the analysed dimensions. They are likely to hire local people, to establish some partnerships and work with other companies (e.g. accommodation providers), to limit the number of participants in each group in order to avoid exceeding the carrying capacity, to involve local communities to some extent, and to use biodegradable products (e.g. fuels). Nonetheless, much still has to be done to increase their sustainable practices. It is important, among other features, to promote the use of a wider variety of environmental and technological practices and to increase awareness both of the relevance of promoting linkages and of avoiding leakages, namely by buying local products. Moreover, it is important to take advantage of the strong potential of sports tourism concerning social cohesion. The paper also identifies a large range of sustainable management practices, covering the five aforementioned sustainability dimensions, which may be useful to the managers of sports tourism companies and for the sustainable development of sports tourism destinations.

1. Introduction

It is widely recognised that sports tourism may play a crucial role in the development of tourism destinations (Briedenhann, 2011; Fredline, 2005). However, it is also known that tourism development is a complex process, and that sports tourism development can also generate negative impacts on tourism destinations, including on their communities (Fredline, 2005; Orams, 2005). It is, therefore, of utmost importance to understand the practices that ensure the sustainable development of sports tourism. Coastal destinations are particularly suited to sports tourism due to their physical characteristics, offering diverse natural assets to visitors, specifically water resources – e.g. sea, rivers, lagoons. Due to their specificities, however, these are also very fragile areas, where the adoption of sustainability principles assumes high relevance.

There is growing interest in the sustainability of sports tourism (Gibson, Kaplanidou, & Kang, 2012; Ma, Egan, Rotherham, & Ma, 2011), although much research in this field is confined to assessing tourism impacts and to specific topics, such as mega-events (Ma et al., 2011; Ziakas & Boukas, 2012), or to specific activities, such as golf or surfing (Markwick, 2000; Ponting & O'Brien, 2014). Moreover, such studies are associated with the most traditional dimensions of sustainability – economic, sociocultural, and environmental (Andersson, Armbrecht, & Lundberg, 2015; Fernández & Sánchez Rivero, 2009; Fredline, 2005; Gibson et al., 2012; Kožić & Mikulić, 2014) – and ignore other important dimensions such as technological and policy factors. Recognising the importance of sustainability in the field of tourism, there have also been several attempts to identify sets of indicators of sustainable tourism development (Choi & Sirakaya, 2006; Kožić & Mikulić, 2014; Marzo-Navarro, Pedraja-Iglesias, & Vinzón, 2015; Miller, 2001; Roberts & Tribe, 2008; Tanguay, Rajaonson, & Therrien, 2013; World Tourism Organization, 2004). There is limited research on practices of tourism companies designed to ensure sustainability. Moreover, much of the research assessing the sustainable practices adopted by tourism companies (Alonso-Almeida, Bagur-Femenias, Llach, & Perramon, 2015; Bagur-Femenías, Martí, & Rocafort, 2015; Bonilla-Priego, Font, & Pacheco-Olivares, 2014; Mihalič, Žabkar, & Cvelbar, 2012; Pérez & del Bosque, 2014; Roberts & Tribe, 2008; Ruiz-Molina, Gil-Saura, & Moliner-Velázquez, 2010; Wickham & Lehman, 2015) refers to tourism firms in general, or to specific types of business such as hotels. Research on the practices of companies that supply sports tourism products has been largely neglected. Through an in-depth case study of managers of sports tourism companies, the present paper aims to fill this gap by providing a global perspective of practices that such companies may adopt to ensure the sustainable development of sports tourism products, considering the several relevant dimensions of sustainability. It is also intended to contribute to a better understanding of how these practices may be implemented.

First, a literature review on the relevance of sports tourism in the development of coastal areas is carried out. This is followed by a discussion on the concept and dimensions of sustainability in the context of tourism, and more specifically sports tourism, with the aim of providing a global perspective on the practices that may be adopted by companies developing sports tourism products. An empirical study is carried out on a Portuguese coastal area – the coastal area of the Aveiro region – targeting the practices implemented by small and medium enterprises (SMEs) that supply sports tourism products in that geographical area. Results are discussed and, finally, conclusions are drawn on the adoption of these practices, and some implications that may help tourism entrepreneurs to develop more sustainable sports tourism products are presented.

2. The role of sports tourism in the development of coastal areas

Coastal areas are unique places of great environmental importance and rich in terms of cultural practices and traditional pastimes, particularly related to fishing. Therefore, they become very desirable for tourist activities. Although a coastal area can be roughly defined as a transition zone between the mainland and the sea (Sorensen & McCreary, 1990), its definition is not straightforward, as it varies depending on the author and often depends on the context in which it is used (Martins, 1998). However, taking into account several perspectives, it can be considered as the contact area between the marine and the terrestrial zone, covering coastal and adjacent environments, including areas that have influence on the coast (even if located far away from it), and resources such as rivers, beaches, coastal plains, lagoons, among others (Albuquerque, 2013).

Recently, there has been significant growth in the pursuit of water-based experiences as forms of sport, leisure, recreation, and tourism (Jennings, 2006). Coastal areas have great potential for their development, as well as for the expansion of other sports tourism activities (Tsartas, 2004). Being nature-based destinations, close contact with nature, and the escape from the daily routine and stress of the city are major attractions, allowing relaxation and enjoyment of the scenic landscape.

Interest in coastal areas is not new; they have long been popular tourism destinations for visitors. Their natural beauty, cultural wealth, and great diversity of landscape make them preferred destinations for many holidaymakers, offering a wide range of facilities and activities for those who seek recreation (European Commission [EC], n.d.a). These areas are a huge asset for tourism, but, in turn, it puts a strain on local ecosystems. Traditional seaside resort destinations, associated with the declining '3S' (sun, sea, and sand) model, are facing severe pressure on their natural, cultural, and socio-economic environments. Thus, the challenge for coastal areas is to use their potential sustainably while providing a major source of development.

The growing trend for the design of alternative tourism products and activities therefore comes as no surprise, with the potential to stimulate sustainable local and regional development. Nowadays, tourists have higher expectations, demanding a wide variety of associated leisure activities and experiences, including sports, culture, and natural attractions (Centre for Industrial Studies & Touring Servizi, 2008). These changes on the demand side require reaction and adaptation on the part of destinations. The sector should develop new products that promote the attractiveness and accessibility of coastal resources through innovative activities.

The tourism development potential that outdoor sports activities offer is high. Since they are very much dependent on the environmental quality of the destinations, integrating biodiversity conservation practices into companies' management systems can become a positive force for sustainability (Hall, 2005). Although sports tourism activities are mainly provided by small-sized companies, they positively affect growth and employment dynamics at the local level, sometimes contributing to the revitalisation of local economies by absorbing workers from declining industries (Centre for Industrial Studies & Touring Servizi, 2008). Sports tourism can also influence geographical and seasonal redistribution of visitor flows, allowing the extension of the high season (Francis & Murphy, 2005).

However, the increase in coastal tourism flows raises concerns about potentially negative impacts on local/regional development from an environmental, economic, and social point of view (the so-called 'triple bottom line'). Tourism in coastal areas can also increase pressure on these fragile environments (Vera Rebollo & Ivars Baidal, 2004). In particular, the natural ecosystems that support coastal areas can experience degradation, higher water use, increased waste generation, and accumulated emissions from air, road, and sea transport in peak seasons (EC, n.d.a). It can also create competition for space, leading to conflicts with traditional activities (such as fishing and agriculture), and cause large seasonal variations in population and employment (Centre for Industrial Studies & Touring Servizi, 2008). There is a need to recognise the negative effects often associated with tourism in coastal areas. A sustainable approach to tourism development may minimise damage and maximise the benefits for this kind of destination.

3. Global perspective on sports tourism sustainable development

The growing awareness of the negative impacts of development has motivated the search for sustainable forms of development. Sustainable development was described by the World Commission on Environment and Development (WCED), in the *Our common future* report, as development that 'meets the needs of the present without compromising the ability of future generations to meet their own needs' (WCED, 1987, p. 43). This definition has become very popular in both political and academic discourses (Choi & Sirakaya, 2006), replacing old development paradigms exclusively centred on economic growth (Eusébio & Figueiredo, 2014; Hunter, 1997). The term was quickly accepted and promoted by many international and national organisations, being also widely incorporated into tourism development policies and strategies (Anderson, Bakir, & Wickens, 2015), and the object of analysis in numerous academic publications. This proliferation confirms the importance of designing adequate tourism development strategies to achieve sustainability.

In the literature, there are many approaches and ways of defining the concept of sustainable tourism, most of them making a transition from the concepts of sustainability or sustainable development. Despite several studies exploring this issue, they tend to focus on a limited number of aspects of sustainability, rather than looking at it across the triple bottom line.

Notwithstanding the growing relevance of sports tourism, research on sustainable management practices adopted by companies supplying sports tourism products has been much neglected and tends to focus on sports tourism impacts (e.g. economic, environmental, social) (Fredline, 2005; Ma et al., 2011). Other literature that may provide interesting insights into sustainability practices is scattered over many areas. Literature on management (e.g. Bocken, Short, Rana, & Evans, 2014; Global Reporting Initiative [GRI], 2002; Labuschagne, Brent, & Van Erck, 2005; Rahdari & Anvary Rostamy, 2015; Veleva & Ellenbecker, 2001; Wiedmann, Lenzen, & Barrett, 2009) suggests important practices that companies may adopt to promote sustainability, identifying sustainability principles, models or indicators that may be used to assess the organisation performance regarding sustainability. In the context of tourism, there are broader studies on the sustainability of tourism destinations (Choi & Sirakaya, 2006; Marzo-Navarro et al., 2015) and literature related more to practices adopted by tourism companies engaged in activities other than sports (Bagur-Femenías et al., 2015; Ruiz-Molina et al., 2010). It is of utmost importance that organisations engaged in sports tourism development or supplying sports tourism products deeply understand the specificities of sports tourism impacts (Hinch & Higham, 2008) and their implications, and adopt sustainable practices designed to maximise the positive and minimise the negative impacts.

In policy documents such as the *Our common future* report or the Rio Declaration on Environment and Development (United Nations Environment Programme, n.d.), sustainable development has traditionally been embedded in environmental and economic principles: preserving biodiversity, ensuring the normal functioning of ecosystems, guaranteeing efficient use of resources, promoting economic growth, and contributing to poverty alleviation. These documents also encompass a sociocultural sustainability perspective which advocates meeting essential human needs, promoting equity, fostering peace, and preserving cultural identity and heritage.

Research undertaken in the management field regarding the sustainability in tourism companies (e.g. GRI, 2002; Labuschagne et al., 2005; Veleva & Ellenbecker, 2001; Wiedmann et al., 2009) is highly based on the 'triple bottom line' approach. In this literature, at the economic level, special emphasis is provided to the financial health and economic performance of the company, but references are also made to external impacts of the companies, namely through taxes. Regarding social sustainability, the main concern seems to be related to issues such as: (ii) employees' satisfaction and perception of equity concerning salaries; (ii) training of the employees; (iii) the customers' protection by ensuring product safety; (iv) community development; and (v) non-discrimination and social exclusion. Principles identified to ensure environmental sustainability are associated with features such as low resources consumption, pollution avoidance, and environmental training.

Tourism is a multidimensional phenomenon with various specificities. However, the discussion on sustainable development in the field of sports tourism (Andersson et al., 2015; Fredline, 2005; Gibson et al., 2012) has largely relied on three approaches to sustainability – the environmental, economic, and sociocultural dimensions. It is worth to note, in contrast to what happens in management, the important role that cultural sustainability assumes in the scope of tourism, due to its important contributions to promote the culture of tourism destinations. Few researchers go beyond the traditional approaches of sustainability and directly focus on other important dimensions, especially those related to technologies (Choi & Sirakaya, 2006; Ruiz-Molina et al., 2010) and policy features (Choi & Sirakaya, 2006; Roberts & Tribe, 2008). This trend is also observed in management, where some research, especially more recently, is emphasising the relevance of some dimensions such as technology (namely to better protect the environment and do a more efficient use of resources) (e.g. Bocken et al., 2014), as well as governance and ethics (e.g. Bos-Brouwers, 2010; Rahdari & Anvary Rostamy, 2015).

Another limitation in the scope of tourism is the lack of research on practices adopted by tourism companies and, particularly, by sports companies. The next section will present a literature review on sustainable tourism and on sports tourism, in order to provide useful insights on management practices that sports tourism companies may adopt to promote the sustainable development of sports activities at destinations.

3.1. Economic dimension

Some tourism research (Markwick, 2000; Pérez & del Bosque, 2014; Wickham & Lehman, 2015) refers to the importance of the economic performance of companies, namely profitability, to economic sustainability. However, when compared to the management literature, tourism research seems less likely to focus this issue and more likely to consider the economic contribution of companies to the community and the whole economy through, for example, expenditure generated in the economy (Bonilla-Priego et al., 2014; Briedenhann, 2011; Choi & Sirakaya, 2006; Roberts & Tribe, 2008). It is particularly important for sports tourism companies to implement sustainable management practices in order to promote the sustainable development of destinations. Attention devoted to sports tourism partially results from recognition of its high potential economic impact. Assessment of the economic impact and sustainability of sports tourism has often centred on the direct expenditure of participants and spectators of sports tourism activities (Andersson et al., 2015; Briedenhann, 2011; Gibson et al., 2012). These impacts relate (i) directly to the sport activity itself (e.g. tickets) or to complementary goods and services (e.g. accommodation, food and beverages, and souvenirs), and (ii) to the creation of jobs (Briedenhann, 2011; Markwick, 2000).

Many suggestions for improving economic sustainability in tourism also relate to these issues, largely to creating employment opportunities (Font, Garay, & Jones, 2014; Marzo-Navarro et al., 2015) and developing measures to increase the number of visitors or their average expenditure (Choi & Sirakaya, 2006; Roberts & Tribe, 2008). Decreasing the seasonality of tourism businesses is also a very important goal (Choi & Sirakaya, 2006) in order to avoid limiting revenue, by diversifying the product supply (Ma et al., 2011).

Recognition of the great potential of tourism, particularly sports tourism, to stimulate local economies, has led researchers to note the importance of encouraging the tourism industry to buy products from local suppliers and to create intersectoral linkages locally, in order to avoid leakages from the community (Choi & Sirakaya, 2006; Miller, 2001; Roberts & Tribe, 2008). Finally, fixing appropriate price and taxation levels is also desirable to avoid potential dissatisfaction with tourism development on the part of local residents, as a result of increases in prices and taxes generated by tourism (Briedenhann, 2011; Fredline, 2005; Markwick, 2000).

3.2. Environmental dimension

The environmental sustainability dimension is one of the most discussed in terms of sports tourism impacts and sustainability. Sports tourism activities may lead to the loss of valuable tourism resources such as flora and fauna (Fredline, 2005; Higham, 2005; Markwick, 2000; Orams, 2005). They can also provoke soil erosion (Fredline, 2005; Orams, 2005) due, among other reasons, to the intrusion of visitors into the habitat of certain species, an increase in the human presence in fragile places, damage caused by trampling, and the practice of sports activities.

The relevance of preserving natural resources and biodiversity is highly remarked in tourism research (Bonilla-Priego et al., 2014; Mihalič et al., 2012; Pérez & del Bosque, 2014), perhaps because of the high dependency of tourism activities on the whole destination. Sports tourism activities are more likely to generate such negative effects when compared to other tourism activities, given their dependence on natural settings and the fact that most of them take place outdoors. Actions designed to avoid these impacts are, therefore, desirable to ensure environmental sustainability. Growing awareness regarding the potential negative effects of additional pressure on resources and the crucial relevance of landscape in the context of tourism sport activities have led some researchers to support the idea of defining limits to growth and number of participants (Mykletun, 2009; Ponting & O'Brien, 2014). Others stress the relevance of implementing forms of development that are visually appealing, or at least acceptable (Markwick, 2000). Pollution and the high use of resources such as air, water, and energy due to sports and other tourism activities should also be avoided (Andersson et al., 2015; Bonilla-Priego et al., 2014; Fredline, 2005; Markwick, 2000; Orams, 2005; Wickham & Lehman, 2015), namely through the adoption of strategies involving the implementation of measures and plans for conserving and monitoring both the quality and use of resources (Alonso-Almeida et al., 2015; Ma et al., 2011; Roberts & Tribe, 2008). These strategies are especially important in fragile sites and destinations with a high number of endangered species (Choi & Sirakaya, 2006).

Given the characteristics of sports activities, some researchers remark that special care should be taken to avoid water pollution, as well as litter and noise production (Fredline, 2005; Ma et al., 2011; Orams, 2005). These measures may also be complemented by the adoption of recycling practices (Font et al., 2014; Gibson et al., 2012; Ma et al., 2011; Roberts & Tribe, 2008; Vellecco & Mancino, 2010), the use of renewable energy and more environmentally friendly forms of locomotion such as public transport, walking, or cycling (Font et al., 2014; Ma et al., 2011). In the line of the previous arguments, the use of existing sports infrastructure rather than purpose-built new facilities has also been strongly recommended (D'Hauteserre, 2005; Ma et al., 2011), with this strategy having been already adopted in several sports tourism contexts (D'Hauteserre, 2005; Gibson et al., 2012). Providing environmental education training to employees is also emphasised, in the scope of tourism, as a very important strategy to achieve environmental sustainability (Alonso-Almeida et al., 2015; Bagur-Femenías et al., 2015; Choi & Sirakaya, 2006; Mihalič et al., 2012).

Other researchers go one step further and refer to less frequently mentioned sustainable management practices that may assume a crucial role in increasing environmental sustainability, such as: (i) creating taxes associated to tourism services in order to raise funds to preserve or improve areas with important natural resources (Gibson et al., 2012); and (ii) developing environmental activities that contribute to raising environmental quality (Alonso-Almeida et al., 2015; Bagur-Femenías et al., 2015).

3.3. Sociocultural dimension

As far as sociocultural impacts are concerned, the development of sports tourism is twofold. On one hand, local residents are likely to perceive negative impacts, particularly in the case of mega-events, associated with crowding (Fredline, 2005; Higham, 2005; Ponting & O'Brien, 2014), increased pressure on existing facilities (e.g. roads, public transport) (Fredline, 2005; Markwick, 2000), inappropriate behaviour of visitors, and lack of security (Higham, 2005). These considerations suggest the relevance of adopting sustainable management practices that avoid congestion. This may be achieved, among other measures, by limiting visitor volume, taking into account the carrying capacity of the destination in order to avoid dissatisfaction on the part of residents, which, as shown in Butler's (2006) destination life-cycle model, tends to rise as the number of visitors increases. Examples of such measures include limiting accessibility to the destination, imposing an entrance fee, establishing visitor quotas, or requiring an accompanying guide for the visit (Deprest, 1997). Other sustainable management practices relate to the spatio-temporal dispersion of visitors and social awareness. Measures to ensure the safety of both residents and visitors, and to prevent residents from losing access to sites they previously visited, seem also to be useful policies.

On the other hand, sports tourism may bring important benefits to tourism destinations and their residents. Measures that are crucial to maximise these impacts, and thus promote the sustainable sociocultural development of sports tourism, include the following: (i) to promote local community involvement in the planning and supply of sports tourism services (e.g. as volunteers) (Choi & Sirakaya, 2006; Fredline, 2005; Ma et al., 2011; Miller, 2001; Roberts & Tribe, 2008; Wickham & Lehman, 2015); (ii) to increase the pride of local residents (Fredline, 2005); (iii) to combat social exclusion and isolation through this kind of tourism (Font et al., 2014; Ma et al., 2011; Wickham & Lehman, 2015); (iv) to ensure a fair distribution of tourism benefits (Fredline, 2005); (v) to guarantee a high percentage of local employment (Font et al., 2014; Ma et al., 2011; Roberts & Tribe, 2008); (vi) to ensure job satisfaction, by minimising part-time and seasonal jobs and offering appropriate wages (Alonso-Almeida et al., 2015; Bagur-Femenías et al., 2015; Bonilla-Priego et al., 2014; Choi & Sirakaya, 2006; Ma et al., 2011; Markwick, 2000; Mihalič et al., 2012; Miller, 2001; Pérez & del Bosque, 2014; Roberts & Tribe, 2008); and (vii) to promote the creation or maintenance of facilities only if they may be used by residents, even after sports events (Fredline, 2005).

From a cultural perspective, the development of sports tourism has a crucial role in creating an appealing image for the destination (Andersson et al., 2015) and in generating entertainment and social cohesion opportunities (Fredline, 2005). Some researchers also highlight the potential of the tourism in promoting culture (Mihalič et al., 2012; Pérez & del Bosque, 2014) and preserving cultural heritage, including retaining local traditions (Choi & Sirakaya, 2006; Font et al., 2014; Wickham & Lehman, 2015). However, in this context, special attention should be paid to the information provided to visitors on local culture (Choi & Sirakaya, 2006) and to the way the visitors' contact with the territory is managed. If such sociocultural practices are properly managed, this may result in residents becoming prouder of living in the destination (Choi & Sirakaya, 2006; Fredline, 2005).

3.4. Technological dimension

The growing relevance of technology in the field of tourism (Buhalis & Law, 2008; Middleton, Fyall, & Morgan, 2009; Pan & Fesenmaier, 2006) has led to the identification of a technology dimension in the scope of tourism sustainability. This may be used by destinations to mitigate some of the negative impacts of tourism and effectively achieve sustainable development. According to Choi and Sirakaya (2006), this dimension encompasses the adoption of low-impact technologies as well as technologies designed to allow data collection, information exchange, and benchmarking.

Ali and Frew (2010) discuss the use and application of information and communication technology (ICT) for sustainable tourism development. They argue that these technologies can be useful in mitigating some of the negative impacts of tourism, and they present an array of ICT-based tools or applications available to destination managers: destination management systems; intelligent transport systems; environment management information systems; location based services; global positioning systems; geographical information systems; community informatics; carbon calculators; virtual tourism; computer simulation. These ICT tools were found to be innovative for the management and distribution of information for critical decision-making. It is argued that the use of ICT fosters innovation for sustainable tourism by leading to a better understanding of the tourism product; monitoring, measuring, and evaluating; forecasting trends; developing partnerships; and engaging and supporting stakeholder relationships (Ali & Frew, 2014). ICT also provides novel ways of approaching marketing, energy monitoring, waste management, and communication for destinations. Other potential contributions of information technologies to sustainable tourism are also highlighted by Gössling (2016). This researcher, among other features, argues that this kind of technologies, providing access to a wider range of information, may offer visitors a deeper knowledge and increase awareness on the destination, as well as facilitate the choice of sustainable services.

Yaw (2005) discusses the importance of implementing clear technologies (e.g. those related to the use of treated sewage for irrigation, renewable energy sources, and lighting and cooling systems) in the tourism industry, and assesses the extension of the use of these technologies in hotels and resorts in the Caribbean. Ruiz-Molina et al. (2010) performed a study to analyse the impacts of the implementation of technology on sustainability. They note its usefulness in reducing paper waste, in optimising efficiency (by using internal and external networks to improve connections within and outside the company) and in controlling and minimising the use of resources such as energy and water. They conclude, however, that the companies are not exploiting the full potential of these technologies.

3.5. Policy dimension

Although policy has always been embedded in the concepts of sustainability and sustainable tourism (Sharpley, 2000; WCED, 1987), it only emerges as an autonomous tourism sustainability dimension in some research (Choi & Sirakaya, 2006; Roberts & Tribe, 2008; Sharpley, 2000; WCED, 1987). This probably happens because many researchers include features related to policy in another dimension, considering policy an instrumental dimension for achieving other sustainability objectives such as social equity goals or sustainable environmental aims. For example, while Choi and Sirakaya (2006) include 'community involvement in planning' in the political dimension, Ma et al. (2011) consider this feature under the scope of social sustainability. This dimension is essentially related to: (i) the existence of tourism policies, plans, and codes of ethics; (ii) the provision of training; (iii) the availability of funding; (iv) forms of organisation that ensure partnerships and linkages; and, more generally, (v) policy formulation (Choi & Sirakaya, 2006; Roberts & Tribe, 2008). Some researchers, although not specifically identify this dimension, also remark the important role of training (Mihalič et al., 2012; Pérez & del Bosque, 2014) and codes of conduct (Pérez & del Bosque, 2014). In the scope of policy-making, Mihalič et al. (2012) point the importance of being involved in the global sustainability strategy for the destination. Timur and Getz (2008) have focused on destination governance, having applied both network and stakeholder perspectives to examine the structure of inter-stakeholder relationships and the potential influence of this relational structure on sustainable destination development. Other studies have also made use of the network theory to investigate the role of collaboration in attaining sustainable development (Erkuş-Öztürk & Eraydın, 2010; Fadeeva, 2005; Halme, 2001; Jamal & Stronza, 2009; Pavlovich, 2001). This approach provides more insights on sustainability, especially since the managers at the top are usually those who belong to networks, having the capacity to lead to sustainable outcomes.

The nature of tourism pushes service providers to develop relationships, both formal and informal, leading to the emergence of inter-organisational networks in destinations, which can provide comprehensive and thus more diversified tourism products (Scott, Baggio, & Cooper, 2008), while simultaneously yielding long-term goals and sustainable destination development. Through a network management system, local stakeholders have more opportunities to participate in the tourism management and planning process, their participation being essential (Gunn & Var, 2002). The fragmented nature of tourism, where small companies dominate (Fyall & Garrod, 2005), makes relationships between the various stakeholders of a destination a crucial factor from a strategic point of view. In this scope, cooperation with the municipality, with local residents, non-governmental environment organisations (Mihalič et al., 2012), and with other suppliers may assume high importance.

Bagur-Femenías et al. (2015) provide evidence of the positive impact that training practices may have on the competitiveness of destinations. According to Choi and Sirakaya (2006), community managers and planners need to provide information and training programmes to all destination stakeholders in order to raise public and political awareness of the planning and conservation of the community's tourism resources. Mykletun (2009) discusses in depth the great relevance of organisation to the sustainable development of sports tourism. The practices included in this context may not only help to preserve resources, as suggested by Higham (2005), but also help tourism companies to operate at peak efficiency and in a way that maximises the benefits of tourism to the destination, namely by reinforcing linkages and avoiding leakages. Information, monitoring systems, and processes may help adjust destination planning and management in a manner that yields sustainable development (Choi & Sirakaya, 2006).

4. Methods

4.1. Geographical context

The area under analysis is the coastal area of the Aveiro region, located in the Centre of Portugal (NUT II), in the Baixo Vouga (NUT III) (Figure 1). More specifically, this area is composed of 10 municipalities that are located on the coast or include some wetlands. The region is an essentially sandy wetland, and this plain landscape is dominated by the tributaries of the river Vouga basin – e.g. Águeda, Alfusqueiro, Cértima, and Vouga – and by the Aveiro lagoon. The existing hydrographic network is also a major factor for landscape quality, as it provides several river beaches, small lagoons, and waterfalls, among other characteristics, which can be harnessed to boost tourism in the region, focusing on sustainability.

This group of municipalities has great potential as a tourism destination, not only because of the abundant water resources, but also due to the quality of its surrounding

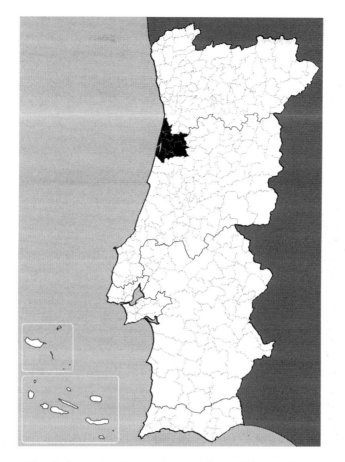

Figure 1. Location of the Aveiro region. Source: Adapted from Wikimedia Commons.

environment. The area is surrounded by mountains and sea, encompassing several blue flag beaches. It also includes the nature reserve of São Jacinto Dunes and offers the opportunity to practice many sports such as sailing, canoeing, and surfing. This range of natural resources is complemented by some appealing cultural heritage such as buildings representative of important architectonic styles – e.g. *Art Nouveau* – and interesting traditional activities linked to salt production, fishing, and agriculture.

Notwithstanding the great potential of this region as a tourism destination, it has a reduced expression in terms of the number of existing accommodation establishments, representing only 10% of the total in the Centre region (NUT II) (INE, 2015). This might in part be explained by the large size of the NUT II region, which is composed of 11 sub-regions. The same pattern emerges with the accommodation capacity, overnight stays, and number of guests. The proportion of foreign guests is a little higher in the sub-region (46.8%) than in the region (40.6%), which may imply greater international recognition. Although with a minimal difference, the sub-region of Aveiro has also higher bed occupancy rate (28.8% vs. 27.7%), and the same average stay (1.8).

According to the National Strategic Plan for Tourism (Ministério da Economia e do Emprego, 2012), the main tourism products of the region are sun and sea tourism, city breaks, cultural tourism, food and wine tourism, nature tourism, nautical tourism, business tourism, and second-home tourism.

Sun and sea is a very popular and well-developed product; however, it is in need of new strategies for its rejuvenation. With a great diversity of natural environments, from the lagoon to ocean and river beaches, this region has the potential to offer a wide range of outdoor activities related to this product.

Cultural tourism is a consolidated product, supported by a diverse material and intangible heritage that allows for the creation of distinct tourist itineraries.

Food and wine is a complementary tourism product, as it is not the primary motivation to travel to this region. Nevertheless, this product allows visitors to get to know typical regional products, thus improving their knowledge of the destination.

Nature tourism is gaining prominence in the region, which is reflected in the growing number of companies providing activities in this area. The awareness of the need to promote sustainable development through nature conservation is pushing forward the growth of this tourism product. In the Aveiro Lagoon, there are several resources for the development of different nature-based activities. The existence of key projects that highlight this kind of tourism and related activities, such as footpaths in the dunes that cross different municipalities, and the BioRia project, are contributing to the visibility of the region as a nature tourism destination.

Despite a long coastal tradition, nautical tourism is at an early stage of development. Due to its extensive coastline, the existence of the lagoon and a river system of considerable size, the region has huge potential to offer different sports activities.

City breaks, business tourism, and second-home tourism are, at present, products under development, since little tourism activity is generated by them.

4.2. Data collection and data analysis methods

Considering that the main objective of this study is to identify sustainable management practices implemented by companies supplying sports tourism products, data were collected through semi-structured interviews with the managers of tourist entertainment companies of the coastal area of the Aveiro region. According to the Portuguese legislation (Decree-Law 95/2013 of 19 July), tourist entertainment companies are firms that supply outdoor recreational, sports, or cultural activities that have relevance to tourists in the region in which they are developed. These are usually micro-companies, with a very small number of workers, ranging from two to three in the low season and employing additional labour in the high season. The population under analysis is composed of the 31 tourist entertainment companies located in the coastal area of the Aveiro region that supply sports tourism activities. These companies were identified through searches in the national register of tourist entertainment companies (an official database compiled by the national tourism administration, comprising data regarding such companies), through complementary searches of the web pages of national and regional organisations with responsibility for tourism management and development, and in social networks. After a first contact, the managers of only 15 companies proved available to participate in the study. The sample therefore corresponded to about 48% of the population.

Semi-structured interviews were considered an appropriate research method due to the exploratory nature of the research. The purpose of this empirical research was to get a deeper perspective of the potential sustainable management practices of sports tourism companies, understanding the specificities of their implementation, rather than a representative view of the adoption of these practices by such companies. Semi-structured interviews are particularly useful in this research context, offering researchers great flexibility in the way questions are phrased and the order in which they are asked (Quivy & Campenhoudt, 1992).

The semi-structured interviews were undertaken in May 2015, with an average duration of 20 minutes. The managers were asked some questions designed to obtain information to briefly characterise the company regarding the following issues: (i) date of creation; (ii) activities developed; (iii) human resources (number of workers and their skills); and (iv) market profile. Further questions were asked to identify the sustainable management practices implemented by the analysed companies in the following domains: (i) economic – including number of workers, having local providers and strategies to deal with seasonality; (ii) environmental – impacts on the environment and strategies to minimise them; (iii) sociocultural – the involvement of the local community, hiring local workers, promotion of cultural heritage to the customers, involvement of customers in local cultural activities; (iv) policy – partnerships or other forms of cooperation with other organisations, creation of codes of conduct; and (v) technological – types of technologies adopted and purpose for which they are used.

The discourse of the interviewees was transcribed and analysed using content analysis. As Quivy and Campenhoudt (1992) remark, this method enables the organisation of information in categories and its analysis in a more methodical and orderly way, allowing specific inferences to be made (Krippendorff, 2013). This kind of analysis aims to understand both the implicit and explicit logic of communications, content, and interpretations (Chizzotti, 2006). Quivy and Campenhoudt (1992) identify three types of content analysis: (i) thematic analysis, which aims 'to reveal the social representations or judgements of the speakers based on some elements of the discourse' (p. 228); (ii) formal analysis, which focuses on the form of the discourse and the way words are linked (encompassing the vocabulary used, size of sentences, and hesitations); and (iii) structural analysis, based on the 'way the elements of the message are arranged' (p. 229) (including the sequence of the elements and the association among themes). Given the objective of the present study, the content analysis of the interviews was performed using thematic analysis. The themes emerged from the literature review undertaken in Section 3, since the literature provides a comprehensive overview of the different themes representing the various sustainability dimensions.

4.3. Characterisation of the companies

In the region under study, the companies offering recreational sports-related tourism activities analysed in the present research are located in six municipalities. The activities provided by them are usually undertaken in the municipality where they are located. However, six firms offer activities in different locations, sometimes across different municipalities. The activities offered by them range from adventure to cultural activities, developed in land, water, or air, thus showing great diversity (Table 1).

Only three companies were created more than 10 years ago, suggesting recent dynamics in the development of new businesses in the tourism sector, especially concerning companies that offer sports tourism activities. Not all of these companies are operating full-time: six run only by request from customers, and, although they are always available to carry out activities, not all of them have an office open to the public.

Regarding the customer profile, the age range is wide and varies according to the company. Overall, participants, who are mainly groups (companies, families, schools, scouts, friends), are between 20 and 50 years old, showing that sports tourism activities are available to a wide age range.

The activities provided by almost all companies are arranged by only one or two people – usually the company's manager with the collaboration of one employee, or more if necessary in a particular activity. However, these employees are usually requested only when needed, especially in the high season or at specific times throughout the year. There are a few larger companies, with greater recognition at national and international level, that generally offer different activities from the rest of the companies.

The educational background of those running the companies is wide (e.g. marketing, engineering, informatics, physical education), with little training in tourism and sports. However, managers hire employees who have some sort of training in these areas. Almost all people working in these companies have enough expertise in languages, with English and Spanish being the most spoken.

5. Analysis of results

Sustainability is a challenge for all the companies under study, as can be seen in the following analysis. The answers provided by the companies are analysed in order to understand how sustainable management practices were adopted to ensure sustainable development, taking into account each of the various sustainability dimensions.

5.1. Economic sustainability

The companies under analysis are important generators of local employment. Although the majority do not sustain more than two jobs during the low season, they tend to hire more employees during the high season. As one manager stated: '[…] There is a list of monitors that we are going to call depending on the extent of the activities and of our needs' (C4). One of the companies even reaches 12 or 14 workers during the high season. In one case, there is the intention of hiring more workers: 'initially there was only the manager and now there are already four of us, and the objective is to increase the list of co-workers even more' (C8).

Seasonality was identified as one of the main challenges ahead for maritime and coastal tourism (EC, n.d.b). It affects all the surveyed companies, since demand varies significantly between high and low season, probably because the majority of the activities offered by these companies are aquatic, taking place outdoors, and being highly dependent on specific weather conditions. Seasonality gives rise to many challenges in achieving sustainability (Choi & Sirakaya, 2006; Martín Martín, Jiménez Aguilera, & Molina Moreno, 2014).

Table 1. General characterisation of the surveyed companies.

Companies	Creation date	Municipality	Sports tourism activities organised by the companies	Operation
C1	2008	Albergaria-a-Velha	Equestrian tourism; paintball; hiking	Full time
C2	2006	Sever de Vouga	Several sports and adventure activities such as canoeing; team building; paintball; climbing; rappel; slide; group dynamics; canyoning; stand up paddleboarding (subcontracting)	Not full time
C3	1999	Ovar	Bowling; karting	Full time
C4	2010	Sever do Vouga	Adventure sports; organisation of sports activities such as mountain biking; rope sports; canoeing; aquatic hiking	Full time
C5	2013	Aveiro	Van tours; hiking; transfers	Not full time
C6	2013	Aveiro	Production of ecological surfboards; outdoor activities such as hiking, sports baptisms, activities with schools	Full time
C7	2014	Ovar	Surfing; kayak; racing; paddle surfing; birdwatching	Full time
C8	n.a.	Vagos	Kayak; paintball; hot air balloon; horse riding; summer camps; activities for seniors	Full time
C9	2010	Aveiro	Sports and recreational instruction; sale and maintenance of sports equipment; equipment rental; diving	Full time
C10	2013	Ílhavo	Canyoning; paintball; hiking trekking; climbing; rappel; rope sports; cultural tours; archery; crossbow; blowgun; paintball for kids; aquatic hiking; team building; bike tours; orientation	Not full time
C11	2014	Sever do Vouga	Cultural activities; sport activities (biking; hiking); leisure activities	Full time
C12	2014	Aveiro	Outdoor activities such as urban hiking	Not full time
C13	1997	Ílhavo	Sports instruction (windsurfing; kitesurfing; sail; kayak; surfing); equipment rentals; events; tours; equipment sales; repairs	Not full time
C14	2014	Ovar	Radical sports; jet ski; boards; ...	Full time
C15	1997	Sever do Vouga	River and sea canoeing; other adventure sports	Not full time

Source: Own elaboration

However, the majority of the companies studied are trying to combat seasonality with complementary offerings, such as indoor activities (alternative aquatic sports or paintball), activities at weddings or other events, and even training sessions, as reported by some managers: 'These training actions are helping us to reduce seasonality across the year [...], as well as group dynamics and indoor activities' (C4). One manager is even investing money in purchasing premises that allow the supply of indoor activities: 'I am negotiating a pavilion' (C2). This study corroborates thus what has been argued by researchers, such as Ma et al. (2011), that product diversification may be a useful tool for achieving economic sustainability (see Section 3.1), not only through attracting diversified market segments but also by enabling the extension of the operating season. The creation of partnerships to diversify the product supply will be further discussed in Section 5.5. Promotions and vouchers during specific periods, such as Christmas and Easter, are other strategies to continue offering different activities to consumers throughout the year.

Regarding the sustainability problematic of linkages and leakages already raised by several researchers (Choi & Sirakaya, 2006; Lacher & Nepal, 2010; Lejárraga & Walkenhorst, 2010; Roberts & Tribe, 2008), it is noteworthy that more than half of the interviewees prefer local providers. For example, one manager reported: 'Whenever possible I try to work with people from here' (C11). However, this is not always feasible. Service providers, particularly of accommodation and food and beverages, are usually local. However, the providers of certain goods, especially materials and equipment needed to perform the activity, are generally from outside the region, since they do not usually exist within it, as stated by six managers: 'Suppliers are foreigners, unfortunately we do not have this kind of supply here' (C6); 'In services, [suppliers are] local ones. In merchandise, [they are] mainly from outside' (C9).

5.2. Environmental sustainability

Usually, from the perspective of managers, the activities offered by these companies do not have an impact on resources, as companies take special care with environmental issues when organising them, and environmental management is one of the companies' chief concerns. Nevertheless, about one third of the firms impose a maximum number of participants in some activities, either to ensure security or to avoid major disturbances in local activities and on resources such as fauna, flora, and habitats. The careful attention assigned to this issue can be well observed in some discourses: '[there is a] limit to the number of participants by activity' (C12); '[...] in some activities there are maximum limits of persons [...] to prevent degradation of trails [and] streams among other resources' (C4). It is worth noting that these companies, perhaps because of the character of their activities, try to not exceed the limits of carrying capacity mainly for environmental reasons: that is, to avoid degradation of the environment. Only a minority of companies report the adoption of other practices to preserve resources. Two examples of these efforts are an attempt to '[...] implement activities without extraordinary impact on the different resources' (C12) and another manager states that '[the destination] has a very rich fauna and flora and so we keep the horses apart, not allowing them to move to the middle [of the destination] with us' (C1). Only one company mentions being involved in an environmental certification process: '[we are] dealing with the ISO 14001 certification process' (C8).

Despite being a very current topic, reuse and recycling is not a practice adopted by all people. Therefore, it is important to value the importance given by some companies to recycling and reuse: 'We recycle the oils we use in karting' (C3); '[...] We work with natural fibres with resins that are made based on the use of industrial waste' (C6); 'I keep all that is rubbish [...] and do the separation of waste' (C11).

Pollution is one of the factors that most affects the environment, so it must be taken into account when the different activities are carried out. Several companies make a strong effort to minimise the negative effects of pollution by opting to use various biodegradable products: 'the paintball balls we use are biodegradable' (C10); 'Our machines use biodegradable fuels and there are strict inspections' (C14).

Litter is also a concern pointed out by a lot of managers, and some companies are even trying to develop interesting efforts to promote more sustainable behaviour among people:

We try to help ... whenever we take a walk and see some garbage; we encourage people to bring the trash back on the surfboard. (C6)

I would like people to collect all the garbage they produce [...] the water bottle and the ice cream wrapper, and I see no excuse for not doing so. A little more education, and we can get this through to people, making posts on Facebook, I have already left some informative papers here, these are things that take time. Everything requiring a behavioural change takes a long time. I try to make it happen, but it's almost impossible. (C11)

Although environmental actions to promote a better environment mentioned by researchers such as Bagur-Femenías et al. (2015) are not so usual, it is worth noting that two of these companies are already organising some actions such as cleaning: '[...] carrying out eco-activities, i.e. activities to clean up the river' (C5); 'we also try to do some clean-up operations' (C4).

5.3. Sociocultural sustainability

An interesting aspect to note is that most of the managers and remaining workers live in the region (only one manager lives outside the region under analysis). Besides adopting local employment practices, companies also promote interaction with the local community. This interaction undoubtedly provides added value to tourism, and many managers underline the relevance of this issue, stating that it is always important to create a link between all those involved in activities with the local community. The involvement of the community is based on two different axes with distinct objectives. The first, pursued by a minority of firms, refers to the prevention of social exclusion, as mentioned by the following respondent: 'Here there are two or three associations, one of them is that of the disadvantaged teens. [...] We promote an activity with these kids, for them to participate with us' (C2). Another aim of several companies is to directly involve local communities in performing activities that may be offered in the scope of adventure sports packages. Some companies have already taken interesting action in this context, as reported by their managers: 'Whenever possible we integrate craftsmen, historians, ethnographic groups [...]' (C12); and 'Yes, the boatmen of river Vouga' (C15). This involvement makes residents prouder and increases their likelihood of cooperating in the future development of different activities. Besides, these strategies also enable richer and more differentiated experiences that offer a combination of adventure sports and cultural activities, where residents can act as cultural brokers, providing a deeper insight into the region.

It is possible to understand that these companies also play a vital role in promoting the cultural heritage of the region. Many of the companies offer interesting and memorable experiences to their customers by promoting direct contact with attractive and relevant regional tourism attractions and engagement in traditional activities, with opportunities for interaction with local hosts, as may be noticed in some discourses:

> We have a tour that is to Sever do Vouga, [...] we do activities with the village people of Couto de Esteves, [...], we pick blueberries accompanied with tasting of traditional and regional products [...] we can make bread in a wood oven, people knead it, and then taste the bread made in the wood oven, and can milk a cow too. (C5)

> We are planning to offer, in local events, the opportunity to participate in some activities available [...] and, thus, helping people to get to know the area. (C8)

These practices not only allow visitors to learn about local traditional activities, but also to experience and taste local products such as blueberries and local bread. Furthermore, companies also intend to offer opportunities to better know the built cultural heritage and natural attractions that are important landmarks of the destination region, as may be observed in the words of some respondents.

I refer again to Costa Nova because it is our preferred place to work with in Aveiro, typical houses, people collecting mussels, and we attempt a bit to show this. (C6)

One of the last hikes we had was to Macinhata Museum, we have this concern to always pass striking sites, […] but we always try to get people to visit [these places] such as the bridge, the Cabreia Cascade […], but then I always invite people to make a tour through the village, to eat our veal, to visit other sites. (C11)

5.4. Technological sustainability

The adoption of technology by the analysed companies is mainly confined to promotion and, therefore, to having a website and using social media. This is one important function of the technology in the scope of sustainability, already reported by some researchers (Ali & Frew, 2010; Choi & Sirakaya, 2006), according to which technology may have a crucial role in facilitating the collection and delivery of information (see Section 3.4). While increasing promotion may help to attract more customers, collecting information about these customers, for example, through social media, may help in designing more appealing products and increasing consumer satisfaction, and thus improving the economic performance of the company. The managers of the companies feel the need to take advantage of social networks to share information and promote the activities they offer, for example, reporting that: 'We have Facebook […] I am going to invest in the use of social networks' (C14); 'It is important to us that, when people come here, they know we exist. We focus a lot on social networks to spread information, such as Twitter, Instagram, YouTube and Facebook' (C6); and 'The goal is that the sale of all products is online' (C6).

It is worth noting that managers also use these networks to analyse and better understand the kind of people that visit the companies' websites, deepening their research on each person and thus obtaining more knowledge on visitor flows. This analysis has been carried out in several ways, such as using Facebook or Google analytics: 'We have software which effectively monitors who visits the site, where the IPs are from and what are the countries that most visit us' (C6) and 'We have Google analytics linked to our website, Facebook also gives us statistics that must be analysed to understand the flow of visits per month' (C8).

Although a considerable amount of literature reinforces the importance of mitigating environmental impacts by, for example, controlling the use of some resources and promoting their reuse (Ali & Frew, 2010; Ruiz-Molina et al., 2010; Yaw, 2005), only a minority use technology to manufacture equipment that has low environmental impact (e.g. ecological surfboards) or to achieve energy efficiency. In this context, some managers reported adopting technology to achieve energy efficiency, having replaced old lamps by more efficient ones – 'We are changing what can be changed in terms of energy efficiency. We have changed some lighting' (C3) – and only one intends to use of renewable energy – 'We will install solar panels, we have some concerns in this regard' (C1).

5.5. Policy sustainability

The majority of the companies consider training given to employees to be essential, as it remedies skill deficiencies and imparts knowledge of new trends (Patterson, 2016). It is usually done by the company itself and, in specific contexts, employees accompany the manager on training sessions outside the company. In addition to specific training programmes related to the sports tourism activities provided by the company (e.g. the operation of equipment), in some companies employees also receive training in foreign languages, safety and security, and communication, among other topics. Only a limited number of firms reported having a code of conduct.

A considerable number of companies have some cooperation with public entities concerning operational issues related to the organisation of activities and there is general satisfaction in this scope – '[they] permit the use of some spaces, [...] help to establish contact with other city councils' (C8); 'We have partnerships with the city council, [...] and whenever it is possible we work together, and they have been very solicitous concerning the ideas I propose' (C11). However, involvement in planning is not so generalised and seems to be limited in scope. Some managers reveal that SMEs have the opportunity to give their opinion and communicate with official bodies such as city councils. However, some also note that this is sometimes not feasible and one respondent said that, when the idea of creating an event emerges, some public institutions prefer to take decisions without consulting tourist entertainment companies. Some of the companies studied have interesting dynamics in terms of partnerships. They collaborate with associations and public entities – city councils, parishes – in order to decrease social exclusion and cooperate in promoting the region.

Companies have also created partnerships with other kinds of business, mainly with accommodation establishments (e.g. rural companies) and restaurants, since many customers request these services due to the duration of the activities and, consequently, the length of stay in the region. However, a few managers have also developed partnership relationships with other types of company such as 'a gym and an organic farm' (C7) and 'surf and language schools' (C13). Also noteworthy are the partnerships that some of these companies create with other tourism entertainment companies in order to share equipment or to complement the range of tourism adventure activities supplied:

> I work a lot with [entertainment firm X], the [entertainment firm X] does not have paintball [...] I do the paintball for them. [...] As I work with [entertainment firm Y], [...] I only have 10 canoes [...] I have annually groups of 40/50 persons [...] I have to rent some of their canoes. (C2)

However, creation of the types of partnership mentioned above is still far from being a generalised practice among the analysed companies.

Few companies have access to funding and some do not use it by choice, due to the specific conditions of financing. Some of the funding comes from the National Strategic Reference Framework and from competitions promoted, for example, by the University of Aveiro and by the Aveiro city council.

6. Discussion of results

Considering the results of the empirical study, one of the main contributions of this paper is the identification of a wide array of strategies that sports tourism companies may adopt to improve the sustainability of sports tourism destinations, encompassing the diverse sustainability dimensions identified in the literature – economic, environmental, sociocultural, policy, and technological. Table 2 provides an overview of the plethora of sustainability practices adopted by the entertainment companies under analysis. It is possible to observe that these companies have adopted a high range of practices representing the various sustainability dimensions before mentioned.

A deeper analysis of the results obtained and the comparison of these results with the literature review enables to draw interesting conclusions that highlight specificities related to the sustainability practices adopted by sports companies and that are certainly related to the specificities of this kind of companies and of sports tourism. It is also worth to note that all the practices identified may provide important contributions to improving the sustainability of the sports tourism destinations where they operate.

As far as economic sustainability is concerned, in the empirical study, in contrast to the management literature reported in the literature review section (Bocken et al., 2014; GRI, 2002; Labuschagne et al., 2005; Rahdari & Anvary Rostamy, 2015; Veleva & Ellenbecker, 2001; Wiedmann et al., 2009) and to some of the tourism literature (Markwick, 2000; Pérez & del Bosque, 2014; Wickham & Lehman, 2015) (see Section 3.1), the respondents do not directly refer to the economic performance of the company, although this issue seems to underlie their discourses. Hence, results corroborate the relevance of strategies designed to decrease seasonality, already mentioned in tourism literature (Choi & Sirakaya, 2006) and, thus, increase the number of consumers, due to the great relevance that seasonality assumes in the scope of the tourism industry. The specific strategies adopted by entertainment companies in order to decrease seasonality seem to be more related to supply indoor sports activities (diversifying their product portfolio) or to offer other indoor complementary activities (e.g. wedding events). As entertainment companies cooperate with other tourism companies, namely accommodations and restaurants, the efforts towards diminishing sustainability will also be reflected in other companies of the destination and on the destination as a whole. Strategies associated with establishing links with local organisations and avoiding leakages, already referred in the tourism literature (Choi & Sirakaya, 2006; Miller, 2001; Roberts & Tribe, 2008) (Section 3.1), are partially adopted by the sports companies under analysis, since half of them work with local accommodations and restaurants. However, sports companies have to purchase equipment to companies outside the region due to the absence of this type of suppliers inside the region.

Looking in much detail to the environmental sustainability dimension, several entertainment companies already implement recycling and reusing practices, widely mentioned in the tourism literature (Font et al., 2014; Gibson et al., 2012; Ma et al., 2011; Roberts & Tribe, 2008; Vellecco & Mancino, 2010) as important measures (see Section 3.2). However, in contrast, while the management and tourism literature refer the importance of measures to decrease pollution, the entertainment companies analysed only explicitly refer to avoid leaving litter on sites where activities take place and, additionally, to develop efforts to increase environmental awareness among consumers. The limited reference to measures designed to avoid pollution is probably related to the small size of these companies, when compared to hotels, for example, and to the kind of activities they develop that are less likely to provoke negative environmental impacts. In this line of thought, one strategy specifically applied by this type of companies is the establishment of a maximum number of participants (already mentioned by Mykletun, 2009; Ponting & O'Brien, 2014) (Section 3.2). A strategy that differentiates these companies from other

Table 2. Sustainable tourism practices adopted by the companies under analysis.

Sustainability dimensions	Examples of sustainable tourism practices
Economic sustainability	Creating linkages and avoiding leakages • Provision of local employment • Working with regional accommodation and food and beverage providers • Buying equipment and other goods from regional providers Reducing seasonality • Complimentary supply of indoor sports activities (e.g. alternative aquatic activities) • Supplying other complimentary indoor activities (e.g. weddings and other events) • Building premises to carry out indoor activities • Offering promotional prices during some periods
Environmental sustainability	Implementing activities without extraordinary negative environmental impact Reuse and recycling • Using recycled products • Promoting products' recycling Using biodegradable products (e.g. fuels, equipment) Establishing a maximum number of participants in activities to avoid damaging the environment Providing environmental education and training Environmental actions (e.g. cleaning up lands and rivers)
Sociocultural sustainability	Recruiting local staff with knowledge and experience regarding the region Promoting interaction with local community • Interaction to offer traditional appealing activities • Interaction to prevent social exclusion in the local community Promoting the local heritage of the region • Opportunities to learn about local traditions • Opportunities to taste traditional products • Opportunities to know the built cultural heritage
Technological sustainability	Adopting technology to promote the company to customers and increase the number of consumers Adopting technology to collect information from customers (e.g. through social media) that enables the design of more appealing products Adopting technology to mitigate environmental negative impacts by controlling the use of some resources and promoting their reuse
Institutional/policy sustainability	Offering training to staff regarding the sports activities Offering other training to staff that may help provide a better service Having a code of conduct Cooperating with public entities in planning and organising activities Cooperation with other entertainment companies Cooperation with other type of companies (e.g. accommodation and food & beverage providers)

Source: Own elaboration

tourism companies and that, therefore, is only rarely mentioned in the tourism literature (by Alonso-Almeida et al., 2015; Bagur-Femenías et al., 2015), is the development of environmental activities such as cleaning rivers.

The entertainment companies analysed adopt one of the social sustainability strategies most mentioned in the tourism literature (Font et al., 2014; Ma et al., 2011; Roberts & Tribe, 2008) – recruiting local people – (see Section 3.3) although they only hire a very small number of employees due to their small size. This feature provides added value to the companies since local workers are more likely to have a deeper knowledge of the region and valuable contact networks. As some authors (Kastenholz, Carneiro, Eusébio, & Figueiredo, 2013) state, they can act as important cultural brokers. In this role, residents may share their experiences with visitors and create deeper ties with them. These are important factors in developing interesting sports tourism products and meaningful experiences. Moreover, the high percentage of local workers may represent a relevant contribution to the development of sports tourism destinations. However, entertainment companies under analysis still have a high percentage of part-time jobs, contrary to what is desirable, as suggested by many tourism researchers. The respondents do not directly mention other issues related to social justice in work and job satisfaction, often previously addressed both in the management and tourism literature (Alonso-Almeida et al., 2015; Bagur-Femenías et al., 2015; Bonilla-Priego et al., 2014; Choi & Sirakaya, 2006; Ma et al., 2011; Markwick, 2000; Mihalič et al., 2012; Miller, 2001; Pérez & del Bosque, 2014; Roberts & Tribe, 2008) in part, perhaps because the seasonality of the jobs is one of the main causes of potential dissatisfaction with jobs in the case of these companies. In contrast to what happens in the tourism literature (Fredline, 2005), respondents do not also refer to the creation or maintenance of infrastructures that may also be used by residents, possibly because the activity of these companies does not require many infrastructures. In addition, it is possible to observe the great ability of these entertainment companies in promoting the involvement of the local communities (an important issue already highlighted by Choi & Sirakaya, 2006; Fredline, 2005; Ma et al., 2011), mainly supplying some services in the activities they offer and, thus, increasing social cohesion, reducing local communities' isolation, and making them prouder (Fredline, 2005; Ma et al., 2011) (Section 3.3).

It is interesting to find that the companies under analysis also greatly contribute to the cultural sustainability of destinations of the sports destinations where they operate, a sustainability dimension that assumes special relevance in the tourism industry (see Section 3). Hence, they also offer cultural activities and incorporate some of these activities in their sports activities programmes. This enables to preserve cultural heritage (aspect already highly valued by Choi & Sirakaya, 2006; Font et al., 2014; Wickham & Lehman, 2015) (Section 3.3) and to do a better promotion of the region's image, which is already pointed as one of the most important impacts of sports tourism (Andersson et al., 2015).

Although the tourism literature suggests several domains where the technology may contribute to foster sustainability (e.g. decreasing pollution, developing partnerships), in entertainment companies technology was found to be mainly used to promote the company and support some decision-making in this scope (strategies already mentioned by Ali & Frew, 2010) and, therefore, to obtain economic advantages. Technology is not so much used by entertainment companies to minimise environmental impacts, as proposed in the literature (Ali & Frew, 2010; Bagur-Femenías et al., 2015; Choi & Sirakaya, 2006; Ma et al., 2011; Ruiz-Molina et al., 2010) (see Section 3.4), although a small group of companies already adopt technologies that permit an efficient use of resources (strategy already suggested by Ruiz-Molina et al., 2010 and Yaw, 2005).

The respondents also address many issues concerning the policy sustainability dimension considered in the literature review. Although training has been advocated to be one of the most important policies to achieve sustainability (Bagur-Femenías et al., 2015; Choi & Sirakaya, 2006; Mihalič et al., 2012; Pérez & del Bosque, 2014; Roberts & Tribe, 2008) (see Section 3.5), the training provided by the entertainment companies analysed is mostly related to languages and to very specific issues related to the activities supplied than to environmental conservation. Nevertheless, a small number of companies provide training on safety and security. Safety and security have an impact on a destination's reputation and image and can affect visitation. If visitors' health and safety is not well managed, adverse incidents can negatively influence the profitability and sustainability of individual businesses or of a destination. Other areas where companies need to provide training to their staff in order to ensure sustainable practices include local culture and history, customer service, natural history and conservation, code of ethics, and sustainable behaviour, among others (Patterson, 2016). Although the adoption of codes of conduct has already been considered an important measure both in management and in tourism (Choi & Sirakaya, 2006; Pérez & del Bosque, 2014; Roberts & Tribe, 2008), in particular, only a small number of the companies analysed reports having a code of conduct. Having this kind of tool would be important to ensure both the safety and satisfaction of visitors and to foster the sustainability of the destinations.

Cooperation and partnerships have been identified as other important policy issues that contribute to sustainability (Choi & Sirakaya, 2006; Gunn & Var, 2002; Mihalič et al., 2012; Roberts & Tribe, 2008; Scott et al., 2008) (see Section 3.5). The cooperation of entertainment companies with public entities seems to be most related to operational issues, where public entities offer some support to these companies, and not so much with the involvement of entertainment companies in planning. It would be of utmost important to promote the active participation of entertainment companies in planning so that they could be more satisfied and would be more likely to cooperate in the global sustainable strategy of the sports tourism destinations in the long run. Some entertainment companies studied show a great dynamic in cooperating with other companies (restaurants, accommodation, other entertainment companies and other kind of companies), specifically in sharing equipment and in complementing and diversifying their supply, certainly to overcome some of their constraints related to limited financial and human resources. These partnerships are extremely important to promote sustainability, not only because they permit companies to save resources, but also because a more diversified portfolio of activities may enable to attract and better satisfy a wider set of customers. This is in line to what is stated by several researchers who argue that, nowadays, it is increasingly important to work with different partners, in order to share resources, to avoid unnecessary expenditure and to ensure that the various companies grow and derive benefits (Costa, Breda, Costa, & Miguéns, 2008). It is essential to realise the need to create partnerships rather than competition, thereby reducing the problems faced. These partnerships bring benefits, such as improving the quality of supply, ensuring the existence of customers with greater regularity, and creating integrated packages, allowing a greater range of services (Breda, Costa, & Costa, 2005; Costa et al., 2008). Obtaining funds is still a major problem for this type of companies, which may be greatly associated with the small size and low negotiating power of these companies. Further conclusions on the sustainable practices adopted by the entertainment companies under analysis will be presented and discussed in the next section.

7. Conclusions and implications

The present paper is a rich in-depth case study of managers perspectives across the five dimensions of sustainability. It extends previous research carried out in the fields of management and tourism by providing a deep insight on the adoption of sustainable management practices by tourism companies, specifically those offering sports tourism products, and, therefore, offers important contributions to maximise potential benefits of tourism in all the sustainability dimensions.

The paper provides important theoretical and practical contributions. As far as the theoretical contributions are concerned, the paper enables a better understanding of the complex and multifaceted character of sustainability in tourism, which encompasses several important sustainability dimensions previously identified in this paper. This research also permits a thorough comprehension of the adaptation of these sustainability dimensions to the field of sports tourism. One of the major theoretical contributions of this paper is the identification of a wide set of sustainable management practices that may contribute to a sustainable development of sports tourism destinations. These practices can be used in the field of sports tourism with several aims: (i) performing sustainability audits in certain regions and identifying the practices that are being adopted by sports companies and (ii) providing insights on sustainable practices that sports companies may adopt. This set of practices has an important added value, not only due to its adaptation to sports tourism, but also because, unlike several studies, it is not restricted to the most traditional sustainability dimensions – economic, sociocultural, environmental (Andersson et al., 2015; Fredline, 2005; Gibson et al., 2012) – but encompasses practices representing a wide range of tourism sustainability dimensions (economic, sociocultural, environmental, policy, and technological). Moreover, this set of practices is broad, and is not confined to issues concerning big companies or mega-events, as is frequently the case, consisting of a useful framework to be used by managers of companies operating in the sports tourism field and to increase their sustainable development.

The paper also provides important practical contributions. First, it highlights the importance of coastal areas as sports tourism destinations and the relevance of adopting sustainable practices to manage companies offering sports tourism products. Moreover, it enables the sustainable practices most widely adopted by the entertainment companies of the region of Aveiro to be identified. In this context, the empirical research suggests that sports tourism companies usually concentrate their efforts regarding sustainability on practices that ensure their economic sustainability, such as reducing seasonality by offering promotions, supplying indoor sports activities or other complimentary activities (Choi & Sirakaya, 2006; Martín Martín et al., 2014). Some policy practices are also considered important to achieve these goals. A considerable set of companies supplying sports tourism activities are already exploiting the benefits of cooperating and creating partnerships with other companies – suppliers, other sports tourism activities and public entities – (some of them already noted in previous research – Choi & Sirakaya, 2006; Fyall & Garrod, 2005; Gunn & Var, 2002; Higham, 2005), such as reducing costs, obtaining support and complementing their supply. The present research also highlights the adoption of sustainable environmental practices previously identified in the literature (Fredline, 2005; Markwick, 2000; Ponting & O'Brien, 2014), such as defining limits regarding the number of participants and picking up trash.

In addition, this empirical research highlights the importance of supporting sports tourism companies, since it reveals that they may have a relevant role in boosting local economies, and identifies sustainable management practices to achieve this objective. In fact, tourism entertainment companies in the coastal area of the Aveiro region, despite their small size and low number of workers, have a high proportion of local employees. Moreover, some of them also have an important role in creating dynamics in local communities, particularly in local economies, due to their preference for local providers and the partnerships they establish with other companies, increasing business opportunities at the local level. Furthermore, this study also shows that sports tourism firms may have a crucial role in promoting and creating an appealing image of coastal areas, as suggested by Andersson et al. (2015) (see Section 3.3). This may be a result of providing information on significant natural and cultural heritage during the activities organised by some of the studied companies (e.g. guided walking tours).

However, the present research also highlights that there may be a limited adoption of sustainable management practices among sports tourism companies, and these may be further explored by some companies. Firstly, the study highlights the importance of increasing the awareness of the managers of the region's sports tourism companies of the relevance of specific environmental and technological practices that, despite being recognised as extremely valuable by many researchers (Ali & Frew, 2010; Bagur-Femenías et al., 2015; Choi & Sirakaya, 2006; Ma et al., 2011; Ruiz-Molina et al., 2010), are only implemented by a minority of the surveyed companies. These include the use of renewable energy; environmental education in order to change mentalities and promote more environmentally friendly behaviours; the use of more environmentally friendly forms of locomotion; the development of environmental actions (e.g. cleaning rivers or land); the adoption of technologies to permit energy efficiency; and a more efficient use of other resources. Some of these practices are not so widely adopted among these firms, perhaps due to their small size and consequently limited budget, but also because the legislation concerning their activities is probably more flexible than that of other sectors. However, they are of utmost relevance to promote the sustainable development of destinations where these firms operate, due to the fragility of these destinations.

Furthermore, although the potential of partnerships and other forms of cooperation has already been discovered by some companies, it would be worthwhile to disseminate the value of such practices to other sports tourism companies in order to increase linkages among the local community and avoid leakages, maximising the benefits of sports tourism development to all the stakeholders of coastal destinations. In this context, it is especially important to reinforce the dialogue between the various stakeholders so that they can better understand each other's needs and opportunities offered. For example, increasing agents' awareness of the importance of supplying certain sustainable materials and equipment that are not available to the managers of entertainment companies at this moment would be extremely important. Finally, it would be of great value to take advantage of the strong potential for social cohesion offered by sports tourism (also mentioned by Choi & Sirakaya, 2006 and Fredline, 2005), by promoting greater involvement of local residents in the activities of sports tourism companies. Simple participation in a sports activity could create positive emotions and promote higher satisfaction among the local community, while perhaps also preventing social exclusion. Direct participation in the supply of tourism products, by conjointly performing a traditional activity with visitors (e.g. cooking, dancing) or sharing information about the region during a guided trip, could enlarge the social network and increase the pride of residents regarding their community (Fredline, 2005), while at the same time enabling the creation of more interactive, sensorily enriching and memorable sports tourism experiences (Schmitt, 1999).

Despite the contributions provided, the empirical study carried out has some limitations, considering the limited number of companies analysed and, specifically, the number and length of interviews done. Although the main objective is not to undertake a representative research on the sports tourism companies, undertaking more interviews could permit to have a richer perspective on sustainable management practices implemented by these companies and on specificities associated with this implementation. This study is also limited in terms of geographical context. It would be of value to extend this work to a larger number of companies supplying sports tourism products in other coastal areas in Portugal and other countries, in order to examine whether the results and conclusions drawn are consistent with the reality found elsewhere. A study that gives a more detailed insight into the main facilitators and constraints to the adoption of the sustainable management practices analysed in this study would also be of great value, to increase the adoption of these practices among sports tourism companies operating in coastal areas. Another interesting challenge would be to extend this work beyond the borders of coastal areas and analyse the sustainable management practices adopted by sports tourism companies operating in other types of tourism destinations (e.g. mountain areas, countryside, urban areas) and eventually supplying a different range of sports tourism activities. In this scope, quantitative studies could be useful to compare the range of activities and sustainable practices implemented by companies operating in different geographical contexts.

Disclosure statement

No potential conflict of interest was reported by the authors.

References

Albuquerque, H. (2013). *Estratégia de desenvolvimento sustentável do turismo na Ria de Aveiro* [Sustainable tourism development strategy in the Aveiro Lagoon] (PhD thesis). University of Aveiro.

Ali, A., & Frew, A. J. (2010). ICT and its role in sustainable tourism development. In U. Gretzel, R. Law, & M. Fuchs (Eds.), *Information and communication technologies in tourism 2010: Proceedings of the international conference in Lugano, Switzerland, February 10–12, 2010* (pp. 479–491). Vienna: Springer.

Ali, A., & Frew, A. J. (2014). ICT and sustainable tourism development: An innovative perspective. *Journal of Hospitality and Tourism Technology, 5*(1), 2–16. doi:10.1108/JHTT-12-2012-0034

Alonso-Almeida, M. D. M., Bagur-Femenias, L., Llach, J., & Perramon, J. (2015). Sustainability in small tourist businesses: The link between initiatives and performance. *Current Issues in Tourism*. doi:10.1080/13683500.2015.1066764

Anderson, E., Bakir, A., & Wickens, E. (2015). Rural tourism development in Connemara, Ireland. *Tourism Planning & Development, 12*(1), 73–86. doi:10.1080/21568316.2014.965844

Andersson, T. D., Armbrecht, J., & Lundberg, E. (2015). Triple impact assessments of the 2013 European athletics indoor championship in Gothenburg. *Scandinavian Journal of Hospitality and Tourism*. doi:10.1080/15022250.2015.1108863

Bagur-Femenías, L., Martí, J., & Rocafort, A. (2015). Impact of sustainable management policies on tourism companies' performance: The case of the metropolitan region of Madrid. *Current Issues in Tourism, 18*(4), 376–390. doi:10.1080/13683500.2014.932757

Bocken, N. M. P., Short, S. W., Rana, P., & Evans, S. (2014). A literature and practice review to develop sustainable business model archetypes. *Journal of Cleaner Production, 65*, 42–56. doi:10.1016/j.jclepro.2013.11.039

Bonilla-Priego, M. J., Font, X., & Pacheco-Olivares, M. D. R. (2014). Corporate sustainability reporting index and baseline data for the cruise industry. *Tourism Management, 44*, 149–160. doi:10.1016/j.tourman.2014.03.004

Bos-Brouwers, H. E. J. (2010). Corporate sustainability and innovation in SMEs: Evidence of themes and activities in practice. *Business Strategy and the Environment, 19*(7), 417–435.

Breda, Z., Costa, R., & Costa, C. (2005). Clustering and networking the tourism development process: A market driven approach for a small backwards tourist region located in central Portugal (Caramulo). In C. Petrillo & J. Sawrbrooke (Eds.), *Networking and partnerships in destination development and management* (Vol. II, pp. 469–484). Naples: Enzo Albano.

Briedenhann, J. (2011). Economic and tourism expectations of the 2010 FIFA World Cup: A resident perspective. *Journal of Sport and Tourism, 16*(1), 5–32. doi:10.1080/14775085.2011.568085

Buhalis, D., & Law, R. (2008). Progress in information technology and tourism management: 20 years on and 10 years after the Internet – the state of eTourism research. *Tourism Management, 29*, 609–623. doi:10.1016/j.tourman.2008.01.005

Butler, R. W. (2006). The concept of a tourist area cycle of evolution: Implications for management of resources. In R. W. Butler (Ed.), *The tourism area life cycle: Applications and modifications* (Vol. 1, pp. 3–12). Clevedon: Channel View.

Centre for Industrial Studies & Touring Servizi. (2008). *The impact of tourism on coastal areas: Regional development aspects*. Brussels: European Parliament.

Chizzotti, A. (2006). *Pesquisa em ciências socias e humanas* [Research in social and human sciences]. São Paulo: Cortez.

Choi, H. C., & Sirakaya, E. (2006). Sustainability indicators for managing community tourism. *Tourism Management, 27*(6), 1274–1289. doi:10.1016/j.tourman.2005.05.018

Costa, C., Breda, Z., Costa, R., & Miguéns, J. (2008). The benefits of networks for small and medium sized tourism enterprises. In N. Scott, R. Baggio, & C. Cooper (Eds.), *Network analysis and tourism: From theory to practice* (pp. 96–112). Aspects of Tourism Book Series. Clevedon: Channel View.

Decree-Law 95/2013 of 19 July. [Legislation on tourist entertainment companies]. Retrieved November 20, 2015 from http://www.turismodeportugal.pt/PortuguC3AAs/conhecimento/legislacao/licenciamentoeutilidadeturistica/empresasdeanimacaoturistica/Anexos/AlteraC3A7C3A3oRNAAT_DL95_2013.pdf

Deprest, F. (1997). *Inquérito sobre o turismo de massa: A ecologia face ao território* [Survey on mass tourism: Ecology in view of the territory]. Lisboa: Instituto Piaget.

D'Hauteserre, A.-M. (2005). Tourism, development and sustainability in Monaco: Comparing discourses and practices. *Tourism Geographies, 7*(3), 290–312. doi:10.1080/14616680500164716

Erkuş-Öztürk, H., & Eraydın, A. (2010). Environmental governance for sustainable tourism development: Collaborative networks and organisation building in the Antalya tourism region. *Tourism Management, 31*(1), 113–124. doi:10.1016/j.tourman.2009.01.002

European Commission [EC]. (n.d.a). *A European strategy for more growth and jobs in coastal and maritime tourism*. Retrieved December 12, 2015, from http://ec.europa.eu/maritimeaffairs/documentation/publications/documents/coastal-and-maritime-tourism_en.pdf

European Commission. (n.d.b). *Challenges and opportunities for maritime and coastal tourism in the EU: Summary report of the online public consultation results*. Retrieved May 10, 2016, from http://ec.europa.eu/dgs/maritimeaffairs_fisheries/consultations/tourism/summary-report-consultation-on-tourism-in-the-eu_en.pdf

Eusébio, C., & Figueiredo, E. (2014). Desenvolvimento sustentável de destinos rurais [Sustainable development of rural destinations]. In E. Kastenholz, C. Eusébio, E. Figueiredo, M. J. Carneiro, & J. Lima (Coords.), *Reinventar o turismo rural em Portugal: Cocriação de experiências turísticas sustentáveis* [Reinventing rural tourism in Portugal: Co-creation of sustainable tourism experiences] (pp. 89–106). Aveiro: UA Editora.

Fadeeva, Z. (2005). Translation of sustainability ideas in tourism networks: Some roles of cross-sectoral networks in change towards sustainable development. *Journal of Cleaner Production, 13*(2), 175–189. doi:10.1016/S0959-6526(03)00124-0

Fernández, J. I. P., & Sánchez Rivero, M. (2009). Measuring tourism sustainability: Proposal for a composite index. *Tourism Economics, 15*, 277–296.

Font, X., Garay, L., & Jones, S. (2014). Sustainability motivations and practices in small tourism enterprises in European protected areas. *Journal of Cleaner Production*, 1–10. doi:10.1016/j.jclepro.2014.01.071

Francis, S., & Murphy, P. (2005). Sport tourism destinations: The active sport tourist perspective. In J. Higham (Ed.), *Sport tourism destinations: Issues, opportunities and analysis* (pp. 73–92). Amsterdam: Elsevier.

Fredline, E. (2005). Host and guest relations and sport tourism. *Sport in Society, 8*(2), 263–279. doi:10.1080/17430430500087328

Fyall, A., & Garrod, B. (2005). *Tourism marketing: A collaborative approach*. Clevedon: Channel View.

Gibson, H. J., Kaplanidou, K., & Kang, S. J. (2012). Small-scale event sport tourism: A case study in sustainable tourism. *Sport Management Review, 15*(2), 160–170. doi:10.1016/j.smr.2011.08.013

Global Reporting Initiative. (2002). *Sustainability reporting guidelines*. Boston, MA: Global Reporting Initiative.

Gössling, S. (2016). Tourism, information technologies and sustainability: An exploratory review. *Journal of Sustainable Tourism*. doi:10.1080/09669582.2015.1122017

Gunn, C. A., & Var, T. (2002). *Tourism planning: Basics, concepts, cases* (4th ed.). New York, NY: Routledge.

Hall, C. M. (2005). Sport tourism planning. In J. Higham (Ed.), *Sport tourism destinations: Issues, opportunities and analysis* (pp. 103–121). Amsterdam: Elsevier.

Halme, M. (2001). Learning for sustainable development in tourism networks. *Business Strategy and the Environment, 10*(2), 100–114. doi:10.1002/bse.278

Higham, J. (2005). Introduction to sport tourism impacts and environments. In J. Higham (Ed.), *Sport tourism destinations: Issues, opportunities and analysis* (pp. 223–232). Oxford: Elsevier Butterworth-Heinemann.

Hinch, T., & Higham, J. (2008). Sport tourism: A framework for research. In M. Weed (Ed.), *Sport & tourism: A reader* (pp. 40–56). New York, NY: Routledge.

Hunter, C. (1997). Sustainable tourism as an adaptive paradigm. *Annals of Tourism Research, 24*(4), 850–867. doi:10.1016/S0160-7383(97)00036-4

INE. (2015). *Anuário estatístico da Região Centro 2014*. Lisboa: Instituto Nacional de Estatística.

Jamal, T., & Stronza, A. (2009). Collaboration theory and tourism practice in protected areas: Stakeholders, structuring and sustainability. *Journal of Sustainable Tourism, 17*(2), 169–189. doi:10.1080/09669580802495741

Jennings, G. (2006). Water-based tourism, sport, leisure, and recreation experiences. In G. Jennings (Ed.), *Water-based tourism, sport, leisure, and recreation experiences* (pp. 1–20). Oxford: Butterworth-Heinemann.

Kastenholz, E., Carneiro, M. J., Eusébio, C., & Figueiredo, E. (2013). Host-guest relationships in rural tourism: Evidence from two Portuguese villages. *Anatolia, 24*(3), 367–380.

Kožić, I., & Mikulić, J. (2014). Research note: Measuring tourism sustainability: An empirical comparison of different weighting procedures used in modelling composite indicators. *Tourism Economics, 20*(2), 429–437. doi:10.5367/te.2013.0283

Krippendorff, K. (2013). *Content analysis: An introduction to its methodology* (3rd ed.). London: Sage.

Labuschagne, C., Brent, A. C., & Van Erck, R. P. G. (2005). Assessing the sustainability performances of industries. *Journal of Cleaner Production, 13*(4), 373–385. doi:10.1016/j.jclepro.2003.10.007

Lacher, R. G., & Nepal, S. K. (2010). From leakages to linkages: Local-level strategies for capturing tourism revenue in Northern Thailand. *Tourism Geographies, 12*(1), 77–99. doi:10.1080/14616680903493654

Lejárraga, I., & Walkenhorst, P. (2010). On linkages and leakages: Measuring the secondary effects of tourism. *Applied Economics Letters, 17*(5), 417–421. doi:10.1080/13504850701765127

Ma, S.-C., Egan, D., Rotherham, I., & Ma, S.-M. (2011). A framework for monitoring during the planning stage for a sports mega-event. *Journal of Sustainable Tourism, 19*(1), 79–96. doi:10.1080/09669582.2010.502576

Markwick, M. C. (2000). Golf tourism development, stakeholders, differing discourses and alternative agendas: The case of Malta. *Tourism Management, 21*(5), 515–524. doi:10.1016/S0261-5177(99)00107-7

Martín Martín, J. M., Jiménez Aguilera, J. D., & Molina Moreno, V. (2014). Impacts of seasonality on environmental sustainability in the tourism sector based on destination type: an application to Spain's Andalusia region. *Tourism Economics, 20*(1), 123–142. doi:10.5367/te.2013.0256

Martins, F. M. (1998). *Políticas de planeamento, ordenamento e gestão costeira: Contributo para uma discussão metodológica* [Planning, zoning and coastal management policies: Contribution to a methodological discussion] (PhD thesis). University of Aveiro.

Marzo-Navarro, M., Pedraja-Iglesias, M., & Vinzón, L. (2015). Sustainability indicators of rural tourism from the perspective of the residents. *Tourism Geographies*, 17(4), 586–602. doi:10.1080/14616688.2015.1062909

Middleton, V. T. C., Fyall, A., & Morgan, M. (2009). *Marketing in travel and tourism* (4th ed.). Oxford: Butterworth-Heinemann.

Mihalič, T., Žabkar, V., & Cvelbar, L. K. (2012). A hotel sustainability business model: Evidence from Slovenia. *Journal of Sustainable Tourism*, 20(5), 701–719.

Miller, G. (2001). The development of indicators for sustainable tourism: Results of a Delphi survey of tourism researchers. *Tourism Management*, 22(4), 351–362. doi:10.1016/S0261-5177(00)00067-4

Ministério da Economia e do Emprego. (2012). *Plano Estratégico Nacional do Turismo: Horizonte 2013-2015* [National Strategic Plan for Tourism: Horizon 2013–2015]. Lisboa: Ministério da Economia e do Emprego.

Mykletun, R. J. (2009). Celebration of extreme playfulness: Ekstremsportveko at voss. *Scandinavian Journal of Hospitality and Tourism*, 9(2–3), 146–176. doi:10.1080/15022250903119512

Orams, M. (2005). Introduction to sport tourism impacts and environments. In J. Higham (Ed.), *Sport tourism destinations: Issues, opportunities and analysis* (pp. 248–259). Oxford: Elsevier Butterworth-Heinemann.

Pan, B., & Fesenmaier, D. R. (2006). Online information search: Vacation planning process. *Annals of Tourism Research*, 33(3), 809–832. doi:10.1016/j.annals.2006.03.006

Patterson, C. (2016). *Sustainable tourism: Business development, operations and management*. Stanningley: Human Kinetics.

Pavlovich, K. (2001). The twin landscapes of Waitomo: Tourism network and sustainability through the Landcare Group. *Journal of Sustainable Tourism*, 9(6), 491–504. doi:10.1080/09669580108667416

Pérez, A., & del Bosque, I. R. (2014). Sustainable development and stakeholders: A renew proposal for the implementation and measurement of sustainability in hospitality companies. *Knowledge and Process Management*, 21(3), 198–205. doi:10.1002/kpm.1452

Ponting, J., & O'Brien, D. (2014). Liberalizing nirvana: An analysis of the consequences of common pool resource deregulation for the sustainability of Fiji's surf tourism industry. *Journal of Sustainable Tourism*, 22(3), 384–402. doi:10.1080/09669582.2013.819879

Quivy, R., & Campenhoudt, L. V. (1992). *Manual de investigação em ciências sociais* [Research guide in social sciences]. Lisboa: Gradiva.

Rahdari, A. H., & Anvary Rostamy, A. A. (2015). Designing a general set of sustainability indicators at the corporate level. *Journal of Cleaner Production*, 108, 757–771. doi:10.1016/j.jclepro.2015.05.108

Roberts, S., & Tribe, J. (2008). Sustainability indicators for small tourism enterprises: An exploratory perspective. *Journal of Sustainable Tourism*, 16(5), 575–594. doi:10.1080/09669580802159644

Ruiz-Molina, M.-E., Gil-Saura, I., & Moliner-Velázquez, B. (2010). Good environmental practices for hospitality and tourism. *Management of Environmental Quality: An International Journal*, 21(4), 464–476. doi:10.1108/14777831011049106

Schmitt, B. (1999). Experiential marketing. *Journal of Marketing Management*, 15, 53–67. doi:10.1362/026725799784870496

Scott, N., Baggio, R., & Cooper, C. (2008). *Network analysis and tourism: From theory to practice*. Clevedon: Channel View.

Sharpley, R. (2000). Tourism and sustainable development: Exploring the theoretical divide. *Journal of Sustainable Tourism*, 8(1), 1–19. doi:10.1080/09669580008667346

Sorensen, J., & McCreary, S. (1990). *Institutional arrangements for managing coastal resources and environments*. Washington, DC: National Park Service, U.S. Department of the Interior.

Tanguay, G. A., Rajaonson, J., & Therrien, M.-C. (2013). Sustainable tourism indicators: Selection criteria for policy implementation and scientific recognition. *Journal of Sustainable Tourism*, 21(6), 862–879. doi:10.1080/09669582.2012.742531

Timur, S., & Getz, D. (2008). A network perspective on managing stakeholders for sustainable urban tourism. *International Journal of Contemporary Hospitality Management, 20*(4), 445–461. doi:10.1108/09596110810873543

Tsartas, P. (2004). Tourism development in Greek insular and coastal areas: Sociocultural changes and crucial policy issues. In B. Bramwell (Ed.), *Coastal mass tourism: Diversification and sustainable development in Southern Europe* (pp. 68–84). Clevedon: Channel View.

United Nations Environment Programme. (n.d.). *Rio Declaration on Environment and Development*. Retrieved November 20, 2015, from http://www.unep.org/Documents.Multilingual/Default.Print.asp?documentid=78&articleid=1163

Veleva, V., & Ellenbecker, M. (2001). Indicators of sustainable production: Framework and methodology. *Journal of Cleaner Production, 9*(6), 519–549. doi:10.1016/S0959-6526(01)00010-5

Vellecco, I., & Mancino, A. (2010). Sustainability and tourism development in three Italian destinations: stakeholders' opinions and behaviours. *The Service Industries Journal, 30*(13), 2201–2223. doi:10.1080/02642060903287500

Vera Rebollo, J. F., & Ivars Baidal, J. A. (2004). Measuring sustainability in a mass tourist destination: Pressures, perceptions and policy responses in Torrevieja, Spain. In B. Bramwell (Ed.), *Coastal mass tourism: Diversification and sustainable development in Southern Europe* (pp. 176–199). Clevedon: Channel View.

Wickham, M., & Lehman, K. (2015). Communicating sustainability priorities in the museum sector. *Journal of Sustainable Tourism, 23*(7), 1011–1028. doi:10.1080/09669582.2015.1042483

Wiedmann, T. O., Lenzen, M., & Barrett, J. R. (2009). Companies on the scale comparing and benchmarking the sustainability performance of businesses. *Journal of Industrial Ecology, 13*(3), 361–383.

World Commission on Environment and Development. (1987). *Our common future*. New York: Oxford University Press.

World Tourism Organization. (2004). *Indicators of sustainable development for tourism destinations: A guidebook*. Madrid: Author.

Yaw, F., Jr. (2005). Cleaner technologies for sustainable tourism: Caribbean case studies. *Journal of Cleaner Production, 13*, 117–134. doi:10.1016/j.jclepro.2003.12.019

Ziakas, V., & Boukas, N. (2012). A neglected legacy. *International Journal of Event and Festival Management, 3*(3), 292–316. doi:10.1108/17582951211262710

Motivation of active sport tourists in a German highland destination – a cross-seasonal comparison

Alexander Hodeck and Gregor Hovemann

ABSTRACT

Sport tourism plays an important role as part of the economy in German highland destinations. Effects of seasonality have been creating challenges for these destinations for a long time. Climatic and demographic changes force destination management organisations to develop new all-season marketing strategies. At the same time, there is a lack of knowledge regarding sport tourism in highland destinations. Although a large number of existing studies elaborate on the motivation of active sport tourists, the results of these studies are not applicable to highland destinations. This study compares active sport tourists of one highland destination during two seasons by segmenting them according to their initial motivation. Results reveal that there is almost no significant difference between summer and winter sport tourists regarding the importance of motivational factors. Twenty-two motives were reduced to six factors by using a factor analysis (principal component analysis). A cluster analysis was then used to segment active sport tourists based on different motivational factors. Considerable seasonable differences between three generated segments of active sport tourists in terms of touristic behaviour (e.g. length of stay) were found. The findings of this study contribute to developing future marketing strategies for highland sport destinations and to reducing effects of seasonality.

Introduction

It was found that the sport tourism phenomenon has increased in importance over the last two decades as one of the fastest growing sectors in tourism. For example, the German tourism industry generated approximately 278.3 billion euros in 2011. This direct contribution of tourism to the gross value added amounts to 4.4% of the GDP and is comparable to that of the construction industry (Bundesministerium für Wirtschaft, 2012, p. 9). Sport or physical activity has become a major aspect of tourism in general. This is illustrated by the fact that sport has been among the seven central travel motives for German tourists for some time now (Aderhold, 2011, p. 90). The winter sport sector, whose share in overnight stays amounts to 3% of all touristic activities, is especially relevant for local stakeholders in destinations such as the Alps or German highland destinations. A large number of researchers have already contributed to developing sport tourism as a research field by working on both theoretical and empirical papers. Empirical studies vary widely. Studies on passive sport tourists (i.e. sport event tourists) differ from studies on active sport tourists. Active tourists are often divided into summer sport tourists and winter sport tourists. As these studies analyse various kinds of sports and destinations and use different methodical approaches, it is almost impossible to compare individual results to each other.

Although sport tourism and particularly winter sport tourism in highland destinations (peaks of up to 2000 m) have a long tradition and are also central to the economy (Ronge, 2012), highlands only play a minor role in scientific studies. Apart from a few exceptions (Konu, Laukkanen, & Komppula, 2011; Tsiotsou, 2006; Vassiliadis, Priporas, & Andronikidis, 2012; Won, Bang, & Shonk, 2008), studies on winter sport tourism mainly concentrate on high mountain areas (Dolnicar & Leisch, 2003; Hallmann, Zehrer, & Müller, 2013; Matzler, Füller, Renzl, Herting, & Späth, 2008; Perdue, 2004). As a consequence, the profiles and the behaviour of sport tourists in highland destinations have been barely investigated so far.

This research compares active sport tourists of one German highland destination (the Ore Mountains) in the summer and in the winter season. Climate change (Landauer, Pröbstl, & Haider, 2012) as well as demographic change (Grimm, Metzler, Butzmann, & Schmücker, 2010) pose great challenges for tourism organisations in highland destinations even more than in high mountain areas, which have been in the scientific spotlight of research for a long time. Up to two of three tourists travelling to highland areas are visiting these destinations for winter sport activities (Ronge, 2012). Highland destinations are forced to develop new marketing strategies because of significantly shorter winter sport seasons and ongoing climate change. At the same time, the number of German winter sport tourists has remained relatively stable over the last years (Aderhold, 2011), and traditional German winter sport destinations (e.g. the Alps, German highlands) have not expanded their portfolio. However, destinations in Eastern European countries (Poland, Czech Republic) have constantly increased their offers (e.g. Klínovec in Czech Republic) and entirely new destinations are now entering the market, such as Plesivec in Czech Republic or Bansko in Bulgaria. Ramped-up competition in the winter sport market increases the need for developing new marketing strategies.

The lack of research on sport tourism in highland destinations results in a higher uncertainty for decision makers in the respective destinations in terms of reorientation strategies. This is the starting point of the present paper. Using one highland destination as an example, active summer and winter sport tourists are segmented based on their motivations. This work delivers scientific insights into motivations of active sport tourists, while also generating practice-relevant results. The method of market segmentation was chosen in order to take both of these aspects into account. Market segmentation is a popular approach for developing marketing strategies and has already been applied in the area of (winter) sport tourism before (i.e. Dolnicar & Leisch, 2003; Füller & Matzler, 2008; Perdue, 2004; Tsiotsou, 2006). Thus, the main objective of this paper is to better understand the motivation of active sport tourists in highland destinations and, as it has not been investigated yet, to analyse whether differences exist between active sport tourists in winter and summer. Existing studies compare different destinations with each other (e.g. Hodeck & Hovemann, 2015; Hudson, Ritchie, & Timur, 2004), yet there is no study that compares active sport tourists of one highland destination over different seasons with each other. This study will contribute to bridging the existing research gap. The results will also be useful for the development of future marketing strategies of this highland destination. The lack of knowledge regarding cross-seasonal sport tourism in highland destinations needs to be overcome, both from a theoretical and a practical point of view. This study is an important first step in that direction as it segments active sport tourists of a highland destination in two seasons.

Theoretical background

Destination choice and segmentation in sport tourism

Literature on sport tourism offers different destination choice models (Hsu, Tsai, & Wu, 2009; Klenosky, Gengler, & Mulvey, 1993; Pearce, 2005; Um & Crompton, 1990). We can generally distinguish between two kinds of destination choice models. According to Pearce (2005, S. 104), there are structured economic approaches (i.e. Means-End Approach) and choice set models.

Using the 'Means-End Approach', Klenosky et al. (1993) discovered that varied and challenging ski slopes and cross-country trails play an important role in satisfying the tourists' desire for fun and excitement. Other important aspects also included snow conditions, social atmosphere, cost-saving opportunities as well as a local and familiar culture. Based on the findings of Klenosky et al. (1993), Dickson and Faulks (2007) studied the destination choice of Australian skiers and snowboarders. Again, snow quality proved to be the most important aspect. British skiers in Canada also stated that snow quality and the variety of ski slopes were the most essential factors for the selection of their destination (Godfrey, 1999).

Pearce (2005, p. 18) pursued the choice set model approach, which is fundamentally based on the studies of Um and Crompton (1990). The approach starts out with the assumption that travel decisions of tourists, which range from the initial idea and the destination selection to actual travel behaviour, depend on different individual characteristics such as age, nationality, gender and other demographic factors as well as internal and external factors. Konu et al. (2011) also pursued this approach and identified four major factors for the destination selection process by means of a factor analysis. The factors were downhill skiing offer, cross-country skiing offer, restaurants and other social offers as well as spa and wellness offers. Six different tourist clusters were identified with the help of these factors.

This research is based on the approach of Pearce (2005) and the findings of Konu et al. (2011). The destination choice process itself is influenced by internal and external factors. Internal factors relate to the traveller (i.e. characteristics and motivation). External factors refer to characteristics of the destination; facts that tourists know about from their personal experience or learn about through marketing measures of the destination or through information from a different source in order to make a travel decision. Other personal aspects (money, time and social environment) can further influence the destination choice.

Based on motivation theory, this study strives to segment active sport tourists in terms of their motivation within the destination choice process. In doing so, the focus is put on internal factors (according to the model of Pearce, 2005; adapted by Konu et al., 2011). Hodeck and Hovemann (2013) have already segmented winter sport tourists of a German highland destination, but without taking into account the internal factors that influence the destination choice process. Their study revealed six types of active sport tourists, which differed significantly from each other with regard to the relevance of certain destination characteristics and travel behaviours. By comparing summer and winter sport tourists, this study realised a cross-seasonal segmentation of active sport tourists for the first time in sport tourism research.

Segmentation is used in order to divide customers into homogenous groups following specific criteria or characteristics. The groups should differ considerably from each other. According to Böhler (1977, p. 10), there are basically two different approaches to defining segmentation. Market segmentation is either considered a process or a marketing strategy. However, this paper will not discuss this delineation in detail. There are various reasons why market segmentation can be helpful (Freyer, 2009; Schneider, 2009; Tsiotsou, 2006). Segmentation is a precondition for successful target marketing. It is the basis for developing effective marketing strategies making it easier to satisfy the needs of the customers. In addition, segmentation contributes to the identification of market opportunities and risks. Segmentation is usually carried out according to demographic, geographic, behavioural or psychographic variables. There are a priori and a posteriori approaches to segmentation (Freter, 2008, p. 196). When pursuing the a priori approach, variables such as age or gender are determined prior to the segmentation process. In contrast, the data used in a posteriori approaches have to be collected through interviews first (Freter, 2008, p. 198).

Segmentation in the field of sport tourism has already been realised according to different sports and destinations. These studies can hardly be compared to each other on account of different research objectives and designs. Existing studies often lead to a comprehensible number of segments of between two and six. Table 1 gives an overview of segmentation studies in sport tourism and compares these studies according to the

Table 1. Overview of segmentation studies in active sport tourism.

Authors	Types of tourists	Destinations/countries	Segmentation variables	Number of segments
Dolnicar and Leisch (2003)	Winter sport tourists	Austrian Alps	Travel motivation/ activities	5
Füller and Matzler (2008)	Ski resort customers	Austria, Switzerland and Italy (Alps)	Lifestyle	5
Perdue (2004)	Active winter sport tourists	Rocky Mountains	Frequency of travel	2
Won et al. (2008)	Students	North America	Destination choice factors	5
Tsiotsou (2006)	Ski resort customers	Greece	Frequency of travel	2
Konu et al. (2011)	Ski resort costumers	Finland	Destination choice criteria	6
Hodeck and Hovemann (2013)	Active winter sport tourists	German highlands	Destination choice criteria	6
Dolnicar and Fluker (2003)	Surfers	Australia / New Zealand	Motivation	6
Dickson and Dolnicar (2006)	Climbers	Australia (Mt. Kosciusko)	Motivation	6
Woratschek, Hannich, and Ritchie (2007)	Climbers	Europe	Motivation	4
Reynolds and Hritz (2012)	Surfers	USA	Motivation	3
Boukas and Ziakas (2013)	Golfers	Cyprus	Motivation	4

type of tourists and destination they investigated as well as the variables of segmentation and the number of created segments they chose. Segmentation studies in winter sport tourism concentrate on high mountain destinations in northern or southern Europe. There is only one study (Hodeck & Hovemann, 2013) dealing with segmentation in a central European highland. Segmentation in summer sport tourism focuses on climbing, water sports and golf tourism. To date, there are no studies on the motivation of active summer sport tourists in highland destinations. Beyond that, there is still no study that compares active sports tourists of one destination in different seasons.

Dolnicar and Leisch (2003) have segmented sport tourists according to their behaviour and motivation. They segmented winter sport tourists of the Austrian Alps using data gathered from a general tourism survey. Five behaviour-related segments and seven motivation-related segments could be identified among all sport tourists. These twelve segments were then grouped into five new clusters. Perdue (2004) segmented active winter sport tourists in the Rocky Mountains. Here, tourists were divided into two groups according to their frequency of travel. One group consisted of tourists that travel very frequently, while the second group contained tourists with a low frequency of travel. Füller and Matzler (2008) analysed winter sport tourists in alpine ski resorts in Austria, Italy and Switzerland. In their study, they segmented tourists into five different lifestyle groups. Won et al. (2008) clustered North American students based on the relative importance of certain factors. This analysis also revealed five segments. They observed significant differences in the relevance of individual factors for the distinctive groups. 'Snow conditions' proved to be the only factor which was the most important one for all groups alike.

If all existing studies are taken into account for the segmentation in winter sport tourism, it soon becomes apparent that they almost exclusively focus on high mountain areas (peaks above 2000 m). Only three studies conducted segmentation analyses of other types of winter sport destinations, including the analysis of Tsiotsou (2006), who segmented Greek winter sport tourists based on their frequency of travel. Konu et al. (2011) divided Finnish winter sport tourists into six different clusters using destination choice criteria. The individual segments differ from each other in terms of gender, age, travel behaviour, frequency of travel and travel companion. Vassiliadis et al. (2012) clustered winter sport tourists in 13 Greek ski areas according to their behaviour during three time blocks (before arrival, upon arrival and during their stay).

Compared to winter sport tourism, there are even fewer studies on destination selection in summer sport tourism. Dolnicar and Fluker (2003) asked 430 surfers about their motivation for choosing a certain travel destination. It became apparent that there was a correlation between motivation and selected destination. Using a factor analysis, Dickson and Dolnicar (2006) segmented 524 climbers into six clusters of different motivations. Similarly, Woratschek et al. (2007) also studied climbers by using a cluster analysis. They identified four segments of varying motivations. Reynolds and Hritz (2012) carried out a survey with 347 surfers. Their findings revealed very heterogeneous groups that differed from each other in terms of age and motivation. Boukas and Ziakas (2013) analysed 100 golf tourists in Cyprus. Their study resulted in four segment clusters that also varied in motivation.

In conclusion, it can be stated that although there are several studies dealing with the motivation of active sport tourists, these studies are usually limited to one kind of sports and one season only. So far, there are no studies on summer sport tourism in Central European highland destinations. Likewise, there are no all-season destination segmentation studies either.

Seasonality in sport tourism

It is obvious that seasonality is a major challenge in tourism (Commons & Page, 2001). This also applies to sport tourism. Sport tourism activities usually depend on geographic and climatic conditions. Due to that and the almost entirely seasonal character of sport touristic activities, seasonality has a considerable impact on them. At the same time, however, possible ways of reducing seasonality through sport tourism have been developed, too (Higham & Hinch, 2002). BarOn (1975) offered the first definition of seasonality. In his opinion, there are either natural (e.g. climate or snow fall) or institutional (e.g. bank holidays and religious aspects) reasons for seasonality. Later, Butler (1984) added three different dimensions (social pressure or fashion, sporting seasons and inertia or tradition) so that both approaches are often combined in order to define seasonality in tourism. This is also true for sport tourism.

Seasonality is generally associated with negative impacts such as inefficient use of infrastructure (i.e. hotels and sports complexes) or services (i.e. employee surplus). This implies insufficient use during off season as well as overcrowding effects during high season. Pegg, Patterson, and Vila Griddo (2012) rightly pointed out the positive effects of seasonality. Yet from an economic point of view, the negative impacts seem to outweigh the positive effects. Therefore, various authors have developed strategies for mitigating the effects of seasonality. These strategies chiefly focused on product and market diversification (Getz & Nilsson, 2004; Higham & Hinch, 2002). In this respect, the segmentation of customers is particularly suitable (Baum & Hagen, 1999; Pegg et al., 2012; Tkaczynski, Rundle-Thiele, & Prebensen, 2015).

Destinations with a clear focus on sport tourism are facing serious challenges in coping with seasonality, especially winter sport destinations (Tkaczynski et al., 2015). These destinations do not only suffer from negative impacts caused by the excessive exposure and use of the region during high season (Hudson, 2000, 2004), but also from the effects of climate change, which have already led to shorter ski seasons or questioned winter sport tourism altogether (Landauer et al., 2012). European highland destinations are particularly affected by these challenges. Consequently, they have to develop new, all-season strategies for sport tourism in the future. Yet, as stated earlier, it is still unclear whether this is possible or not.

There is a research gap concerning the motivation of active sport tourists related to seasonality in general and to sport tourism in highland destinations in particular. The present study strives to reduce this lack of knowledge. At the same time, the results of segmentation based on motivation are essential for destination management organisations in highland destinations for the development of theoretically sound marketing strategies.

Methodology

A self-constructed questionnaire was used for the survey. It consisted of three parts. The first part focused on socio-demographic variables. Questions about motivation formed the second part of the survey. Motives were taken from the German Travel Analyses (Aderhold, 2011), which have been used in German tourism research for over 30 years, including sensory, aesthetic, entertainment-related, social and health aspects (Beier, 2001, p. 205). Finally, sport tourists where asked about their travel behaviour and satisfaction.

The data ($n = 256$) were collected during the winter season of 2013/2014 and during the summer season of 2014 in one German highland destination (the Ore Mountains). The Ore Mountains rank third in the analysis of all German highlands and they rank first among East German tourism destinations. There are more than three million overnight stays in the Ore Mountains every year (TV Erzegebirge, 2014). Most of the tourists visit this destination in winter, as it is known for its long winter sport tradition. The Ore Mountains are located in the federal state of Saxony in the southeast of Germany next to the border to Czech Republic. Due to its location, the Ore Mountains used to be a politically divided area. In fact, even today this destination appears to have no borders at all. The majority of the tourists visiting the region come from Germany, most of them from the eastern part, but the numbers of tourists from Czech Republic, Poland and Slovakia and even from the Netherlands have slightly risen over the last few years.

A multi-level process was used for the selection of the sample. A cluster sampling (area sampling) method was chosen (Berekoven, Eckert, & Ellenrieder, 2001). Data were collected at several locations within each destination on four different dates. The subjects at the pre-selected places were chosen randomly. Four dates for each destination had been selected before the season started in order to reduce the effects of weather conditions. The sampling during winter season took place between the end of December 2013 and the end of February 2014. Two of the samplings were carried out on a weekend and two took place during the week. In the summer season, data were collected between the end of June 2014 and the end of August 2014 on four different points in time, too. Data were collected with the help of standardised questionnaires and trained personal consisting of Master's Degree students in a Sports Management programme. Interviews were conducted close to relevant touristic sport complexes (ski slopes, ski tracks, bike routes, walking trails and hotels).

The sample only considered people who spent at least one night at the destination or visited the destination for one day, and lived more than 50 kilometres away from where the interviews were carried out. Only persons who considered sport as a main aspect of their visit were included in the sample.

IBM SPSS 21 was used for the statistical analysis. Active sport tourists were compared to each other on the basis of socio-demographic variables in order to compare the sample with the population. Segmentation based on travel motives of active summer and winter sport tourists was carried out in a multi-level process. Initially, a factor analysis (principal component analysis (PCA) with varimax rotation) was used to reduce the 22 motives to a smaller number of factors. Afterwards, a two-step cluster analysis helped create the optimal number of segments among active sport tourists. The single-linkage method was used for the extraction of extreme values. Homogenous segments were then created using the Ward method (Bergs, 1981, p. 97). This method has been applied in other studies dealing with the segmentation of winter sport tourists in highland areas before (Hodeck & Hovemann, 2013). Finally, differences between clusters regarding various socio-demographic variables were analysed in order to accumulate information for marketing strategies.

Results

The sample matches the average population of active sport tourists of this destination, which becomes apparent when comparing data such as average age (41.50 years) or length of stay (3.65 days) as well as the distribution of gender (52.50% female sport tourists) with data of the destination management organisation (TV Erzgebirge, 2014) or other studies on this destination (Hodeck & Hovemann, 2013).

There are no significant differences between summer and winter sport tourists regarding age or gender. Yet, the study revealed significant differences between active sport tourists regarding their length of stay ($T = 5.487$; $p < .001$) and the distance travelled to reach the destination ($T = 6.314$; $p < .001$). In winter, active sport tourists travel 289.81 kilometres to the Ore Mountains and stay for 4.92 days within the destination while summer tourists travel only 65.08 kilometres and stay for 2.84 days.

Active summer and winter sport tourists of the Ore Mountains were segmented according to the relevance of specific internal destination selection criteria (motives) within the destination choice process. As a first step, the 22 motives taken from the German Travel Analyses (Aderhold, 2011) were boiled down to eight factors based on their relevance in the destination choice process. This accounted for the percentage of 65.5% of the total variance of the variables, which was generated by using a PCA (Table 2). The data suitable for this type of analysis, as both the Kaiser–Meyer–Olkin (KMO) measure of sampling adequacy (0.688) and Bartlett's test of sphericity ($p < .001$) confirmed that the

Table 2. Results of the PCA.

	1. Do something and have fun together	2. Take a Break	3. Experience the environment	4. Just relax	5. Be active and healthily	6. Experience the destination	7. Spend time with the family	8. Experience nature
Experience a lot	.814							
Move around	.733							
Experience something with friends	.645							
Fun, pleasure	.629							
Away from it all		.733						
Refuel		.689						
Leave a polluted city		.536						
Enjoy free time			.708					
Healthy climate			.696					
Gain new impressions			.688					
Be free, have time				.710				
Rest				.689				
Relax, no stress				.640				
Do sport actively					.741			
Soft sport/fitness					.666			
Do something for your health					.626			
Talk to inhabitants						.709		
Enjoy nice weather						.693		
Meet nice people						.552		
Play/spend time with children							.848	
Spend time with partner/family							.553	
Experience nature, landscape								.884

Notes: KMO measure of sampling adequacy = 0.688; $p < .001$; cumulative percentage of variance explained: 65.5

Table 3. Differences between active summer and winter sport tourists regarding average importance of motivational factors (1: not important at all; 5: very important).

Motivational factors (average)	Summer	Winter	t-Value	Significance
Do something and have fun together (3.85)	3.93	3.79	−1.62	n.s.
Take a break (3.83)	3.95	3.75	−1.68	n.s.
Experience environment (3.47)	3.63	3.31	−3.53	$p < .001$
Just relax (3.76)	3.89	3.61	−3.21	$p < .001$
Be active and healthy (3.45)	3.43	3,58	1.64	n.s.
Experience the destination (3.09)	2.85	3.25	−4.22	$p < .001$
Spend time with the family (3.90)	3.69	4.17	−4.28	$p < .001$
Experience nature (4.16)	4.23	4.13	−0.93	n.s.

analysis is acceptable as 'mediocre' (Kaiser & Rice, 1974, 112). All of the eight factors have an eigenvalue higher than one. The importance of four out of eight factors differs significantly depending on the season (Table 3). 'Experience nature' was the most important factor for both groups with insignificant differences between summer and winter sport tourists. 'Experience the destination' seemed to be the least important factor for all sport tourists, but differences between the groups were considerable.

Eight created motivational factors were used for the two-step cluster analysis. Five subjects had to be excluded from the sample after the first step. A three-cluster solution seemed to be the best solution after the second step of clustering. As there are no clear statistical rules for defining the most suitable number of clusters, the authors determined the number in two steps. According to the elbow criteria (Backhaus, Erichson, Plink, & Weiber, 2011, p. 436f.), the three-cluster solution was deemed the most suitable solution. The test of Mojena (1997, p. 359ff.) confirmed three clusters as the best solution. The largest cluster of active sport tourists can be described as 'Want-it-all tourists', as the average importance of all factors in this cluster is higher than the average of the whole sample. 'Have time with the family' is the only factor of high importance for 'Family tourists'. The smallest cluster with only 25 persons can be described as 'Active and recreational tourists'. There are significant differences between seven out of eight motivational factors regarding the average importance among the clusters (Table 4). Only the factor 'Be active and healthy' is equally important for all three segments. Of course, sport in general is the main aspect of all subjects included in the sample, but other factors were also decisive for the destination choice of the active sport tourists.

Table 4. Differences between segments of sport tourists regarding average importance of motivational factors (1: not important at all; 5: very important).

Motivational factors (average)	Want-it-All tourists ($n = 162$)	Family tourists ($n = 64$)	Active and recreational tourists ($n = 25$)	Significance (of ANOVA)
Do something and have fun together (3.85)	**4.00**	3.35	**4.17**	$p < .001$
Take a break (3.83)	**4.04**	3.38	3.60	$p < .001$
Experience environment (3.47)	**3.73**	2.73	**3.63**	$p < .001$
Just relax (3.76)	**3.93**	3.21	**4.04**	$p < .001$
Be active and healthy (3.45)	3.45	3.36	**3.71**	n.s.
Experience the destination (3.09)	3.20	2.62	**3.56**	$p < .001$
Have time with the family (3.90)	3.89	**4.03**	3.60	$p < .05$
Experience nature (4.16)	**4.60**	3.84	2.12	$p < .001$

Table 5. Differences between segments of sport tourists regarding several variables.

Variables (average)	Want-it-all tourists ($n = 162$)	Family tourists ($n = 64$)	Active and recreational tourists ($n = 25$)	Significance (of ANOVA)
Age in years (41.50)	**43.55**	40.92	30.68	$p < .001$
Distance from home in kilometres (164.01)	**171.88**	159.35	127.86	n.s.
Length of stay in days (3.65)	3.38	**4.75**	2.60	$p < .05$
Total money spent per day per person in Euro (96.50)	98.15	**104.20**	77.59	$p < .05$

Some differences between the three created segments of tourists regarding their socio-demographic profile and touristic behaviour (Table 5) have been revealed, which is of interest for destination management organisations. The clusters differ considerably from each other in terms of average age. For example, 'active and recreational tourists' are more than 10 years younger than the other tourists. Gender did not influence the affiliation to one of the clusters. 'Family tourists' stay within one destination for the longest time and spend the highest average amount of money per person and per day. While a typical 'Active and recreational tourist' spends only 201.73 euros per stay (money spent per person and day multiplied with the length of stay), a 'Family tourist' spends 494.95 euros on average when visiting the destination. There is a significant correlation between season and segment of tourists (chi-square = 30.161; $p < .001$ and Cramer's $V = 0.347$; $p < .001$). There are actually more 'Family tourists' than expected in the winter season and less than expected in the summer season. A similar observation was made for 'Want-it-all tourists', only vice versa: there were more tourists of this cluster than expected in summer and less than expected in winter. There is no seasonal divergence for 'Active and recreational tourists'.

Discussion

Seasonality of sport tourism is a relevant factor for the investigated highland destination. Statistical data indicate that a higher number of tourists visit this destination in winter (Ronge, 2012). Apart from that, active sport tourists spend more time at the destination in winter. The investigation proves that in addition to segmentation conducted in previous studies, active sport tourists of a highland destination can be segmented based on internal destination choice criteria as motivation, too. As shown in existing studies, active sport tourists of different clusters of segmentations, based on external (e.g. Hodeck & Hovemann, 2013; Konu et al., 2011; Won et al., 2008) or internal (e.g. Boukas & Ziakas, 2013; Dickson & Dolnicar 2006; Dolnicar & Fluker, 2003; Reynolds & Hritz, 2012; Woratschek et al., 2007) destination choice criteria, differ notably from each other in terms of socio-demographic variables and touristic behaviour.

Recent studies on the comparison of active sport tourists in different highland destinations imply that there are major differences between the sport tourists of different destinations (Hodeck & Hovemann, 2015) within one season. Differences detected in these studies were more significant than the differences discovered by this study, which compares active sport tourists of one destination in different seasons. As a consequence, destination choice must be regarded as a destination-specific phenomenon. Thus, study results concerning different destinations can hardly be compared to each other, regardless of whether the same methodology was used or not, as sport tourism depends on the location, people and activities (Weed & Bull, 2002). However, the segmentation of active sport tourists in the Ore Mountain illustrates that there is a correlation between season and cluster. On the other hand, the importance of motivational factors for summer and winter sport tourists does not differ notably. Thus from a practical point of view, it can be assumed that the destination is attractive for the same profiles of tourists all year round.

Yet, effects of seasonality on the destination can still be observed. One reason could be the lack of a suitable strategy for all-season sport tourism. Three created clusters of tourists are interesting for destination management organisations and for understanding active sport tourists in general. While 'Want-it-all tourists' can be found in most of segmentation studies (e.g. Konu et al., 2011; Park & Yoon, 2009) and, thus, do not appear to be special sport tourists or particular for this destination, 'Family tourists' are a typical cluster of active sport tourists in highland destinations (Hodeck & Hovemann, 2013). These tourists create a high economic impact for the chosen destination, as they spend more than twice as much as tourist from other segments. From a practical point of view, future destination strategies should focus on this segment, especially for the summer season, where they are still under-represented at the moment. Based on the collected data, the following recommendations for the necessary development of future marketing strategies can be derived. All-season concepts for sport tourism should be developed in order to overcome seasonality effects as a result of this first cross-seasonal segmentation of active sport tourists in highland destinations.

At the same time, the results that form the basis for interpretation should be considered as a snapshot and ought to be treated cautiously. Due to the design of the study, unavoidable seasonal particularities might occur. Both the number of people questioned and the number of interview locations is limited. Impacts caused by weather conditions or the interviewer must be taken into consideration, too. General statements based on the results should be reduced to a minimum, and the consequences drawn from the findings should be seen as preliminary indications for the development of future strategies. Further studies on multiple seasons are necessary in order to prove the results obtained in this study. Additional destinations (beyond highland destinations) should also be taken into account. This investigation indicates that it might be possible to attract the same segments of active sport tourists to a traditional highland winter sport destination throughout the whole year. More generally, we still do not know whether all-season strategies in active sport tourism in highlands are also suitable for other sport tourism destinations.

Without neglecting the restrictions mentioned before, this study illustrates that destination choice in active sport tourism is a phenomenon, which depends less on the time of travel or the kind of sport than on the chosen destination. This should be explored in future studies. From a practical point of view, all-year-round destination-specific marketing strategies directed toward active sport tourism appear as a promising way to manage the effects of seasonality in German highland destinations.

Disclosure statement

No potential conflict of interest was reported by the authors.

References

Aderhold, P. (2011). *Reiseverhalten der Deutschen. Kurzfassung der Deutschen Reiseanalyse 2011* [Travel behaviour of the Germans. Short version of the German Travel Analysis 2001]. Kiel: FUR.

Backhaus, K., Erichson, B., Plink, W., & Weiber, R. (2011). *Multivariate Analysemethoden. Eine anwendungsorientierte Einführung* [Multivariate methods of analysing. A practical introduction] (13th ed.). Berlin: Springer.

BarOn, R. (1975). *Seasonality in tourism: A guide to the analysis of seasonality and trends for policy making*. London: Economist Intelligence Unit.

Baum, T., & Hagen, L. (1999). Responses to seasonality: The experiences of peripheral destinations. *The International Journal of Tourism Research, 1*(5), 299.

Beier, K. (2001). *Anreizstrukturen im Outdoorsport* [Incentive structures in outdoor sports]. Schorndorf: Hoffmann.

Berekoven, L., Eckert, W., & Ellenrieder, P. (2001). *Marktforschung. Methodische Grundlagen und praktische Anwendungen* [Market research. Methodical basics and practical applications] (9th ed.). Wiesbaden: Gabler.

Bergs, S. (1981). *Optimalität bei Cluster-Analysen* [Optimality in cluster analysisi]. (Dissertation). Münster.

Böhler, H. (1977). *Methoden und Modelle der Marktsegmentierung* [Methods and models of market segmentation]. Stuttgart: Poeschel.

Boukas, N., & Ziakas, V. (2013). *Golf tourist motivation and sustainable development: A marketing management approach for promoting responsible Golf tourism in Cyprus*. Retrieved from http://www.academia.edu/3568662/Golf_Tourist_Motivation_and_Sustainable_Development_A_Marketing_Management_Approach_for_Promoting_Responsible_Golf_Tourism_in_Cyprus

Bundesministerium für Wirtschaft. (2012). *Wirtschaftsfaktor Tourismus Deutschland* [Economic factor tourism in Germany]. München: PRpeptum.

Butler, R. (1984). Seasonality in tourism. Issues and problems. In A. Seaton (Ed.), *Tourism, the state of the art* (pp. 3323–339). Chichester: Wiley.

Commons, J., & Page, S. (2001). Managing seasonality in peripheral tourism regions: The case of Northland, New Zealand. In T. Baum & S. Lundrop (Eds.), *Seasonality in tourism* (pp. 153–172). New York, NY: Pergamon.

Dickson, T. J., & Dolnicar, S. (2006). *Ascending Mt Kosciuszko: An exploration of motivational patterns*. CD Proceedings of the 15th International Research Conference of the Council for Australian University Tourism and Hospitality Education (CAUTHE 2006): To the City and Beyond, 1030. Retrieved from http://ro.uow.edu.au/commpapers/75/

Dickson, T. J., & Faulks, P. (2007). Exploring overseas snowsport participation by Australian skiers and snowboarders. *Tourism Review, 62*(3/4), 7–14.

Dolnicar, S., & Fluker, M. (2003). Behavioural market segments among surf tourists: Investigating past destination choice. *Journal of Sport Tourism, 8*(3), 186–196.

Dolnicar, S., & Leisch, F. (2003). Winter tourist segments in Austria: Identifying stable vacation styles using bagged clustering techniques. *Journal of Travel Research, 41*(3), 281–292.

Freter, H. (2008). *Markt- und Kundensegmentierung. Kundenorientierte Markterfassung und –bearbeitung* [Market and customer segmentation. Customer-orientated market control and strategy] (2nd ed.). Stuttgart: Kohlhammer.

Freyer, W. (2009). *Tourismus-Marketing. Marktorientiertes Management im Mikro- und Makrobereich der Tourismuswirtschaft* [Tourism marketing. Market-oriented management in the micro and macro field of the tourism industry] (6th ed.). München: Oldenbourg.

Füller, J., & Matzler, K. (2008). Customer delight and market segmentation: An application of the three-factor theory of customer satisfaction on life style groups. *Tourism Management, 29*(1), 116–126.

Getz, D., & Nilsson, P. A. (2004). Responses of family business to extreme seasonality in demand: The case of Bornholm, Denmark. *Tourism Management, 25*(1), 17–30.

Godfrey, K. B. (1999). Attributes of destination choice: British skiing in Canada. *Journal of Vacation Marketing, 5*(1), 18–30.

Grimm, B., Metzler, D., Butzmann, E., & Schmücker, D. (2010). Auswirkungen des demografischen Wandels auf touristische Nachfragestrukturen in Deutschland und ausgewählten Quellmärkten. Das zukünftige Reisevolumen und –verhalten verschiedener Altersgruppen [Impacts of demographic change on tourism demand structures in Germany and selected source markets. The future travel volume and behaviour of different age groups]. *Tw Zeitschrift für Tourismuswirtschaft, 2*(2), 111–132.

Hallmann, K., Zehrer, A., & Müller, S. (2013). Perceived destination image: An image model for winter sports destination and its effect on intention to revisit. *Journal of Travel Research, 54*(1), 94–106.

Higham, J., & Hinch, T. (2002). Tourism, sport and seasons: The challenges and potential of overcoming seasonality in the sport and tourism sector. *Tourism Management, 23*, 175–185.

Hodeck, A., & Hovemann, G. (2013). Typisierung von Wintersporttouristen in deutschen Mittelgebirgen am Beispiel des Erzgebirges [Typification of winter sport tourists in German highlands using the example of the Ore Mountains]. *Sciamus – Sport und Management, 4*(4), 1–13.

Hodeck, A., & Hovemann, G. (2015). Empirical findings regarding the destination choice in two German winter sport destinations. *Polish Journal of Sport and Tourism, 22*(2), 114–117.

Hsu, T.-K., Tsai, Y.-F., & Wu, H.-H. (2009). The preference analysis for tourist choice of destination: A case study of Taiwan. *Tourism Management, 30*, 288–297.

Hudson, S. (2000). *Snow business: A study of the international ski industry*. London: Continuum International Publishing Group.

Hudson, S. (2004). Winter sport tourism in North America. In B. Richie & D. Adair. (Eds.), *Sport tourism: Interrelationships, impacts and issues* (pp. 188–204). Clevedon: Channel View.

Hudson, S., Ritchie, B., & Timur, S. (2004). Measuring destination competitiveness: An empirical study on Canadian ski resorts. *Tourism and Hospitality Planning & Development, 1*(1), 79–94.

Kaiser, H. F., & Rice, J. (1974). Little Jiffy, Mark IV. *Educational and Psychological Measurement, 34*, 111–117.

Klenosky, D., Gengler, C., & Mulvey, M. (1993). Understanding the factors influencing Ski destination choice: A means-end analytic approach. *Journal of Leisure Research, 25*(4), 362–379.

Konu, H., Laukkanen, T., & Komppula, R. (2011). Using ski destination choice criteria to segment Finnish ski resort customers. *Tourism Management, 32*, 1096–1105.

Landauer, M., Pröbstl, U., & Haider, W. (2012). Managing cross-country skiing destinations under the conditions of climate change – scenarios for destinations in Austria and Finland. *Tourism Management, 33*, 741–751.

Matzler, K., Füller, J., Renzl, B., Herting, S., & Späth, S. (2008). Customer satisfaction with alpine Ski areas: The moderating effects of personal, situational and product factors. *Journal of Travel Research, 46*(4), 403–413.

Mojena, R. (1977). Hierarchical clustering methods and stopping rules: An evaluation. *The Computer Journal, 20*, 359–363.

Park, D., & Yoon, S. (2009). Segmentation by motivation in rural tourism: A Korean case study. *Tourism Management, 30*, 99–108.

Pearce, P. L. (2005). *Tourist behaviour: Themes and conceptual schemes*. Clevedon: Channel View.

Pegg, S., Patterson, I., & Vila Griddo, P. (2012). The impact of seasonality on tourism and hospitality operations in the alpine region of New South Wales, Australia. *International Journal of Hospitality Management, 31*, 659–666.

Perdue, R. (2004). Sustainable tourism and stakeholder groups: A case study of Colorado ski resort communities. In G. Crouch, R. Perdue, H. Timmermanns, & M. Uysal (Eds.), *Consumer psychology of tourism, hospitality and leisure* (pp. 253–264). Wallingford, CT: CABI.

Reynolds, Z., & Hritz, N. M. (2012). Surfing as adventure travel: Motivations and lifestyles. *Journal of Tourism Insights, 3*(1), 14–23.

Ronge, C. (2012). Die Entwicklung des Tourismus in Sachsen 1992 bis 2011 [Development of tourism in Saxony from 1992 to 2011]. In C. Ronge (Ed.), *Statistik in Sachsen 3/2012* (pp. 30–33). Kamenz: Statistisches Landesamt.

Schneider, W. (2009). *Marketing und Käuferverhalten* [Marketing and consumer behaviour] (3rd ed.). München: Oldenbourg.

Tkaczynski, A., Rundle-Thiele, S., & Prebensen, N. (2015). Segmenting potential nature-based tourists based on temporal factors: The case of Norway. *Journal of Travel Research*, *54*(2), 251–265.

Tsiotsou, R. (2006). Using visit frequency to segment ski resorts customers. *Journal of Vacation Marketing*, *12*(1), 15–26.

TV Erzegebirge (2014). *Destinationsstrategie Erzgebirge* [Destination strategy of the Ore Mountains]. Annaberg-Buchholz: Tourismusverband Erzgebirge e.V.

Um, S., & Crompton, J. L. (1990). Attitude determinants in tourism destination choice. *Annals of Tourism Research*, *17*, 432–448.

Vassiliadis, C., Priporas, C.-V., & Andronikidis, A. (2012). An analysis of visitor behaviour using time blocks: A study of ski destinations in Greece. *Tourism Management*. doi:10.1016/j.tourman.2012.03.013

Weed, M., & Bull, C. (2002). *Sports tourism: Participants, policy, and providers*. Oxford: Elsevier.

Won, D., Bang, H., & Shonk, D. (2008). Relative importance of factors involved in choosing a regional Ski destination: Influence of consumption situation and recreation specialisation. *Journal of Sport & Tourism*, *13*(4), 249–271.

Woratschek, H., Hannich, F. M., & Ritchie, B. (2007). Motivations of sport tourists – an empirical analysis of several European rock climbing regions. Retrieved from http://www.fiwi.uni-bayreuth.de/de/download/WP_02-07.pdf

Determining the influence of the social versus physical context on environmentally responsible behaviour among cycling spectators

Elizabeth A. du Preez ⓘ and Ernie T. Heath

ABSTRACT
The paper explores the relationships between three factors and environmentally responsible behavioural intentions among cycling spectators: place attachment, subculture identification and subjective norms. Two categories of behavioural intentions are presented namely situational (while spectating) and future (before attending similar events). Analysis of covariance is used to test the relationships in a sample of 619 spectators from both road race and mountain bike events. The paper supports previous research highlighting the importance of the social dimension of sport spectating and the link to social norms that drive environmental behaviour. It also adds to existing research on place attachment as a precursor to environmentally responsible behaviour with reference to sport spectating.

Introduction

Many outdoor sporting codes depend on the natural environment in which they are performed and the quality thereof directly affects participants' experiences (Hinch & Higham, 2011). An increasing number of studies explore the role of the sports organisation, management and policies to promote environmentally responsible behaviour among consumers (for example, Casper & Pfahl, 2012; Casper, Pfahl, & McCullough, 2014; Inoue, Kent, & Smart, 2012; Kellison & Kim, 2014; Pfahl, 2010), an important endeavour as the behaviour of consumers is essential to the success and effective execution of environmental management initiatives (Sheth, Sethia, & Srinivas, 2011; Stanford, 2008). Still not enough is known about the environmentally oriented behaviour of spectators as one group of these consumers (Nguyen, Iacono, & Stratmann, 2011), despite recent advances in the field of environmental sustainability for sport events (discussed in Sotiriadou & Hill, 2015).

Environmental behaviour is strongly influenced by individual differences in people (Dolnicar & Grün, 2009; Mehmetoglu, 2010; Miao & Wei, 2013) while also taking place within a social context (Günther, 2009; Winkel, Seagert, & Evans, 2009). Behaviour takes place within a specific 'situation' known as the behavioural setting – a point in time and place (Belk, 1975; Pearce, 2005) and includes the physical as well as the social surroundings (Belk, 1975). To study environmentally responsible behaviour of individuals in a sport spectating context, it is thus important to define the relevant situational characteristics and to explore behaviour against the backdrop of a particular spatial setting (Günther, 2009). King, Kahle, and Close (2011) similarly argue that to explore consumer behaviour in sport, aspects unique to sport consumption as the social context should be considered. Environmental behaviour therefore has to be explored within the behavioural setting of the sport type under investigation to understand the influence on behaviour of individuals.

Cycling tourism is a growing niche market (Ritchie, Tkaczynski, & Faulks, 2010) and cycling routes and cycle tourism developments are increasingly being integrated into sustainable development and transport policies (Pucher, Buehler, & Seinen, 2011; Pucher, Garrard, & Greaves, 2011; Ritchie et al., 2010). The growing interest in cycling has also been witnessed in South Africa as country where the research was conducted, surpassing golf in popularity among corporates and with a proliferation of cycling events attracting international attention (Barry, 2014; Du Toit, 2013; Hardisty, 2014). The sport has become synonymous with environmental responsibility, healthy living and carbon-free transport (Aldred, 2010; Cupples & Ridley, 2008) with bicycle tourism even being named an environmentally sustainable niche market (Lamont, 2009). Yet, not a lot is known about the environmental behaviour of both active and passive participants of cycling events.

Cycling races attract large crowds with spectators spread along the route of the race. As races mostly occur outdoors in public spaces, there is arguably less control over the environmental behaviour of the spectators than in the case of gated events where appropriate facilities are provided in a confined space. The active participants (cyclists) may be guided by sporting codes of conduct and unofficial norms that develop among them (after Fink & Smith, 2012), while this may not be the case among spectators and even more so in the case of environmental behaviour. Spectators have a big environmental impact, travelling to the event and spending time in the event's surrounding environment. The ecological footprint of spectators to the opening of the Tour de France has, for example, been equated to 57,990 global hectares or 143 times the area of London's Olympic Park, mainly due to transport, accommodation and consumables (Collins, Roberts, & Munday, 2012). Where the cyclists may be focused on the sporting activity and be less inclined to engage with the wider environmental setting, the opposite may be true of spectators who often interpret the space as a leisure setting (Snelgrove & Wood, 2010). Furthermore, spectators at outdoor events do not play the same significant role in the income model of event organisers as is the case with stadium spectators that bring income through ticket sales, refreshments and merchandise purchases (Szymanski, 2003). This may have added to the current situation where research is dominated by a focus on participants in the case of outdoor events.

Using cycling with its two distinct forms (Kruger & Saayman, 2014) as sport type where the surrounding environment forms an essential part of the experience (Kulczycki & Halpenny, 2014), this paper explores the relative importance of the social versus the physical context to encourage environmental behaviour in an outdoor spectator sport setting.

Literature overview

The literature overview starts off with a definition of environmental behavioural, followed by an exposition of three factors from social psychology theory that could have relevance as influencers of behaviour within the setting of cycling spectators.

Desirable environmental behaviour

Definition and measurement of environmentally responsible behaviour

Environmentally responsible behaviour is defined as:

> ... either repeated or occasional concrete behavioural choices made in everyday environments. They concern specific natural and common resources of these daily environments such as choices of use/maintenance of specific resources, including water, air, land, sources of energy ... and other more or less recyclable materials ... as well as of life forms present in the environment. (Bonnes & Bonaiuto, 2002, p. 35)

The aim of understanding environmental behaviour of individuals should be to prepare, guide and establish behavioural choices that are more or less pro-environmental (Bonnes & Bonaiuto, 2002).

The study of individuals' behaviour towards the environment falls within the interdisciplinary field of environmental psychology where theory from among others social psychology is used to explain behaviour. Environmentally responsible behaviour can be viewed from two perspectives, with each perspective being represented by specific theoretical models (Bamberg & Möser, 2007; Klöckner & Blöbaum, 2011). Firstly, it can be seen as a matter of self-interest, where the focus is on strategies to minimise one's own health risks. Researchers following this view rely on rational choice models such as Ajzen and Fishbein's (1980) Theory of Reasoned Action and Ajzen's (1991) Theory of Planned Behaviour (TPB) where behaviour is driven by behavioural, normative and control beliefs and mediated by behavioural attitude. Secondly, it can be seen as something that is pro-socially motivated with the focus on concern for other people, future generations, or biospheric systems. Researchers following this view refer to models such as Schwartz's (1977) Norm-Activation-Model or Stern's (2000) Values-Beliefs-Norms model as theoretical frameworks. Still, it is never just one of these, but rather a mixture of both as attested to in the multitude of models depicting the factors that drive behaviour (for example, Bamberg & Möser, 2007; Klöckner & Blöbaum, 2011; Milfont, Duckitt, & Wagner, 2010; Steg, Bolderdijk, Keizer, & Perlaviciute, 2014). Kollmuss and Agyeman (2002) argued that the question of what shapes environmentally responsible behaviour is such a complex one that it cannot be visualised in one single framework or diagram.

The readiness to perform certain behaviour is known as behavioural intention (Ajzen, 1991).

> This readiness to act can be operationalised by asking whether people intend to engage in the behaviour, expect to engage in the behaviour, are planning to engage in the behaviour, will try to engage in the behaviour, and indeed, whether they are willing to engage in the behaviour.

These various expressions of behavioural readiness reflect the same underlying construct – intention (Ajzen, 2011). The stronger a person's intention to engage in a behaviour, the more likely he or she is to perform it (Ajzen, 1991). The majority of behavioural studies focus on behavioural intention as opposed to actual behaviour (Nigbur, Lyons, & Uzzell, 2010), with various models using intention as a strong predictor for actual behaviour (such as Bamberg & Möser, 2007; Milfont et al., 2010; Montaño & Kasprzyk, 2008; Klöckner & Blöbaum, 2011). When a series of behaviours have to be reported on, each situation has to be 'imagined' by the individual and then judged according to whether, given the opportunity, it will be done or not. Still, a prominent feature of behaviour research is the occurrence of the attitude–behaviour gap (Blake, 1999; Kollmuss & Agyeman, 2002) and very few studies measure behavioural intention as well as resultant actual behaviour.

Taking cognisance of the multitude of factors that could possibly be influencers of environmental behaviour, three constructs have been identified that could be relevant to represent the social and physical dimensions in the context of sport spectating. Before presenting these factors, a description of the behavioural 'setting' of this research is provided.

Responsible behaviour within the sports event context

The essential behaviour that should be measured among outdoor sport even spectators can be linked back to the environmental management practices employed by the event organiser. Yang, Yang, and Peng (2011) identify the environmental management system as all efforts to minimise the negative environmental impacts of an organisation's processes and product throughout the entire production life cycle. Pertinent activities include those related to transport, eco-design, water management, waste management, recycling, re-use, sporting goods, energy management, CO_2 offset, public awareness, and policy (taken from GSA, 2006; Laing & Frost, 2010; Schmidt, 2006). Other examples include signposts, banning traffic and movement in certain areas, route marking, setting up obstacles, restricting activities during certain periods of time (Jagemann, 2003). Having appropriate facilities available to spectators are extremely important to encourage desired behaviour. For example, while 90% of spectators to the London opening of the Tour de France indicated being regular recyclers at home, 30% indicated that they did not recycle while spectating due to a lack of accessible recycling facilities (Collins et al., 2012).

In the context of managing sports event spectator behaviour, there can arguably be two broader categories. Firstly, preparing attendees for and guiding them to act responsibly once they step into the behavioural setting (at an event). Secondly, contributing to a sense of commitment towards the environment that will encourage the desired behaviour in future. These two 'stages' are visible in Sahler's (2007) layout of the five phases of an event's production process. Environmentally responsible behaviour will play a part of the sports consumption process to a greater or lesser extent during the different phases and it is appropriate to undertake an investigation of not only the behavioural intention while in the setting, but also future intended behaviour. Funk (2008) similarly explains that behavioural outcomes can include purchase behaviour (or, in this case, the decision to attend the event), post-decision activities of the purchase behaviour (transport, activities undertaken while spectating), and post-experience behaviour (activities after attending the event). Not a lot is known about the effects that a travel experience may or may not have on the individual. Even though environmental learning and behavioural change as a result of experiences have been explored in both tourism (see Kachel &

Jennings, 2010; Lee & Moscardo, 2005; Moscardo, 2009) and sports (see Brymer, Downey, & Gray, 2009; Ray, 2009), there is said to be no strong evidence of significant or substantial changes to the individual tourist/traveller/participant's knowledge (Moscardo, 2009; Wu, Huang, Liu, & Law, 2013).

To effectively address sustainability challenges, tourists have to be provided with guidelines beyond the mere 'reduce, re-use, recycle' approach through the communication of specific principles (Middleton & Hawkins, 1998 in Pearce, 2011). Firstly, recognition of the impacts of one's own actions; secondly, refusal to make unethical purchases; thirdly, replacing of high impact with lower impact experiences; fourthly, retraining oneself in order to be less dependent on high-impact activities; fifthly, rewarding oneself by making use of incentives that promote sustainable; and lastly, re-education to change one's personal behaviour based on tourists experiences. Once tourists have undergone a personal change in thinking on the issue, the sustainability of an event may become a part in the decision to attend these types of events in future (Laing & Frost, 2010) or even refraining from travel at all for the sake of the environment (Puczkó & Smith, 2012). However, most tourists (as consumers) are 'superficial environmentalists' who are 'concerned' but very reluctant to undertake any corrective actions that inconvenience them (Weaver, 2012).

In summary, environmentally responsible behaviour of sport event spectators can be divided into two aspects, namely the *situational intention* and *future intention*, comprising the aspects discussed (summarised in Table 1). Situational intention will be the readiness to perform behaviour in a more or less pro-environmental direction while spectating; future intention will be the readiness to perform pro-environmental behaviour related to, but away from, the event and before future attendance.

After establishing the relevant aspects of the behavioural setting under investigation, the next three sections present three context-specific factors that could influence the behaviour of individuals, namely place attachment, subculture identification, and subjective norms.

Place attachment

Place attachment can be defined as any positive or negative relationship that a person has with the location of the sports event or the specific sports event, creating an emotional bond with that place or event (adapted from Kyle, Graefe, Manning, & Bacon, 2003). It is concerned with the specific meaning attached to a space (physical and geometric) (Hinch & Higham, 2011; Weed & Bull, 2004).

Place attachment may be an important factor underlying or providing impetus to a spectator's intention to behave responsibly during an event (McCullough & Kellison, 2016) and this attachment is regarded as a vital consideration in natural resource management strategies (Lee, 2011; López-Mosquera & Sánchez, 2012; Ramkissoon, Smith, & Weiler, 2013; Snider, Hill, Luo, Buerger, & Herstine, 2011). Different levels of place attachment will lead to different levels of concern about the state of the natural resources in a specific setting (Kyle, Graefe, Manning, & Bacon, 2004; Snider et al., 2011) and a heightened sense of attachment could lead to greater propensity to display responsible behaviour in such a setting (Halpenny, 2010; Ramkissoon et al., 2013). In some instances, place attachment may lead to a greater willingness to sacrifice resources towards protection of the

Table 1. Environmentally responsible behaviour to be measured.

Environmental management component	Possible spectator behaviour	Situational intention	Future intention
Water management	Closing taps	✓	
	Refilling water bottles with tap water	✓	
	Not polluting natural water sources	✓	
Waste management	Making use of the ablution facilities provided	✓	
	Throwing rubbish in the bins provided	✓	
	Participating in recycling activities	✓	
	Picking up litter (during or after the race)	✓	
	Making a financial contribution towards an event's clean-up and recycling initiatives		✓
Energy management	Making use of public transport/car-pooling to reduce the carbon footprint of an event		✓
Protection of biodiversity	Parking cars in designated parking areas	✓	
	Staying within the designated viewing areas	✓	
	Respecting plants and animals	✓	
Aesthetics and noise pollution	Refraining from making noise	✓	
Information communication (encouragement)	Reading the information signs to guide behaviour	✓	
	Reading the event's environmental rules and regulations before actual attendance		✓
Management of non-compliance	Reporting inappropriate behaviour of other spectators	✓	
Marketing communication	Following an event's environmental initiatives in the media before deciding to return		✓
	Supporting a sustainable event's sponsors because of the association with responsible practices		✓
Other	Willingness to make a financial contribution towards the event's environmental initiatives		✓
	Willingness to watch the race on television or over the internet in order to reduce the environmental impact of the event		✓
	Sign a petition against the event if it becomes known that the event has a negative impact on the environment where it takes place		✓

Source: Taken from Greening the WSSD (2003), GSA (2006), Jagemann (2003), Kang and Stotlar (2011), Laing and Frost (2010), Pearce (2005), Sahler (2007), Schmidt (2006), and Responsible Traveller Magazine (2014).

place (Kyle et al., 2003; López-Mosquera & Sánchez, 2012). Once individuals feel a sense of ownership towards a place where they participate in recreational activities, they are inclined to display responsible behaviour (Trendafilova, 2011). This may depend on the number of visitations to a place (Snider et al., 2011), the perceived benefits received through visitation (López-Mosquera & Sánchez, 2012), and the specific meaning attached to a place by the visitor (Wynveen, Kyle, & Sutton, 2012). Increased knowledge about a place through information provision (Halpenny, 2010) or through regular use (Thompson, Davidson, & Hutson, 2008) also increases the likelihood that an individual will display responsible behaviour in order to protect the place. Similar to the findings of Laing and Frost (2010) in corporate events, there may be instances where a stronger sense of attachment may be developed towards a sports event or activity if it is associated with socially responsible practices (Filo, Funk, & O'Brien, 2008).

Sport event spectators will have different drivers of attachment than active participants. Where participants may, for example, be attached to an event due to its level of organisation and ability to prove their skills (Kruger & Saayman, 2014), spectators may have a bond based on the socialisation opportunities, entertainment value or the nature of the event setting. Some spectators may feel attachment to the wider destination or place, while others focus on the event and its participants. These varied focuses will arguably influence their orientation towards the environment in which the event takes place, affecting the extent of their concern with and intention to act responsibly in the setting (McCullough & Kellison, 2016).

Subculture identification and subjective norms

The desire to be part of the subculture of the sport at an event remains one of the key motives driving attendance (Green & Chalip, 1998; Snelgrove, Taks, Chalip, & Green, 2008). Understanding the subculture of a sport is important to drive consumer behaviour in the desired direction (Green, 2001) and event organisers are increasingly engaging with 'sport fan consumption communities' to do so (Hedlund, 2012).

Subculture identification is a process whereby the beliefs and values held by a particular sports consumption community are adopted and internalised by individual consumers. Individuals use their affiliations with sports to express aspects of their self-concept to others (Hirt & Clarkson, 2011; Scammon, Fuller, Karniouchina, & Masters, 2011; Shipway & Kirkup, 2011). They may see themselves as a 'typical' supporter or fan and they may also be known as such. Individuals with a strong sense of subculture identification will possibly be more inclined to change behaviour in the spectator setting in order to feel an increased sense of belonging and to make a connection with peers.

Some outdoor sports cultures have become synonymous with either being unsustainable or 'green' (Mansfield & Wheaton, 2011), though very little research has been done on this topic. The so-called 'lifestyle sports' also referred to as 'free sports', 'alternative sports', and 'fringe sports' have been associated with environmentally conscious participants and nature-friendly practices (Brymer & Gray, 2010; Salome, Van Bottenburg, & Van den Heuvel, 2013), spurred on by the fact that these sports codes are highly dependent on the natural resources where they take place. The surfer culture has effectively been harnessed to address water pollution issues (Wheaton, 2007). Similarly, disc golf players have been encouraged to display responsible behaviour through the culture among golfers at a park (Trendafilova, 2011). In a different context, a resident subculture built around affiliation with a local football club has also been used in a campaign to promote pro-environmental behaviour (Baldwin, 2010).

It is argued that the more a spectator associates with other spectators of the specific sport, the more they are inclined to follow the group's behaviour in terms of specific activities (in this case, environmentally responsible behaviour) (McCullough & Kellison, 2016). The distinct subculture of cycling participants as consumers has been researched (discussed in Kruger & Saayman, 2014), but not a lot is known about the existence of subcultures among the spectators of these events.

Group affiliation is closely linked to the concept of social norms (Andorfer & Liebe, 2013; Hedlund, 2012). Social norms are defined as rules and standards that are understood by members of a group, and that guide and/or constrain social behaviour without the force of laws' (Cialdini & Trost, 1998, p. 152). Social norms influence personal norms, or an individual sense of obligation to engage in a particular action (Cameron, 2002). It is one of the main predictor variables in the widely applied TPB and has been directly linked to behavioural intention (Bamberg & Möser, 2007; Klöckner & Blöbaum, 2011; Milfont et al., 2010; Montaño & Kasprzyk, 2008). It would be appropriate to strengthen the predictive power of subjective norms through the addition of social aspects of behaviour such as a sport subculture (Nigbur et al., 2010).

Norms are categorised by various terms including moral norms, personal norms, social norms and ecological norms, depending on the context in which they are being applied. Subjective norms refer to norms as a social factor regarding 'the perceived social pressure to perform or not to perform the behaviour' (Ajzen, 1991, p. 188). They are the 'rules and standards that are understood by members of a group, and that guide and/or constrain social behaviour without the force of laws' (Cialdini & Trost, 1998, p. 152). Social norms influence personal norms, or an individual sense of obligation to engage in a particular action (Cameron, 2002) in order to obtain favourable results (Iconaru, 2012; Steg et al., 2014) such as approval by important referent individuals or groups (Ajzen, 1991). Several studies have indicated this approval to be a strong predictor of a person's intention to perform a specific behaviour (Iconaru, 2012).

Social norms are followed conditionally upon the satisfaction of two expectations, namely normative expectations (what one thinks others expect from you) and empirical expectations (what one has observed or knows about the behaviour of others in similar situations) (Bicchieri, 2006). For social norms to exist, there have to be a sufficient number of people who know that the norm exists and who share the same expectations (Bicchieri, 2006; Elster, 1999). Furthermore, there should be a sufficient number of people who have a conditional preference to comply with the norm (Bicchieri, 2006). Another feature of social norms is that they are enforced by sanction mechanisms directed at violators, where the fear of punishment (in the form of being seen by others doing something inappropriate) can motivate people to comply with the norm. Therefore, the activation of social norms depends strongly on the fact that the individual is 'being observed by others' (Elster, 1999, p. 196).

Behaviour often takes place in a social context, such as this study's context of sport spectating. It is therefore likely that the behaviour of others will influence the behavioural decision of individuals (Biel & Thogersen, 2007). The extent of this influence will also vary according to the behavioural situation (Fishbein & Ajzen, 1975 in Iconaru, 2012). For example, a study by Goldstein, Cialdini, and Griskevicius (2008) found that hotel guests were more encouraged to participate in an environmental conservation programme through signage that used descriptive norms (other guests are performing the behaviour), than signage that focused on environmental protection. Furthermore, normative appeals that described the behaviour of other individuals in the same setting (the same floor/room) proved to be even more effective. Similarly, McCullough and Cunningham (2011) and McCullough (2013) found that seeing other spectators partaking in recycling and seeing famous sport stars participating in recycling, and hearing them make announcements to encourage recycling, had different effects on spectator recycling. They also found subjective norms (other families at the tournament and significant others) as one of the greatest influences on spectators' recycling intentions.

It is argued that the discussed constructs are important dimensions of sport spectatorship and that all three contain aspects that may link to environmental behaviour. Items derived from the literature to construct the factors for statistical measurement are indicated in Table 2.

The question is posed whether they have equally important interactions with a spectator's intentions to display environmentally responsible behaviour within the

Table 2. Measurement scales for place attachment, subculture identification and subjective norms.

Place attachment
- I am very attached to visiting this place specifically
- I have a special connection to attending this cycling race
- Attending this particular event is more important to me than attending a cycling event in another place

Subculture identification
- My friends and family know me as a cycling supporter/fan
- The sport of cycling describes me as a person
- I strongly relate with other spectators and feel 'at home'

Subjective norms
- Seeing other spectators being environmentally responsible
- Being looked down upon if I am not environmentally responsible
- Knowing that other spectators expect me to behave in an environmentally responsible manner
- Being frowned upon if I go out of my way to be too environmentally responsible
- Knowing that no one else is being environmentally responsible
- Seeing the cyclists being environmentally responsible

situational setting, but also in terms of future behaviour. Furthermore, whether these variables are the same across different spectator groupings based on the type of events (road versus mountain bike). An article by McCullough and Kellison (2016) developed a conceptual model to test the influence of sense of place (which incorporates place attachment) and fan identification on environmental behaviour. However, the model proposes fan identification as a variable that moderates the relationship between sense of place and behaviour and only looks at behaviour while attending a sport event.

Methodology

Sample

Self-completion surveys were completed at seven different cycling events (both mountain bike and road races) in South Africa. Non-probability sampling in the form of convenience sampling was used to solicit participants (spectators) along the various routes. Because the quality of the research would be affected by using convenience sampling (Saunders, Lewis, & Thornhill, 2007), the researchers employed heterogeneous or maximum variation sampling to include different (heterogeneous) individuals. A final sample of 619 spectators was included.

Measurement instrument

A self-completion questionnaire was chosen, as self-administered surveys improve anonymity (Keyton, 2011). Situational and future intentions were measured using 4-point Likert-type scales, ranging from 1 = 'Definitely not', 2 = 'Unlikely', 3 = 'Maybe' to 4 = 'Definitely'. The question for situational intention was stated as 'Activities that you undertake as a spectator at this event'. With the scale using 'unlikely' and 'maybe' as descriptors, the scale measured intention and not actual behaviour, as it asked people whether they intended, expected or planned to engage in the behaviour (Ajzen, 2011). Asking people whether they had actually performed the behaviour only ('definitely not' or 'definitely') would most likely have resulted in 'over-reporting of admirable attitudes and behaviors' known as social desirability bias (Krosnick, 1999, p. 545). True measurement of behaviour would arguably require a qualitative methodology such as participant observation or other forms of 'evidence' for the actual behaviour. The decision to test intentions could therefore be considered a limitation of the study. Place attachment and subculture identification were also measured on a 4-point scale, ranging from 1 = 'Strongly disagree' to 4 = 'Strongly agree'. The researchers opted not to include a middle value ('not sure'/'don't know'), as people often perceive the middle of the scale as the 'normal' or 'typical' value and tend to place themselves near that point, regardless of the label given (Krosnick, 1999, p. 544). Subjective norms were measured on a 3-point scale where 1 = 'not at all encouraging', 2 = 'to some extent encouraging', 3 = 'very encouraging'.

Data analysis

Initial descriptive statistics were used to describe the sample and data. Cronbach's *a* coefficients were used to test internal reliability of the scales. *T*-tests were firstly used to determine the differences between the two spectator groups for all of the scale items as well as the scale composite scores. Thereafter, the relationships between the three independent variables (place attachment, subculture identification and subjective norms) and two grouping categories (mountain bike versus road cycling) were tested to see which of these variables had the largest effect size with the two outcome variables (situation and future intention). Analyses of variance techniques such as ANOVA and MANOVA are well-established and frequently used technique in tourism studies (Tang, 2014). However, it only allows for testing the relationship between one independent continuous variable and categorical variables. A procedure known as univariate analysis of covariance (ANCOVA) effectively combines ANOVA with regression (interaction between more than one continuous independent variable) into a linear model (Field, 2013). It allowed the researchers to simultaneously test the effect of the setting (mountain bike versus road race) and the three factors on behavioural intentions by systematically including each variable through step-wise regression. This technique has been used in research with a similar theme, including to test the differences in environmental attitudes of nature-based tourists based on their motivations (Luo & Deng, 2008); the differences in pro-environmental product choices between different consumers based on environmental concern (Cornelissen, Pandalaere, Warlop, & Dewitte, 2008); and differences in behaviour based on environmental attitudes and knowledge between different cultural groups (Laroche, Tomiuk, Bergeron, & Barbaro-Forleo, 2002).

Description of the sample

The sample consisted of 446 (72%) road race spectators and 173 (28%) mountain bike spectators. The profile of the different events is indicated in Table 3.

The majority participants were female (68%), held a tertiary qualification (70%) with an average age of 37 (minimum age of 18). Spectators originated primarily from neighbouring towns/cities (42%) or neighbourhoods surrounding the event (40%). Majority (67%) of the spectators were day visitors (not sleeping over in the host destination), with an average stay of three nights. The vast majority attended with friends (52%), followed by family (19%), friends and family (15%), alone (4%), as part of a cyclist support team (3.6%) or other (including work colleagues, a sports club or educational group).

Descriptive statistics and reliability of the scales

Descriptive statistics and Cronbach's a levels of the scales are indicated in Table 4. The two independent variables achieved satisfactory Cronbach's a levels. The dependent variable 'Future Intention' also achieved a satisfactory a level. 'Situational intention' at first achieved a low score of .608, but after the removal of two negatively worded items, the scale's reliability increased to a satisfactory level. Table 3 indicates the descriptive statistics and a levels of the scales. The Cronbach's a for 'Subjective Norms' was low. The two reverse-coded items were removed, but the scale still presented a low score. An exploratory factor analysis indicated that one item had a negative cross-loading and this problematic item was also removed. The remaining three items had a Cronbach's a of .56, which is low but approaching .6 and can be considered (George & Mallery, 2003). In the case of these three items, the item inter-correlations were low, which reduces a. Furthermore, items with low scale points (three in this case) may also produce an underestimate (Gliem & Gliem, 2003; Takavol & Dennick, 2011). It was therefore decided to retain this scale for further analysis.

Based on the item mean scores of each factor, spectators agreed mostly to the statement that they had a special connection to attending the specific cycling race ($M =$ 2.69). No distinct differences were found between mountain bike versus road race spectators on any of the individual place attachment items or the overall scale composite score. Spectators agreed mostly to the statement that they could strongly relate with other spectators ($M = 2.69$). No distinct differences were found between mountain bike versus road race spectators on any of the subculture identification items or the overall scale composite score. Seeing cyclist being environmentally responsible would be the most encouraging aspect from a social norm viewpoint ($M = 2.64$). Road race spectators were more encouraged by seeing other spectators behaving responsibly than mountain bike spectators ($F = 6.880, p < .05$). However, no significant difference was found based on the overall scale composite score.

Table 3. Profile of events.

Province	Type	Sample size	Years[a] running	Number of cyclists	Landscape
Gauteng (inland)	Road	191	18	30,000	Urban spaces (from inner city to suburbs and peripheral areas of large city)
Gauteng (inland)	Road	32	17	3000	Peripheral areas of large city
Eastern Cape (coastal)	Road	78	30	4000	Urban spaces (from inner city to suburbs and peripheral areas of large city)
Eastern Cape (coastal)	Mountain bike	45	30	150	Farmlands and mountain
Western Cape (coastal)	Road	145	37	35,000	Urban spaces (from inner city to suburbs)
Western Cape (coastal)	Mountain bike	41	14	3000	Farmlands and mountain (conservancy area)
Western Cape (coastal)	Mountain bike	87	12	1200	Farmlands and mountain

[a]In 2015.

Table 4. Descriptive statistics and reliability of the scales.

Item	Mean	Std. dev.	Cronbach's α
Place attachment			.730
Very attached to visiting this place specifically	2.33	0.931	
Has a special connection to attending this cycling race	2.69	0.996	
Attending this particular event is more important than any other	2.41	0.970	
Subculture identification			.805
Friends and family know me as a cycling supporter/fan	2.60	0.991	
The sport of cycling describes me as a person	2.11	0.903	
Strongly relate with other spectators and feel 'at home'	2.69	0.893	
Subjective norms			.567
Seeing other spectators being environmentally responsible	2.62*	0.546	
Knowing that other spectators expect me to behave in an environmentally responsible manner	2.46	0.628	
Seeing the cyclists being environmentally responsible	2.64	0.534	
*Situational intention***			.707
Stay in designated viewing areas	3.64	0.682	
Read information signs to guide behaviour	3.57	0.665	
Throw rubbish in the bins provided	3.86*	0.460	
Make use of the ablution facilities	3.69	0.648	
Pick up any visible litter	3.06*	0.886	
Volunteer to pick up litter after the race	2.44	0.933	
Report inappropriate behaviour of others	2.64	0.924	
Refill water bottle with tap water	2.73*	1.103	
Park vehicle only in designated areas	3.63	0.740	
Take note of the surrounding natural environment	3.50	0.701	
*Future intention***			.755
Read the event's environmental rules and regulations before attendance	2.99	0.908	
Willingness to make a financial contribution towards the event's environmental initiatives	2.54	0.847	
Make use of public transport or car-pooling to reduce the carbon footprint of the event	2.70	0.964	
Willingness to watch the race on television or over the internet in order to reduce the environmental impact of the event	2.18*	0.956	
Follow the event's environmental initiatives in the media before deciding to return next year	2.44	0.909	
Sign a petition against the event if it becomes known that the event has a negative impact on the environment where it takes place	2.62	1.015	
Buy more products of the event sponsoring company because they support this environmentally friendly event	3.00	0.835	

*Significant difference for the item between two groups ($p < .05$).
**Significant difference for the overall scale between two groups ($p < .05$).

The three most likely environmentally responsible activities while spectating would be throwing rubbish in bins ($M = 3.86$), reading information signs to guide behaviour ($M = 3.57$), and using ablution facilities ($M = 3.69$). Least likely behaviour would be to volunteer to pick up litter after the race ($M = 2.44$). Mountain bike spectators displayed higher intentions than road race spectators to throw rubbish in bins ($F = 4.068$), volunteer to pick up litter after the race ($F = 3.590$) and to refill water bottles with tap water ($F = 8.938$). A significant difference was found based on the overall scale composite score with mountain bike spectators having higher overall levels of responsible situational intentions ($F = 7.885$).

The three most likely activities in future would be buying more products of the event-sponsoring company because they support this environmentally friendly event ($M = 3.00$), reading the event's environmental rules and regulations before attendance ($M = 2.99$), and making use of public transport or car-pooling to reduce the carbon footprint of the event. Least likely activities were to avoid physical attendance in order to reduce the event's carbon footprint ($M = 2.18$). Mountain bike spectators were, however, more likely to avoid physical attendance in order to reduce the event's carbon footprint ($F = 4.559$). Again, a significant difference was found based on the overall scale composite score with mountain bike spectators having higher overall levels of responsible future intentions ($F = 14.634$).

Univariate ANCOVA

ANCOVA was performed to determine the interaction effects of the three factors, place attachment, subculture identification and subjective norms on the outcome variables, situational intention and future intention when distinguishing spectators based on event type. Where the previous analyses indicated differences in terms of specific dimensions of the factors as well as outcome variables based on item-level statistics, this analysis tests the relationships between the factors and the outcome variables based on the composite scores of the scales.

Table 5 shows the results of the effects of the factors on behavioural intention when compared between road race and mountain bike spectators.

Place attachment has a large significant relationship ($F = 38.082$) with behavioural intention. The model only explains 6% of the variability in behavioural intentions. When subculture identification is added, place attachment still has a significant but smaller relationship with behavioural intention ($F = 4.530$). Subculture identification has a larger significant relationship with behavioural intention ($F = 12.844$). The explanatory power of the model increases slightly to 8%. However, when the factor subjective norms is added, the relationship between place attachment and behavioural intention becomes insignificant. Subculture identification still has a large significant relationship ($F = 8.944$), while the factor subjective norms has a very large significant relationship ($F = 46.573$). The predictive power of the model also increases to 14%. Event type retains a significant relationship with behavioural intention throughout the process.

Table 6 shows the results of the effects of the factors on future intention when compared between road race and mountain bike spectators.

Table 5. Interaction effects of factors with behavioural intention based on event type.

Source	F	Sig.	R^2
Place attachment entered into the model			
Corrected model	22.432	.000	.062
Intercept	2603.243	.000	
Place attachment	38.082	.000	
Event type	7.383	.007	
Subculture identification entered into the model			
Corrected model	19.497	.000	0.080
Intercept	2163.959	.000	
Place attachment	4.530	.034	
Subculture identification	12.844	.000	
Event type	6.376	.012	
Subjective norms entered into the model			
Corrected model	27.250	.000	.139
Intercept	486.782	.000	
Place attachment	2.836	.093	
Subculture identification	8.944	.003	
Subjective norms	46.573	.000	
Event type	5.000	.026	

Table 6. Interaction effects of factors with future intention based on event type.

Source	F	Sig.	R^2
Place attachment entered into the model			
Corrected model	31.620	.000	.086
Intercept	661.870	.000	
Place attachment	50.204	.000	
Event type	14.144	.000	
Subculture identification entered into the model			
Corrected model	27.295	.000	0.108
Intercept	514.076	.000	
Place attachment	5.866	.016	
Subculture identification	17.136	.000	
Event type	12.509	.000	
Subjective norms entered into the model			
Corrected model	23.561	.000	.123
Intercept	108.473	.000	
Place attachment	4.786	.029	
Subculture identification	14.506	.000	
Subjective norms	11.130	.001	
Event type	11.413	.001	

Place attachment has a large significant relationship (*F* = 50.204) with future intention. The model only explains 9% of the variability in future intentions. When subculture identification is added, place attachment still has a significant but much smaller relationship with future intention (*F* = 5.866). Subculture identification has a larger significant relationship with future intention (*F* = 17.136). The explanatory power of the model increases slightly to 11%. When the factor subjective norms is added, the relationship between place attachment and future intention remains significant (*F* = 4.786). Subculture identification still has a large significant relationship (*F* = 14.506) while the factor subjective norms has a large significant relationship (*F* = 11.130). The predictive power of the model also increases to 12%.

Conclusion and recommendations

Descriptive data analysis indicated that there were no significant differences in the levels of place attachment, subculture identification or subjective norms between road race and mountain bike spectators. However, for both situational and future intentions, mountain bike spectators displayed higher levels of responsible behavioural intention.

The ANCOVA analysis indicated changes in the significance and effect size of the physical context (place attachment and event type) with the introduction of the social context. In the case of situational intention, both place attachment and event type initially had significant effects on intention. However, after the inclusion of subculture identification, their effect sizes decreased and after the inclusion of subjective norms, place attachment did not have a significant relationship with behavioural intentions and effect of the physical setting decreased further. It could be concluded that within the setting (while spectating), the social context (the behaviour and expectations of fellow spectators) had more potential than the physical setting or the attachment thereto, to influence behavioural intentions. This finding is significant, as it proves the relative importance of a person's identification with the social context at a sports event to influence behaviour; supporting McCullough and Kellison's (2016) statement that when fans attend a sport event and 'engage in the spectacle around the event', their social identity (as a fan) may dominate other identities such as an environmental identity. It corresponds with previous research, suggesting that communication strategies at an event should be built around subjective norms (Casper et al., 2014; McCullough & Cunningham, 2011), making use of appropriate 'message framing' (Cheng, Woon, & Lynes, 2011) to encourage pro-environmental behaviour. Based on the descriptive data analysis, using cyclists as 'environmental ambassadors' could be especially relevant, corresponding with research indicating the positive influence of sport teams to encourage pro-environmental behaviour among fans (Inoue et al., 2012).

In terms of future intention, all three factors retained significant levels of interaction, indicating that both the social and physical contexts could potentially influence responsible decision-making in the future. Once outside of the setting and direct contact with other spectators, individuals may be more inclined to turn to their sense of attachment to the place or event along with what individuals expect other spectators would be doing. By showing the varied influence of the social context on behavioural intentions, this study contradicts findings by Dolnicar and Grün (2009) arguing that tourists' environmental behaviour is not context-/environment-dependent but that individuals display similar behaviour at home and in holiday settings. In terms of the physical setting, a strong attachment to the place or event may prove beneficial, as these spectators appreciate the place and are more prone to support event organisers' environmental management initiatives through using public transport to the event and reading the rules and regulations before actual attendance. Communicating to spectators based on place attachment and referral to the quality of the setting which they may plan to attend again in future may encourage them to convert some of their responsible behaviour of the past into future behaviour, especially with reference to the same event (Wu et al., 2013). It is important to note that some of the future intentions measured are not necessarily all favourable for event organisers and include following an event's environmental initiatives in the media before deciding to return or even not attending if an event becomes known to be unsustainable (corresponding with studies by Laing & Frost, 2010; Puczkó & Smith, 2012).

Limitations of this study include limiting the spectator groupings only to event type, while other variables could also add to explaining differences (for example, place of origin, travel group and demographics). Research could also explore the three factors as drivers of environmentally responsible behaviour among sport spectators in different sport settings and sport codes. This can be linked to research exploring the extent to which different sporting codes are perceived as being 'green' by attendees. The finding that mountain bike spectators showed higher levels of responsible intentions could be explored further to determine whether the sport itself is associated with environmentally responsible behaviour or whether it is the physical (natural) setting that encourages these intentions. If the former is the case, there would be the potential for these values to be adopted and internalised by individuals who strongly associate with the subculture and use it to express this aspect of their self-concept (after Hirt & Clarkson, 2011; McCullough & Kellison, 2016; Scammon et al., 2011; Shipway & Kirkup, 2011). If the latter is true, the influence of the natural setting on behaviour should be explored through factors not tested in this research such as environmental awareness. The fact that behavioural intentions and not actual behaviour were measured is a further limitation. Future research should focus on actual pro-environmental behaviour in addition to intentions.

Disclosure statement

No potential conflict of interest was reported by the authors.

ORCiD

E. A. du Preez http://orcid.org/0000-0001-8144-1999

References

Ajzen, I. (1991). The theory of planned behavior. *Organizational Behavior and Human Decision Processes*, *50*(2), 179–211.
Ajzen, I. (2011). The theory of planned behaviour: Reactions and reflections. *Psychology & Health*, *26*(9), 1113–1127.
Ajzen, I., & Fishbein, M. (1980). *Understanding attitudes and predicting social behavior*. Englewood Cliffs, NJ: Prentice-Hall.
Aldred, R. (2010). 'On the outside': Constructing cycling citizenship. *Social & Cultural Geography*, *11*(1), 35–52.
Andorfer, V. A., & Liebe, U. (2013). Consumer behavior in moral markets. On the relevance of identity, justice beliefs, social norms, status and trust in ethical consumption. *European Sociological Review*, *29*(6), 1251–1265.
Baldwin, R. M. (2010). *Can (a football) community tackle climate change? A case study analysis of Ipswich Town Football Club's Campaign to encourage pro-environmental behavioural change amongst its fans*. CSERGE Working Paper EDM 10-05, School of Environmental Sciences, University of East Anglia, Norwich [Online]. Retrieved March 13, 2012, from http://prototype2010.cserge.webapp3.uea.ac.uk/sites/default/files/edm_2010_05.pdf
Bamberg, S., & Möser, G. (2007). Twenty years after Hines, Hungerford, and Tomera: A new meta-analysis of psycho-social determinants of pro-environmental behaviour. *Journal of Environmental Psychology*, *27*, 14–25.
Barry, H. (2014). *Cycling is the New Golf* [Online]. Retrieved May 2, 2016, from http://www.moneyweb.co.za/archive/cycling-is-the-new-golf/
Belk, R. W. (1975). Situational variables and consumer behaviour. *Journal of Consumer Research*, *2*(3), 157–164.
Bicchieri, C. (2006). *The grammar of society*. New York: Cambridge University Press.
Biel, A., & Thogersen, J. (2007). Activation of social norms in social dilemmas: A review of the evidence and reflections on the implications for environmental behaviour. *Journal of Economic Psychology*, *28*, 93–112.
Blake, J. (1999). Overcoming the 'value-action' gap in environmental policy: Tensions between national policy and local experience. *Local Environment*, *4*(3), 257–278.
Bonnes, M., & Bonaiuto, M. (2002). Environmental psychology: From spatial–physical environment to sustainable development. In R. B. Bechtel & A. Churchman (Eds.), *Handbook of environmental psychology* (pp. 28–54). New York: John Wiley & Sons.
Brymer, E., Downey, G., & Gray, T. (2009). Extreme sports as a precursor to environmental sustainability. *Journal of Sport and Tourism*, *14*(2–3), 193–204.
Brymer, E., & Gray, T. (2010). Developing an intimate 'relationship' with nature through extreme sports participation. *Leisure/Loisir*, *34*(4), 361–374.
Cameron, L. D. (2002). *Promoting positive environmental behaviours through community interventions: A case study of waste minimisation*. Environment Waikato Technical Report No. 13. Hamilton: Waikato Regional Council [Online]. Retrieved August 19, 2013, from http://www.waikatoregion.govt.nz/PageFiles/2493/tr02-13.pdf
Casper, J. M., & Pfahl, M. E. (2012). Environmental behavior frameworks of sport and recreation undergraduate students. *Sport Management Education Journal*, *6*, 8–20.

Casper, J. M., Pfahl, M. E., & McCullough, B. (2014). Intercollegiate sport and the environment: Examining fan engagement based on athletic department sustainability efforts. *Journal of Issues in Intercollegiate Athletics*, 7, 65–91.

Cheng, T., Woon, D. K., & Lynes, J. K. (2011). The use of message framing in the promotion of environmentally sustainable behaviors. *Social Marketing Quarterly*, 17(2), 48–62.

Cialdini, R. B., & Trost, M. R. (1998). Social influence: Social norms, conformity, and compliance. In D. T. Gilbert, S. T. Fiske, & G. Lindzey (Eds.), *The handbook of social psychology* (4th ed., Vol. 2, pp. 151–192). New York: McGraw-Hill.

Collins, A., Roberts, A., & Munday, M. (2012). *The environmental impacts of major cycling events: Reflections on the UK stages of the Tour de France*. Cardiff: Cardiff University [Online]. Retrieved May 2, 2016, from http://orca.cf.ac.uk/53325/1/Tour-de-France.pdf

Cornelissen, G., Pandalaere, M., Warlop, L., & Dewitte, S. (2008). Positive cueing: Promoting sustainable consumer behaviour by cueing common environmental behaviours as environmental. *International Journal of Research in Marketing*, 25, 46–55.

Cupples, J., & Ridley, E. (2008). Towards a heterogeneous environmental responsibility: Sustainability and cycling fundamentalism. *Area*, 40(2), 254–264.

Dolnicar, S., & Grün, B. (2009). Environmentally friendly behavior: Can heterogeneity among individuals and contexts/environments be harvested for improved sustainable management? *Environment and Behavior*, 41(5), 693–714.

Du Toit, N. (2013, October/November). *Did the African cycling dream impact on the cycling trade? Sports trader – for the sport, outdoor & leisure industries* [Online]. Retrieved May 2, 2016, from http://www.sportstrader.co.za/pages/issue%20articles/2013OctNov/Cyclingimpactsonsales.php

Elster, J. (1999). *Strong feelings*. Cambridge: MIT Press.

Field, A. P. (2013). *Discovering statistics using SPSS: And sex and drugs and rock 'n roll* (4th ed.). London: Sage.

Filo, K., Funk, D. C., & O'Brien, D. (2008). *The influence of social responsibility on sport tourists*. Paper presented at the CAUTHE 2008 conference [Online]. Retrieved March 13, 2012, from http://132.234.243.22/conference/cauthe2008/refereed-papers/RP014.pdf

Fink, A., & Smith, D. J. (2012). Norms in sports contests: The tour de France. *Journal of Sport Management*, 26, 43–52.

Funk, D. C. (2008). *Consumer behaviour in sport and events: Marketing action*. Oxford: Elsevier.

George, D., & Mallery, P. (2003). *SPSS for windows step by step: A simple guide and reference. 11.0 update* (4th ed.). Boston, MA: Allyn & Bacon.

Gliem, J. A., & Gliem, R. R. (2003, October 8–10). *Calculating, interpreting, and reporting Cronbach's alpha reliability coefficient for Likert-type scales*. Midwest research to practice conference in adult, continuing, and community education, The Ohio State University, Columbus, OH [Online]. Retrieved May 1, 2016, from http://www.ssnpstudents.com/wp/wp-content/uploads/2015/02/Gliem-Gliem.pdf

Goldstein, N. J., Cialdini, R. B., & Griskevicius, V. (2008). A room with a viewpoints: Using social norms to motivate environmental conservation in hotels. *Journal of Consumer Research*, 35(3), 472–482.

Green, B. C. (2001). Leveraging subculture and identity to promote sport events. *Sport Management Review*, 4, 1–19.

Green, B. C., & Chalip, L. (1998). Sport tourism as the celebration of subculture. *Annals of Tourism Research*, 25(2), 275–291.

Greening the WSSD. (2003). *Responsible tourism handbook – a guide to good practice for tourism operators*. Not known: Greening the WSSD [Online]. Retrieved April 16, 2012, from https://www.globalnature.org/bausteine.net/f/5801/Tourismhandbook.pdf?fd=2

GSA. (2006, November 30–December 1). *Mainstreaming the environment in major sports events*. Report of the global forum for sport and environment, Lausanne [Online]. Retrieved February 5, 2012, from http://www.unep.org/Spanish/Sport_env/Activities/gf2006.asp

Günther, H. (2009). The environmental psychology of research. *Journal of Environmental Psychology*, 29, 358–365.

Halpenny, E. A. (2010). Pro-environmental behaviours and park visitors: The effect of place attachment. *Journal of Environmental Psychology*, 30, 409–421.

Hardisty, C. (2014, November). *Boom time for cycling. Sports trader – for the sport, outdoor & leisure industries* [Online]. Retrieved May 2, 2016, from http://www.sportstrader.co.za/pages/Issue%20articles/2014November/boomtimeforcycling.php

Hedlund, D. (2012, September 18–21). *An empirical model of sport fan consumption communities*.Workshop: ESMQ 2013 Special Issue: Value co-creation in sport management, Aalborg. Retrieved from www.easm2012.com

Hinch, T., & Higham, J. (2011). *Sport tourism development* (2nd ed.). Bristol: Channel View Publications.

Hirt, E. R., & Clarkson, J. J. (2011). The psychology of fandom: Understanding the etiology, motives and implications of fanship. In L. R. Kahle & A. G. Close (Eds.), *Consumer behavior knowledge for effective sports and event marketing* (pp. 59–85). New York: Routledge.

Iconaru, C. (2012). Modeling the impact of normative beliefs in the context of online buying: Direct and moderation effects. *The Romanian Economic Journal, 44*, 243–262.

Inoue, Y., Kent, A., & Smart, D. L. (2012). Sport teams as promoters of pro-environmental behavior: An empirical study. *Journal of Sport Management, 26*(5), 417–432.

Jagemann, H. (2003, September 22). *Sports and the environment: Ways towards achieving the sustainable development of sport*. Paper presented at the 4th Pierre de Coubertin School Forum Arenzano (MUVITA) [Online]. Retrieved April 24, 2012, from http://www.thesportjournal.org

Kachel, U., & Jennings, G. (2010). Exploring tourists' environmental learning, values and travel experiences in relation to climate change: A postmodern constructivist research agenda. *Tourism and Hospitality Research, 10*, 130–140.

Kang, K. J. & Stotlar, D. (2011). An investigation of factors influencing decision making for participation in the olympic partners sponsorship: A case study of Samsung. *International Journal of Applied Sports Sciences, 23*(1), 225–250.

Kellison, T. B., & Kim, Y. K. (2014). Marketing pro-environmental venues in professional sport: Planting seeds of change among existing and prospective consumers. *Journal of Sport Management, 28*, 34–48.

Keyton, J. (2011). *Communication research: Asking questions, finding answers* (3rd ed.). New York: McGraw-Hill.

King, J., Kahle, L. R., & Close, A. G. (2011). Introduction: The study of sports and events consumer behavior. In L. R. Kahle & A. G. Close (Eds.), *Consumer behavior knowledge for effective sports and event marketing* (pp. 1–28). New York: Routledge.

Klöckner, C. A., & Blöbaum, A. (2011). A comprehensive action determination model: Toward a broader understanding of ecological behaviour using the example of travel mode choice. *Journal of Environmental Psychology, 30*, 574–586.

Kollmuss, A., & Agyeman, J. (2002). Mind the gap: Why do people act environmentally and what are the barriers to pro-environmental behavior? *Environmental Education Research, 8*(3), 239–260.

Krosnick, J. A. (1999). Survey research. *Annual Review of Psychology, 50*, 537–567.

Kruger, M., & Saayman, M. (2014). How do mountain bikers and road cyclists differ? *South African Journal of Research in Sport, Physical Education and Recreation, 36*(2), 137–152.

Kulczycki, C., & Halpenny, E. A. (2014). Sport cycling tourists' setting preferences, appraisals and attachments. *Journal of Sport and Tourism, 19*(2), 169–197.

Kyle, G., Graefe, A. R., Manning, R., & Bacon, J. (2003). An examination of the relationship between leisure activity involvement and place attachment among hikers along the Appalachian trail. *Journal of Leisure Research, 35*(3), 249–273.

Kyle, G., Graefe, A. R., Manning, R., & Bacon, J. (2004). Effects of place attachment on users' perceptions of social and environmental conditions in a natural setting. *Journal of Environmental Psychology, 24*, 213–225.

Laing, J., & Frost, W. (2010). How Green was my festival: Exploring challenges and opportunities associated with staging Green events. *International Journal of Hospitality Management, 29*, 261–267.

Lamont, M. (2009). Reinventing the wheel: A definitional discussion of bicycle tourism. *Journal of Sport & Tourism, 14*(1), 5–23.

Laroche, M., Tomiuk, M., Bergeron, J., & Barbaro-Forleo, G. (2002). Cultural differences in environmental knowledge, attitudes, and behaviours of Canadian consumers. *Canadian Journal of Administrative Sciences, 19*(3), 267–282.

Lee, K. (2011). The role of media exposure, social exposure and biospheric value orientation in the environmental attitude-intention-behavior model in adolescents. *Journal of Environmental Psychology, 31*, 301–308.

Lee, W. H., & Moscardo, G. (2005). Understanding the impact of ecotourism resort experiences on tourists' environmental attitudes and behavioural intentions. *Journal of Sustainable Tourism, 13*(6), 546–565.

López-Mosquera, N., & Sánchez, M. (2012). Theory of planned behaviour and the value-belief-norm theory explaining willingness to pay for a suburban park. *Journal of Environmental Management, 113*, 251–262.

Luo, Y., & Deng, J. (2008). The new environmental paradigm and nature-based tourism motivation. *Journal of Travel Research, 46*(4), 392–402.

Mansfield, L., & Wheaton, B. (2011). Leisure and the politics of the environment. *Leisure Studies, 30*(4), 383–386.

McCullough, B. P. (2013). Identifying the influences on sport spectator recycling behaviours using the theory of planned behaviour. *International Journal of Sport Management and Marketing, 14*, 146–168.

McCullough, B. P., & Cunningham, G. B. C. (2011). Recycling intentions among youth baseball spectators. *International Journal of Sport Management and Marketing, 10*(1/2), 104–120.

McCullough, B. P., & Kellison, T. B. (2016, February). Go Green for the home team: Sense of place and environmental sustainability in sport. *Journal of Sustainability Education, 11*.

Mehmetoglu, M. (2010). Accurately identifying and comparing sustainable tourists, nature-based tourists and ecotourists on the basis of their environmental concerns. *International Journal of Hospitality and Tourism Administration, 11*(2), 171–199.

Miao, L., & Wei, W. (2013). Consumers' pro-environmental behavior and the underlying motivations: A comparison between household and hotel settings. *International Journal of Hospitality Management, 32*, 102–112.

Milfont, T. L., Duckitt, J., & Wagner, C. (2010). A cross-cultural test of the value-attitude-behavior hierarchy. *Journal of Applied Social Psychology, 40*(11), 2791–2813.

Montaño, D. E., & Kasprzyk, D. (2008). Theory of reasoned action, theory of planned behaviour, and the integrated behavioral model. In K. Glanz, B. K. Rimer, & K. Viswanath (Eds.), *Health behavior and health education – Theory, research and practice* (pp. 67–92). San Francisco, CA: Jossey-Bass.

Moscardo, G. (2009). Tourism and quality of life: Towards a more critical approach. *Tourism and Hospitality Research, 9*(2), 159–170.

Nguyen, S., Iacono, V., & Stratmann, W. (2011). *To be 'Green' or not to be 'Green': The perspectives of sport consumer on the relationship between sport and the environment*. In NASSM 2011: Book of Abstracts, NASSM, London [Online]. Retrieved March 13, 2012, from http://hdl.handle.net/10536/DRO/DU:30036823

Nigbur, D., Lyons, E., & Uzzell, D. (2010). Attitudes, norms, identity and environmental behaviour: Using an expanded theory of planned behaviour to predict participation in a kerbside recycling programme. *British Journal of Social Psychology, 49*, 259–284.

Pearce, P. L. (2005). *Tourist behaviour – Themes and conceptual schemes*. Clevedon: Channel View Publications.

Pearce, P. L. (2011). *Tourist behaviour and the contemporary world*. Ontario: Channel View Publications.

Pfahl, M. E. (2010). Strategic issues associated with the development of internal sustainability teams in sport and recreation organizations: A framework for action and sustainable environmental performance. *International Journal of Sport Management, Recreation and Tourism, 6*, 37–61.

Pucher, J., Buehler, R., & Seinen, M. (2011). Bicycling renaissance in North America? An update and re-appraisal of cycling trends and policies. *Transportation Research Part A, 45*, 451–475.

Pucher, J., Garrard, J., & Greaves, S. (2011). Cycling down under: A comparative analysis of bicycling trends and policies in Sydney and Melbourne. *Journal of Transport Geography, 19*, 332–345.

Puczkó, L., & Smith, M. (2012). An analysis of tourism QOL domains from the demand side. In M. Uysal, R. R. Perdue, & M. J. Sirgy (Eds.), *Handbook of tourism and qualify-of-llife research – Enhancing the lives of tourists and residents of host communities* (pp. 263–277). New York: Springer.

Ramkissoon, H., Smith, L. D. G., & Weiler, B. (2013). Relationships between place attachment, place satisfaction and pro-environmental behaviour in an Australian national park. *Journal of Sustainable Tourism, 21*(3), 434–457.

Ray, S. J. (2009). Risking bodies in the wild: The 'corporeal unconscious' of American adventure culture. *Journal of Sport and Social Issues, 33*(3), 257–284.

Responsible Traveller Magazine. (2014). *Responsible traveller – Be the difference.* [Online] Retrieved April 10, 2014, from http://www.responsibletraveller.co.za/responsibletraveller1.co.za

Ritchie, B. W., Tkaczynski, A., & Faulks, P. (2010). Understanding the motivation and travel behavior of cycle tourists using involvement profiles. *Journal of Travel & Tourism Marketing, 27*(4), 409–425.

Sahler, G. (2007). *Green champions in sport and environment.* Berlin: Federal Ministry for the Environment, Nature Conservation and Nuclear Safety [Online]. Retrieved August 10, 2010, from http://www.unep.org/sport_env/FinalGreenChampions_Guide_070928.pdf

Salome, L. R., Van Bottenburg, M., & Van den Heuvel, M. (2013). We are as Green as possible: Environmental responsibility in commercial artificial settings for lifestyle sports. *Leisure Studies, 32*(2), 173–190.

Saunders, M., Lewis, P., & Thornhill, A. (2007). *Research methods for business students* (4th ed.). Essex: Prentice Hall.

Scammon, D. L., Fuller, D. A., Karniouchina, E. V., & Masters, T. (2011). Sport-related subculture as a useful basis of market segmentation. In L. R. Kahle & A. G. Close (Eds.), *Consumer behavior knowledge for effective sports and event marketing* (pp. 103–143). New York: Routledge.

Schmidt, C. W. (2006). Putting the earth in play: Environmental awareness and sports. *Environmental Health Perspectives, 114*(5), A286–A295 [Online]. Retrieved April 13, 2012, from http://www.ncbi.nlm.nih.gov/pmc/articles/PMC1459948/

Schwartz, S. H. (1977). Normative influences on altruism. In I. Berkowitz (Eds.), *Advances in experimental social psychology* (pp. 221–279). New York: Academic Press.

Sheth, J. N., Sethia, N. K., & Srinivas, S. (2011). Mindful consumption: A customer-centric approach to sustainability. *Journal of the Academy of Marketing Science, 39,* 21–39.

Shipway, R., & Kirkup, N. (2011). Understanding sport tourism experiences: Exploring the participant-spectator nexus. In R. Sharpley & P. R. Stone (Eds.), *Tourist experience – Contemporary perspectives* (pp. 127–140). London: Routledge.

Snelgrove, R., Taks, M., Chalip, L., & Green, C. (2008). How visitors and locals at a sport event differ in motives and identity. *Journal of Sport & Tourism, 13*(3), 165–180.

Snelgrove, R., & Wood, L. (2010). Attracting and leveraging visitors at a charity cycling event. *Journal of Sport & Tourism, 15*(4), 269–285.

Snider, A., Hill, J., Luo, S., Buerger, B., & Herstine, J. (2011). Implications for place attachment in coastal reserve management. *Ocean and Coastal Management, 54,* 612–620.

Sotiriadou, P., & Hill, B. (2015). Raising environmental responsibility and sustainability for sport events: A systematic review. *International Journal of Event Management Research, 10*(1), 1–11.

Stanford, D. (2008). 'Exceptional visitors': Dimensions of tourist responsibility in the context of New Zealand. *Journal of Sustainable Tourism, 16*(3), 258–275.

Steg, L., Bolderdijk, J. W., Keizer, K., & Perlaviciute, G. (2014). An integrated framework for encouraging pro-environmental behaviour: The role of values, situational factors and goals. *Journal of Environmental Psychology, 38,* 104–115.

Stern, P. C. (2000). New environmental theories: Toward a coherent theory of environmentally significant behavior. *Journal of Social Issues, 56*(3), 407–424.

Szymanski, S. (2003). The economic design of sporting contests. *Journal of Economic Literature, 41,* 1137–1187.

Takavol, M., & Dennick, R. (2011). Making sense of cronbach's alpha. *International Journal of Medical Education, 2,* 53–55.

Tang, L. (2014). The application of social psychology theories and concepts in hospitality and tourism studies: A review and research agenda. *International Journal of Hospitality Management, 36,* 188–196.

Thompson, J., Davidson, J., & Hutson, G. (2008). A case study on environmental perspectives of boulderers and access issues at the niagara glen nature reserve. *Australian Journal of Outdoor Education, 12*(2), 24–31.

Trendafilova, S. (2011). Sport subcultures and their potential for addressing environmental problems: The illustrative case of disc golf. *The Cyber Journal of Applied Leisure and Recreation Research, 13*(1), 1–14 [Online]. Retrieved March 13, 2012, from http://larnet.org/2011-03.pdf

Weaver, D. (2012). Organic, incremental and induced paths to sustainable mass tourism convergence. *Tourism Management, 33,* 1030–1037.

Weed, M., & Bull, C. (2004). *Sports tourism: Participants, policy and providers.* Oxford: Elsevier Butterworth-Heinemann.

Wheaton, B. (2007). Identity, politics and the beach: Environmental activism in surfers against sewage. *Leisure Studies, 26*(3), 279–302.

Winkel, G., Seagert, S., & Evans, G. W. (2009). An ecological perspective on theory, methods and analysis in environmental psychology: Advances and challenges. *Journal of Environmental Psychology, 29,* 318–328.

Wu, J., Huang, D., Liu, J., & Law, R. (2013). Which factors help visitors convert their short-term pro-environmental intentions to long-term behaviors? *International Journal of Tourism Sciences, 13*(2), 33–56.

Wynveen, C. J., Kyle, G. T., & Sutton, S. G. (2012). Natural area visitors' place meaning and place attachment ascribed to a marine setting. *Journal of Environmental Psychology, 32,* 287–296.

Yang, C. C., Yang, K. J., & Peng, S. Y. (2011). Exploration strategies and key activities for the system of environmental management. *Total Quality Management and Business Excellence, 22*(11), 1179–1194.

Index

Note: Page numbers in *italics* refer to figures
Page numbers in **bold** refer to tables
Page numbers with "n" refer to notes

academic discourse 4
acceptable behaviour 59
active event travel 19
active-sport-event travel careers (ASETC) 14, 16–17
active sport tourism 14–15, 102, 103–4; events 102, 103, 105, 114, 117; segmentation studies in **176**
active sport tourists 24, 28, 72, 115, 174, 176, 179; in highland destinations 182; summer and winter sport tourists 180, **181**
Agyeman, J. 189
Ajzen, I. 189
Alegre, J. 74
Ali, A. 150
Altman, I. 35
amateur cyclists 19
ANCOVA, univariate 199–200
Anderson, B. 59
Anderson, E. 167
Anderson, J. 37
Andersson, T. D. 16
Anfield-Breckfield regeneration plan 63
Anfield Project (2013) 62, 63
Anfield Stadium 55
Appadurai, A. 58
ASETC *see* active-sport-event travel careers (ASETC)
Assaker, G. 90
attractive destinations 14
authenticity 59
Aveiro region, Portugal 144, 152–4, *153*, 161, 166
average variance extracted (AVE) values 83

Bagur-Femenías, L. 152, 159
Baldwin, J. 36
Banff National Park (NP) 72, 76, 77; appropriateness as location of race **79**, 82, 94; attachment to **81**; limitations and recommendations for improvements 93; plans to return and recommend **82**; practical implications 92–3; sustainable tourism to 91–2
BarOn, R. 178
Beaumont, E. 37, 49
Becken, S. 3
behaviour: acceptable 59; consumer 125; cycling 109–11, **110**, **111**; decision-making 24; environmental 187–8; model 90
behavioural intention 189, 199; interaction effects of factors with **199**
bicycle tourism *see under* cycling; cyclists; mountain biking
bikers, mountain *see* mountain bikers
biking tourism, mountain *see under* mountain biking
binary logistic regression analysis 109, 113, **113–14**
biodiversity, natural resources and 148
Böhler, H. 176
Boukas, N. 177
boundaries 35–6, 43
Breda, Zelia 143
Brown, D. 37, 49
Brown, G. 77, 90
Bruun, T. J. 73
Bull, C. J. 17, 26, 27, 94, 137
Buning, R. J. 13, 14, 16, 17, 25
Butler, R. W. 149, 178
Buultjens, J. 18

Callarisa-Fiol, L. J. 74
Campenhoudt, L. V. 155
Canada: mountain bike event 16; Rocky Mountain parks 92
Carneiro, Maria Joao 143
Carragher, Jamie 66
Central America, cultural norms of 40
Chalip, L. 14, 27, 72, 91, 93, 103
charity events 18

INDEX

Chen, C. F. 18, 74, 94
Chen, F. S. 74
Chen, H. M. 138
Chen, P. 18
Chi, C. G. Q. 74
Chinese heritage tourists 73
chi-square goodness of fit 82
Choi, H. C. 150–2
Christian, L. M. 19
Cialdini, R. B. 194
Cladera, M. 74
Close, A. G. 188
coastal areas, sports tourism role in development of 145–6
coastal destinations 144
coastal tourism 145–6, 156
cognitive dissonance 75
cognitive interviewing procedure 20
Cohen, J. 79
Coleman, R. J. 108
Comley, C. 37
companies: characterisation 155–6, **157**; entertainment 163; sports tourism 144, 166, 168; tourism 144, 147; tourist entertainment 154
comparative fit index (CFI) 82
community, sport programmes fostering 2
confirmatory factor analysis 83, **83**
conflicts 45
Conn, D. 62–3
consumer behaviour 125
Cordeiro, Catarina 143
Costa Rica: Pavones 40–2, *41*; resident foreigners in 38
CRM *see* customer relationship management (CRM)
Crompton, J. L. 25, 175
crowding 46, 50
cultural heritage 104–5
cultural norms, Central America 40
cultural programmes 2
cultural sustainability 147
cultural tourism 154
Cunningham, G. B. C. 194
customer relationship management (CRM) 92
cycling 101; behaviours 109–11, **110, 111**; events 102, 118; races 188; routes 18; tourism 17–18, 124, 125, 188; *see also* mountain biking
cyclists 26; amateur 19; non-career 16; non-cyclists 25, 28; road racing 17; touring 17; traveling to an event solo or with other cyclists (TS/OC) 20, 21; travel with non-cycling travel companions (Tw/NC) 20, 21; *see also* mountain bikers

Daskalos, C. T. 36, 49
decision-making behavior 24
Delphi study 18

Denizci-Guillet, B. 72
Derom, Inge 101
destination: attributes 25; characteristics 17–19; loyalty 72, 74, *76*; preferences 22, **23**
Dickson, T. J. 175, 177
Dillman, D. A. 19
discriminant validity 83; of measurement model **84**
Dolnicar, S. 177, 201
Dorset, W. 37
Downward, P. 18, 28
Driver, B. L. 77
du Preez, E. A. 187

ecological footprint, of spectators 188
economic dimension, sustainable development 147–8
economic sustainability 148, 156–8, **163**
ecosystem, natural 146
The Endless Summer II (1994) 41
English football 66
entertainment companies 163
entrepreneurs 92
environmental ambassadors 201
environmental behaviour 187–8
environmental dimension, sustainable development 148–9
environmentally responsible behaviour: defined 189–90; measurement **192**
environmental management practices 190
environmental programmes 2
environmental sustainability 158–9, 162, **163**
ETC *see* event travel career (ETC)
ethnography 39
European sun holiday tourists 74
Evans, Daniel 55
event: attachment 87–9; characteristics 17–19; leverage 103–4; loyalty *76*; organizers 92; owners 103; participation, motivation 111–13, **112**; predicting sustainability of 79, 83, *85*; preferences 21, **22**; spectators 116; sport tourism 102; stakeholders 103; sustainability 79, 83, *85*, 87, 89, 91; *see also specific types of event*
event active sport tourism, sport tourism as 14
event travel career (ETC) 14, *15*, 15–16
Everton FC 63–5; Everton-West Ham game 64
exercise motivations inventory 109

family tourists 182, 183
Faulks, P. 17, 139, 175
Fédération Internationale de Football Association (FIFA) 57
FIFA World Cup (2006) 2
Filo, K. 72, 73
First Division of the Football League 62
Fishbein, M. 189
Flanders, cycling heritage of 105, 109, 116
Flora London Marathon (2007) 73

INDEX

Fluker, M. 177
food and wine tourism 154
football 56–60; environment, construction 61–3; globalization 57; spectatorship 59
football club 63; globalization 56–8; identifiers 59; in Liverpool 63; revenues (2012–2013) **57**
foreigners, Ticos and 43–9
Forgas-Coll, S. 74
Frazer, R. 47
Freeman, R. 27
Frew, A. J. 150
Füller, J. 177
Funk, D. C. 28, 72, 73, 190

Gammon, S. 104, 105
German tourism 173, 179; winter sport tourists 174
German Travel Analyses 179
Gerrard, Steven 66
Getz, D. 14, 16, 18, 26, 151
Gibson, H. J. 6, 13–14, 16, 17, 24, 25, 27, 72, 102
global environmental change 6
globalization: football 57; football clubs 56–8
Goffman, E. 47
Gold Coast Airport Marathon (2005) 73
Goldstein, N. J. 194
golf tourism 131
Gómez, Edwin 33
good scale reliability 78–9
Gordon, E. 36
Gössling, S. 151
Green, B. C. 72, 91, 126, 137
Griskevicius, V. 194
group affiliation 193
Grün, B. 201
Gubb, K. 16
Gursoy 72, 73, 89

Hall, C. M. 4
Halpenny, E. A. 14, 17, 71, 74, 75, 77, 94
Harrison-Hill, T. 93
Heath, E. T. 187
heavy localism 36–8, 48
heritage: active sport tourism events based on 114; Chinese tourists 73; cultural 104–5; Flanders' cycling 105, 109, 116; motivation, prediction of 113; sport-based 104; sport tourism 102
Highamand, J. E. S. 1
Higham, J. 72, 104, 127, 152
highland destinations, sport tourism in 174
Hinch, T. D. 1, 104
Ho, C. I. 138
Hodeck, A. 173, 176
Holdnak, A. 27
host communities, in sport tourism destinations 33
Hovemann, G. 173, 176
Hritz, N. M. 177

Hsu, F. Y. 73
Huang, H. 18
Huang, S. C. 138
human territoriality *see* territoriality
Humphreys, C. 127, 137

identity, performances of 56
information and communication technology (ICT), for sustainable tourism development 150–1
institutional/policy sustainability **163**
interaction effects, of factors with future intention **200**
interpretivism 127
interviews 127–8; semi-structured 155

Jenkins, J. 18
Jones, I. 73, 126
Jordan, J. S. 28
Joseph, J. 104
Journal of Sport & Tourism 1, 4

Kaffine, D. T. 34, 37, 48
Kahle, L. R. 188
Kang, S. J. 72
Kaplanidou, K. 14, 17, 24, 27, 28, 72, 88–94
Karabaxoglou, I. 93
Karadakis, K. 27, 93
Keep Everton in our City (KEIOC) 63
Keep Flags Scouse 66
KEIOC *see* Keep Everton in our City (KEIOC)
Kellison, T. B. 195, 200
Kerstetter, D. 34, 38, 42, 48, 50
Kerwin, S. 27, 93
Kesenne, S. 72, 91
Khachadoorian, M. A. 37
King, J. 27, 188
Kirkup, N. 75
Klenosky, D. 175
Kollmuss, A. 189
Konu, H. 175, 177
The Kop 68n3
Krause, S. 38, 41
Kulczycki, C. 14, 17, 71, 74, 75, 77
Kyle, G. 73, 75

Lamont, M. 18, 19
Larson, D. J. 17
Lawson-Remer, T. 37
Lee, C. 18
Lee, J. J. 75
Lee, T. H. 73, 75
Lefebvre, Henri 35, 55, 57, 58, 67
Leichenko, R. 57
Leisch, F. 177
Leong, J. K. 74
Leou, C. H. 73
Levene's test 109
leveraging process 103

Liao, T. Y. 138
life-cycle model 149
lifestyle sports 193
Likert scale 111
Little, R. J. A. 78
Liu, Z. 138
Liverpool: clubs 63; culture 58; de-urbanization of 61; economy 55, 57; Everton's place in 63; football club in 63; football matches in May 2013 60; football space in 58; football spaces of 57; globalization of football clubs in Liverpool 56; tourism economy of 62
Liverpool FC 64–6; Anfield Stadium 55
localism 34, 36–8; enactment of 37; heavy 36–8, 48; mild 36; moderate 36; of Nicaraguan surfers 38; origins of 37; at Pavones 48; as territoriality 37–8
logistic regression analysis, binary 109, 113, **113–14**
López-Mosquera, N. 75
loyalty promotion 71
Lumsdon, L. 18, 28
luxurious accommodations 26

MacCannell, D. 47
market segmentation 174
Martyn, S. 72, 91
Ma, S.-C. 151, 157
maturity 16–17
Matzler, K. 177
McConnell, A. 16, 18, 26
McCullough, B. P. 194, 195, 200
McGuirty, J. 14, 27
McKercher, B. 72
means-end approach 175
Mediterranean golf resorts 6
Melissa's Road Race: attachment to **81**; plans to return and recommend **82**; sustainability of 91
Miami marathon tourists 90
Mihaliè, T. 151
mild localism 36
Millward, P. 60, 66
model fit indices **84**
moderate localism 36
Moghimehfar, Farhad 71
Morley, D. 117
Mosedale, L. 27
motivation 73, **79**, 89; for event participation 111–13, **112**; factors **181**; theory 175
Moularde, Julie 123
mountain bike event, Canadian 16
mountain bikers 123, 126–8, 138; racers 18; serious 138
mountain biking: ethos 134, 135; racers 18; spectators 201; subculture 139; tourism 123–5, 130, 131
Mowen, A. J. 73
Moyle, B. D. 1

multicollinearity 78
multiple imputation method 78
Mykletun, R. J. 152

National Strategic Plan for Tourism 154
national tourism administration 154
natural ecosystems 146
natural resources and biodiversity 148
nature tourism 154
nautical tourism 154
Nazer 48–9
Ng, E. 72
Nicaraguan surfers 47; localism of 38
non-career cyclists 16
non-cyclists 25, 28; non-cycling companions 25
Norcliffe, Glen 55
Norm-Activation-Model 189
Normed Fit Index (NFI) 82
Novelli, M. 139

O'Brien, D. T. 36, 49, 72
O'Brien, K. 57
Olive, R. 40
Olympic sponsors 2
O'Neill, M. 60
outdoor sporting codes 187
outdoor sports cultures 193
ownership 35, 42–3

Palau-Saumell, R. 74
Paris (2015) global climate agreement 3
park associations **82**
Park Attachment 88–9
parks: managers 92; sustainability, predictor of 90
Park Visitation Sustainability 76, 79, 83, *85*, 89, 91
participatory sport events 13, 14, *15*, 28
Patterson, I. 16, 178
Pavlidis, A. 40
Pavones, Costa Rica 40–2, *41*; localism at 48
PCA *see* principal component analysis (PCA)
Peace Corps volunteer 40
Pearce, P. L. 16, 175
Pearson, G. 60
Pegg, S. 178
Peng, S. Y. 190
people's sport 57
perceived appropriateness 90
perceived value 90–1
Perdue, R. 177
Phou, S. 94
place attachment 191; descriptive statistics and reliability of scales 197–9, **198**; measurement scales for **195**
policy dimension, sustainable development 151–2
policy sustainability 160–1; dimension 164
pollution 149, 158

INDEX

Ponting, J. 49
pragmatists 38
Prayag, G. 94
predicting event sustainability 79, 83, *85*
predicting heritage motivation 113
Premier League 62, 66; clubs 63
principal component analysis (PCA) 179, 180, **180**; factor analysis 78, 80
private sector partnerships 4
pseudonyms 39
public address (PA) club 64
public sector: agencies 103, 117; partnerships 4

Qu, H. 74
Quivy, R. 155

race organizers 91
racing cyclists: mountain 18; road 17
Raffestin, C. 35, 47
Ramchandani, G. M. 108
Ramshaw, G. 101, 104, 105, 117
Raymond, C. M. 77
regulation 36, 44
resilience theory 3
respect 45–6
respondents' enthusiasm 129
responsible behaviour, within sports event context 190–1
Reynolds, Z. 177
Rickly-Boyd, J. M. 105
riders, attracting 139
Rio Declaration on Environment and Development 147
Rio 2016 Olympic Games 2
Ritchie, B. W. 17, 27, 139
Rittichainuwat, B. N. 74
road racing cyclists 17
Robins, K. 117
Roggenbuck, J. W. 77
Rookwood, J. 60, 66
root-mean-square error of approximation (RMSEA) 82
Ruiz-Molina, M.-E. 151
running travel motives 89
Ryan, C. 94

Sack, R. D. 35
Sahler, G. 190
Sánchez-García, J. 74
Sánchez, M. 75
satisfactory fit 83
Sato, M. 28
Schanzel, H. A. 26
Schellhorn, M. 3
Schwartz, S. H. 189
Scott, D. 75
seasonality 9, 156, 178; effects of 183; sport tourism 178, 182

segmentation, in sport tourism 175–8, **176**
self-awareness 67
semi-structured interviews 155
serious leisure 15, 125–8; durable benefits 132–3; framework 137–8; perseverance of participation 129–30; progression through a long-term career 130–1; significant personal effort 131–2; social identification 136–7; unique ethos 133–6
SES *see* socio-ecological systems (SES)
Shen, Y. L. 75
Shipway, R. 73
Sirakaya, E. 150–2
situational intention 191, 197, 200
small and medium enterprises (SMEs) 144
small-scale sport tourism event 94
SMEs *see* small and medium enterprises (SMEs)
Smith, A. 90
Smyth, J. D. 19
Sobel test 84
social desirability bias 196
social enthusiasm 102
social equity goals 151
social impacts of sport events 2
social interactions 133
social media 139, 160
social norms 193, 194
social sustainability 147, 151
social worlds 16
sociocultural dimension, sustainable development 149–50
sociocultural sustainability 159–60, **163**
socio-ecological systems (SES) 3
Soper, D. S. 79
spectators 188
Spion Kop 68n3
sport events 13; mega-events 103; national/global impacts of 2; profile of events **197**; social impacts of 2; spectator behaviour 190, 191; spectators 192; *see also* participatory sport events
sport heritage 104: activities 1; and tourism development 104–5
sport meccas 127
sport programmes, in fostering community 2
sport-specific motivational items 93–4
sport tourism: activities 145, 148, 178; companies 144, 166, 168; development 1, 3, 6; as *event active sport tourism* 14; events 5, 73; in highland destinations 174; products 5–6; propensity of 5; role in development of coastal areas 145–6; seasonality 178, 182
sport tourism destinations: choice and segmentation in 175–8, **176**; host communities in 33; planning and policy 4; sustainability of 5
sport tourism sustainable development 146–7; economic dimension 147–8; environmental dimension 148–9; policy dimension 151–2;

sociocultural dimension 149–50; technological dimension 150–1
sport tourists, segments of **181**, **182**
stand-up paddleboarders (SUP) 34, 43
Stebbins, Robert 15, 126
Stern, P. C. 189
Storey, D. 36
strategic destination partnerships 4
structural model analysis: direct effects **85**; indirect effects and mediation analysis **86**
structural regression model (SRM) 79, 82, 83
subculture identification 193–5; descriptive statistics and reliability of scales 197–9, **198**; measurement scales for **195**
subjective norms 193–5; descriptive statistics and reliability of scales 197–9, **198**; measurement scales for **195**
sun and sea tourism 154
Sun, X. 74
SUP see stand-up paddleboarders (SUP)
surfers 37; culture 193; local 38; Nicaraguan 47; resident 48; Tico 39, 40, 42, 47
surfing 36–7; etiquette 38; universal rules 37
surf schools, proliferation of 36
surf tourism destinations 33; sustainability of 34
surf tourists 33–4
survey instrument 107–8, **108**
sustainability: cultural 147; economic 156–8; indicator of 82; issues of 2; of Melissa's Road Race 91; social 147; of sport tourism 144; of sport tourism destination 5, 34; in tourism companies 147; see also specific types of sustainability
sustainable development 1, 124
sustainable environmental aims 151
sustainable management practices 149, 150, 154
sustainable sport tourism destinations, contributions and implications for **7–8**
sustainable tourism 3, 72, 151; to Banff National Park 91–2; development, ICT for 150–1; framing of 3; practices **163**
sustainable tourism indicators 81–2; re-visitation and positive recommendations as 73–6
Sutherland, M. 75

Taks, M. 27, 72, 91
Tantamjarik, P. A. 47, 49
Tarrant, M. 73
TCP see travel career pattern (TCP)
technological dimension, sustainable development 150–1
technological sustainability 160, **163**
territoriality 34–6, 56; localism as 37–8
Theodorakis, N. D. 93
Theory of Planned Behaviour (TPB) 189
Theory of Reasoned Action 189
Thoman, D. 37

Thomlinson, E. 27
Ticos: and foreigners 43–9; surfers 39, 40, 42, 47
Timur, S. 151
Tkaczynski, A. 17, 139
tourism: cycling 17, 18; decisions related to 24; development 104–5; economic sustainability in 148; see also specific types of tourism
tourism companies 144; sustainability in 147
tourism-tourist entertainment companies 154
Tour of Flanders Cyclo event 105–6, 108, 112
Tour of Flanders Visitor Centre 105
TPB see Theory of Planned Behaviour (TPB)
travel: behavior 23; careers 15, 20; characteristics 17–19; conditions 14, 19, 20
travel career pattern (TCP) 16
travel style 25; preferences 23, **24**
tribalism 66
'triple bottomline' approach 147
Tsai, S. P. 94
Tsiotsou, R. 177
TS/OC see under cyclists
T-test 196
Tw/NC see under cyclists

Um, S. 175
univariate ANCOVA 199–200
universal surfing rules 37
Unruh, D. R. 16
Usher, Lindsay E. 33, 34, 38, 42, 48, 50

Valderrama, A. 37
Values-Beliefs-Norms model 189
Vaske, J. J. 77
Vassiliadis, C. 177
Vila Griddo, P. 178
Vogt, C. 14, 17, 72, 89, 91, 93
volunteers, Peace Corps 40

Waitt, G. 37, 47
Wang, X., 73
'Want-it-all tourists' 183
water territories 47
Waterton, E. 104
Watson, S. 104
WCED see World Commission on Environment and Development (WCED)
Weaver, Adam 123
Weber, D. 77
Weed, M. 2, 5, 27, 94, 137
Welch t test 109
Westland, J. C. 79
Weston, R. 28
Williams, D. R. 77
Willming, C. 27
WoM see word-of-mouth (WOM) recommendations
Won, D. 17, 177

INDEX

Woratschek, H. 177
word-of-mouth (WOM) recommendations 24, 71, 74
World Commission on Environment and Development (WCED) 146

Xu, H. 74

Yang, C. C. 190
Yang, K. J. 190
Yaw, F., Jr. 151
Yeoman, I. 26
You'll Never Walk Alone 65

Ziakas, V. 177